AF763820

Jeremy Geddert brings Grotius down from the shelf of dusty old international law books, and presents to us a thinker who is at once innovative and bold, and yet has deep roots in the venerable tradition of political thought. Geddert's Grotius challenges many of the assumptions embedded in our political vernacular – the language of rights – and compels us to reconsider our fundamental ideas about matters of enduring moral concern involving war and peace, constitutionalism and criminal law.

Lee Ward, *Alpha Sigma Nu Distinguished Associate Professor of Political Science, Campion College at the University of Regina*

Geddert has produced an analysis of the key notion of justice in the thought of Hugo Grotius that now constitutes a new benchmark within the relevant scholarship. It is notable for the way it challenges the prevailing orthodoxy that Grotius originates modern rights theory as mere subjective claims. In its place Geddert locates the development of rights within a far broader conception of justice. He mines a wide range of texts, political and theological, to show how Grotius addresses the priority of the common good as the framework for our most cherished convictions.

David Walsh, *Professor of Politics, The Catholic University of America*

Hugo Grotius and the Modern Theology of Freedom

Human rights are thought to guarantee pluralism by protecting individual liberty from imposed religious conceptions of virtue. Yet critics often argue that this secular focus on merely avoiding violations can also enable unfettered individualism and undermine appeals to the common good.

This book uncovers in secular rights pioneer Hugo Grotius a rights theory that points toward the enlargement of individual responsibility. It grounds this connection in Grotius' unexplored theological corpus, which reveals a dual metaethics and jurisprudence. Here a deontological natural law undergirds a secular theory of rights that is self-aware of its own limitations. A teleological practical reason then guides the exercise of these rights, so as not to compromise the political order that defends them. The book then illustrates this symbiosis of rights and responsibilities in five areas: consent theories of government, rights of rebellion, criminal punishment, war and international responsibility, and Atonement theology. This reassesses Grotius' legacy as a secularist opponent of classical political thought, and suggests that modern liberalism and universal human rights are compatible with a world of resurgent religion.

Jeremy Seth Geddert is Assistant Professor of Political Science at Assumption College. He has published on natural rights, early modern political thought, religion and politics, and the just war tradition.

Routledge Innovations in Political Theory

56 **Kantian Theory and Human Rights**
Edited by Reidar Maliks and Andreas Follesdal

57 **The Political Philosophy of Judith Butler**
Birgit Schippers

58 **Hegel and the Metaphysical Frontiers of Political Theory**
Eric Lee Goodfield

59 **Time, Memory, and the Politics of Contingency**
Smita A. Rahman

60 **Michael A. Weinstein**
Action, Contemplation, Vitalism
Edited by Robert L. Oprisko and Diane Rubenstein

61 **Deep Cosmopolis**
Rethinking World Politics and Globalisation
Edited by Adam K. Webb

62 **Political Philosophy, Empathy and Political Justice**
Matt Edge

63 **The Politics of Economic Life**
Martin Beckstein

64 **The Temporality of Political Obligation**
Justin C. Mueller

65 **Epistemic Liberalism**
A defence
Adam James Tebble

66 **Hegel, Marx, and 21st Century Social Movements**
Democracy, Dialectics, and Difference
Brian Lovato

67 **Ideologies of Experience**
Trauma, Failure, and the Abandonment of the Self
Matthew H. Bowker

68 **Post-Politics in Context**
Ali Rıza Taşkale

69 **Claus Offe and the Critical Theory of the Capitalist State**
Jens Borchert and Stephan Lessenich

70 **Equality Renewed**
Christine Sypnowich

71 **Rethinking Utopia**
Place, Power, Affect
David M. Bell

72 **Hugo Grotius and the Modern Theology of Freedom**
Transcending Natural Rights
Jeremy Seth Geddert

Hugo Grotius and the Modern Theology of Freedom

Transcending Natural Rights

Jeremy Seth Geddert

Routledge
Taylor & Francis Group
LONDON AND NEW YORK

First published 2017 by Routledge

2 Park Square, Milton Park, Abingdon, Oxfordshire OX14 4RN
711 Third Avenue, New York, NY 10017

Routledge is an imprint of the Taylor & Francis Group, an informa business

First issued in paperback 2018

Library of Congress Cataloging in Publication Data
A catalog record for this book has been requested

ISBN: 978-1-138-69594-8 (hbk)
ISBN: 978-1-138-36826-2 (pbk)

Typeset in Times New Roman
by Wearset Ltd, Boldon, Tyne and Wear

Contents

Acknowledgments

I originally began the research for this book in 2008 as a paper for David Walsh, inspired by Oliver O'Donovan's thoughts on Grotius' justice of assignment. I expanded it into a doctoral dissertation exploring how Grotius' twin categories of justice play out in a variety of political areas. In the four years since, I reconceived it to incorporate the wider epistemological, metaethical, and jurisprudential foundations of Grotius' twin categories, as they began to reveal themselves among the thickets of his ornate prose.

Critics will undoubtedly argue that I have tried to do too much in this book, especially as a junior scholar. They are presumably correct; indeed, Plato trusts in public only the political reflections of those over fifty. I can only respond that children often wonder – much like Socrates – at questions whose answers transcend their comprehension. They pre-reflectively trust in the unity of the whole, intuiting that the sun gives them life even if their eyes cannot behold it for more than a glimpse. In that spirit I offer this book, fully owning its limitations, which are surely legion. If my prose seems at times unduly assertive, I aim not to profess ontological certainty but to make some sense of Grotius' argument in economical language.

I could not have written this book without the help and guidance of many. I gratefully acknowledge my debt to them all, even though I have space here to name only a few. I would like to start by thanking David Walsh for his guidance, insight, encouragement, and support over the past decade. His courage to revisit deeply held premises exemplifies not only the academic life but the philosophic one. More immediately, I thank him for the opportunity to present the introduction to this project at the 2014 Eric Voegelin Society meetings. I also thank Claes Ryn and Stephen Schneck for their feedback over the years.

I am grateful to Steve McGuire for inviting me to participate in the 2015 Agora Institute conference *Nature: Ancient and Modern*, and to contribute to the volume of the same name. My chapter there, "Natural Rights and History: Hugo Grotius' Modern Translation of Aristotle" helps to shape parts of my conclusion here. Steve's insights, support, education, and friendship through the years have been indispensable, and this book could not have been written without them.

I am thankful for the thoughts and suggestions of Jesse Covington at the Agora conference, and those of Thomas Heilke, Wolfgang Leidhold, Peter Haworth, and Mark Polachic at the American Political Science Association,

Ciceronian Society meetings, and elsewhere. I also thank the editors and reviewers at the *Review of Politics* for their feedback on my 2014 article "Beyond Strict Justice: Hugo Grotius on Punishment and Natural Right(s)," which helped to shape the argument in Chapters 6–7.

My colleagues at Assumption College have fostered an environment most conducive to philosophic reflection on politics. I would like to thank Dan Mahoney, Geoffrey Vaughan, Greg Weiner, B. J. Dobski, and Dan Maher for reading my work, considering my argument, offering feedback, and discerning unwritten rules. I am also grateful to Nalin Ranasinghe for his in-depth feedback on an earlier draft in a time of need, and to Jim Lang for his invaluable and timely insight on the publication process. Provost Louise Carroll Keeley provided funding that allowed me to participate in several conferences, and the Faculty Development Committee made possible the Summer 2014 and 2016 development and revisions of the manuscript.

I am truly grateful to Natalja Mortensen for her guidance, advocacy, and support through the publication process. Lillian Rand was very helpful throughout the final stages, and two anonymous reviewers provided in-depth feedback that helped to greatly refine the project.

Finally, I would like to thank my parents, Ron and Joy, for fostering my intellectual curiosity from a young age. Their seriousness about important questions set the tone for the educational journey of which this book is only a small part. In pursuing the academic vocation I have surely added to my debt, and I can only hope that this manuscript represents a down payment.

1 Grotius and Modern Natural Rights

Beyond a Secular History

"Respect for human life, liberty and well-being must be enshrined as rights beyond the power of any force to diminish." Nelson Mandela spoke this phrase as he signed into effect the 1996 Constitution of South Africa. His words carried an obvious poignancy; during twenty-seven years of imprisonment, his own liberty had been greatly diminished by government force. Many observers saw this inauguration as the final victory of an anti-Apartheid campaign championed by Mandela from within and assisted by international pressure from without. But observers around the globe praised not only the event of the constitution but the content. The South African constitution enshrines not only the rights of traditional liberal-democratic societies, but also a host of socio-economic rights, and even "third-generation rights" to information and to a healthy environment (to sample but two).

Rights have become the language of politics today. When ordinary Americans invoke the gravity and authority of the Constitution, it is often done in order to defend a claim-right. Rights are no less revered in France, home of the "Rights of Man and Citizen." Even Brits compromised Parliamentary sovereignty to conform to the EU charter of rights. Why the currency of rights? First, they are impersonal. The constitutional courts tasked with their interpretation carry an air of political rectitude that contrasts with the horse-trading of legislatures. Judges, after all, are supposed to be restrained by the text of the rights charter, whereas politicians are apt to be swayed by personal considerations of re-election and patronage. Second, rights are secular. They do not depend on what John Rawls calls "comprehensive doctrines," which means they can be justly imposed on all in a way that political interests cannot. Third, rights are universal. Rights apply equally to everyone, meaning that nobody can be denied and that favouritism is out of bounds. Indeed, rights language is both employed globally and aimed globally, from imprisoned journalists in Egypt to sacrilegious rock bands in Russia to democratic activists in China.

South Africa needed not labour to attract global attention when Nelson Mandela passed away. Yet as statesmen from East to West rushed to honour his legacy, the phrase "human rights" was conspicuously scarce in their tributes.[1] What, then, motivated their homages? One clue might lie in a word used repeatedly: reconciliation. Mandela's most enduring legacy was his ability to unify a highly divided country, one on the brink of civil war mere days before he was elected as its President.[2] And no single policy was more integral to this unity than the Truth and Reconciliation Committee (TRC). Mandela's African National Congress proposed this approach during the anti-Apartheid campaign, he himself endorsed it before the election, and he then implemented it as President.[3] Yet Mandela would have been well within his rights to reject this approach and instead indict Apartheid criminals. As an individual, he would have gained satisfaction for his long years of imprisonment. As a chief executive, he would have carried out the standard governmental task of punishing criminals. And as a party leader, he would have satisfied a sizable constituency demanding retribution. Yet by exercising such a right in the strict sense, Mandela would have stoked the flames of civil war, a condition that would jeopardize the practical realization of even the most basic right of life.[4]

In other words, Mandela is uniquely revered not for advocating and fighting for rights, but instead for how he exercised his own right to punish. While genuine political order and unity in South Africa certainly required a respect for rights, it also required the active willingness to give up the right to punish by reference to a higher good. How could Mandela fight for rights, then preach giving them up? Were the impersonal and universal character of rights – generally thought to be a benefit – actually an impediment to a policy of amnesty? Does this explain why so many revolutions in the name of rights – however potentially justifiable – end in a reign of terror? Is there a flaw, or at least an internal tension, in the concept of rights? Must rights refer to something beyond themselves?

These questions lead us to consider the origin of secular rights theories. The conventional narrative begins in the mid-seventeenth century with Thomas Hobbes, who argues that authority arises only from the consent of those who will be subject to that rule. Locke subsequently recognizes that Hobbes' theory gives *carte blanche* to the exercise of sovereign authority, and thus remedies this defect by stipulating that even legitimately constituted sovereigns must adhere to limits. That is, citizens retain natural rights that cannot be given to government. These rights theories are seen as a repudiation of the classical teleological conception of justice that relies on a rich philosophical anthropology. Indeed, Hobbes and Locke are clear about their distaste for the Aristotelian provenance of such ontologies.

Yet Hobbes' conception can hardly be called a foundation for natural rights, because the right of one person to self-preservation does not imply the corresponding duty of another not to harm that one. Few would be reassured by a state of nature in which "every man has a right to every thing, even to one another's body."[5] Locke's theory of rights may be more sound, but the secularity of its foundation is debatable. If rights come from property, and property comes from labour, then the very reason that "no one ought to harm another in his life, health, [and] liberty ..." is precisely that men are all "... the workmanship of one omnipotent, and infinitely wise maker."[6]

A slightly more sophisticated history of rights begins earlier in the seventeenth century, with the writings of Dutch polymath Hugo Grotius. After enumerating a list of basic rights, he (in)famously argues that "what we have been saying would have a degree of validity even if we were to assert ... that there were no God." Most political theorists can at least identify the name of Grotius with this "impious hypothesis," and the literature has increasingly cited him as the true beginning of secular rights-based political thought. The claim has a modicum of merit, even if the originality of his hypothesis is overstated by a good two centuries. But if this history were the chief reason we should be interested in Grotius, it would only lead us back to the philosophical problem of the limits of rights. Rather, we should be interested in Grotius because he establishes a foundation for secular natural rights in full awareness of this problem – and because he shows how we can transcend it.

In what follows, I argue that Grotius indeed has a deontological theory of individual rights, but it is oriented toward a teleological and ultimately Christian conception of person and politics. Rights point to responsibilities. These two elements are anchored in Grotius' division of justice into two categories much noticed but little understood: "expletive" (or "strict" justice), and "attributive" (or "wider" justice). Expletive justice is grounded in secular and 'objective' theoretical reason. It outlines universal laws and rights, the implementation (*explere*) of which confers on the holder of such a right a formal legal status of immunity from accusations of injustice. By contrast, attributive justice is grounded in a practical reason that ascertains the character of individuals and the ends of human existence, dealing with persons whose ontologically higher essence transcends the final solutions of pure reason. While it is technically non-justiciable, it guides the action of assigning (*attribuere*) benefits and burdens and carrying out the actions associated with each. Hence, it governs the exercise of the rights previously guaranteed in law by expletive justice, and is oriented toward a trans-political reality that can never be fully instantiated in politics. Expletive justice is demanded in natural reason as a starting point, and sets out the formal preconditions for just political action. However, attributive justice adds a "harmony with nature" that transcends the flat two-dimensionality of depersonalized reason and promotes the fulfilment of a fully human existence.

In other words, Grotius establishes an independent and nonsectarian theoretical foundation for rights, while remaining fully conscious of the limits of this formal status on its own. If the exercise of this status is not guided by a virtue located in the person and ultimately grounded in God, a nation may undermine the very order that makes rights possible. This means that the holder of a right has an inherent responsibility, a duty that may in fact call forth a sacrifice on behalf of the polity. Hence, if individual rights are the beginning of Grotius' political thought, they are not the end. Grotius provides the concept of individual rights with a secure but limited place that keeps alive the wider horizon of higher goods. Rights are best protected by a regime that transcends natural rights.

This thesis about Grotius' concept of natural rights begins by outlining the history of justice (Chapter 2). This traces the development of Aristotle's two categories of justice throughout the middle ages. It also shows the interplay of his categories of theoretical and practical reason and highlights the Christian development of the concept of history. This historical sketch leads to a conceptual distinction between natural Right, natural law, and individual natural rights.

Chapter 3 begins by examining the philosophical anthropology that grounds Grotius' defence of natural Right. It then traces Grotius' dual metaethics: a naturalism grounded in God as creator and a voluntarism based on God as governor. This leads to a tripartite epistemology that includes reason, history, and revelation. When combined, these philosophical foundations lead to a five-fold taxonomy of justice from which expletive and attributive justice emerge. The chapter will then compare these two categories of justice on seven axes, and show how the "negative liberty" of expletive justice leads to the "positive liberty" of attributive justice.

Because Grotius' explicit references to expletive and attributive (or "strict" and "wider" justice) are somewhat sparing, the project then shows how they are implicit in five areas of his political thought (Chapters 4–8). These chapters are respectively organized around a particular right: the right to consent, the right of rebellion and civil disobedience, the right to punish, the right to wage war, and the right to pardon. Each chapter will show how the right in question points toward a wider responsibility to exercise it wisely. Chapter 4 begins by examining the creation of governing institutions, which requires a people to exercise its right to consent. Grotius here addresses the question of why a people would exercise this formal right, making reference to a substantive and trans-political natural Right. He outlines five purposes of government that enjoin its creation, including a justification for positive law. Positive law does not simply protect property but also makes the practical realization of natural Right more likely. Government also provides a forum in which to further discover and promulgate truths of natural Right through their instantiation in particularities of time and place. However, if the people irresponsibly exercise their right to make a constitution, or the ruler his to enact positive laws, civil society will fail to reach the substantive aims that motivated its very creation. Grotius' treatment of civil society as salutary – but not strictly necessary – helps to draw out both the validity of individual choice under expletive justice, and the responsibility to the common good under attributive justice.

Chapter 5 explores Grotius' oft-misread right of rebellion and civil disobedience. Here he argues that the expletive status of authority is nearly unassailable once constituted through expletive consent. However, he permits a wide latitude for civil disobedience, as attributive justice holds the ruler's actions to a lofty standard. He unites these two seemingly paradoxical elements through a four-fold taxonomy of types of rule, which reveals informal sources of authority. This framework also shows how indicative moral judgment carries a weight of its own, apart from imperative coercive force. This implicitly Christian balance between naturalism and voluntarism envisions a sovereign responsible to a standard outside himself. When the conceptual right to govern is used irresponsibly, the effect of governing is rendered nearly inert.

Chapter 6 outlines Grotius' philosophy of punishment. It begins by showing how Grotius separates civil and criminal law in order to distinguish restoration of property from punishment of persons. Expletive justice can govern the former but is incomplete for the latter. While it deductively grants the political authorities a strict natural right to punish lawbreakers, unlike in civil law it cannot suggest a course of action that fulfils the (now forward-looking) purposes of punishment. This calls for attributive prudence to understand social particulars, foresee consequences, and ascertain (and shape) the intention of the perpetrator. The ruler must also exercise the classical virtue of equity, which transcends the letter of the positive law, and ought to consider the Christian concept of pardon, which refers to a reality that transcends even the spirit of the law. Hence, the capacity to punish is not a claim-right but in fact a difficult responsibility. Only by punishing responsibly can the ruler protect the very political order that secures his original right to punish.

Chapter 7 explores the right to apprehend international criminals by waging punitive war. Grotius' expletive natural right to punish in the pre-political 'state of nature' permits nations to punish others in the continuing international 'state of nature.' This right is attentive to religious pluralism, as it limits the grounds for punitive war to those crimes against humanity whose proscriptions are knowable in pure reason to all. Yet this right alone is unlikely to motivate the imperfect responsibility of apprehending international criminals. Nor can its pure reason mandate a limited war that demands a proportionality of means to these just ends. Only attributive (and perhaps Christian) virtues will motivate states to sacrifice their soldiers or observe limits in carrying out the war. Attributive justice thus protects even the secular and procedural expletive rights of nations in international society.

Chapter 8 brings Grotius' themes to a climax in his concept of divine government. Grotius' Atonement doctrine not only addresses the fundamental issue of grace and works in justification that made Christian unity impossible after the Protestant Reformation, but also outlines a theology of justice, law, punishment, pardon, and political virtue. He conceptualizes sin as not a civil debt against God as creditor (or even judge) but a criminal offence against the entire moral universe of which God is governor, thus presenting a conception of God more fundamentally political than any previous Atonement theologian. Expletive justice grants God the right to damn all of humanity, but this just course of action would mean the end of attributive (and Christian) virtue. Hence, God the governor prudently accepts Christ's substitutionary death not as expletive repayment of the civil liability of humanity, but as attributive substitution of criminal punishment. This prudence at the centre of God's character steers a 'middle way' between universal damnation and 'cheap grace,' and preserves the possibility of virtue among imperfect humans by maintaining some link to extrinsic reward. Christ's charity also demonstrates sacrificial virtue, which inspires the intrinsic motives that alone can produce genuinely free virtue. What is more, Christ's act of justification does not merely declare humanity as innocent, but inspires the sanctification that brings the development of positive virtue. This Atonement theology substantiates government as not simply the value-neutral arbitration of private property claims, but a public practice requiring both prudence and charity in a governor. It aims to build up the moral dignity and stature of the government not as an end in itself, but as a means to promote virtue in the entire populace. In sum, if God does not exercise his right to punish with responsibility (and indeed charity), humanity will not take up its responsibility to religion and virtue that both preserves rights and transcends them.

Chapter 9 will conclude with some thoughts on Grotius' place in the history of political thought by drawing together his classical and Christian roots. Grotius' attributive justice reflects the classical concept of natural Right by transcending the abstract formulations of expletive justice. His classical teleology is fulfilled in a personal God who steps into history to inspire positive virtues in a way that Aristotle's virtuous man cannot (or will not). His Christian concept of the will undergirds rights by underscoring the centrality of conscience and freely chosen virtue. Finally, his Christian concepts of forgiveness and sacrifice inspire the exercise of those rights by reference not to one's own self-interest but to an interpersonal common good. Grotius' secular and formal natural rights are thus conceptually suitable for a pluralistic world, but the prospect of their practical implementation draws on a teleological and ultimately Christian vision of human flourishing. His language of rights suggests not a rejection of classical and Christian political thought but an attempt to preserve it in a modern idiom.

While this project is on one level a thesis about Grotius' political justice, it is on another level a supra-political argument. The narrow thesis about the relation between rights and responsibilities points toward several philosophical themes that bring a wider coherence to his thought. The first theme traces Grotius' implicit metaphysics, and questions the implicit reduction of his thought to a deontological series of universal rules. The second deals with Grotius' metaethics. Some portray Grotius as a voluntarist in whom ethical obligation proceeds from command, while others see his *etiamsi daremus* as liberating nature from any divine command. Grotius implicitly makes room for both naturalism and voluntarism in his Christian conception of God. The third theme explores Grotius' jurisprudence, which outlines his concept of the interplay of law and politics and provides an unexpected defence of the latter. This points toward his surprisingly explicit epistemology, which implicitly situates Aristotle's categories of *techne* (making) and *phronesis* (doing). His jurisprudence and epistemology leads to a fourth theme that also integrates the first, in which Grotius explores the interplay of the rule of law and the discretion of personal rulers – including a theological analogy of rule. The fifth theme explores the implications of Grotius' epistemology for political coercion, as pure reason brings the benefit of universal application but limits the content that can be applied. His epistemology of practical reason and history – both secular and sacred – will then address and overcome the limits of pure reason. This emphasis on Grotius' boundaries of coercion, together with his metaethics, leads to a sixth theme that explores his concept of free will. Here Grotius' rights confer a realm of freedom that permits a realm of moral indifference yet also – paradoxically – enables the fullest exercise of natural virtue. Finally, Grotius' seventh wider theme deals with nature and supernature, showing how the natural justice of rights is theoretically self-sufficient but may depend on a higher source to enable its practical realization. This theme brings us back to the primary political theme: if rights lack a standard of responsible exercise, liberty may become licence, thus undermining itself.

Grotius thus ennobles rights discourse and protects the practical implementation of rights by promoting the distinctively human responsibility to transcend the merely human.

While this is a project wide-ranging in its scope, it is also a set of theses somewhat unconventional in its findings. While the thesis amplifies a minority strain of interpretation whose lineage goes back to Grotius' own day, it runs counter to the dominant Grotian legacy shaped by the French Enlightenment as well as the mainstream school of interpretation in contemporary academic literature. Before outlining the scope and methodology of the project, it is worth examining the narrative of Grotius as the father of modern natural rights, and its recent discontents.

Grotius' Legacy: Father of Modern Natural Rights?

Hugo Grotius was born in 1583 in Delft, in the United Provinces of Holland and Zeeland. Young Hugo gained an early reputation as a child prodigy, entering the university of Leiden at age eleven and mastering his education in the classics of Greece and Rome. At the age of fifteen, he was taken to visit the inquisitive King of France, who pronounced the boy "the miracle of Holland." He would live up to the appellation, becoming a true Renaissance man of thought and action: one might imagine a contemporary combination of Ronald Dworkin, Vaclav Havel, Henry Kissinger, and Michael Walzer. At the age of sixteen, he was called to the bar, and two years later, in 1601, he was chosen (over a distinguished professor of letters) to be the official historiographer of Holland. Grotius' career soon became intertwined with that of Johann van Oldenbarnevelt, a leading politician, and in 1613, at the age of twenty-eight, he became pensionary (mayor) of Rotterdam. By this time he had begun publishing in earnest in literature, history, theology, and politics, as well as wading boldly into the political and religious controversies of the day. Having earned the wrath of the orthodox Calvinist party, he was imprisoned for life in 1619. Two years later, after a daring escape from prison in a chest of books, he found refuge in Paris, where he would spend most of his remaining decades. Here he was granted a royal pension by the King of France, and in 1634 became a diplomat for Sweden, working for the cause of peace and religious unity during the tumult of the Thirty Years' War. He continued to write until his death in 1645, producing more works of jurisprudence, legal commentary, poetry, tragedy, philology, theology, political thought, and a massive four-volume Biblical commentary.

For two centuries, Grotius' works were almost continuously in print. While his practical efforts for Christian unity failed, his apologetic work *de Veritate Religionis Christianae (On the Truth of the Christian Religion)* would be published over 100 times in a dozen languages. His doctrinal work *de Satisfactione Christi (The Satisfaction of Christ)* would form the Atonement theology for much of Arminian Protestantism, especially the Methodist church. Grotius was also read and recommended by Founding Fathers such as Benjamin Franklin, John Adams, Alexander Hamilton, and Thomas Jefferson, and (unlike Locke) cited in the *Federalist.* Likewise, he influenced jurists such as James Kent, whose *Commentaries on American Law* have been described as "the first great American law treatise."[7]

Yet Grotius' twentieth-century legacy is largely shaped by remnants of the eighteenth-century continental European interpretation of *de Jure Belli ac Pacis* (*DJB*). The most influential of over fifty editions was Jean Barbeyrac's idiosyncratic French translation of 1724, which Onuma describes as "strongly colored by his own bold interpretations."[8] Barbeyrac argued that Grotius' systematic method had separated natural law from its theological and metaphysical entanglements. He thus portrayed Grotius as having "broken the ice" after the long winter of medieval ethics. This edition would become highly influential; for example, most of the French *philosophes* owned a copy.[9] Rousseau would oppose Grotius several times in *The Social Contract*, and Kant would also use him as a foil.[10] A contemporary of Rousseau, Emer de Vattel, would emphasize Grotius' writings on positive law, thus opening the door for the portrayal of Grotius as the "father of the modern science of law."[11] Hersch Lauterpacht's now-(in)famous 1946 article entitled "The Grotian Tradition in International Law" would read in(to) Grotius "the subjection of the totality of international relations to the rule of law."[12] Barbeyrac's influence carries on today, as the most recent complete English edition is based on his French edition.

If this was the background for studying Grotius, Quentin Skinner more broadly set the tone for exploring early seventeenth-century thought with his revolutionary 1978 *Foundations of Modern Thought*. Here he set out to challenge the standard story that modern rights theories arose in opposition to Christianity. His *Foundations* Volume II, entitled "The Reformation," argues that a study of political thought up to and including the seventeenth century requires understanding the theological side of these thinkers. This is a surprising approach for someone who has described Christianity as "intolerant" and "dangerously irrational."[13] Yet it may dovetail with another of his aims: to show that the resultant development of the modern state took a negative conception of liberty. Skinner uses the term "negative" in the sense introduced by Isaiah Berlin: merely protecting citizens from outside interference, rather than enabling them to make good use of their liberty. Elsewhere, however, he implies that the term also describes his value judgment. Taken together, this suggests a reading of Grotius as a genuinely Christian thinker, one who borrows or builds on earlier Christian rights theorists to reduce justice to an (unfortunate) minimum standard.

Curiously, however, Skinner barely mentions Grotius in *Foundations*, and his subsequent work declines to build on his earlier exploration of Christianity. His student Richard Tuck would take up at least the first of these tasks, identifying a clear turning point in Grotius. First, Tuck argues that Grotius sees systematic mathematical rationality covering the whole of morality, which opens the door to "a definite and *a priori* science of ethics." His rejection of the distinction between theoretical and practical sciences is the reduction of the latter to the former. Second, this leads Grotius to develop the first theory of secular natural rights, built on premises that even a relativist could accept. Lacking a philosophical anthropology, Grotius need not talk about virtue. Rather, his justice is limited simply to upholding the rights of others, and ignores the question of how those rights might be exercised. One need no longer aspire to a vision of human flourishing; one need only avoid breaking rules. Third, social life is nothing but "the peaceable exercise by each member of his rights." Self-interest is the primary human drive, and politics needs reference to little beyond it.[14] Grotius uniquely "treats liberty as a piece of property."[15] Fourth, Tuck then infers that Grotius leaves "little room for individual judgment or the exercise of *phronesis*," the latter being Aristotle's central political virtue. Hence, Grotius is the herald of the modern world, because his deontological rights theory excises any influence of teleology. Fifth and finally, Grotius makes a "final and public break" with Aristotle, the effects of which remain with us today. In Tuck's words, "after the *De Jure Belli*, it was impossible for anyone who wished to think about politics in a modern way – that is, in terms of natural rights and the laws of nature – to pretend that they were still Aristotelians."[16]

Tuck's scholarship has set the agenda for studies of Grotius, beginning with his 1979 *Natural Rights Theories* and continuing in several subsequent works. His reading is echoed both in the works of Skinner's other intellectual descendants within the so-called "Cambridge School," as well as those outside. One of the former is Jerome Schneewind, who further cites Grotius' rejection of virtue as a mean as a repudiation of Aristotle. More fundamentally, he argues that Grotius rejects virtue ethics by grounding morality on law. This metaethics leads to a theory of rights that grounds a realm of "nonmoral choices among permissible acts."[17] Another, Annabel Brett, reflects this position in asserting that "beyond [expletive justice] there is only the free play of utility."[18]

One of the latter is Charles Taylor, whose 2007 *magnum opus* identifies the beginning of our secular age in what he repeatedly describes as the "Grotian-Lockean" theory of order. Natural law is now based on geometric reason rather than teleology. This inaugurates a new modern politics concerned only with physical security and economic exchange, while making possible the religious "disenchantment" of the world. Yet Taylor does not impugn the professed Christian faith of Grotius (or indeed of Locke). In fact, he suggests that these developments open up the beneficial possibility of humanism, especially when – contra Skinner's adamant protestations – infused with a Christianity that must be individually chosen now that it can no longer be taken for granted. Yet this work cites few of Grotius' many theological writings.[19]

Michael Gillespie offers a variant of this reading of Grotius as modern but Christian. He suggests that modernity arose out of the nominalist challenge to scholasticism in the fourteenth century. This challenge arises from a latent tension in the Christian idea that a transcendent God makes possible the regularities of nature, yet creates humans bearing – in his image – freedom of will. To Gillespie, this ultimately theological debate between nature and freedom is at the heart of all of the significant debates of modernity, culminating in Kant's attempt to separate the phenomenal and noumenal worlds. However, because Grotius lacks any explicit metaphysical writings, he is off Gillespie's radar.[20]

Political theologian Oliver O'Donovan further explores these religious themes by relating Grotius' theology to his overall project. He argues that Grotius' Atonement theory vindicates a traditionally thick Christian moral understanding of politics, and a high regard for the virtue of prudence in the character of God himself. This calls into question Grotius' supposed groundwork for possessive individualism and negative rights. O'Donovan asserts in his deliberately entitled *From Irenaeus to Grotius* that Grotius "is the last great figure in whose thought a unity of theology, law, philology, and history is effective." If modernity is a radical change, the turning point does not occur until Hobbes.[21]

Christoph Stumpf builds on this reading in his systematic *The Grotian Theology of International Law*. He suggests that Grotius' conception of *jus* is not in fact a theory of subjective rights, but rather a traditional conception of natural Right. In other words, he counters Tuck's reading of Grotius by agreeing with four interpretive threads: Skinner's (and Gillespie's) contention that Christianity is relevant; Taylor's belief that Grotius' Christianity is genuine; O'Donovan's demonstration that Grotius' theology is central to his political theory; and O'Donovan's conviction that Grotius is continuous with the classical political concern for the soul. However, Stumpf does so by denying in Grotius the rights theory that Tuck and others see as central to Grotius.[22]

This project will attempt to show how the secular (or deontological) rights identified by Tuck and Schneewind are only a starting point. Grotius' Christian humanism (in Taylor's words) is not so much the foundation for his rights as a standard for their subsequent exercise. Rights are meant to preserve the Christian emphasis on freedom that Gillespie identifies, allowing the exercise of this higher standard to be undertaken virtuously. Such a standard is, as O'Donovan and Stumpf emphasize, a Christian development of classical teleology and Aristotelian prudence. In other words, Grotius' ostensibly modern conception of rights is formulated in a way that remains faithful to the classical spirit of Aristotle and his Christian interpreters.

The Secular Challenges of Reading Grotius

Grotius is a notoriously difficult figure to understand. While most are vaguely familiar with *DJB*, few have ventured beyond the most notorious passages of its Prolegomena. One reason is Grotius' florid prose; his 'impious' sentence is 111 words long in the Latin original. Another is his penchant for references to ancient Greece and Rome that do little for many modern readers. A third is the fact that *DJB* is not strictly a work of political theory; rather, the theory must be inferred from Grotius' international relations and his jurisprudence.

However, the greatest difficulty is the fact that Grotius' writings often appear to be at odds with each other, even within one work, and only a sense of the whole can help to resolve the contradictions. Grotius was a true Renaissance man, described by one contemporary as "the greatest universal scholar since Aristotle."[23] To read him solely through selections of *DJB* would be like reading into Aristotle's *Politics* a simple defence of modern pluralism, ignoring the teleology in the *Metaphysics* or the defence of the philosophic life in the *Ethics*.

The dominant interpretive approach to Grotius is heavily inspired by the contextualist methodology laid out in successive treatises in the late 1960s by J. G. A. Pocock, John Dunn, and Skinner. Skinner has stated that one of his primary purposes in *Foundations* was to challenge the then-regnant positivism, but without recourse to the traditional approach. To do so, Skinner avoids reading texts as clues to the overall mind of thinker, or as "timeless meditations on perennial themes" that might speak to our own condition.[24] Rather, he reads texts in isolation as "speech-acts": instruments of political action that advance the author's partisan interests at a given moment.

In this spirit, Cambridge School figures such as Tuck, Knud Haakonssen, Jerome Schneewind, and Martine Julia Van Ittersum have situated Grotius' writings within the political and economic milieu of early seventeenth-century Holland, often showing considerable historical erudition. Tuck's work is particularly noteworthy, especially his attention to Grotius' early *de Jure Praedae (DJP)*. This work was written to defend the actions of the Dutch East India company (VOC) of which Grotius' father was an official. Tuck points out that the theory of property rights outlined therein was expedient to the Dutch opposition to the claimed Portuguese monopoly over the East Indies trade. The same is true of Grotius' belief (one of "extreme originality") that sovereignty over the sea requires countries to concede the right of innocent passage.[25] He also argues that Grotius here grants permission to Christian rulers to conduct treaties with non-Christians in order to assuage domestic Dutch concerns about the VOC's dealings (which indirectly included Grotius himself) with the Sultan of Johor. (Van Ittersum provides even more detail about the context of *DJP*, arguing for instance that Grotius withheld its publication due to the political events of 1606.[26])

Tuck continues this approach when he turns to *DJB* and its more robust view of natural punishment. Here he argues that Grotius altered his position in order to legitimize the post-1619 Dutch practice of forcibly annexing native territory.[27] Tuck also provides a detailed comparison of later editions to buttress his contextual claims. Of particular note are the differences between the first edition of *DJB* in 1625, which remains untranslated into English to this day, and the second edition in 1631, now standard. He provides an original translation of selections from the former, including a passage subsequently excised from the latter about the self-interested nature of man in the (presumably counter-factual) absence of reason. He suggests that this revision was calculated to appeal to the "Aristotelian, Calvinist" culture of Holland in an attempt to secure Grotius' return from exile.[28] These portraits, rich in historical and contextual detail, helped to reinvigorate the study of Grotius and his era in an age of positivism.[29]

While this contextual approach has produced prolific results, its internal tensions suggest that Grotius' value for political life may actually endure beyond the early seventeenth century. A relatively simple illustration arises from Skinner's rejection of the belief that ideas shape power; rather, he asserts that power shapes ideas. This leads him to follow Nietzsche's rejection of a canon.[30] Yet Van Ittersum points out that Skinner's own work still primarily focuses on the canonical figures of Machiavelli and Hobbes, as does the work of many other Cambridge school authors.[31]

A further – and more substantive – tension arises from the methodological attempt to divorce the study of history from prescriptive considerations of our own day. In a key early text, Dunn famously stated that "I simply cannot conceive of constructing an analysis of any issue in contemporary political theory around the affirmation or negation of anything which Locke says about political matters." Yet twenty years later, Tuck began his own methodological reflections by pointing out that while Cambridge School practitioners assert "very little relevance for modern theory, they have also been distinguished contributors to discussions on republicanism, democracy and justice." Skinner's own work on negative and positive rights is a prime example of the practice belying the method. Perhaps for this reason, Dunn has later recanted his earlier assertion, despite its apparent centrality to the method.[32]

Finally, there is some evidence that the contextual approach to Grotius may have unduly coloured the reading itself. In particular, its practitioners seem to prioritize those works for which the method is particularly illuminating, while de-emphasizing other works or shoehorning them into procrustean readings. For instance, the contextual approach works particularly well for *DJP*, a work written to justify a particular action: the seizure of a Portuguese ship by the Dutch East India company. This may help to explain why Tuck judges it "the most impressive and remarkable of all of Grotius' writings."[33] However, Tuck's implicit reduction of Grotius' later texts to political interests of the day (such as the 1631 revisions of *DJB*) is less plausible. The orthodox Calvinists who had originally arrested and imprisoned Grotius likely would have been unmoved by Aristotelian arguments about the nature of man; it was from precisely these pagan influences that they sought to reform the Church.

Indeed, Tuck's emphasis on the centrality of *DJP* also appears to lead to an implicit break with Skinner's belief that there is no comprehensive and unified mind of the author, and the consequent methodology of looking "for coherence only at the level of each individual text."[34] While Tuck sees Grotius' early works as outgrowths of his three main political interests (republicanism, free seas, and tolerance), Tuck seems to imply that these interests coalesced early and remained consistent throughout Grotius' life. Hence, he can argue that "most of the substantive theory of the *DJB* was in fact an expansion of the themes of [*DJP*]," advancing this claim at length in his introduction to the 2005 edition of *DJB*.[35] Hence, while Tuck goes beyond *DJB* to *DJP*, and implies some unity of thought, he does not continue to look at the rest of Grotius' corpus to search for substantive shifts or further insights. Rather, the later works (particularly those of theology) are merely fields for Grotius to illustrate the implications of the foundational moral and political minimalism of *DJP*.

I do not wish to dispute Tuck's claim for the originality and surprisingly mathematical approach of *DJP*. The work does, indeed, sound remarkable notes that would later be echoed in Hobbes' work, a fact that would be little appreciated without Tuck's careful attention. However, there are several reasons to question his bold claim that the work is paradigmatic. The first is the aforementioned fact that *DJP* was written for expressly partisan reasons in a way that most of Grotius' later works were not. The second is the fact that Grotius wrote *DJP* at the tender age of twenty-one, several years before the beginning of his own practical education in politics. Grotius surely would not be the first thinker to prioritize mathematical thinking in his earlier years, only to later appreciate the prudential wisdom that only time and experience – hard-won, in the case of Grotius the exile – can confer. (Indeed, Plato begins his education of the Guardians with mathematics, but judges them fit to rule only after age fifty.[36]) Grotius was indisputably a child prodigy, but I would hesitate to suggest – as Tuck does, I think it is fair to say – that his defining text was the work of a twenty-one-year-old.

Indeed, this leads to the third and most theoretically substantive misgiving: between the 1604 *DJP* and Grotius' productive decade from 1611 to 1621,[37] he altered his more radical, proto-Hobbesian positions on at least half a dozen important premises, including four that cannot be ignored here. The first is an explicit repudiation of his earlier agreement with Horace in *DJP* that society is formed purely due to self-interest; by contrast, *DJB* states that men would enter political society to fulfil their uniquely human nature even if unnecessary for physical needs.[38] The second is an acknowledgement already in the *Meletius* of 1611 that God does not simply command and prohibit actions that are known by natural law (as in *DJP*), but actually issues truths of special revelation that transcend secular reason.[39] The third is that Grotius' early enumeration of strict justice as limited to the protection and restitution of property now includes a positive duty of punishment in the 1617 *de Satisfactione* (later echoed in *DJB*). The fourth is that he abandons the purely negative conception of virtue in *DJP* as a 'mean' between suffering injustice and committing it, and returns to the traditional Socratic-Christian conception that virtue may consist in suffering injustice. These are not minor changes, and Tuck recognizes many of them. Yet, having helpfully marshalled the evidence for the reader, he declines to press a substantively revised case.

Hence, while Cambridge scholarship has produced many insights on Grotius, time has revealed some internal difficulties in its interpretive approach. An alternative approach to Grotius, unconstrained by rigid adherence to a particular method, offers a way forward. Indeed, Tuck has acknowledged that many of the best studies "have worn their methodological commitments (on the whole) fairly lightly."[40]

This study presupposes some element of timeless truth in Tuck's profession that a historical study of ideas can illuminate and even guide our own political situation.[41] The approach here does not seek to read the texts as pure abstractions divorced from the phenomena of politics. Even perennial questions would have to be asked by ensouled bodies in time, and lead to implications requiring prudential application in particular contexts. In this way, it follows Tuck's approach of attempting to "work out what the people were up to."[42] However, it suggests that Grotius was "up to" more than mere political advancement. Rather, he sought to understand politics for its own sake, and to place it within a comprehensive vision of human existence involving dialogue with law, history, theology, and philosophy. For this reason, I presume that Grotius' insights into politics advanced with his age and experience in the school of political hard knocks, and that his writings demonstrated a greater degree of cohesion as time went on. In this, I follow Tuck's example of looking beyond *DJB* for insight into Grotius' mind, but I seek to do for Grotius' later works what Tuck has done for *DJP*. Indeed, the historical record shows that Grotius' later years saw a deepening of interest in Biblical scholarship, to the point where his final decade was devoted almost entirely to his *Annotationes* – a ten-inch-thick commentary on the Bible. He also devoted significant practical energies as a diplomat in an (obviously futile) attempt to reunite the three branches of Christianity. This seems to confirm that his increasingly theological emphasis, already evident in the 1611 *Meletius*, is not derivative, but integral to his overall project. If anything, it should have pride of place in understanding Grotius' mature thought.

Such a pursuit has been hampered by the absence – until recently – of contemporary English translations of Grotius' theology. Until 2003, the most recent translation of *de Imperio* – Grotius' primary work of political theology – was the 1651 edition. Grotius' most doctrinal work of theology, *de Satisfactione*, was republished in 1990, as the previous edition approached the end of its third century. An early work detailing the commonalities between branches of Christianity, *Meletius*, lay completely undiscovered until 1988. Moreover, the (primarily European) secondary scholarship that has since arisen around these works encounters the same tension as Tuck.[43] On the one hand, most scholars imply that Grotius' pioneering approach to historical criticism make him less than genuine (and certainly unorthodox) in his Christian conviction.[44] On the other hand, they tend to question the possibility of reading Grotius as a comprehensive thinker, preferring the historical reading of Grotius as a product of his time.[45] The field is ripe for a study that explores the impact of Grotius' theological and theo-political writings on his political thought.

Reconsidering the Modern Political Self-Understanding

If Skinner's *Foundations* largely overlooked Grotius, it has nonetheless shaped the last generation of scholarship by showing the importance of religion in political thought of the seventeenth century. However, despite his protestations that such findings should have little relevance for today, his own impact (intentional or not) suggests otherwise. We continue to live in a world shaped by the questions and the political structures of that pivotal time period. Our politics are explicitly nonteleological, and religiously particularistic only in a superficial sense. Yet the phenomena – the quest for distinctively human purposes and the experience of religion – remain with us. A revised account of such a key figure as Grotius points toward several broader implications.

The first implication of this study arises from its exploration of the systematic, rational nature of Grotius' expletive justice. This superficially substantiates the long-standing claim, most recently put forward by Tuck and Taylor in their different ways, that Grotius makes possible a world without teleology. Taylor believes that a nonteleological politics is a more humane vision that prevents coercion of heretics, but argues that its underlying society still needs a higher conception of human life. Yet while Grotius creates a space for nonteleological society that can qualify as distinctly human, he also shows that a *fully* (and not merely distinctly) human social existence transcends the formalism of this approach. Grotius' vision may not merely be a precondition for the humane modernity that Taylor advocates, but may actually anticipate that substantive vision. Grotius may offer insights on how to live in a pluralistic world, without reducing political life to the emaciated condition that Nietzsche sees as inherent in modernity.

The coexistence of formal (expletive) and teleological (attributive) categories in Grotius further suggests that the two are not mutually exclusive. This leads to the second implication: that a teleological vision of life need not be hostile to a nonteleological science (whether natural or human). This portends a cooling of the so-called conflict between religion and science, as it speaks not only to those who would substitute reason with revelation, but also to those whose faith in the fact-value distinction leads to contempt for the normative language of wisdom. Grotius' purely rational expletive justice carves out a space for a scientific approach to the 'facts' of the humanities. Yet he also points out the losses that come from ignoring the teleology of 'values.'[46]

Skinner himself seems to have an intimation of this problem when he discusses rights. He has argued that the formalism of a purely 'negative' approach to rights (corresponding to Grotius' expletive justice) undercuts the very viability of rights in the first place. Grotius' attributive justice vindicates exactly this assessment. However, it does so by advocating the teleology (both natural and religious) that Skinner opposes. This implies that the problem identified by Skinner in fact follows from his very rejection of teleology, because that rejection eclipses the need (and ability) to carry out the 'positive' duties that will sustain a regime of rights. It also suggests a reconsideration of Skinner's implicit thesis that Grotius is a modern 'negative rights' thinker seeking to undercut the Renaissance conception of 'positive rights.'[47]

A third major implication of this re-reading is to emphasize the importance of free will and individual responsibility, but within a framework that is Christian rather than Nietzschean. Grotius everywhere emphasizes the importance of teleology, and yet insists that it must be freely chosen; comprehensive doctrines cannot be imposed. He maintains a characteristic Protestant emphasis on the importance of the will, while yet rejecting the Reformed idea that nature is so fallen as to be unintelligible to human reason. This is evident is the way that he affirms both sides of the naturalist-voluntarist debate introduced in Plato's *Euthyphro*. Here he implicitly affirms the mystery of a God who simultaneously grounds both goodness and existence, a mystery surely no less central than that of a Christ both God and man. Without addressing the mystery in ontological terms – nay, even criticizing the propositional metaphysics that seek to drain the question of its mysterious depths – he remains fully aware of the potential tension between nature and freedom that Gillespie sees as animating modernity. If this story reaches a climax in Kant's twin doctrines of right and virtue, as Gillespie has suggested, Grotius may prepare the ground.

This account of modernity is unlikely to convince many who, like Skinner, reject the prescriptions of Christianity as irremediably anti-humanistic. Yet even if we bracket normative questions, surely a value-free, descriptive political science must acknowledge the importance of religion. Although the 'secularization hypothesis' has been surprisingly impervious to contrary evidence, the events of 9/11 are particularly difficult to ignore or explain away. In any case, political theorists from John Rawls to William Connolly to Jeremy Waldron had begun to grapple with the question of religion and public reason even prior to that event.[48] All the same, Taylor is surely correct to observe that this religious fervour (for both good and ill) takes place in a pluralistic context where belief can no longer be taken for granted.

Perhaps the coexistence of religious practice in a disenchanted world is not as new as we think. Consider Grotius' context: he came from a devout but mostly tolerant country (his own imprisonment and exile being the exception that proved the rule); he moved in the upper circles of Paris – the centre of the non-teleological avant-garde – while defending orthodox Christianity; he dealt seriously and sensitively with the question of justice in non-Christian societies; his apologetic work was directed to those for whom Christianity was not self-evident or even familiar; and he served as a diplomat during a war fuelled at least partly by religious fanaticism. In short, his religious context and concerns are surprisingly similar to our own.

Indeed, while Grotius (like Hobbes) recognizes the problems of religious dogmatism, Grotius (unlike Hobbes) sees the solution *within* religion. If Grotius is – unlike Hobbes and Locke – the true progenitor of modern nonsectarian rights theories, he was animated to do so not by rejecting Christianity but by embracing it. Although he made it possible to speak about politics in a secular language, he did not aim to disenchant the world. This leads to a final implication: a re-evaluation of the conventional wisdom that modern liberal politics arose in reaction to religion and can survive only on secular terms. No less a liberal luminary than Jurgen Habermas has recently acknowledged that human rights and democracy "continue to draw on the substance of this [Judeo-Christian] heritage. Everything else is just idle postmodern talk."[49] If we wish to explore the sources of our own political self-understanding today, Grotius is a good place to start.

Notes

1 Government of South Africa, "Nelson Rohlilahla Mandela, 18 July 1918–5 December 2013: Tributes From World Leaders," available at www.mandela.gov.za/quotes/index.html, accessed 21 November 2016.

2 Henry Kissinger had predicted a million deaths.

3 Alex Boraine, *A Country Unmasked: Inside South Africa's Truth and Reconciliation Commission* (Oxford: Oxford University Press, 2000), 11–14, 34–38, 45–46. As Boraine states,

> there were those who argued then and still do that the ANC was divided and that Mandela, in his commitment to reconciliation, had not been keen on the TRC. Clearly this was not [Mandela's minister Dullah] Omar's view, and it certainly wasn't my experience when we met with the President.... He was remarkably supportive ... [and] quick to defend the Commission.

4 Many observers have highlighted the political facets of the Truth and Reconciliation Commission (TRC). In particular, they have pointed out that the TRC was not simply

a prerogative of President Nelson Mandela or the ANC, but a precondition for the end of White minority rule (see Lynn Graybill, "Review: Assessing South Africa's Truth and Reconciliation Commission," *Canadian Journal of African Studies*, Vol. 36, No. 2 (2002), 360; Richard A. Wilson, *The Politics of Truth and Reconciliation in South Africa: Legitimizing the Post-Apartheid State* (Cambridge: Cambridge University Press, 2001), 5–9. Yet even in 1993, the ANC still had a choice; like many other African liberation movements, it could have resorted to armed force rather than to negotiate with the White minority. To consider the interests of the White minority was to consider the interests of every person in South Africa, all of whom would suffer from civil war. In my reading, Grotius suggests that to use the word 'political' in a pejorative sense is to adopt a posture toward rights discourse that may be detrimental to a regime of human rights.

There is also a significant literature evaluating the results of the TRC. Many sources observe that the TRC is considered more successful by overseas observers than by South Africans. It is worth pointing out one South African's response: "the [TRC] report was widely criticized, which is perhaps the best evidence of its intellectual integrity" (Mark Wolf, "Quality of Mercy," *New York Times Review of Books*, May 27, 2001, 4). The first specific critique is that the TRC did not air all crimes of Apartheid, as some victims did not come forward and some perpetrators refused to participate or gave incomplete testimonies (Elizabeth Stanley, "Evaluating the Truth and Reconciliation Commission," *Journal of Modern African Studies*, Vol. 39, No. 3 (September, 2001), 531). However, this would seem a critique of the imperfect implementation of the idea rather than of the idea itself; the problem is that the idea was not carried to its fullness. A second critique argues that the continuation of South African socio-economic inequality compromises any possibility of racial reconciliation (Stanley, "Evaluating," 527). However, one might argue that radical economic redistribution (such as the forced land transfers of neighbouring Zimbabwe) would have precipitated a civil war in which surviving Africans would have been further impoverished. A third critique argues that the ethic of reconciliation was inconsistent with the customs of traditional South Africans, which favoured retribution over reconciliation (Wilson, *Politics of Truth*, 9–13, 89, 129). A related argument is that TRCs "are highly ambiguous in human rights terms" (Paul Gready, "Review of Alex Boraine, *A Country Unmasked: Inside South Africa's Truth and Reconciliation Commission* and Dorothy Shea, *The South African Truth Commission: The Politics of Reconciliation*," *Bulletin of the School of Oriental and African Studies, University of London*, Vol. 64, No. 3 (2001), 448). However, while a policy of retribution might have been more true to custom, and perhaps even more faithful to rights (in the strict sense of justice), it would also have been far more likely to stoke a civil war whose many victims (mostly African) would be unable to enjoy the right of retribution. As Archbishop Desmond Tutu argued, "you say to those who say 'we want justice,' that if there were no amnesty, then we would have justice and ashes" (M. Woollacott, "Reconciliation, or Justice and Ashes?," *Guardian*, 17 February 1997, 17; see also Olayiwola Abegunrin, "Review: Truth and Reconciliation," *African Studies Review*, Vol. 45, No. 3 (December, 2002), 32).

5 Thomas Hobbes, *Leviathan*, ed. C. B. MacPherson (New York: Penguin, 1968), Ch. 14.

6 John Locke, *Second Treatise of Government*, ed. C. B. MacPherson (Indianapolis, IN: Hackett, 1980), Sec. 6, 9. Some would argue that Locke's foundation for rights is secular; at minimum, his right to property seems to fit this description.

7 Mark W. Janis, *America and the Law of Nations 1776–1939* (Oxford: Oxford University Press, 2010), 50.

8 Onuma Yasuaki, *A Normative Approach to War* (New York: Oxford University Press, 1993), vi.

9 Martine Julia Van Ittersum, *Profit and Principle: Hugo Grotius, Natural Rights Theories, and Dutch Power in the East Indies* (Boston: Brill, 2006), xxviii.

10 Rousseau describes Grotius as "a child, and what is worse, a dishonest child," while Kant labels him a "sorry comforter." See Jean-Jacques Rousseau, *Political Writings*, vol. II, ed. and trans. by C. E. Vaughan (Cambridge: Cambridge University Press, 1997), 147; Immanuel Kant, *Toward Perpetual Peace*, ed. Pauline Kleingeld, trans. David L. Colclasure (New Haven, CT: Yale University Press, 2006), 79.

11 Renée Jeffery, *Hugo Grotius in International Thought* (Basingstoke: Palgrave MacMillan, 2006), 70–74.

12 Ibid., 86–88, 92–96, 105–09.

13 Quentin Skinner, "Modernity and Disenchantment: Some Reflections," in *Philosophy in an Age of Pluralism*, ed. James Tully *et al.* (Cambridge: Cambridge University Press, 1995), 46–48.

14 Richard Tuck, *Philosophy and Government, 1572–1651* (New York: Cambridge University Press, 1993), 171–73, 197.

15 Richard Tuck, *Natural Rights Theories: Their Origin and Development* (New York: Cambridge University Press, 1979), 60.

16 Richard Tuck, "Grotius and Selden," in *The Cambridge History of Political Thought 1450–1700*, ed. J. H. Burns (New York: Cambridge University Press, 1991), 506–07, 515–19. For a variation on this specific line of thought, see Villey, 619–20, or John Finnis, *Natural Law and Natural Rights* (New York: Oxford University Press, 1980), 205–08.

17 Jerome Schneewind, *The Invention of Autonomy: A History of Modern Moral Philosophy* (New York: Cambridge University Press, 1998), 76–77.

18 Annabel Brett, "Natural Right and Civil Community: The Civil Philosophy of Hugo Grotius," *Historical Journal*, Vol. 45, No. 1 (March, 2002), 44.

19 Charles Taylor, *A Secular Age* (Cambridge, MA: Belknap Press of Harvard University Press, 2007), 115–27, 157–70.

20 See Michael Gillespie, *The Theological Origins of Modernity* (Chicago: University of Chicago Press, 2008).

21 Oliver O'Donovan and Joan Lockwood O'Donovan, "Grotius (1583–1645)," in *From Irenaeus to Grotius: A Sourcebook in Christian Political Thought, 100–1625*, ed. Oliver O'Donovan and Joan Lockwood O'Donovan (Grand Rapids, MI: Eerdmans, 1999), 787–88.

22 See Christoph Stumpf, *The Grotian Theology of International Law* (New York: Walter de Gruyter, 2006).

23 Hugh Trevor-Roper, *From Counter-Reformation to Glorious Revolution* (Chicago: University of Chicago Press, 1992), 79.

24 Quentin Skinner, "Surveying the *Foundations:* A Retrospect and Reassessment," in *Rethinking the Foundations of Modern Political Thought*, ed. Annabel Brett *et al.* (Cambridge: Cambridge University Press, 2007), 242–44.

25 Grotius substantially alters this position in *de Jure Belli.*

26 Martine Julia Van Ittersum, *Profit and Principle: Hugo Grotius, Natural Rights Theories and the Rise of Dutch Power in the East Indies (1595–1615)* (Boston: Brill, 2006), 188.

27 Richard Tuck, *The Rights of War and Peace: Political Thought and the International Order from Grotius to Kant* (New York: Oxford University Press, 1999), 88–94, 103–04; Richard Tuck, "Introduction," in Hugo Grotius, *De Jure Belli ac Pacis (The Rights of War and Peace)*, ed. Richard Tuck, from the Edition by Jean Barbeyrac (Indianapolis, IN: Liberty Fund, 2005).

28 Tuck, *Rights of War and Peace*, 99.

29 This portrait of Grotius serves Tuck's more wide-ranging and original hypothesis in *The Rights of War and Peace.* Tuck turns on its head the standard narrative that liberal political theory led to state sovereignty, arguing instead that the invention of modern individual rights was a by-product of the interests of early modern states (such as Holland). For more detail, see Knud Haakonssen, "Review: *The Rights of War and Peace*," *Mind*, Vol. 111, No. 442 (April, 2002), 499–502.

30 Skinner, "Surveying the *Foundations*," 241.
31 Van Ittersum, xli–xlii.
32 John Dunn, "What is Living and What is Dead in the Political Theory of John Locke," in *Interpreting Political Responsibility* (Cambridge: Cambridge University Press, 1990), 9–25; Richard Tuck, "History," in *A Companion to Contemporary Political Philosophy*, 2nd ed., ed. Robert E. Goodin *et al.* (Chichester: Wiley-Blackwell, 2012), 69. Tuck concludes his thoughts by re-asserting that political history is not about writing a policy program for today, but leaves an unsatisfying account of what the historical method has actually produced.
33 Tuck, *Natural Rights Theories*, 59.
34 Skinner, "Surveying the *Foundations*," 241.
35 Tuck, *Philosophy and Government*, 176–81; Tuck, *Rights of War and Peace*, 95; Tuck, "Introduction."
36 One can even discern this tendency in contemporary research. Most groundbreaking work today in mathematics and the hard sciences is accomplished by young scholars in their thirties or even twenties. By contrast, scholars in the humanities typically produce their best work later in life. Hobbes himself is a testament to this fact, as he published *Leviathan* at the age of sixty-three. In contrast to Grotius' mathematical musings, those of Hobbes are clearly the fruit of a mature and settled mind, the culmination of thoughts percolating for a half-century.
37 This period produced *Meletius*, *Ordinum Pietas*, *de Imperio*, *de Satisfactione*, *Inleydinge* (though not published until much later), and the beginnings of *DJB*; Grotius' only major works outside this period were *DJP*, *de Veritate*, and the *Annotationes*.
38 Richard Tuck, *Philosophy and Government 1572–1651* (Cambridge: Cambridge University Press, 1993), 197–98; Brett, "Natural Right and Civil Community," 40–41.
39 Tuck, *Philosophy and Government*, 185–86.
40 Richard Tuck, "History of Political Thought," in *New Perspectives on Historical Writing*, 2nd ed., ed. Peter Burke (University Park, PA: Pennsylvania State University Press, 2001), 229.
41 Tuck puts it even more clearly in his introduction to *DJB*, as he concludes with the observation that "the world Grotius depicted is indeed recognizably our world, for good or ill."
42 Tuck, "History of Political Thought," 220–21.
43 See, for instance, *Hugo Grotius – Theologian*, ed. Henk J. M. Nellen and Edwin Rabbie (Leiden: Brill, 1994); *Politique, droit et theologie chez Bodin, Grotius et Hobbes*, ed. Luc Foisneau (Paris: Kimé, 1997); J. P. Heering, *Hugo Grotius as Apologist for the Christian Religion: A Study of His Work* De veritate religionis christianae (Leiden: Brill, 2002).
44 See, for instance, G. H. M. Posthumus Meyjes, "Grotius as a Theologian," in *Hugo Grotius: A Great European, 1583–1645*, ed. National Committee for the Commemoration of Grotius' Birth, trans. P. J. E. Hyams (Delft: Meinema, 1983), 51–58.
45 Harm-Jan Van Dam, "Introduction," in Hugo Grotius, *de Imperio Summarum Potestatum Circa Sacra*, ed. Harm-Jam Van Dam (Leiden: Brill, 2001), 5–6.
46 This is evident not least in Grotius' pioneering approach to historical-critical methods of Biblical scholarship – an approach that even Pope Benedict XVI has endorsed in his "Relationship between Magisterium and Exegetes," Address to the Pontifical Biblical Comission, in *L'Osservatore Romano*, Weekly Edition in English (23 July 2003), available at www.vatican.va/roman_curia/congregations/cfaith/pcb_documents/rc_con_cfaith_doc_20030510_ratzinger-comm-bible_en.html, accessed 21 November 2016. This approach allows believers to accept as legitimate knowledge the contributions of nonbelievers, while acknowledging that even the most comprehensive knowledge *about* God's revelation is insufficient to know God personally. Grotius takes this very approach to pagan and Jewish religion. He treats Judaism with great respect, and his commentary on the Old Testament gives great weight to the Jewish tradition

of interpretation. Nonetheless, he maintains that it has an incomplete understanding of redemption that is fulfilled – but not overturned – in Christ. This suggests that Rawls' overlapping consensus is sufficient for description, but that a comprehensive doctrine is necessary for an adequate prescription.

47 Skinner, "Surveying the *Foundations*," 256–60.

48 John Rawls, *Political Liberalism* (New York: Columbia University Press, 1996); Rawls, "The Idea of Public Reason Revisited," *The University of Chicago Law Review*, Vol. 64, 765–807; William Connolly, *Why I Am Not a Secularist* (Minneapolis: University of Minnesota Press, 1999); Jeremy Waldron, *Law and Disagreement* (Oxford: Oxford University Press, 2001). See also Jeffrey Stout, *Democracy and Tradition* (Princeton, NJ: Princeton University Press, 2004).

49 Jurgen Habermas, "A Conversation about God and the World," in *Time of Transitions* (Cambridge: Polity Press, 2006), 150–51.

2 Natural Right and Natural Rights

If one were drawing up a job advertisement for the available position of "United States President," several requirements would immediately spring to mind. In designing the prerequisites, one would begin by listing an elite education, and then proceed to executive experience – the higher the better. Political savvy and an electoral track record would be essential, and military honour or business success a benefit. Organizational skill would rank highly, with charisma and photogenic appearance only slightly lower.

One of the most important presidential elections in American history featured a candidate with such traits aplenty. Stephen Douglas held a New York law degree, and was a Democratic party power broker. He had a track record as a skilful legislator, and had won three straight elections to the United States Senate. He was a dominant personality, a forceful negotiator, and a practiced debater. When he looked across at his chief opponent, he must have praised his luck: his challenger lacked a single one of these characteristics. This rival had less than two years of formal schooling, lacked executive experience both political and military, and had failed in business. He had lost eight elections – including the most recent Senatorial race to none other than Douglas himself. He was a lean man who once suffered a nervous breakdown, was not possessed of great charisma or personal dominance, and would have been utterly ignored for the cover of his generation's *GQ* magazine.

Yet despite failing to meet a single criterion on the checklist, Abraham Lincoln emerged the winner in 1860. Indeed, the mere term "winner" seems rather an understatement, considering Lincoln's place in the American Pantheon. Yet if the voters of 1860 struggled to define what made Lincoln fit for office, even political historians with the great benefit of hindsight have some difficulty explaining their high estimation of him. Glenn Tinder frames his discussion of Lincoln by establishing that "One of the constant characteristics of great historical figures is their inscrutability. Their lives are apt to be pervaded by ambiguities and contradictions, their greatness strangely undefinable." He describes the "mystery of Lincoln" as the archetypal example of this phenomenon: "He has often seemed, in comparison with other men of power and high station, a quintessential 'common man.'"[1] Why does this not cause us to question Lincoln's greatness? Can Lincoln really be an ideal President if we cannot even define what makes him great?

This is the very underlying question that Socrates faces in Plato's *Republic*. What defines the ideal of justice? Yet when Socrates is asked this question, he does not answer it, but turns around and asks his inquisitors for suggestions. He then rejects their efforts. Indeed, throughout the *Republic*, he will argue that the highest sense of justice is ultimately beyond definition – nay, even beyond words. Why, then, is Plato's ontological realism considered the origin of natural Right, especially if one can discern in his thought no definite individual natural rights – such as those for which Lincoln fought so memorably? What is natural Right without natural rights?

One alternative would be to characterize greatness as the promotion of natural rights – a criterion that could easily be applied to Lincoln. This would naturally suggest a return to the origins of modern natural rights theories, which some have identified in Grotius. If we want to explore Grotius' concept of natural rights, we must first explore his more foundational concept of justice. Yet when we do, we will find that Grotius' concept of justice in fact draws heavily on pre-modern thinkers; for example, his *de Jure Belli* cites eight ancient figures over 100 times each. In order to situate Grotius' conceptions of justice, we must begin by exploring classical conceptions of virtue, law, epistemology, theory, and practice. These themes will converge around three paradigmatic approaches to justice: the ancient concept of natural Right, the medieval concept of natural law, and the ostensibly modern concept of individual natural rights. If Grotius is great, it cannot simply be because he develops natural rights; it must have something to do with his own implicit admission that he stands on the shoulders of giants.

Natural Right in Plato

The classical tradition of political philosophy is often said to have originated when Socrates 'brought down philosophy from the heavens.' Socrates asserts that the study of the highest things – that of Being – has implications for human action, which includes political existence. However, politics is a derivative, second-order reality of Being. The tripartite structure of the polis, including the virtues of each part, reflects the ontologically pre-existent tripartite structure and virtues of the soul. Indeed, to say that political justice mirrors justice in the soul is to say that the former is the imprint and the latter the cause. Put another way, justice is not reducible to institutional solutions. It is not simply about organizing the polis in a particular way. Rather, true justice resides in the soul of the philosopher-king. As a result, political order points toward philosophical order – the order of the soul – which transcends the political realm.

If discursive reason connects human existence to Being, its human language is also inadequate to fully express philosophical order. When Socrates' interlocutors demand a definition of justice in the soul, Socrates hesitates to provide one. As he says, "I won't be up to it and I'll disgrace myself and look ridiculous by trying." However, Socrates does offer a substitute: "I am willing to tell you about what is apparently an offspring of the good and most like it." Accordingly, in the following books, Socrates provides metaphors: the sun, the divided line, and the cave.[2] Thus, the Form of the Good, the higher justice by which the philosopher-kings justly rule the polis, transcends concrete propositional formulations. The words Glaucon and Adeimantus want to hear cannot be anything more than second-order realities in relation to the justice which resides in the souls of the philosopher-kings. It may not be accidental that Plato writes in dramatic form, using allegory and metaphor, rather than writing a treatise aiming for scientific exactitude.

Plato expresses these themes even more clearly in his *Statesman.* Here he sets up a six-fold typology of regimes, one more famously repeated in Aristotle's *Politics.* These types are divided according to institutional categories of rule by the one, the few, or the many, and rule by law or by the interests of the ruler. However, Plato makes it clear that each of these institutional types is limited in its ability to realize justice – even those ruled by law. For this reason, Plato adds a seventh type of rule, which corresponds to true statesmanship.[3]

This statesmanship is characterized by the art of ruling, an art that transcends the rule of law. While the law is rigid and inflexible, the art of ruling may counsel different prescriptions for each unique individual in a particular situation. Just as a good doctor considers each patient individually rather than slavishly adhering to the guidelines of the textbook, the justice of the true statesman is manifested in his wise action in unique situations. Indeed, law is one step removed from the art of ruling; it is only an imitation of the true art.[4] The propositions contained in a written constitution or set of laws are akin to a bridle, not to the skill of horsemanship. The wise ruler is a sort of 'living law,' because the law dwells within his or her soul. This further testifies to the personal and existential character of justice.

Thus, for Plato, justice in its highest sense concerns not political institutions but the soul. It is not about the procedural forms of law-making but the substantive content of virtue that it seeks to cultivate. Yet because it is fundamentally personal, it cannot be fully defined in logical propositions or laws any more than an individual person could be defined. Indeed, it receives its being from participation in a higher reality to which words are inadequate. It is known inasmuch as that eternal order is realized in the human world of actions in time, change, and the particularity of human history.

Natural Right in Aristotle

Aristotle is not the same thinker as Plato, as the student famously breaks with the teacher in Book II of the *Politics*. Yet for all their differences, Plato and Aristotle agree on a great many fundamental issues, especially in contrast with modern political thought. In many ways, Aristotle simply further develops Platonic themes in a more concrete and scientific fashion. For instance, Plato had begun with the right ordering of the philosophical soul and then conceived of political justice as merely a second-order manifestation of it. Aristotle begins likewise, outlining "complete" justice as a characteristic (*hexis*) of the soul that makes people desire to act justly.[5] However, he then establishes "partial" (or political) justice as a separate category of its own with a distinct and not merely mirrored structure.

Aristotle subdivides the genus of political justice into two species: "arithmetic" (or "rectificatory") justice, and "geometric" justice. Arithmetic justice (which would later be termed "commutative" justice) deals not with the public matters involving the citizenry as a whole, but with private matters between two individuals. More specifically, arithmetic justice deals with the external goods of economic transactions, not with the character of the actors; that is, it deals with objects, not subjects. As Aristotle says, "it makes no difference whether a decent man has defrauded a bad man or vice versa.... The only difference the law considers is that brought about by the damage."[6] This makes the judge's decision much easier, as he need not consider intangible realities of internal character.

In order to bring about arithmetic justice, the judge must consider the share of external goods held by each individual. Imagine an initial just distribution in which both persons possess [x]. The first person then unjustly comes to possess a portion [y] of the second person's stock. The first now possesses [x+y] and the second [x−y]. In order to rectify the injustice, the judge performs an arithmetic calculation: he simply subtracts [y] from the stock of possessions of the first and adds [y] to that of the second. Arithmetic justice is thus the mathematical inverse of the original unjust act.[7] It thus appears to require no virtue beyond simple calculation. As a result, its prescriptions are much more amenable to systematization. All it requires is a universal rule that one must repay exactly as much as they have borrowed or taken. When the judge gives the verdict, there is no question about the extent to which justice has prevailed; it is clear that the original state of justice has been restored.

Aristotle further points out that arithmetic justice involves transactions both voluntary and involuntary.[8] The first corresponds to what is known today as contract law: if a debtor fails to pay back the mutually agreed sum, the creditor can take the debtor to court to recover the lost amount. The second lines up with tort law: if a person destroys an object lent to him, its owner can sue for damages.

By contrast, geometric justice (subsequently termed "distributive" justice) deals with public matters involving the state and the citizenry. It governs the distribution of public honours, material goods, or any other common goods that a state may allocate. The state allocates these goods in order to publicly recognize the merit or desert of the recipient and thus to encourage similar virtue in others. For this reason, it requires insight into the character of the person.

In order to bring about geometric justice, the governor must consider not only the two (or more) shares of external goods but also the two (or more) persons. Here the size of each person's share should be geometrically proportionate to his merit. If one person is twice as meritorious as another, the first should receive twice the honours.[9] However, while the honours in question are external goods (as in arithmetic justice), the merit they reward is nonetheless intangible (unlike arithmetic justice) and thus difficult to quantify. Hence, the distribution of these honours first requires a *spoudaios*, or man of practical wisdom, to ascertain the internal character of each person. Indeed, the judgment needed in such prudential considerations can only be developed through experience. While young men may be excellent mathematicians, they cannot have any genuine practical wisdom.[10] Moreover, it seems that this proportionality must be determined on a case-by-case basis. No predetermined, universal rule can specify the just course of action prior to assessing the particulars of the situation.

Aristotle's political justice might appear to be value-neutral. In the case of geometric justice, one might argue that a polis could choose any definition of merit that it desires, even one akin to "honour among thieves." Yet Aristotle makes it clear that a polis oriented around simple preservation of life might be a state of animals (reminiscent of Glaucon's evaluation of the *Republic*'s unphilosophical city as one fit for pigs). The purpose of the state is not simply "to provide an alliance for mutual defence against injury, or to ease exchange and promote economic intercourse." Rather, the good state exists to ensure a "particular quality of character" among its members, and thus to promote philosophical or "complete" justice in the soul. Absent this aim, law simply becomes a guarantee of each person's rights against one another: an offer of collateral to guarantee payment of a debt. It merely has the outward appearance of just external behaviour, rather than being a rule of life meant to inculcate virtue in the souls of people.[11]

Unlike Plato, however, Aristotle argues that politics plays an inherent role in human flourishing. It is not simply a formal vehicle for the transmission of philosophy to the nonphilosopher, but the arena in which the good of every person is discerned, developed, and instantiated. Politics is not a threat to human flourishing but an aid; man is fundamentally political. Indeed, Aristotle notes that the human desire for sociality would lead people to a common life even if it were not needed for self-preservation.[12]

To put this another way, the full development of the philosophical or intellectual virtues requires politics. Aristotle lists several types of such philosophical virtue, including pure science (*episteme*), applied science (*techne*), and practical wisdom (*phronesis*). *Episteme* refers to ascertaining those things that cannot be otherwise, that is, the immutable laws by which the universe operates. *Techne*, often translated as "making," refers to the process of first visualizing a particular immutable form in the mind, and then acting on an object in the physical world to reify this abstract form in a finished product. Contrary to both *episteme* and *techne*, *phronesis* refers to the action of "doing" in the human world. It involves a deliberation that considers how to "act rationally in matters good and bad for man."[13] Hence, *phronesis* is a uniquely political virtue, one that is both exercised and developed in politics.

Phronesis is often translated as "prudence." However, it is important to distinguish Aristotle's understanding of prudence from the modern Cartesian-Hobbesian approach of current linguistic usage. Aristotle's prudence deals with the particulars of a human situation: those elements that change based on the time, place, and person. For this reason, its judgments are contingent rather than universal. The prudent man must imagine a future that will not be exactly like the past. By contrast, Hobbes eliminates as "knowledge" anything involving contingency, and specifically dismisses the ancient notion of prudence as mere guessing. In his view, one can know the future only if one makes it through *techne*. True foresight thus belongs alone to the sovereign Providence "by whose will [future events] actually come."[14]

Aristotle also sees prudence as a virtue unique to citizen-rulers, which links this human activity of doing to the practice of politics. Politics does not consist in acting on inanimate nature to make something out of (or into) an object, but rather in dealing with personal subjects. By contrast, Hobbes sees politics as a thing: its essence is the Leviathan, or sovereign state, which acts for the entire political realm. Political science studies consequences from the accidents of this body politic, and derives tangible and concrete conclusions about its object of study.

Most fundamentally, Aristotle's prudence differs from the modern conception by being a purposive end and by lacking a temporal end.[15] The prudent man is like a flute-player, whose purpose is to play the flute himself, and whose task of instantiating beauty is never truly complete.[16] In other words, prudence is a virtue that enables one to carry out the dynamic reality of politics – a politics whose purpose is intrinsically self-validating and whose task has no temporal end.[17] Here Aristotle's conception of prudence contrasts most starkly with the familiar modern usage of the term. Webster's dictionary defines prudence as "careful good judgment that allows someone to avoid danger or risks." This defines prudence as a means toward an end beyond itself, such as physical security. The man of modern prudence is not like a flute-player, but rather a flute-maker – one whose immediate task of *techne* is to see through to completion the production of the flute, and whose wider purpose is to enable the flute-player to make music. In other words, modern prudence is not like the virtue of playing music that is worth cultivating for its intrinsic value, but a skill cultivated for an extrinsic gain. Indeed, modern prudence often connotes a skilful economization of scarce resources to best maximize one's physical benefit. For instance, the flute-maker of modern prudence may forego immediate pleasures in order to read instruction on how to sell flutes to tone-deaf customers. Inasmuch as this calls for the short-term virtue of self-discipline, such virtue is only a means toward the end of enlightened self-interest. Modern prudence may also advise one how to avoid the risk of danger, in order to ensure physical self-preservation. For example, one might enlist as a Marine Band flautist in order to avoid the possibility of a combat role. The paradigmatic form of such calculated, self-interested, and risk-avoidant prudence is Hobbes' establishment of the Leviathan. Hobbes' politics is an instrumental means to avoid physical harm, and Hobbes' technical solution to this collective action problem brings political thought to its completion. By contrast, Aristotle's *phronesis* is not an instrumental skill but an intrinsic virtue. Its purpose is to help oneself and others achieve final goods, and is rooted in a comprehensive vision of human flourishing. Julia Annas uses implicitly Grotian terminology of "narrow" and "wide" to distinguish between [modern] prudence "in a narrow sense" of a self-regarding good, and [ancient] prudence "in a wider sense," which "guides the agent to what is required for happiness."[18] This ancient happiness, of course, is meant in the eudaimonistic sense of attaining human perfection rather than simply possessing external goods.

Natural Law in Thomas Aquinas

Thomas Aquinas stands at a crossroads. As a theologian at the University of Paris he is committed to an understanding of the supernatural, as it is known through revelation. Yet the rediscovery of the naturalistic philosophy of Aristotle creates a challenge for the Christian world: How can the compelling insights of this reasonable pagan thinker be harmonized with a revealed Christian understanding of reality?

Aquinas makes room for both reason and revelation by proposing that God creates humanity with natural ends known by pagan philosophers, but also with supernatural ends only discernible by believers in Christian revelation. The worldly realm of politics thus has a provisional completeness, because (as in Aristotle) it is central to attaining the natural ends of man. However, man's ultimate (and eternal) end is theological, and the flourishing of this-worldly existence is inadequate to enable eternal felicity. Hence, even the completeness of the political realm points toward a moral vision that transcends politics. Thus, Aquinas deepens the tradition of Aristotle and especially Plato in seeing political life as ultimately ordered toward an extra-political realm – one that now offers theological rather than philosophical rewards.

Aquinas thus argues that reason and revelation are parallel (and occasionally interchangeable) sources of knowledge. Yet in adding revelation, Aquinas implicitly endorses history as a source of truth. One cannot know the supernatural end of human existence without a knowledge of the contingent events of Hebraic and Christian revelation. One cannot deduce this end from first principles; one must learn of it through a personal chain of promulgation beginning with witnesses to the original event. While the fullest event of revelation is in Christ's life and death, God continues to reveal truth to his Church through the Holy Spirit, which enables theologians to further understand Christ's revelation in light of reason. Once theologians universally converge on agreement over a particular idea, it becomes official Church doctrine. Sacred history further supplements reason and revelation as a source of law.[19] Hence, Aquinas implicitly puts forward a tripartite epistemology of reason, revelation, and history.

This place for history means that natural law is not only known through deduction from first principles; it can also gradually make itself known in practice. If this is true for Christian doctrine, it is just as true for political practice; if theologians can develop knowledge over time, surely politicians also can do so. Positive laws that have attained universality and long duration can acquire the status of natural law. Hence, positive laws are not simply beneficial because they add imperative sanctions to the truth that natural law has previously indicated; such laws may actually be beneficial by helping to indicate additional truths of natural law. The positive laws of secular history thus have some ontological status as laws, not only descriptively, but also morally. For this reason, Aquinas sees value in even in positive laws that merely co-ordinate morally indifferent matters on a wide scale, because they provide order and peace. He states that positive human laws are valid even when oriented only toward this political good, rather than toward the divine good. Indeed, Aquinas values this secular order highly enough even to prohibit civil disobedience against unfair laws if such disobedience would compromise that order.[20] Hence, Aquinas' Christianity allows for history as a source of sacred (and secular) moral laws.

Indeed, the term "law" is fitting, as Aquinas particularly conceptualizes ethics through the lens of law. His *Summa Theologiae* deals with law before it deals with justice, and his highest sense of justice is termed "legal justice." This tendency to conceptualize rightness as law – perhaps even more than conceiving it as virtue – reflects Aquinas' Roman heritage. While the Greek world focused on political order as residing in persons, the Roman world tended to emphasize institutions. This implicitly refocused attention away from the less tangible virtues of the soul, and toward the more systematizable actions effected by those virtuous souls. One such institution was the tradition of legal cases. When a judge encountered a particular case, he needed only the technical ability to identify similar cases in the past. This guidance of external codes and cases in law could act as a substitute for virtue, allowing a just verdict even if the judge lacked the virtue of practical wisdom.

This legal approach makes possible a proliferation in the terminology of justice or Right. Where Greek used *dike*, Latin employs not only *justitiae*, but also *jus* (with its substantive, *justum*). Aquinas defines *jus* as the object or goal of justice (*justitiae*). Thus, *jus* is a depersonalized condition which obtains as a result of the exercise of justice. Because it is a static reality, it is more easily definable and thus more amenable to systematization. According to Aquinas (and many Roman thinkers before him), the content of *jus* consists of "rendering to others what is due them."[21] He then defines *justitiae* as the will to do exactly this, as if *justitiae* takes its lead from *jus*.[22] This Christian conception of the will leads to a second implication: the 'agent' employing justice is not the cognitive power of reason or intellect but the will. Thus, justice is not merely a part of intellectual virtue, but of practical virtue; merely knowing what is just does not make one just.[23] Hence, on the one hand, Aquinas' terminology makes it possible to talk about *jus* in a depersonalized sense; on the other, he deepens the sense of the will involved in the justice of the soul.

Aquinas also follows Aristotle in his bifurcation of political justice, but changes the category headings of justice from "arithmetic" to "commutative" and from "geometric" to "distributive." While Aquinas thus de-emphasizes the mathematical nature of these types of justice, he does not dispute that they are concerned with external goods (or, more specifically, the virtue involved in the transfer of external goods.) Aquinas' commutative justice thus reflects the economic, private, and transactional nature of Aristotle's arithmetic justice. Aquinas seems to focus more heavily on commutative justice, devoting fifteen different questions of his *Summa* to it. Also like Aristotle, Aquinas' distributive justice concerns public matters between the community and the individual.[24] However, he seems much less interested in this category, devoting only one question to it.

In sum, Aquinas echoes Plato and Aristotle's sense that ethics or natural Right goes beyond political justice. Indeed, he provides a clearer exposition of the trans-political realm, and provides this realm with its own epistemological category of sacred history. By extension, he thus opens up the idea of secular history as revealing truths of natural law. Aquinas also grants to positive law a value on its own for its role in fostering public order. Aquinas follows Aristotle's bifurcation of justice, but appears to emphasize the commutative justice of objects at the expense of the distributive justice that governs subjects. Moreover, his definition of justice includes reference to his Roman-inspired concept of *jus*. This opens the door to a systematized institutional science of politics, as *jus* corresponds to visible states of being or external conditions. When it comes to the wider sense of Right, Aquinas also tends to conceive of natural Right along the lines of a systematized framework of natural laws. This appears to be only a subtle departure from the classical natural Right position. However, in subsequent centuries, this distinction would lead to significant implications for practical virtue, the personal nature of politics, and the connection between the political and the trans-political.

Natural Right and Natural Law

This brief discussion of the classical tradition of justice includes several implicit themes. One is the particularly tricky distinction between natural Right, natural law, and natural rights. Natural Right (as distinguished from natural rights) connotes a virtue-based moral philosophy, as is implicit in Plato and somewhat more explicit in Aristotle. As Jerome Schneewind puts it, this means that "no antecedently statable set of rules or laws can substitute for the moral knowledge the virtuous agent possesses."[25] At the very least, Right cannot be put into a semantic framework, least of all one that is universally valid. Rather, it is manifested in actions of persons, springing forth from its dwelling-place in the soul of the virtuous person. Thus, Right by nature is inherently personal, even if it transcends the person.

Natural Right is thus somewhat difficult to communicate to those who do not already have it in their souls. As a result, one might make an effort to formulate its ineffable, personal characteristics in second-order propositions of law that can more easily be communicated from one to another. The recipient may now carry out acts that conform to specific propositions of natural law. The repeated performance of these acts may, in turn, awaken the recipient's soul to a participation in the transcendent source of natural Right. The reconfiguration of natural Right as natural law may help to make it more widely available.

Yet if natural law is easier to understand, it may also be less rich in meaning. As these natural law propositions come to address more and more situations that the person encounters, the importance of personal judgment and intuitive wisdom may become less obvious. One need not observe others to ascertain the good course of action in a particular situation when the absolute natural law already has the answer. In fact, one does not even need another, wiser person to teach and guide; one can read a book. In other words, the greater and more detailed the formulations of natural law, the more they may begin to act as a substitute for (rather than a second-order sign of) natural Right. To use Platonic terms, correct opinion (*doxa*) may come to eclipse actual knowledge of the good. The letter of the law may begin to diverge from the underlying spirit of the law.

Laws may come to be seen as the final word, and the infinite possibilities of human action may be forced into procrustean beds of legal formulations.

The reformulation of natural Right as natural law also carries the benefit and challenge of of orienting moral and political discourse around acts rather than character or habit. This is especially true because most laws have a negative function of preventing bad acts rather than promoting good ones. For example, laws can – and often do – proscribe the fraudulent acts which weaken social trust. A law commanding every person to trust one another when entering a contract would be practically feeble, and would have little bearing on whether the parties actually come to trust each other. Yet the mere absence of (negative) fraudulent acts does not imply the presence of positive character that inspires interpersonal trust. Thus, although the use of laws or rules in ethical discourse need not necessarily reduce political action to a negative function or separate it from its orienting teleology, it opens the door to doing so in practice.

A focus on natural law might also lead to legalism, as its adherents may increasingly perform only the minimum possible action that qualifies as "legal." This is a particular temptation in cases where the legal process is especially cumbersome, and the associated opportunity costs of pursuing redress must be offset by a high potential payoff. For example, a contract may stipulate that one party must provide a particular quantity of goods. However, it is often difficult to regulate the quality of those goods. In a society with little trust, one can expect the party to provide goods of poor quality that barely suffice to prevent a lawsuit. To be sure, this licit action would be preferable to simply breaking the contract. However, this legalism would clearly be inferior to one in which the party provides adequate or superior goods, reflective of a good working relationship between the two parties.

The English language creates further potential to separate law from its normative source. Most languages employ separate terms for the natural law of morality and the positive laws of the state: in Latin, *jus* and *lex*; in French, *droit* and *loi*; in German, *recht* and *gesetz*. However, in English, the term "law" refers to both. This terminological coincidence tends to conflate the concepts, often reducing natural law to positive law. This compounds the implicit conflation already present when legislative action turns natural laws into positive laws. Because the promulgation and sanctions of natural law are usually less immediately present than those of positive law, one may be inclined to forget that the content of the positive law is derived from the natural law. Indeed, one may come to see law as purely imperative, and thus to see all law as mere positive law grounded in the threats and sanctions of the state. This confusion between natural and positive law creates challenges in understanding Grotius from the beginning. As most observers begin with *de Jure Belli*, their first English impression of Grotius comes from the mistranslated title "The Law of War and Peace." This leads them to assume that Grotius is operating from a primarily or even purely positivistic conception of law, rather than an overarching framework of natural Right.

Natural Right and Natural Rights

The concept of subjective natural rights incorporates these natural law adaptations of natural Right, but then goes one step further. While laws create active duties not to commit the worst of negative actions, rights create passive claims that one not be subjected to the worst of negative actions. Subjective rights thus conceptualize justice not from the perspective of the one who acts but the one who benefits.[26] Subjective rights thus orient moral discourse around the individual, de-emphasizing the multiplicity of agents who might act on him and thus simplifying the inherent social complexity of ethics. Subjective rights also shift the focus from the act (or will) of the duty-bearer to the effect on the right-holder, making it easier to identify breaches of justice. A state can then develop purely objective criteria to measure compliance or lack thereof: namely, the condition of external, tangible objects. Because these inert objects are lifeless and frozen, their essences are static and thus naturally amenable to systematization (as suggested by the term "the justice system"). This is particularly true for the duties of commutative justice.

This benefit of systematization need not inherently undermine natural law or natural Right. Indeed, natural rights may sometimes be reciprocal to the natural law that expresses a portion of natural Right. For instance, if one's own subjective right to life is violated by another's practice of hunting people for sport, one would have to assume that the other person is violating a natural law not to murder, as well as failing to live up to natural Right in his or her being. However, the physical damage to one's own body is only a third-order consequence of the other's breach of natural Right. Natural Right is the first-order reality, requiring people to live in harmony with each other (to use one of many possible – and necessarily imperfect – formulations). The subsequent natural law is a second-order reality that creates in the other person the duty not to commit unnecessary harm. It is fully applicable and legitimate, but it does not completely express the first-order vision of living in harmony with others. From this narrowly defined second-order duty follows one's own reciprocal third-order right to security of person. Thus, while the individual right is consistent with natural Right, it is only a third-order reflection of a higher and more comprehensive vision of human flourishing. The conceptualization of justice as subjective claim-rights may have the effect of turning a third-order reality into a cornerstone.

Subjective rights may also create a perception of radical moral autonomy. Subjective rights operate by protecting a sphere in which an agent has the ability to act autonomously, free from constraints. This does not mean that the individual is radically free to re-create the structure of moral reality. Indeed, by opening a sphere of freedom, one might argue that freely willed goodness – surely the highest kind of goodness – may flow forth. However, this grant is a double-edged sword, because conferring on the individual a sphere of sovereignty may create the impression that such sovereignty is radical and absolute. The holder may feel emboldened to act without moral constraint.

Moreover, the emphasis of subjective rights on passive claims and individual perspective may gradually undermine a sense of justice as interpersonal harmony. Although natural law may turn the active natural Right framework of will or intention into a passive framework of act-avoidance, it still contains the idea of a duty to refrain from committing evil against others. The concept of individual natural rights may remove the element of will as a primary consideration entirely. Rather than demanding that others not commit a particular act, which requires a limitation of will, rights simply stipulate that one's possessions be free of external impediments (in Hobbes' language). Furthermore, political discourse may increasingly come to confer moral approval on possession of things, particularly property, rather than on actions. Unlike actions, possessions are necessarily exclusive and zero-sum. Hence, their holder may begin to take a defensive posture toward others, as one seeks to protect one's own rights. Thus, the concept of rights can begin to eclipse the idea of duties toward others, leading individuals to focus on what they can get for themselves. Subjective rights thus may gradually reshape a polis once focused on the common good into an aggregation of competitive individuals that merely resembles an Aristotelian alliance.

In sum, subjective natural rights should not be mistaken for a return to the concept of natural Right or right by nature seen in Plato's notion of the Good, in Aristotle's understanding of philosophy, or in the medieval understanding of a personal God. Indeed, the grammatical use of an article, definite or indefinite, to indicate "a right to X" or "the right to X" is a clue to the fundamentally possessive nature of rights. Likewise, the grammatical possibility of the pluralization of rights testifies to their quantitative (and thus ontologically monistic) nature. Just as the English language may confuse natural and positive law, it may confuse Right with a right. However, the two terms bring important and distinct implications for politics.

Conclusion

If the fullness of natural Right (and thus of ideals or greatness) is undefinable, one should expect to glimpse it in surprising places. One such surprising manifestation may be Abraham Lincoln's Second Inaugural Address. This oration, delivered as Lincoln led a nation emerging from strife, is not a rousing victory speech. Lincoln takes little personal credit for the impending outcome of the war, and points instead to a higher Providence: he can see (and follow) the right only "as God gives [him] to see the right." His own sense of political justice is valid only inasmuch as it participates in a higher source. Nor does he moralize over his adversary; rather, he invokes upon himself Christ's admonition to "judge not that we be not judged." Greg Weiner concludes that "his substitution of grace for reason between the *Lyceum Address* and the *Second Inaugural* reflects a mature humility that lies at the heart of prudence."[27] In this reading, Lincoln appears to demonstrate this central Aristotelian virtue of prudence precisely by pointing toward a Platonic-Christian source of virtue that transcends politics. One could say that as leader of the Union, Lincoln had a subjective natural right to undertake war, but this speech is surely less a defence of that individual natural right than it is a testament to an overarching natural Right.

(Indeed, Lincoln would soon have an even more tangible right to punish Confederate soldiers, yet would offer pardon to them, displaying – as Chapters 7 and 8 will show – an implicit Grotian inspiration.)

Yet if subjective natural rights are a mere third-order sign of a first-order natural Right, they need not necessarily eclipse or even oppose that higher reality. Indeed, if natural rights ultimately draw their substance from natural Right, there ought to be a way to connect the two. Returning to the *Republic*, if Plato portrays correct opinion (*doxa*) as a third-order sign of the divine Form of the Good (*nous*), he does not disparage it per se. In his Allegory of the Cave, the one who has *doxa* has already begun the ascent from the shadows. While he may still need a guide to bring him into the light of the sun, his current station is not contemptible; the only shame would lie in refusing to continue the journey upward. In the same way, the Lincoln who pointed toward the source of natural Right had, a year and a half earlier, unashamedly spoken in the language of subjective natural rights: a nation "conceived in liberty" with a government "of the people, by the people, and for the people." If the concept of subjective natural rights is capable of pointing beyond itself, perhaps the task is to formulate and promulgate it in such a way as to make clear its limits, and to direct the individual bearers of natural rights toward higher realities. Grotius' theory of natural right(s), grounded in his theory of justice, will take up this commission.

Notes

1 Glenn Tinder, "The Almost-Chosen People: Abraham Lincoln's America," *Weekly Standard*, Vol. 6, No. 11 (2000).
2 Plato, *Republic*, trans. G. M. A. Grube, rev. C. D. C. Reeve (Indianapolis, IN: Hackett, 1993), 506d–518b, 180–90.
3 Plato, *Statesman*, trans. J. B. Skemp, rev. Martin Ostwald (Indianapolis, IN: Hackett, 1992), 300e–303b, 78–84.
4 Ibid., 292a–300e, 63–78.
5 Aristotle, *Nicomachean Ethics*, trans. Martin Ostwald (Upper Saddle River, NJ: Prentice Hall, 1999), 5.1 (1129a7–11), 111.
6 Ibid., 5.4 (1132a1–4), 120–21.
7 Ibid., 5.4 (1131b25–1132b20), 120–22.
8 Ibid., 5.2 (1130b30–34), 117.
9 Ibid., 5.2 (1130b30–34), 117; 5.3 (1131a10–1131b24), 118–20.
10 Ibid., 6.8 (1142a11–20), 160.
11 Aristotle, *Politics* 3.9 (1280a30–1280b14), trans. Ernest Barker (New York: Oxford University Press, 1958), 118–20. The lesser understanding of law is taken from the phrase of the Sophist Lycophron.
12 Aristotle, *Ethics* 3.6 (1278b19–23), 111.
13 Ibid., 6.4–6 (1140a1–1141a1), 151–56.
14 Thomas Hobbes, *Leviathan*, ed. C. B. MacPherson (New York: Penguin, 1985), 97.
15 Ibid.
16 Aristotle, *Politics* 3.4 (1277b24–30), 106 (see also editor's note). The flute-player may perform in a musical production, but unlike the production of a flute, the life of a musical 'production' is not finished at its first curtain call. Likewise, the future presentations of a musical production are always interpretations rather than replications of the original; even a supposedly 'definitive' production can be surpassed.
17 It is true that Aristotle's *Politics* (and Plato's *Laws*) seem to envisage a more realistic system of concrete political structures and laws. However, these systems can never

perfectly reflect order in the souls of the well-ordered rulers, as that order is made manifest in time. Absolute laws enshrining permanent propositional truths about good politics fail to represent the full order of reality.

18 Julia Annas, "Prudence and Morality in Ancient and Modern Ethics," *Ethics* Vol. 105, No. 2 (January, 1995), 244–48.

19 Thomas Aquinas, *Summa Theologiae* I–II, in *On Law, Morality, and Politics*, 2nd ed., ed. William P. Baumgarth, trans. Richard J. Regan (Indianapolis, IN: Hackett, 2002), 97.3, 72–74.

20 Ibid., 90.2, 13; 92.1, 28; 96.4, 64. Aquinas also states that unjust laws ordered to the ruler's private good are perversions of law, but still "partake of the nature of law." Hence, he seems to define the term "law" descriptively as well as prescriptively.

21 Ibid., II–II 57.1–2, 98–101.

22 Ibid., 58.1, 105–06. Aquinas also substitutes the term "will" for "habit" in order to reaffirm that justice is an act rather than a potency (58.1).

23 Ibid., 58.4, 110–11.

24 Ibid., 58.5, 112; 58.7, 115–16; 61.1, 123–24.

25 J. B. Schneewind, *The Invention of Autonomy* (New York: Cambridge University Press, 1998), 76.

26 John Finnis, *Natural Law and Natural Rights* (New York: Oxford University Press, 1980), 205.

27 Greg Weiner, "Of Prudence and Principle: Reflections on Lincoln's Second Inaugural at 150," *Society*, Vol. 52, No. 5 (December, 2015).

3 Two Concepts of Justice

The Germany of 1949 was a country emerging from tumult, oppression, and destruction. For over a generation, human rights had been trampled under militaristic and authoritarian government, culminating in absolute surrender and American-led regime change. The new *Basic Law* aimed to start over. It began with the phrase "Human dignity shall be inviolable," which established the protection of basic negative liberties. The *Basic Law* was quickly embraced by the German people. The country wisely elected as its first Chancellor Konrad Adenauer, and six years later the military occupation ended with Germany's reception into NATO. Within ten years Germany had significantly realized many of the positive liberties listed elsewhere in its *Basic Law*: establishing public enterprises, transportation networks, and banking infrastructure, as well as generally re-empowering the German people to achieve their potential.[1]

The Iraq of 2005 faced a similar recent history of oppressive government, militarism, and disrespect for human rights, culminating in American-led regime change. Its new constitution aimed at a new beginning, as it outlawed terrorism and ethnic cleansing and aimed to promote positive liberties such as equality and democracy.[2] However, elections quickly descended into a sectarian struggle. The withdrawal of occupation troops led to civil war. Soon the Islamic State of Iraq and the Levant began to commit the very acts outlawed in the preamble to the constitution. Despite operating under the rule of these basic rights, Iraq in 2015 was a fragile state with little economy or education, its citizens largely unable to achieve positive aims of individual and political potential.[3]

One of the most helpful (if contested) clarifications of human rights is Isaiah Berlin's famous "two concepts of liberty." "Negative liberty" consists in the "freedom from" external coercion: the absence of a wall separating East and West Berlin permits individuals to enter West Berlin. "Positive liberty" consists in "freedom for": access to motorized transport (or extraordinary physical stamina) enables one to travel from Leipzig to Berlin.[4] Both post-war Germany and post-war Iraq had strong constitutional protections for negative liberty, and even some provisions for positive liberty. Yet only in Germany were the latter actually achieved. The German people exercised well their negative liberty at the ballot box, helping to establish positive liberty in economic growth and education. By contrast, the Iraqi people exercised their negative liberty in a way that divided the country. The Iraqi constitution may have guaranteed positive rights to health care and education, but ten years later, few Iraqis were well-cared-for or well-educated.

J. G. A. Pocock has identified the roots of positive liberty in Aristotle, whose concept of ruling and being ruled in turn implies a capacity for political participation that simultaneously demands and develops the person's fullest human capacities. He traces negative liberty to Hobbes, who famously defined liberty as "the absence of external impediments."[5] Pocock's Cambridge School confrère Quentin Skinner has further argued that negative liberty eclipsed an older (and fuller) form of liberty in the seventeenth century. Skinner traces this change to the development of modern constitutionalism, in which Protestants embraced rights theories developed by Catholics both before and after Luther.[6] This history suggests that if we want to understand rights discourse today, we might turn back to the Christian thinkers of the Renaissance era.

Grotius certainly qualifies as one such. His Renaissance education already informed his prodigious teenage works, as he frequently cites Greek, Roman, and even Hebrew classics in their original tongues. His Reformation milieu led him to pen works of political theology, Christian apologetics, Atonement doctrine, Scriptural drama, and ecclesiology. His wider European citizenship allowed him to move comfortably among Catholic circles, and he worked tirelessly to try to unify Protestant, Catholic, and Orthodox Christianity on the basis of its common classical Greek and Roman origins. Grotius might profitably be seen as a synthesist for his era – an Aristotle, Aquinas, or Hegel of the Renaissance. Yet scholars of this era (including luminaries such as Skinner) often devote only cursory attention to Grotius. Those few who do explore Grotius in detail (such as Skinner's student Richard Tuck) generally see a thinker who takes a decisive step in developing a theory of negative rights, one that rejects not only positive rights but the broader classical framework of natural Right.[7] Hence, a historical genealogy of negative rights seems to call for a closer look at Grotius.

Yet establishing a Grotian historical patrimony would still leave unanswered several important conundrums of negative rights. Are they superior to positive rights? Need they exclude positive rights? Do they threaten their own practical realization without positive rights (or at least positive action) – as in Iraq after Saddam? Grotius' works show not only a foundation for negative rights but an attentiveness to these very questions. Grotius provides an independent grounding for negative rights, but also shows that they are ordered toward a broader framework of positive rights.

Grotius' concept of negative and positive liberty is grounded in his dual framework of justice, which in fact develops the classical taxonomy of Aristotle and Aquinas. Yet a broader study of Grotius' theoretical foundations helps to further situate this framework and points to wider philosophical implications. Grotius' defence of natural justice provides a place for both intrinsic and extrinsic motives, prefiguring both an impersonally objective natural law and a personally subjective natural Right. This metaethics will provide a place for both naturalism and voluntarism, and his theology will respectively ground these in God as creator and God as governor. This leads to a corresponding jurisprudence that recognizes the place and value of both natural and positive law. These categories of law will then help to explain his epistemology, and the important role of both reason and history as sources of knowledge. Grotius systematizes these philosophical foundations in his taxonomy of Right, which he lays out most clearly in an obscure letter of his personal correspondence. This taxonomy provides the groundwork for his two categories of "strict" and "wider" justice. After establishing the foundations of these categories, we can begin to explore their features. There are seven distinct axes of comparison that show the unique and opposing characteristics of each type of justice. This examination will flesh out the categories and show how they express Grotius' earlier philosophical groundwork. The naturalism of pure reason grounds expletive justice, from which flows the "negative" liberty of rights. The voluntarism of history grounds attributive justice and points toward revelation, from which flows the "positive liberty" of responsibilities.

Defence of Natural Right: Intrinsic and Extrinsic

From its title, *de Jure Belli ac Pacis* (*DJB*) purports to be a work of international theory. Grotius begins by noting that there has been much commentary on Roman law but little on the relations between states. Unlike other jurists, he aims not simply to comment on the tradition of positive laws within one particular nation. Rather, he seeks the fundamental principles of natural Right that govern a realm lacking positive law.

Grotius recognizes – much like Plato – that before he can examine the concept of natural Right, he must first justify its very existence. Why ought one act justly? Is justice not simply a cover for self-interest, as Carneades and Thrasymachus had argued? Grotius addresses these sceptical objections very early in his Prolegomena to *DJB*.[8] Here he offers both intrinsic and extrinsic justifications for natural Right by outlining a conception of human nature. Humans have physical self-interest, which they share with animals. However, humans also have a higher desire for social life of which animals have only a premonition. Most distinctively, humans have a further capacity to govern themselves through speech and discursive reason completely foreign to animals. This human reason has two parts. The first is the unique capacity to act in accordance with general and necessary principles. The second is the unique ability to envision the contingent future, and thus to determine what is fitting in particular cases. To be even clearer, these two distinctive capacities are not simply means to the same ends as animals; they are ends in themselves. Our social nature would lead us into society even if we did not lack anything. Hence, political society is oriented toward fulfilling our unique human nature. Grotius' intrinsic defence of natural Right is thus grounded in human nature; his ethics follows his ontology.[9]

However, while political existence is good for us, it is also expedient. The Author of nature made us weak, needing the help of others to live properly. In other words, we directly punish ourselves if we do not act according to the principles of reason that correspond to human nature. This provides an additional incentive to live according to justice. Even if we are not motivated by truth, we may be motivated by fear; God has implanted both intrinsic and extrinsic motivations in us. One might in fact see this as evidence of God's care for creation: our extrinsic need makes us more likely to achieve our highest purposes (and thus our happiness) than would our conscience alone.[10]

Grotius reinforces this idea of two natures, one higher than the other, in his treatment of friendship. He does not deny that individual need or self-interest may lead to friendship. However, friendship cannot be reduced to what he calls first (animal) nature, or need alone. Rather, friendship is also something to which we are spontaneously drawn by our distinctively human nature. From this (second) nature is known something higher than self-interest. Consideration of others suggests – and sometimes commands – individuals to put the interests of others above themselves.[11]

Thus, Grotius' references to expediency do not indicate a wholesale reduction of political existence to the self-interested desire to avoid pain and punishment. Expediency may reinforce the higher human inclination toward acting justly, but one should not thereby conclude that natural Right is justified only by recourse to it. Extrinsic factors do not preclude the existence of intrinsic ones, and Grotius is comfortable with their mutual coexistence.

Dual Metaethics: Naturalistic Reason and Voluntaristic (Divine) Will

This dual justification for the existence of natural Right carries on into Grotius' metaethics. The metaethical debate between naturalism and voluntarism has persisted since Plato formulated its dilemma in the *Euthyphro*: does God command actions because they are good, or do actions become good because God commands them? In other words, does God carry out an indicative (naturalistic) role that identifies for us what is naturally good, or an imperative (voluntaristic) role that sovereignly commands us to act in a certain way? Grotius deals with this tension between naturalism and voluntarism in orthodox Christian fashion: he implicitly denies the either-or nature of the philosophical question by affirming that both are true in the mystery of a God who is both infinitely good and infinitely omnipotent. Throughout his work, Grotius will fastidiously repeat (indeed, almost to the point of tedium) that the indicative moral obligations of reason are also imperatively commanded by God.[12] Thus, natural Right is binding because it is inherent in the nature of creation and because God commands it. The moral laws of God are both intrinsically good and extrinsically beneficial to those who follow them.

Epistemologically, however, Grotius separates God's indicative and imperative roles. God indicates to us some elements of Right in the natural order whose principles we discern through our God-given reason; God commands other elements through his special revelation in Scripture. The former gives rise to the infamously misinterpreted passage through which alone so many have read (and judged) Grotius. After establishing the existence and content of natural Right, Grotius postulates his infamous *etiamsi daremus*, or "impious hypothesis." Here he states,

> what we have been saying would have a degree of validity even if we should acknowledge that which cannot be acknowledged without the greatest wickedness: that God does not exist, or that the affairs of men are of no interest to Him.

Natural Right – or, more precisely, those basic elements of natural law that Grotius has just outlined – could be known even by those ignorant of God's special revelation. However, it is important to parse Grotius' wording with care. He does not – as commonly believed – say that such things could be known if God did not exist. Rather, he says that such things can be known by those who refuse to acknowledge God as the source of their capacity to reason. The fact that some elements of natural law can be known even by atheists does not change the fact that God exists – or the fact that the atheist's knowledge of natural Right is still dependent upon the prior existence of God. Whether acknowledged or not, natural reason is in fact natural revelation. Grotius reinforces this position by asserting that everything we know indicatively in natural Right is given subsequent weight through God's imperative will. God forbids things contrary to nature and enjoins those which naturally have a quality of moral necessity. Yet while God commands it, he is not free to change it. Just as God cannot make two times two equal anything but four, he cannot cause an intrinsic evil to be good. Interestingly, Grotius points out that God allows himself to be judged by such a standard, as is shown in several examples from scripture.[13]

This distinction between the created order of nature and the divine will of God often gives rise to the distinction between the natural and supernatural realms. The natural world is that which proceeds in an orderly and predictable way, according to the logic of God's design; the supernatural world is the domain of the unexplainable, which could only be revealed by God. However, Grotius will offer a somewhat different account when he discusses nature in his theo-political work *de Imperio*. This account blurs the lines between reason and revelation. Here he describes as "natural" even those principles that proceed in a stable and consistent manner from a divine source. He gives as an example the idea that the Trinity is one God, and thus deserving of worship. Thus, he seems to understand the term "natural" not in opposition to "supernatural," but to "arbitrary." The primary characteristic of nature is not its disavowal of sacred matters but its immutability.[14]

The first basic implication of Grotius' approach is to reaffirm that nature is, in fact, God's creation. The atheist need not acknowledge it as such in order to begin to uncover its mysteries. Nonetheless, a complete study of nature should lead even the atheist to its divine source, even if special revelation and grace are prerequisites for a full conversion to Christianity. This sheds a more orthodox light on Grotius' allegedly impious hypothesis, and points to his later conclusion that natural reason leads to natural religion.

The second implication is that Grotius draws a distinct line between nature and free will, even in God. His primary distinction in knowledge is not between reason and revelation; it is between God's natural law and God's positive law.

While the former is an immutable law, the latter follows from God's positive action, and is willed in ways that could have been otherwise. The latter especially portrays God as a person who voluntaristically acts in contingent ways. Because God's subjects cannot penetrate the intention of God from which these acts spring, they may see it as arbitrary (*arbitrario*). However, God cannot contradict himself. His intention flows from his mind, which means it is in fact reasonable, even if those reasons cannot be formulated in propositions fully accessible to human capacities. Indeed, Grotius has just told us that divine Right may reveal truths additional to those knowable through natural Right.[15]

Hence, God is not simply a creator of nature, let alone Aristotle's mere first cause of "thought thinking itself." Rather, God is a person who governs the moral universe – which militates against the common reading of Grotius as a proto-deist who sees God only as creator of nature. God exercises this will by entering into history – that is, intervening into the otherwise immutable natural laws of the created order – and acting out of concern for the good of the people he has created. This 'subjective' character of Divine positive Right makes it uniquely appropriate for the human world, as the person is not an object and can never be treated as one. Right ultimately transcends 'objective' nature.

Tripartite Epistemology: Reason, Revelation, and History

Grotius' multiple sources of ethical obligation point toward multiple sources of knowledge. In fact, in Grotius' first paragraph of *DJB*, he immediately suggests three sources of knowledge for international Right (*jus inter populos plures*). First, Right can be "derived from nature." That which is made binding through the indicative function of nature is known through reason. Second, Right can be "established by divine ordinances." The voluntaristically binding obligations of God's imperative will are known through sacred Scripture. Grotius then adds a third: Right can "hav[e] its origin in custom and tacit agreement." In addition to reason and Scripture, knowledge is available in history. Grotius then uses this tripartite epistemology to defend Right by nature. Reason offers intrinsic motives to obey natural Right, such as those that Plato offers in the *Republic*; history condemns injustice by the "common agreement of good men"; and – most importantly – God reveals that he is a friend of the just soul, promising rewards in this world and the next.[16]

In other words, while God's imperative role makes obligatory the indicative moral truth of nature (such as the fact that injustice enslaves the conscience), it also provides additional moral knowledge beyond that which can be known through reason (such as the fact that injustice leads to eternal torment).[17] The latter moral truths cannot be deduced by reason; they must be known in sacred history. To claim divine positive law as a source of knowledge is to claim history as a source of knowledge. This is particularly true in Christianity, whose revelation comes not in the form of an angel who reveals divine commandments, but in the historical record of God's interaction with the Hebrew people and Christ's life and death. Moreover, this role of history fits with the universalism of Christianity, because it permits even nonexperts to know the highest truths of religion.

After all, knowledge of Christ's example is communicable through Scripture in a way that detailed theology is not.[18] The fact that some people come to know truths of God through the revelation of sacred history in no way invalidates others' simultaneous knowledge of God through reason. The dual role of history and reason tells against Tuck's representative reading of Grotius as reducing morality to mathematical reason.[19]

If Grotius sees both 'secular' reason and sacred history as sources of knowledge, we should not be surprised when he posits secular history as a third source. As he sees it, the purpose of history is twofold: it supplies judgments and illustrations. The convergence of judgments on particular matters through the passage of time may reveal a truth on the same level as the rational knowledge of nature according to principles of reason. Illustrations from history, particularly those from Greece and Rome, further confirm those judgments.[20] Indeed, Grotius chiefly criticizes previous writers on international *jus* either for their unwillingness to rely on history, or for citing controversial historical examples that suit their self-interest rather than examples that offer universally recognized lessons.[21]

Taxonomy of Right

After justifying the existence of natural Right (or, including revelation, simply "Right"), and outlining its three sources, Grotius then provides a taxonomy of categories of Right. His clearest exposition of this structure actually comes from one of his private letters. His prolific personal correspondence, a full seventeen volumes in all, testifies to his tireless energy and his citizenship in the international 'republic of letters.' In one of these, a 1615 letter to his brother (and publisher) Willem, he lays out very clearly the structure of justice implied in his public works. *Jus* (or Right), he says, has a structure with four successive divisions into two.[22] This structure may be organized as shown in Figure 3.1.

As we might already guess, Grotius first implicitly divides Right into categories of divine positive Right and natural Right. The first category corresponds to the positive commands of Divine revelation, the latter to the natural laws inherent in creation. Grotius' first category of Divine positive Right includes those specific divine commands that could not be known through natural reason, even if they originate in a rational God. Elsewhere, Grotius clarifies that divine commands supplement that which God already approves or disapproves of as being in harmony with the rational and social nature he implanted in man. God intervenes into this nature with his free divine will to command or to prevent many other things, "not necessarily, but because it has seemed good to Himself."[23]

As governor of the moral universe, God may issue his positive commands to the entire world, or only to a particular people. According to Grotius, there are only three universal revelations: immediately after creation, immediately after the Flood, and the highest of all, in the Gospel of Christ. Grotius interprets the rest of the Old Testament as given only to the people of Israel, as indicated by the preamble "Hear, O Israel." This helps to explain why, for instance, Levitical prohibitions against some kinds of meat were never applicable to foreigners in

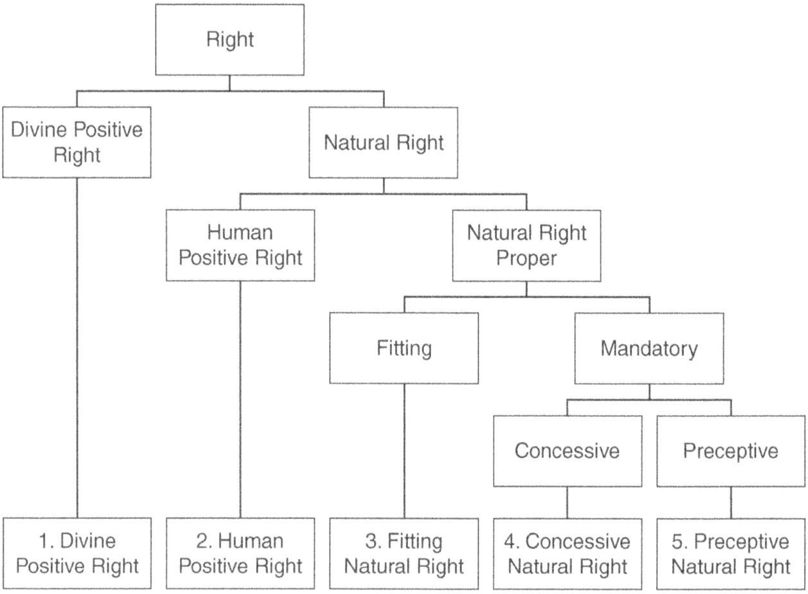

Figure 3.1 Grotius' Structure of Right

Israel. As governor, God may also give commands for a limited duration. In Grotius' view, all of God's commands to the Hebrew nation were impermanent, and corresponded only to the existence of Hebrew nationhood. He argues that the Levitical code no longer applies to the Jews because, after the destruction of Jerusalem, they no longer constitute the nation to whom God issued the code.[24] Because these Temple regulations are geographically particular and temporally mutable, Grotius asserts that they do not set forth the law of nature. Yet nor do they contravene it. Rather, they govern what he calls "indifferent things."[25]

Why would God have given laws only to one people and only for a time? The answer may come from Grotius' comparison of God to a parent, who must give rules for a child.[26] One notes that some parental rules have little to do with the intrinsic content of justice. Instead, they are simply meant to teach adherence to law and obedience to authority. (The command, "Don't sit on the blue chair!" is surely an indifferent thing.) Once the child has learned the principle of obedience, the particular rule may be annulled. Hence, good positive laws display the parental lawmaker's prudent sensitivity to person and context. To extend the analogy, the Hebrews were in the infancy of religion, being the first to slowly learn that divine commands were not the arbitrary dictates of powerful and capricious gods, but rather laws directed toward the good of God's created and called nation. Hence, these otherwise indifferent religious commands helped to inculcate in them an internal adherence to law. Through the Hebrews, God was able to teach this principle to those with ears to hear. Having internalized this principle, Christians are no longer bound by the unnecessary weight of the particulars of the Levitical code.

Grotius further develops this reasoning by noting that even when a parent teaches matters of intrinsic justice, he or she might make less exacting commands to a younger child who is only beginning to learn principles. In morally educating a child, a parent must sometimes "tempt them to learn with a cake."[27] To return to the Old Testament analogy, Grotius implies that God likewise often accommodated his laws to the Hebrews' partially developed capabilities for justice and fidelity, such as when he permitted revenge and divorce. Many Hebrews may have been incapable of following God's full natural law that absolutely forbade the two practices. Had God not relaxed this law, Israel would have seen rampant violations of the law, and might have developed a widespread and counterproductive contempt for the very idea of law itself.[28] Hence, in his beneficent will, God gave to the Hebrews a mutable positive law that reflected the aims of his active government in a way that an immutable natural law could not have done. However, the subsequent New Testament revelation enjoins fuller moral precepts. It instantiates the truths already recognized by the best of the Hebrews, as it counsels against indulging in the sinfully sweet delights of vengeance or 'trading up' (or perhaps both simultaneously).[29] Hence, while the Gospel law abolishes the divine positive Right of the Levitical code that concerns indifferent things, it is not thus a more relaxed code, because it lays out much more exacting standards in regard to non-indifferent intrinsic Right.[30] In doing so, the Gospel also transcends natural law. While natural law sets out the minimum standard by which injustice (and its consequent punishment) may be avoided, the Divine Gospel law points the way toward a higher level of nobility and perfection.[31]

Grotius' first category of divine positive Right is simple, and contains no further sub-divisions. The other category deriving from this first-order division of *jus* is natural Right, which features three subsequent sub-divisions. The first division of natural Right separates human positive Right from natural Right proper. The resulting second category – human positive Right – arises in much the same way as Divine positive right: through ordinances of command, this time human rather than divine. These operate in areas ungoverned by divine (and natural) law. Humans may thus make promises to exercise this freedom in a particular way. Only after making the promise do they take on the natural law obligation to fulfil the promise. Two common examples are those of constitutions and legal statutes, which arise from the mutual promises made by a political society. Here the natural law obligation is contingent rather than pre-existing. Human positive Right is then known by the transmission of its commands through secular history, much like those of Divine positive Right are known in sacred history.[32] One cannot deduce from first principles that a person has made an agreement; one must trust in the word of an authority who can vouch for the historical event.

Just as God's commands may be binding on an individual, or a particular people, or the entire world, the same is true of human positive Right. Human positive Right involves individuals in private promises and contracts. It involves a particular people in state constitutions and subsequent positive statutes. It could conceivably involve the whole of humanity through international law. However, no agent can make promises that contradict divine and natural law.

Next, Grotius divides natural Right proper into two further sub-divisions: fitting and mandatory. This distinction will become central to Grotius' subsequent works through his understanding of "strict" and "wider" justice. Grotius' third category of fitting natural Right corresponds to "that which is appropriate." Unlike divine and human positive Right, the ethical obligation of fitting natural Right does not rest in the will of the agent. Rather, as part of natural Right, it is grounded in the natural order of things. It is not binding because of the imperative will of God or man; it is binding because nature indicates its goodness. Nonetheless, this fitting counsel does not flow from the necessity of nature formulated as a law; one cannot deduce it through pure reason. Rather, fitting natural Right has a "harmony with nature" that transcends absolute propositional formulations. Grotius describes it not as strictly obligatory, but as "becoming" of a person who manifests it. While it is revealed (in a sense) in those actions, the actor himself does not bring into existence a moral obligation; he responds to one. Hence, in order for others to know the content of fitting natural Right, they must discern it through studying the history of those individuals who have demonstrated it.[33]

If fitting natural right has a harmony with nature, mandatory natural right flows strictly, directly, and clearly from nature. Here one can plainly delineate the bounds of justice and injustice through formulations of reason. One needs no knowledge of history, which is largely irrelevant to mandatory natural Right. Rather, one can deduce it from the inherent principles one observes in nature, unaided by authority. Grotius sub-divides mandatory natural Right into two further sub-divisions: concessive and preceptive natural Right. His fourth category of concessive natural Right applies to those areas where the commands and prohibitions of natural (and divine) law are silent. It safeguards a sphere of liberty to act according to one's own free will. This is a realm of moral indifference in which one may licitly choose from a plurality of options with equal moral validity. One may also exercise this freedom by taking on an obligation through promise, thus transforming part of this realm of concessive natural Right into the aforementioned realm of human positive Right.[34]

Grotius' other species of mandatory natural Right is his fifth category: preceptive natural Right. Like concessive natural Right, this is a realm whose pre-existing moral obligations are grounded in natural law and knowable through deduction. However, where concessive natural Right guarantees a freedom of action, preceptive natural Right takes away freedom of action. It commands or forbids a specific course of action.[35]

Like concessive natural Right, preceptive natural Right is known through pure reason. Just as a permission is knowable in the indicative structure of the cosmos, so is a command. Theoretically, one need not rely on any historical authority to know these truths. However, Grotius qualifies this statement by arguing that history may not simply transmit the record of Divine and human positive Right, but may also reveal some additional obligations of preceptive natural Right. This occurs in matters where increasing numbers of individuals have voluntarily taken on the same promise. Once this promise has been accepted by all people, or at least those nations "more advanced in civilization," there is "every probability" that it is in fact a universal moral imperative. The dissent of a few people(s) savage and of unsound mind does not call this judgment into question, just as honey does not cease to be sweet because a sick man is unable to perceive its sweetness.[36] This near-universal contingent positive agreement must indicate a necessary truth, even if undiscoverable by a priori reasoning.

Grotius' chief example of universal promise-making is that of property (to which he will later add *jus gentium*, which consists of international customs and tacit agreements).[37] Pure reason does not demand the division of the world into private property, and primitive humanity lacked this institution. However, individuals increasingly made mutual promises to assign and respect property, promises which are now near-universal. Hence, it is now a universal imperative of preceptive natural Right to respect property rights. Even if one person disputes the legitimacy of property, the person is not free to steal from others. This means that the natural truth of respecting others' property is not (and cannot be) discovered through the pure reason indicated by nature; it can be known only through historical reason. The knowledge must be passed down to them by others, as with divine positive Right and human positive Right. This allows a small opening for secular history in the knowledge of natural Right proper, a subcategory that might be termed historical natural Right.[38]

These five categories of Right, and their constitutive characteristics, can be organized according to Table 3.1.

Table 3.1 Grotius' Categories of Right

	1. Divine Positive Right	*2. Human Positive Right*	*3. Fitting Natural Right*	*4. Concessive Natural Right*	*5. Preceptive Natural Right*
Traditional Name	Revelation	Natural Law	Natural Right ("Right by Nature")	Subjective Natural Rights	Natural Law
Source of Ethical Obligation	Voluntaristic (Imperative) Will	Voluntaristic (Imperative) Will	Naturalistic (Indicative) Reason	Naturalistic (Indicative) Reason	Naturalistic (Indicative) Reason
Source of Knowledge	Sacred History	Secular History	Secular History	Reason (incl. Historical Reason[1])	Reason (incl. Historical Reason)
Grotius' Category of Justice	Charity (Beyond Justice)	Expletive (Strict) Justice	Attributive (Wider) Justice	Expletive (Strict) Justice	Expletive (Strict) Justice

Note

1 The term "historical reason" (that of this author, not of Grotius) corresponds to historical natural right.

Political Justice

In *de Jure Belli*, Grotius provides a treatment of *jus* that will implicitly consolidate several categories from this five-fold taxonomy of Right. After defending the existence of natural Right in his Prolegomena, his proceeds to lay out its content in his first substantive chapter. He begins by defining *jus* itself in an "objective" sense as "that which is not unjust." This objective *jus* seems to imply a status or a condition that obtains when there is an absence of injustice in the world. It also implies a sort of neutrality: an absence of negativity rather than the presence of positive characteristics. This marks a departure from many earlier thinkers, who proposed a positive conception of objective Right. Grotius conspicuously spends little time on this category before moving on.[39]

Grotius then ascribes to *jus* a second and more detailed meaning: a "subjective" sense that is oriented toward the person. This subjective *jus* confers a moral quality on a person, enabling him to justly do or have something. This moral quality may be a particular right over things, or a right over people. Rights over things include categories of "ownership" and "credit" (to which debt corresponds inversely), while rights over people include the category of "powers."

Expletive ("Strict") Justice

Grotius then quietly introduces a crucial distinction into this second sense of justice as a moral quality related to a subject. *Jus* as a moral quality may be either perfect or imperfect. Grotius then begins to describe this perfect *jus*, which he calls a faculty (*facultas*).[40] He formulates it as a right to one's own (*suum*), which follows Aquinas' classic definition of justice. He then links this perfect *jus* to a sub-division of *jus naturale* he earlier outlined in his Prolegomena: *jus* "properly or strictly so called."[41] Notably, Grotius explores this category immediately after having outlined only the first of his two uniquely human faculties: that of discerning general principles. This strict justice appears to reflect God's naturalistic modality as creator of nature. It sets out five general principles: respecting rights, returning unjustly taken objects, protecting promises, providing restitution, and conferring the right to punish crimes (a taxonomy that will serve as an organizing principle of *DJB*). He names this faculty "expletive justice" (*justitia expletrix*). According to Grotius, this is Aristotle's rectificatory justice. Its dictates are "well and truly *jus*," lining up with the strict or perfect sense of *jus*.[42]

Returning to his first substantive chapter, Grotius further explores *jus naturale* in its "proper" or "strict" sense. He states that *jus naturale* commands specific actions, which he elsewhere describes as "morally definite." This includes natural law commands such as worshiping God, and prohibitions such as not harming the innocent.[43] This expletive justice appears to fit into the fifth category of preceptive natural Right. Grotius does not here include actions compelled by the second category of human positive Right as part of natural Right, but he will elsewhere place them also into this "strict" justice.

Grotius states that some additional matters may accord with *jus naturale* not strictly but "by reduction" – a scholastic phrase. In this realm, mandatory natural

Right does not command a particular course of action, but instead commands others not restrict one's freedom. In other words, if the previous two categories of preceptive and human positive Right are the realm of strict obligation, this category is the reciprocal realm of strict non-obligation. One may, of course, use this freedom to take on an obligation of human positive Right. This seems to fit into Grotius' fourth category of concessive natural Right, or subjective natural rights.[44] Hence, when Grotius turns to the political manifestation of justice, he groups together natural law and subjective natural rights under the expletive justice that deals with perfect rights.

Attributive ("Wider") Justice

Returning to Grotius' original treatment of subjective *jus* as a moral quality related to a subject, Grotius stated there that this moral quality may also be imperfect rather than perfect. In this case, it is not labelled a faculty but an aptitude (*aptitudo*). Grotius calls this realm "attributive justice" (*justitia attributrix*). It is rendered as something that is 'fitting' or 'suitable' (*id quod convenit*). Grotius immediately associates it with the Greek term *axian*, which connotes the dignity or honour of a person.[45] In this sense (although not in others), it resembles Aristotle's geometric justice, which sought to attribute public honours to deserving citizens.[46]

Grotius soon illustrates this distinction between expletive and attributive justice with an example from Xenophon's *Training of Cyrus*. In this story, Cyrus gives a small tunic to a smaller boy, and a large tunic to a larger boy. If both tunics had belonged to Cyrus, such an assignment would be an appropriate exercise of attributive justice; it would determine which tunic was more fitting for each boy. However, before determining fit, Grotius points out that one must address a prior issue: the proper ownership of the tunics. In this story, the smaller boy owned the large tunic, and Cyrus took it against the wishes of its rightful owner. Because Cyrus did not satisfy this first criterion of expletive justice, his action could not be just, even if it showed a great deal of fit under attributive justice. Even if the larger tunic was more fitting for the larger boy, he did not have a right to it.[47] Only if Cyrus had owned both tunics, or had been entrusted with the public allocation of the tunics, could this have been a just action.

Grotius continues his treatment of attributive justice by now mentioning virtue for the first time in his treatment of *jus*. Indeed, he crucially states that *jus* in its widest sense corresponds to a higher sense of Right – a fact that sheds a dramatic new light on his title of *de Jure Belli* and thus his overall aim in the work. *Jus* in the wider sense does not simply compel what is objectively just (which is to say, "that which is not unjust"). Rather, it points toward what is honourable, which includes all the virtues. Grotius particularly mentions those virtues that do good to others, such as generosity and compassion.[48] Hence, if Grotius earlier separated virtues from objective *jus*, he now includes them in the wider sense of *jus*.

If expletive perfect *jus* corresponded to Grotius' earlier category of strict *jus naturale*, attributive imperfect *jus* corresponds to an earlier category of "wider" *jus naturale* in his Prolegomena. His discussion of this "wider" sense of *jus* notably followed his discussion of the second uniquely human capacity: the ability to make judgments about things that are good or bad. Hence, it involves not only the determination of how to avoid violating rights, but also how to instantiate positive goods. Grotius further describes this wider justice as concerned with "foresight in matters of government," which relates to the future-oriented concern of "wider" justice.[49] This follows from a further element of his second unique human capacity: the ability to imagine the future. The inherent contingency of the human future emphasizes that its mode is one of judgment rather than logical deduction. However, it is no less natural for this reason; Grotius is quick to add that anything contrary to this judgment is also contrary to *jus naturale*.[50] Finally, Grotius then adds that this wider sense of justice includes the knowledge of how best to use those things that belong to us as part of strict *jus*. For instance, this judgment may lead us to allocate these goods to those who are wise, or to those who are close to us, or to those who have greater need. Thus, strict *jus* may first determine what is ours, but wider *jus* then guides our exercise or distribution of those things that are ours, according to the conduct of the situation or the nature of the thing.[51] This further confirms its link with attributive justice. This category seems to reflect God's imperative modality as governor of the moral universe, in which he freely acts to foresee and affect the future of the temporal human world.

These actions of attributive or wider justice initially appear to be located within concessive natural Right, because they are not the realm of strict commands or prohibitions. Yet nor is the choice to perform it (or to refrain) a morally indifferent one. Attributive justice determines that one among the many licit possibilities is more noble or fitting than the rest. Reason does not discern this action as "right" (or its nonperformance as "wrong"), because many actions are "right." However, reason does commend it as "honourable." Grotius describes it as a "more extended meaning" of *jus*; it may not be natural in the strict sense, but it is harmonious with nature.[52] Hence, if expletive justice covers the strict natural law liberties of concessive natural Right, as well as the natural law obligations of preceptive natural Right and human positive Right, attributive justice covers the wider guidance of fitting natural Right. This category appears to echo the nonpropositional character of classical natural Right.

Grotius and Aristotelian Justice

In this bifurcation of justice, Grotius situates himself as an inheritor to the tradition of Aristotle (and Aquinas). He says that Aristotle would label his expletive justice as "rectificatory" and his attributive justice as "distributive." Aristotle's rectificatory justice was concerned with the shares or external goods possessed by two private persons, often as a result of a contract. Thus, the two shares, not the two persons, were the relevant consideration. By contrast, distributive justice concerned itself with the relation of those two shares to two other independent measures of value in the persons, as in the determination of public honours. Thus, the relevant consideration was the geometric proportion of the share to the measure of public virtue in each. However, Grotius argues that Aristotle's primary criterion of distinction between the two – the type of mathematical reason used – cannot be the fundamental distinction in political justice, because rectification and distribution properly employ both types of mathematical reason. Grotius argues that a private contract may sometimes demand goods geometrically proportionate to some other consideration of value. Likewise, the filling of a public office may employ a simple (if rather metaphorical) arithmetic proportion if there is only one candidate for one position. Hence, the basic distinction of justice is not the type of calculative reason used to determine its content.

In addition to rejecting mathematical criteria of differentiation, Grotius also objects to another axis onto which Aristotle had mapped rectificatory and distributive justice: that of "public" vs "private."[53] According to Grotius, the public realm of political affairs is not limited to the latter category that he now calls attributive justice; politics also involves expletive justice. For example, if the state reimburses a private citizen for something he has provided to the public realm, this is an execution of expletive justice; it repays him what is strictly owed. Nor is the private realm limited to expletive justice; a private actor may also demonstrate attributive justice. For instance, if a person voluntarily donates a property to the state, this is an exercise of attributive justice; it is not a duty but a free gift.[54] Hence, the primary distinction of justice is not a jurisdictional distinction between private and public life.

On the contrary, Grotius argues that the most basic distinction in political justice is the matter with which it is concerned. Expletive justice is concerned with the matter of giving others their due. By contrast, attributive justice is concerned with the matter of doing good to others, which goes beyond what is due.[55] Hence, the distinction between the two categories concerns the type of obligation: whether it is strictly owed, or fitting. Only the former meets the classical definition of justice as "giving one their due." In this sense, both of Aristotle's categories fit into expletive justice. For Grotius, if one is due something, then it is a subjective natural right. By contrast, attributive justice involves considerations of fit that cannot be claimed by right – only by reference to the good.

By declining to formulate distinct categories of private and public justice, or to outline the specifically public nature of justice, Grotius initially appears to depart from the Greek approach, which had emphasized the privative nature of private life.[56] Hence, one might interpret Grotius' thought as an individualistic modern denigration of Aristotle's emphasis on the public practice of politics. However, Grotius clearly states that either form of justice exercised in the public realm is superior to the exercise of justice in the private realm. Instances of public *jus* are exercised by the community (*communitas*), and are ordered by the common good.[57] Hence, his real purpose seems to emphasize instead the applicability of attributive justice to both public and private realms, showing that all areas of life should be the locus of virtue rather than simply of strict rights and duties. In sum, in his two basic categories of justice, Grotius has rejected the arithmetic-geometric and private-public distinctions in favour of the due-fitting distinction. His basic orienting principle is the distinction between deontological right and teleological good.

Characteristics of Expletive Justice

After outlining his categories of expletive and attributive justice, Grotius will further explore this implicit distinction throughout *DJB*. As the work proceeds, he will gravitate to the language of "strict" *jus* (or "*jus* properly so-called") and "wider" *jus* (or "*jus* in the wider sense"). This may account for the lack of scholarly attention to the categories of expletive and attributive justice, as well as the assumption that expletive justice is Grotius' only true sense of justice. Throughout his work, one can come to perceive seven additional axes of comparison between the two types of justice. Each characteristic of expletive justice will set up a contrast with attributive justice.

The first characteristic of expletive justice is its focus on a tangible object or status that a person can possess. This is evident in the matter of property, which Grotius discusses in his first two expletive categories of ownership and credit.[58] Ownership generally describes goods that are external to a person, over which absolute mastery or possession can be claimed. This requires that they be rendered inert and lifeless, such that they are amenable to control. The same is largely true of credit, to which debt inversely corresponds. Credit is simply a good over which one has ownership, but not yet possession. Repayment of the debt does not require a change in the nature of the debtor, but a change in the status of the goods he currently possesses.[59] If it is impossible to restore the object to its rightful owner, expletive justice seeks an equivalent substitute, of which there are often many interchangeable options.[60] These substitutes are typically commodities that can be bought and sold, which further testifies to their impersonal nature. Expletive justice deals with objects, not subjects.

For this reason, expletive justice is not achieved by changing the character of the person, but by transferring a tangible object to the person. As in Aristotle's arithmetic justice, it does not matter whether the person paying the debt is a good person or a bad one; whether the person is freely acting to realize the spirit of the law, or acting against their will simply to avoid imprisonment. Either act fulfils expletive justice. Indeed, from the standpoint of expletive justice, the two acts are identical.

Grotius' third expletive category of "powers" functions in much the same way as ownership and credit. When one has a status of superiority over another person, one can make a demand on that person that is valid regardless of whether it is fitting or appropriate to the person. Likewise, the performance of the demand need not be carried out willingly or happily; expletive justice requires meeting only the defined letter of the law.

These definite (and often quantitative) remedies lead directly to the second element: to determine the obligations of expletive justice requires only calculative reasoning. Whether the calculation is arithmetic or proportional, it operates by strict and inflexible laws of reason. This reflects the first element of the highest distinctive of human nature: the capacity to discern necessary principles. The resulting legal judgment is not really a practical judgment but a logical deduction. The judge uses reasoning processes that are simple rather than complex. The matter at hand need not (and cannot) be known metaphorically or poetically; the text captures all relevant levels of meaning. Hence, one can reduce all relevant considerations into a single measure (such as money), and then quantify them. For this reason, a computer could theoretically perform this calculation, providing a comprehensive and complete output. In other words, merely technical skills suffice to bring about expletive justice. This is why Grotius links expletive justice to a faculty, a capability that automatically obtains – or does not obtain – in a person.[61]

The irrelevance of contingent factors leads to the third characteristic of expletive justice: its universal prescriptions. Once one has determined the descriptive facts of the situation, the prescription is universally clear, because it is exactly comparable to other situations in different particular contexts. Hence, the exercise of expletive justice does not require the long and careful cultivation of personal experience to recognize and respond to the nuances of individual situations. Indeed, in Grotius' earlier discussion of the story of Cyrus, Cyrus' prudential determination that the larger tunic would better fit the larger boy is irrelevant. According to expletive justice, there is only one consideration: namely, ownership of the larger tunic. Just as it is wrong for the larger boy to possess this tunic, so is it wrong for all other individuals (save its owner) to do so. Grotius' frequent references to expletive justice as "strict" justice further underscore its universal and exceptionless character.[62] This also reflects the aforementioned human ability to discern general principles.

The example of debt repayment illustrates a fourth characteristic of expletive justice: its temporal orientation toward the past. Expletive justice seeks to return the defendant to the condition that obtained prior to the injustice.[63] It does so by dictating an equal and opposite reaction, which cancels out the initial unjust action, as if the action never occurred. For example, a debtor must restore funds to the rightful creditor who once had possession of the sum. Expletive justice is unconcerned with the future interactions between creditor and debtor. Indeed, even the very roles of "creditor" or "debtor" cease to exist once the debt is paid and the debtor returned to "that [condition] which is not unjust." Having restored the condition of the creditor, the matter is completed with finality.

This backward-looking focus leads to the fifth element: expletive justice consists in a status rather than an action. It is a condition that applies to the subject matter in its entirety. In other words, it is binary. This follows from the mathematical character of expletive reason, which reduces these objects to a single ontological level and thus allows them to be defined comprehensively and unambiguously. As a result, the determination of expletive justice becomes a singular data point (a term that itself denotes unidimensionality) that is complete within its boundaries. Because each data point in the sequence is one-dimensional, corresponding to one binary status or the other, each bit of information can be manipulated in the same way: on or off, just or unjust. The status of "off" or "on" can be changed instantaneously, as if at the flick of a switch. Indeed, such instantaneity conjures up the digital sequence of a computer alternating (however rapidly) between static states of being. This fundamentally differs from the dynamic character of interpersonal interaction that occurs in time.

As a result, the information can be organized into a neat system in which each data point forms a discrete link in the chain. It then operates sequentially, in a mechanistic fashion, in order to produce an output. This facilitates the reduction of expletive justice to the procedures of the justice system. The system asks a series of questions to which definite answers of "yes" or "no" can be given, or which can be answered in a number. Each successive answer begets another such question, until the final output is determined: "just" or "unjust." This final output confers a status, but does not direct future action. Although a status may imply the need for action, the system cannot carry out the action.

This characteristic is evident in Grotius' third modality of expletive justice, that of powers. A power deals not with a status over a thing, as in ownership and credit, but over a person. It is clear who holds the authority, and who is subservient to that authority. Furthermore, if one has the status of a power, every action that follows is legally valid. Indeed, considerations of proportion are not strictly relevant to the status of authority. This reflects its binary condition: if authority is not absolute, at least within a defined realm, then it is not really authority at all.[64]

This binary nature, in which all components are comprehensively defined, leads to a sixth implication: expletive justice can be fully and perfectly implemented. In the realm of restitution, the debtor can completely satisfy the creditor by fully paying the debt.[65] Indeed, Grotius' term "expletive" is a cognate of the Latin word *explere*, which is variously translated as "to complete, fulfill, discharge, satisfy, or perfect." As its alternate appellation of "perfect *jus*" implies, expletive justice is amenable to full and perfect implementation.[66]

For this reason, it neatly fits Grotius' original "objective" definition of *jus* as the absence of infractions. It is theoretically possible for someone to be perfectly 'not unjust,' because they must only meet the demands of moral neutrality.[67] The state need not demand virtue, but only the status of "not guilty." For this reason, it needs no teleological conception of the person, let alone a transcendent conception of virtue grounded in a particularistic religion. Because of its clarity and independence from comprehensive doctrines, it can legitimately be demanded of all; none can claim that such requirements would violate individual conscience.

The "perfect" connotations of expletive justice testify to its seventh characteristic: its correspondence to a specific and well-delineated duty that can be demanded of a specific person.[68] One knows exactly what is demanded and of whom. The performance of the duty is not honourable or noble; it is mandatory. Its deontological character delineates a clear and indisputable standard.

For these seven reasons, expletive justice corresponds well to Isaiah Berlin's famous concept of 'negative liberty.' Negative liberty asks the question, "What is the area within which the subject ... should be left to do or be what he is able to do or be, without interference by other persons?" This area is the realm of expletive justice. Like negative liberty, expletive justice does not concern itself with the complex question of what it means to be a person; its concern with the "subject" is only a concern with the subject's freedom, not the subject's self-realization as a person. Those in charge of governing a regime of negative liberty do not require great skills in determining the positive content of public policy, of which there is little. Moreover, because expletive justice merely ensures that people are free to choose their own paths, it is universally applicable across a broad range of societies, like negative liberty. Likewise, expletive justice is concerned with the status of freedom, not with the subsequent use of that freedom. Indeed, advocates of negative liberty frequently justify such a regime by reference to – not despite – its greater promotion of nonconformity, originality, and eccentricity.[69] Ultimately, like negative liberty, expletive justice is concerned with protecting claim-rights to credit, ownership, and powers – not with ensuring the best use of those faculties.

Characteristics of Attributive Justice

Throughout *DJB*, Grotius regularly sets out what is owed according to expletive justice. However, he often follows by pointing to the content of a further obligation that transcends expletive justice. For instance, when discussing familiar obligations, he says that one's duty is "sometimes taken strictly … on expletive Justice; sometimes in a larger sense." In this case it also includes that which "cannot be neglected without dishonour." Thus, the duties of justice spring not only from justice understood narrowly (as expletive justice), but also from a wider sense of attributive justice.[70]

As mentioned above, attributive justice is the realm of "aptitudes" rather than "faculties." It is not a power that automatically obtains or does not obtain. Rather, it requires the exercise of human will and virtue both in order to be ascertained, as well as to be carried out. This leads to its first characteristic: attributive justice deals specifically with the internal character of the person, rather than external possessions. For this reason, Grotius frequently uses the term *convenientia* in conjunction with attributive justice. The modern English translation "convenient" is somewhat misleading, because it carries connotations of utilitarian expediency. On the contrary, Grotius' frequent use of the Latin *convenientia* implies several concepts distinct from – or even opposed to – the notion of expediency. The first is fit or suitability. This implies the suitability of a human construction to a pre-existing standard, such as a person acting in accord with their inherent nature or *telos*. The second is agreement. This suggests an interpersonal realm, one that operates in the peaceable manner that Grotius earlier described as distinguishing persons from animals. A third is harmony. This connotation builds on the previous one, suggesting that a person is well-situated within the web of relationships that constitute his or her interpersonal reality. It is worth noting that harmony does not mean unanimity; each of the components maintains its distinct quality. Nonetheless, it suggests that each individual part plays a unique role that, while not strictly essential, enriches the whole. However, harmony also suggests a qualitative difference from unity. It is not only consonant with nature, but builds on it; in musical parlance, it adds another dimension to the symphony. Yet it does so without doing away with the melody from which it takes its lead; the harmonies fit the melody. Of course, a polity that demonstrates these characteristics of fit, agreement, and harmony may also display the efficiency associated with contemporary connotations of "convenience." In this situation, however, the expedient result should be viewed as a second-order by-product.

Each of these three characteristics illustrates how attributive justice deals with the person as a subject, rather than with the objects that the person possesses. Yet for Grotius, this form of justice consists not simply in the correct ascertaining of the internal character, but in the cultivation and expression of that character in the first place. In this sense, the content of attributive justice is "subjective." Indeed, it corresponds to a higher conception of justice than does "objective" expletive justice, which is merely concerned with the second-order worldly consequences of the character of the people involved.

The second characteristic of attributive justice is its call for prudential rather than calculative reason. Because attributive justice deals with the qualities of individual persons who vary from one to the other, its associated reasoning must consider particulars. Its prescriptions do not flow forth as static and propositional forms that automatically inhere in the nature of things, or even as stable elements of the contingent order. It is not like a physical characteristic of the person, such as the height of the adult that can be measured once and for all. Rather, one can only discern the internal character of a person from observing him or her in particular circumstances. Likewise, because the character of the person can change over time, attributive justice cannot provide perfect guidance in advance of particular circumstances. However, this does not make it relativistic. Although it must be manifested in human will in particular situations, such a will (much like the governing will of God) is a manifestation of a pre-existing rectitude.

The fact that the just course of action under attributive justice is not clear to all, as it would be in a mathematical formula, further illustrates why Grotius emphasizes the importance of an "aptitude" (in contrast to a "faculty").[71] This aptitude is not like a faculty of hearing, which automatically obtains in all healthy persons; rather, it requires development. Judgment can only be taught by those who already possess the virtue. He states that those with undeveloped practical judgment are duty-bound to seek instruction from the wise, presumably in order to observe and emulate their virtue.[72] It is not a technical skill that could be learned from intellectual treatises; inasmuch as it could be learned through reason, its medium would be a narrative account of virtuous actors.

This contrasts with the abstract nature of calculative reason. Because mathematics deals with binary logic, there can be no intermediate stages; an object is either fully one thing or fully another. Yet the world of persons is not so easily classified, and mathematical reasoning always involves some distortion of the full reality. Here Grotius repeats one of Aristotle's most crucial insights: "What Aristotle wrote is perfectly true, that certainty is not to be found in moral questions in the same degree as in mathematical science."[73] The 'rightness' of attributive justice cannot be calculated.

The incalculable meaning of attributive justice leads to its third element: its contingent, nonuniversal character. This follows from the etymology of *attribuere*. In Grotius' aforementioned example of choosing the best person to carry out a particular role in public life, there can be no clear, universal instruction, inherent in the nature of things.[74] One would not say that the job is due to the best job applicant, in a strict mathematical sense. Rather, one might say that it is fitting to assign the job to that candidate. As long as the person making the appointment has the right to make the decision, the subsequent appointment does not offend against expletive justice. However, in showing poor judgment, it fails to realize attributive justice.[75]

This echoes Grotius' earlier statements of the 'wider' sense of justice, which involves a creative judgment about how best to use or distribute one's possessions in particular situations. As Grotius states, "In moral questions, ... even trifling circumstances alter the substance." As a result, in some situations the correct action may lean toward one extreme, in other situations the other extreme. There are often moments of doubt, "as when day passes into night, or when cold water slowly becomes warm."[76] Hence, there can be no 'hiring guidebook' for a society that dictates which person should be hired for which job. A constitution can universally mandate that theft must be punished, but it cannot set out in advance which magistrate should punish a particular thief. This contingent mode of reasoning reflects the second half of Grotius' fullest distinctive of human nature: the ability to determine what is fitting in particular cases.

This example of selecting a public official points toward the fourth element of attributive justice: whereas expletive justice looks backward to rectify a past wrong, attributive justice looks forward to promote future positive goods. The true test of a hiring decision is in the future performance of the employee. The hiring manager must anticipate the future needs of the organization and imagine the future ability of the candidate to respond to those changing requirements. For this reason, the hiring decision is not mechanistic, but imaginative. A manager may put specific characteristics into the job description, but if he uses that checklist as a rigid formula, he may force himself to choose a candidate that he knows is inferior. This element reflects Grotius' very first description of the wider sense of Right in *DJB*. It also corresponds to the uniquely human capacity not only to deduce general principles, but the judgment to "discern things pleasant or hurtful, and those not only present but future."[77] One cannot look back to the past; one must use the mind's eye to envision the future.

The temporal outlook of attributive justice also relates to its fifth element: the justice of attribution consists not in changing a status but in carrying out an action. For example, in the aforementioned example of assigning a role, expletive justice might confer on one person the status as "hirer." It may also set out some parameters within which the search must be conducted. For instance, it may designate as 'wrong' choices those candidates who lack an educational credential. However, as long as the correct person makes the hire, and hires a candidate possessing the credential, expletive justice is mute about whether the choice was a good or bad one. Because expletive justice governs one's status, it confers procedural legitimacy on the search. However, once the hire is made, expletive justice has little more to say.

Hence, while expletive justice will guarantee that any procedurally legitimate choice qualifies as a right choice, the manager surely knows that some of the available 'right' choices (those who possess the educational credential) are far better or worse than others. Consequently, he must exercise attributive justice to envision the candidate's capacity to perform the role. Indeed, the purpose of hiring the employee is to enable the (good) future actions of the employee, not simply to cancel out the negative expletive condition of having the position empty. Hence, attributive justice is not best described as residing in decisions (i.e., about the initial hiring), because decisions are taken once and for all. Rather, attributive justice manifests itself in actions. It is ongoing; unlike a change of status, one cannot bring it about in an instant. Moreover, because it endures in time, the (multiple) relevant factors which must be considered in attributive justice are in a constant state of flux. The procedurally 'right' candidate becomes an employee whose performance continually moves in better or worse directions. Unlike expletive justice, attributive justice must be maintained in a dynamic fashion.

In the case of a hiring manager, one might say that a procedurally legitimate hiring choice is not only a 'right' choice, but in fact an expletively perfect choice that entirely fulfils the strict and mathematically definite criteria. But unlike a debt, where the fulfilment is perfectly clear, the standards of attributive justice are seemingly indefinite. No employee can ever perfectly fulfil the function of the office, even if he does so better than any other possible employee. This leads to the sixth element: no decision of attributive justice can ever be perfect. This imperfect nature also follows from Grotius' classically inspired use of the term *convenientia* to describe attributive justice. As Adam Smith noted, "The Stoics … called the imperfect virtues … proprieties, fitnesses, decent and becoming actions … what Cicero expresses by the Latin word *officia* and Seneca, I think more exactly, by that of *convenientia*."[78]

When one says that attributive justice is imperfect, it is tempting to presume its inferiority to an expletive justice that admits of perfection. After all, why stick with criteria of 'better' and 'worse' when one could talk of perfection? A grade of 90 per cent may be better than one of 70 per cent, but why worry about 90 when 100 per cent is available? The problem is that in the human world, it is not clear what action could count as perfect. It would be as absurd as declaring a particular work of music or art to be perfect. The same is true of politics, especially when one recalls that even the greatest leaders in history have committed imperfections. It is rather implausible to think of a political office being carried out in such a way that not a single person suffers a disproportionate burden, and all are not simply better off but actually as well off as they possibly could be within the limits of nature. Once one is dealing with subject and not objects, the category of perfection is a mirage.

The impossibility of perfect satisfaction in attributive justice leads to its seventh and final element. In expletive justice, if something is due another person, the recipient can be said to have a perfect right to it. The demands of justice are clear, as is the determination of how to satisfy it. On the contrary, attributive justice confers no such perfect claim-right. As Grotius says, this "aptitude" or "fitness" is not *jus* "properly so-called," because it confers no property on its holder. One cannot make a justiciable claim simply because one is fit for something. In the example of a hiring manager, no job candidate, not even the best qualified, can ever demand the position as a right. If an inferior candidate is chosen, the better-qualified one has no legal recourse. Likewise, Grotius says that if a person owes something not "from the point of view of strict justice, but aris[ing] from some other virtue, such as generosity, gratitude, pity or charity, this debt cannot be collected by armed force any more than in a court of law."[79] Again, this speaks to the problem of perfection: one might be obligated to show gratitude, but how much gratitude would be due? For this reason, it is inappropriate to use the language of duty when it comes to virtues. The very purpose of conceptualizing attributive justice along the lines of virtue is to go beyond what is strictly due.

Beyond the problem of perfection is the problem of coercive force. While the state can compel one to provide the goods owed in strict justice, it is somewhat problematic to suppose that the state could compel the exercise of virtue. If virtue is produced under compulsion, it is not true virtue, but only the external appearance of the same. A parent can force a child to apologize, but not to be sorry. Unlike the repayment of goods, virtues such as gratitude cannot be carried out grudgingly. As Grotius says, "He who confers a kindness has no right to demand gratitude; otherwise there would be an agreement, not an act of kindness." Likewise, unless it is safe to remain ungrateful, there is no virtue in gratitude.[80] This virtue must be undertaken voluntarily; on some level, it must always be a free gift by a person to a person. Attributive justice cannot create a corresponding claim-right held by the person on whom it ought to be bestowed. As law increases, the possibility of virtue decreases.

Hence, Grotius emphasizes that Right goes beyond a system of rights whose claims can easily be pursued in the legal system. Many of Grotius' rights are nonjusticiable imperfect rights – or imperfect duties. Politics is not simply about perfect claim-rights, which conceptualize justice from the point of view of the one who benefits – and thus tend to orient political discourse around the individual's pursuit to maximize benefits within the constraints of the system.[81] Politics also calls for attributive justice, even if it cannot demand it in law. Reciprocally, the gift-nature of attributive justice calls forth a recognition of the social (and thus political) nature of reality, and of dependence upon others. Rather than orienting political discourse from the perspective of the individual, it orients discourse toward the common good.

Hence, where expletive justice provides a basic standard of justice, attributive justice outlines a richer conception. It is grounded not in pure reason, but in a substantive vision of human flourishing. Where expletive justice is deontological, attributive justice is axiological (as seen by its association with the Greek term *axian*). Where the former deals with natural law dictates grounded in an impersonal order of right, the latter dwells in the personal will (or character) of a virtuous agent. Because attributive justice deals with human actions in time, it requires the virtue of prudence to provide situational guidance. Likewise, because it aims to cultivate virtue in its subjects, it must be able to look into what is internal to a person. Likewise, it looks forward to a vision that may be better instantiated in the future, but which will never be perfectly instantiated. For this reason, it can never be perfectly encapsulated in finite propositional formulations.

Negative and Positive Liberty

Attributive justice aligns closely with Isaiah Berlin's concept of 'positive liberty.' Positive liberty is the concern of the subject who states, "I wish to be a subject, not an object … not acted upon … as if I were a thing." This is precisely the focus of attributive justice, as it treats the person not as a possessor of tangible goods, or even of intangible rights, but as someone capable of attaining a uniquely human purpose. The advocate for positive liberty states, "I wish, above all, to be conscious of myself as a thinking, willing, active being."[82] Attributive justice is concerned not with the status that a person possesses, but the freely willed actions that flow from that status.

According to Berlin, the question of positive liberty is "what, or who, is the source of control or interference that can determine someone to do, or be, this rather than that?"[83] Yet for all Grotius' rich emphasis on positive liberty, his answer appears to be largely this: "a noncoercive authority."[84] In other words, Grotius emphasizes that no matter the desirability of attributive justice, expletive justice is the condition under which it must be realized. If this is the case, why does he devote so much attention to attributive justice?

A look at Berlin's own framework may hint at an answer. Berlin's two concepts are usually taken to be mutually exclusive. The greater the sphere of positive liberty, the smaller the sphere of negative liberty. Berlin himself advocates for negative liberty, arguing that positive liberty is too easily transformed into an overbearing paternalism that turns subjects into objects. Nonetheless, he treats positive liberty with such even-handedness as to give its advocates plenty of ammunition. He asks rhetorically, "What is freedom to those who cannot make use of it?" He then points out that "to offer political rights, or safeguards against intervention by the State, to men who are half-naked, illiterate, underfed and diseased is to mock their condition."[85] He is aware that the aims of positive liberty are desirable, and seems to reject it only reluctantly.

Grotius also outlines two concepts of justice that seem mutually exclusive – indeed, exclusive on seven different axes of comparison. Yet with attributive justice, he makes clear what Berlin only seems to hint at: that individuals ought to use their expletive negative freedom to pursue the positive goods of attributive justice. While Grotius defends basic negative liberties, he simultaneously makes clear his opposition what Berlin calls the "classical form" of negative liberty: the idea that liberty is good per se, even if it fails to produce the hoped-for results of truth, imagination, and human greatness.[86] While demanding expletive justice, and grounding this demand in an order of right, Grotius also argues that expletive justice is ordered toward attributive justice.

Indeed, the nonjusticiability of attributive justice indicates that it is not the lesser, but the greater of the two types. When one gives money to another because the law states that one has an expletive debt, one is not generous, even though the virtue of generosity may involve giving money to another. If the act is simply one's duty, it fails to attain the highest level of righteousness: as Christ asked rhetorically, "do not even the pagans do that?"[87] The actions of attributive justice are virtuous precisely because one has a right not to carry them out; if they are carried out, they are done so as a free gift. Yet while the exercise of attributive justice transcends expletive justice, it is nonetheless still compatible with it; attributive justice does not sweep away expletive justice. Just as the freely chosen higher standards of Christianity fulfil the spirit of the Hebraic law, attributive justice fulfils expletive justice.

Conclusion

Isaiah Berlin begins his "Two Concepts of Liberty" by asserting that social and political theory would not exist if men never disagreed about the ends of life. Once ends are agreed on, he argues, political and moral questions become technological ones, reducible to the "administration of things." This could happen only at the end of history, a condition that is not ours to seek after.[88] Indeed, Berlin advocates for negative liberty over positive liberty precisely because he fears political programs that claim such definitive knowledge.

Yet while the mere deontological consensus about the protection of negative rights may birth and keep alive a society, it does not necessarily foster a *good* society. Few want to think of their common life as simply a set of rules that permits a more peaceful competition of all against all. A positive vision of human flourishing need not imply the "end of history" ideologies of Lenin or Hitler. Even pluralistic liberal democracies have common goals that they hold dear: constitutionally restrained monarchy; life, liberty, and the pursuit of happiness; *liberté, égalité, fraternité*. Indeed, without this common vision, few are likely to put their lives on the line to defend their societies. Had citizens of Western liberal democracies not set aside their fundamental negative rights to security of person after Hitler invaded Poland, they might today suffer the oppression that (Isaiah) Berlin so rightly sought to oppose. Only a vision of shared aims, one that directs the exercise of liberty toward a positive concept of human flourishing, could motivate the supreme sacrifice of self-interest. Political theory might not exist if men never disagreed about the ends of life, but one's own political order may cease to exist if its men never agree about the ends of life.

This is a conundrum that Grotius' twin concepts of justice seek to address. Grotius provides a clear defence of negative rights in his "strict" form of expletive justice. Just as Aristotle had placed his discussion of justice not in his *Politics*, but in his *Nicomachean Ethics*, the "greatest universal scholar since Aristotle" also grounds his exposition of political justice in his moral philosophy, one that – like Aristotle – builds on his metaethics and epistemology. Expletive justice is grounded in God's indicative (or naturalistic) modality as creator, which provides immutable principles of natural Right in the strict sense. It is known through a deontological reason that is theoretically available to all. Indeed, the human capacity to discern general principles is one of the unique characteristics of the human animal. Because deontological reason does not require a substantive vision of human flourishing, it needs no reference to historical examples of persons who have exemplified the aims of human existence. The reason of expletive justice does not demand virtue; it only demands that one refrain from injustice by respecting others' subjective rights. To do so is to act within one's own rights, which is the beginning and end of expletive justice.

However, the permissions of subjective natural rights and the propositional directives of natural law fail to capture the fullness of Right. Their very deontology allows the state to justifiably coerce them, yet such coercion effectively removes the human element of free will that is necessary for true virtue. Grotius' emphasis on freely willed practical virtue (typically associated with Aristotle's *phronesis*) thus leads him to argue that Aristotle's two mathematical categories of justice are properly situated within expletive justice, and thus incomplete. Beyond the natural laws (and reciprocal natural rights) of expletive justice is a "wider" concept of justice. Although wider justice is considered as part of natural Right, as it pre-exists the decisions of the person, it is not grounded in the laws of nature. Rather, wider justice reflects God's imperative (or voluntaristic) modality as governor of the moral universe. Because it is manifested in temporal actions rather than in abstract formulations, it is not discerned through principles of theoretical reason, but in narratives of virtuous examples in secular and sacred history. Yet while these narratives outline external acts, the acts themselves are only second-order signs of the character from which they flow, and which they are meant to cultivate. One such element of character is the further unique human ability not simply to discern general principles of right but to see into the future and to recognize good and evil. Because attributive justice deals with persons and looks toward a future, it requires prudence rather than deduction.

Aristotle had suggested that a standard of justice must be attainable by human beings.[89] Accordingly, Grotius' concept of expletive justice is perfectly fulfillable, and hence reasonably demanded of politics and underpinned by coercive force. One can at least theoretically perfectly refrain from all negative acts. However, one can never perfectly instantiate the positive acts of virtue, because virtue truly resides in the internal intentions never fully known even to oneself. Moreover, the standard is not simply an Aristotelian mean that must be prudently determined. Rather, the standard is unlimited; in Grotius' Christian eyes, one can never be too contemptuous of pleasure or too desirous of heaven. Moreover, it is unclear what would count as perfection when the ultimate standard of virtue rests in an infinite God; as Christ counselled, "Be perfect, therefore, as your heavenly Father is perfect."[90] Hence, natural Right ultimately transcends the propositionality of laws both natural and positive, just as the infinitude of an indicatively omniscient and imperatively omnipotent Creator-God reveals a standard that transcends even the greatest human example.

For this reason, Grotius argues that the deontology of expletive justice guarantees the valid possession of a status or power, but is mute about its exercise. Government ought to guarantee subjective natural rights, but the holders of those rights should then turn to an axiological standard to guide the exercise of those rights. Where expletive justice promotes the quantitatively greatest amount of freedom, attributive justice promotes the qualitatively greatest use of that freedom. Hence, when one exercises attributive justice, expletive justice is not washed away; rather, it is fulfilled. The coercive force of government may be limited to protecting negative liberty, but the ultimate purpose of political life is to cultivate a particular kind of person. Far from focusing on the mere possessive interests of the private individual, Grotius is concerned with the good of both the community and the entire moral universe. Indeed, without the standard of attributive justice that may counsel the sacrifice of one's right, it may ultimately be impossible to uphold the peaceful political existence which also distinguishes man from beast.

It is true that Grotius is sparing in his explicit references to attributive justice (although he does use the "wider" descriptor with more regularity). Perhaps this is appropriate or even intentional. Because it is not abstract, it is not best known in theoretical explication. Rather, it reveals itself more often (and more richly) when Grotius turns to illustrate five elements of his thought: the origins of political authority, rebellion and civil disobedience, punishment, war, and Atonement theology. These examples will show how this structure of expletive and attributive justice is almost universally implicit in Grotius' approach to political life.

All five of these examples presume the first: the origins of government. As Grotius will show us, human government is guaranteed by human positive Right. In other words, the individual entry into civil society is not a command of preceptive natural Right or divine positive Right; it is a choice. Is it then an amoral choice of concessive natural Right, one ungoverned by a higher standard? Or might attributive natural Right, while protecting the right of refusal, nonetheless recommend the entry into (and subsequent contours of) political authority? The next chapter takes up these questions.

Notes

1 German *Basic Law*, Art. 1, 16, 20, 87–90, available at www.bundestag.de/blob/284870/ce0d03414872b427e57fccb703634dcd/basic_law-data.pdf (Accessed 4 August 2015).

2 Constitution of Iraq, Preamble, Art. 4, 7, 14, 15, 20, 31, 34, available at www.iraqinationality.gov.iq/attach/iraqi_constitution.pdf (Accessed 4 August 2015).

3 In 2015, Iraq placed twelfth on the Fragile States Index, and had the second-lowest score on the Human Development Index in its region.

4 Isaiah Berlin, "Two Concepts of Liberty," *Four Essays on Liberty* (Oxford: Oxford University Press, 1969), 2. See also Bruce Baum and Robert Nichols, eds, *Isaiah Berlin and the Politics of Freedom: 'Two Concepts of Liberty' 50 Years Later* (London: Routledge, 2015).

5 J. G. A. Pocock, "Foundations and Moments," in *Rethinking the Foundations of Modern Political Thought*, ed. Annabel Brett *et al.* (Cambridge: Cambridge University Press, 2007), 42–43.

6 Quentin Skinner, *The Foundations of Modern Political Thought, Vol. 2: The Age of Reformation* (Cambridge: Cambridge University Press, 1978), 148–67; Skinner, "Surveying the *Foundations:* A Retrospect and Reassessment," in Brett *et al.*, *Rethinking the Foundations*, 256–60. For his part, Skinner goes beyond the positive-negative dichotomy and posits a third kind of republican liberty in the *vivere libero* of the Renaissance Italian city-states. Nonetheless, he does believe that this *vivere libero* was eclipsed by negative liberty.

7 See, *inter alia*, Richard Tuck, "Grotius and Selden," in *The Cambridge History of Political Thought 1450–1700*, ed. J. H. Burns (New York: Cambridge University Press, 1991), 506–07, 515–19.

8 Hugo Grotius, *The Rights of War and Peace*, ed. Richard Tuck, from the Edition by Jean Barbeyrac (hereafter *DJB*) (Indianapolis, IN: Liberty Fund, 2005), Prol.1, 75; Prol.5, 79; Prol.31, 107. Citations from *DJB* are occasionally taken from Hugo Grotius, *De Jure Belli ac Pacis (The Law of War and Peace)*, trans. Francis W. Kelsey, intro. James Brown Scott, Carnegie Classics of International Law, No. 3, Vol. 2 (New York: Bobbs-Merrill, 1925), or from this author's own translations from the Latin.

9 Grotius, *DJB* Prol.5–7, 79–85; Prol.9, 87; 1.1.10.1–5, 150–56. This philosophical anthropology repeats what Grotius has earlier asserted in his *Inleydinge*, or *Jurisprudence of Holland*. See Hugo Grotius, *The Jurisprudence of Holland*, ed. R. W. Lee (Oxford: Oxford University Press, 1926), 1.2.6, 5–7.

10 Grotius, *DJB* Prol.16, 93; 1.1.10.1–2, 150–53.

11 Ibid., 405–06.

12 See, for instance, Hugo Grotius, *Defensio Fidei Catholicae de Satisfactione Christi (The Satisfaction of Christ)*, ed. and intro. Edwin Rabbie, trans. Hotze Mulder (Assen, NL: Van Gorcum, 1990), 3.1–2, 150–1; 4.23, 172–3; 5.1, 174–5; Grotius, *DJB* 1.1.10.1, 150–1; Grotius, *The Jurisprudence of Holland* 1.2.5, 5.

13 Ibid.

14 Hugo Grotius, *De Imperio Summarum Potestatum Circa Sacra (On the Power of Sovereigns Concerning Religious Affairs)*, critical edition with introduction, translation, and commentary by Harm-Jan Van Dam (Boston: Brill, 2001), 3.3, 208–09. This understanding suggests that natural Right includes God's commands given to all people, which would presumably include those of Christ. Such a definition of natural Right is rather broad, as it includes many distinctives of Christianity, and is somewhat inconsistent with his other works.

15 One might add a third implication: Grotius emphasizes positive law as mutable, even when God is the lawmaker. Positive law follows from the will of the authority that enacts it. If the will is free, it cannot be constrained by immutability. See Grotius, *de Imperio* 3.3, 208–09.

16 Grotius, *DJB* Prol.1, 75; Prol.20–21, 95–96.

17 Ibid., Prol.12, 90–91. This is a departure from Grotius' early *de Jure Praedae*, in which he does not see God as adding any commands through revelation to those already known by reason. See Richard Tuck, *Philosophy and Government 1572–1651* (Cambridge: Cambridge University Press, 1993), 185–6; Tuck, *The Rights of War and Peace: Political Thought and the International Order from Grotius to Kant* (Oxford: Oxford University Press, 1999), 101.

18 This reiterates one of Aquinas' reasons for why God would reveal truths also available to unassisted reason.

19 Tuck, "Grotius and Selden," 506–07, 515–19. For a variation, see Michel Villey, *La Formation de la Pensée Juridique Moderne* (Paris: Montchrétien, 1975), 619–20. Another common piece of evidence in this reading is Grotius' claim in his Prolegomena that he is abstracting himself from knowledge of particulars, much like mathematicians. However, the wider context in which Grotius makes this comment is not a discussion of the sources of knowledge, but a defence of his impartiality. In this statement, Grotius is aiming to transcend partisan desires and interests and to faithfully elucidate the true justice of war and peace (see Grotius, *DJB* Prol.58, 131).

20 Grotius, *DJB* Prol.46, 121–22.

21 Ibid., Prol.38, 109; Prol.55, 118–21.

22 Hugo Grotius, letter to Willem de Groot, 18 May 1615, in Herbert F. Wright, *Some Less Known Works of Hugo Grotius* (Leiden: Brill, 1928), 209–10. The distinction between divine positive Right and natural Right is superimposed here on the taxonomy, and Grotius' final distinction within preceptive natural Right is omitted.

23 Grotius, letter 18 May 1615; Hugo Grotius, letter to Willem de Groot, 21 May 1638, in Wright, *Less Known Works*, 208–10.

24 Grotius, *de Imperio* 3.3, 208–09; *DJB* 1.1.15–16, 164–75. Grotius adds that the

destruction of the nation left no hope of restoration. One wonders how Grotius would have approached this issue after 1948.

25 Grotius, *DJB* 1.1.17.1–2, 175–8; Hugo Grotius, *The Truth of the Christian Religion* (hereafter *de Veritate)*, ed. and intro. Maria Rosa Antognazza (Indianapolis, IN: Liberty Fund, 2012), 5.7, 195–98.

26 Grotius, *de Imperio* 3.13, 224–7; Grotius, *de Veritate* 5.6, 193–95.

27 Grotius, *de Veritate* 5.6, 193–95. One is reminded of Alasdair MacIntyre's account of practices, and his example of teaching a bright young child to play chess using a system of progressively declining extrinsic rewards. See Alasdair MacIntyre, *After Virtue*, 2nd ed. (Notre Dame, IN: University of Notre Dame Press, 1984), 187–89.

28 This is the very reason why Aquinas states that "although God is all-powerful and supremely good, nevertheless He allows certain evils to take place in the universe, which He might prevent, lest, without them, greater goods might be forfeited, or greater evils ensue." Citing Augustine, he uses an example only slightly different from divorce: prostitution. Thomas Aquinas, *Summa Theologiae*, 2nd ed., trans. Fathers of the English Dominican Province (London: Burns Oates and Washbourne, 1922), II–II, Qu. 10, Art. 11; see also I–II, Qu. 96, Art. 2; II–II, Qu. 42, Art. 2.

29 Grotius, *DJB* Prol.49, 124–5; Grotius, *de Veritate* 5.6, 193–95.

30 Christians do enjoy one advantage: the assurance of God's goodness (Grotius, *DJB* 1.1.16, 174–75).

31 Grotius, *DJB* Prol.51, 126.

32 Grotius, letter 18 May 1615, 209–10.

33 Ibid.

34 Ibid.

35 Ibid.

36 Grotius, *DJB* 1.1.12, 159–62.

37 Ibid., 1.1.14, 162–63.

38 Grotius also further sub-divides preceptive natural right into two less important sub-categories: immutable and changeable. Immutable preceptive natural Right might include the moral injunction against murdering people for sport, an obligation that is no less binding after one has killed the person. Changeable preceptive natural right would include the obligation of a debtor to pay a creditor, on obligation that disappears after one has repaid the debt.

39 Ibid., 1.1.3.1, 136.

40 Ibid., 1.1.4–5, 138–39.

41 Ibid., Prol.8, 85–6; 1.1.5–6, 139–41; 1.1.8.1, 141–5; 2.20.6.1, 962.

42 Ibid., Prol.7–8, 84–86.

43 Ibid., 1.1.10.3, 153–4; Grotius, *de Imperio* 7.2, 326–31.

44 Grotius, *DJB* 1.1.10.3, 153–54.

45 Ibid., 1.1.7, 141.

46 Aristotle, *Nicomachean Ethics* 5.6, trans. Martin Ostwald (Upper Saddle River, NJ: Prentice Hall, 1999), 129–30. For Aristotle, of course, human dignity did not carry the inherent qualities which are often assumed today to automatically obtain in any person, simply by virtue of their human nature. Rather, this dignity corresponds more closely to virtue or character, something that must be cultivated. As a result, this dignity will inevitably vary from person to person.

47 Grotius, *DJB* 1.1.8.2, 141–45.

48 Ibid., 1.1.9, 147–50.

49 Ibid., 1.1.8, 141–46.

50 Ibid., Prol.9, 87.

51 Ibid., Prol.10, 87–9; Grotius, *de Imperio* 7.2–3, 326–35.

52 Grotius, *DJB* Prol.10, 87–89.

53 Likewise, Aquinas had subsequently argued that particular commutative (and distributive) justice dealt with goods going to private individuals. Only general justice concerned those goods going to the community.

54 Grotius, *DJB* 1.1.8, 141–46.
55 Ibid., 1.1.8, 141–46.
56 See Hannah Arendt, *The Human Condition*, 2nd ed. (Chicago: University of Chicago Press, 1998), 38.
57 Grotius, *DJB* 1.1.6, 140–41.
58 Ibid., 1.1.5, 138–39.
59 Ibid., 2.7.2.1, 581–82.
60 Ibid.
61 Ibid. See also Oliver O'Donovan and Joan Lockwood O'Donovan, "Hugo Grotius (1583–1646)," in *From Irenaeus to Grotius: A Sourcebook in Christian Political Thought*, ed. Oliver O'Donovan and Joan Lockwood O'Donovan (Grand Rapids, MI: Eerdmans, 1999), 790.
62 Grotius, *DJB* 2.7.4.1, 584–85.
63 Ibid., 2.7.2.1, 581.
64 This will be the subject of Chapters 4 and 5.
65 Ibid., 3.4.1.1, 1270–71.
66 Note, however, that expletive justice can only be perfectly implemented within its own boundaries; it must artificially close off these parameters within the open-ended expanse of higher justice. In similar fashion, a perfect duty – such as the duty to provide a specific payment to a specific creditor – may be morally mundane compared to an imperfect duty that is not owed to anyone in particular and whose performance can never be final. For instance, the perfect duty of a millionaire businessman to pay a billionaire supplier may be prosaic in relation to the millionaire's imperfect duty to promote better health among the world's malnourished. Yet regarding the latter, it is unclear what the parameters of the duty are, to whom it is owed, what would constitute its perfect fulfilment, or whether the millionaire (or billionaire) is even capable of doing so.
67 Ibid., 1.1.2.1, 134. See also 1.2.1.3, 157.
68 Samuel Fleischacker, *A Short History of Distributive Justice* (Cambridge, MA: Harvard University Press, 2004), 20–2, 139–40. See also J. B. Schneewind, *The Invention of Autonomy* (New York: Cambridge University Press, 1998), 78–80, and Haakonssen, Knud, ed. *Natural Law and Moral Philosophy: From Grotius to the Scottish Enlightenment* (New York: Cambridge University Press, 1996), 26–30.
69 Berlin, "Two Concepts of Liberty," 2, 6, 8–9.
70 Grotius, *DJB* 2.7.4.1, 584–85.
71 Ibid., 2.17.3, 886.
72 Ibid., 2.23.4, 1118–19.
73 Ibid., 2.23.1, 1115–16.
74 Ibid., 1.1.8, 141–6; 2.17.3, 886.
75 See Oliver O'Donovan, "The Justice of Assignment and Subjective Rights in Grotius," in *Bonds of Imperfection: Christian Politics, Past and Present*, ed. Oliver O'Donovan and Joan Lockwood O'Donovan (Grand Rapids, MI: Eerdmans, 2004), 181–82.
76 Grotius, *DJB* 2.23.1, 1115–16.
77 Ibid., Prol.9–10, 87–89.
78 Adam Smith, *The Theory of Moral Sentiments*, ed. Knud Haakonssen (Cambridge: Cambridge University Press, 2002), 7.2.46, 344.
79 Grotius, *DJB* 2.22.16, 1112–13.
80 Ibid., 2.20.20, 995; 2.22.16, 1112–13.
81 John Finnis, *Natural Law and Natural Rights* (Oxford: Oxford University Press, 1980), 205.
82 Berlin, "Two Concepts of Liberty," 8.
83 Ibid., 2.
84 Chapter 5 will explore this idea in greater detail.
85 Berlin, "Two Concepts of Liberty," 4, 8–9.

86 Ibid., 6.
87 Matthew 5:47, New International Version: "And if you greet only your own people, what are you doing more than others? Do not even pagans do that?"
88 Berlin, "Two Concepts of Liberty," 1–2.
89 Aristotle, *Ethics* 1.6, 13.
90 Matthew 5:48, New International Version.

4 The Origins of the State

How and Why?

What makes the coercive force of the state legitimate? Classical political thinkers seek to unite coercive force with wisdom. The resulting wise rulership is naturally good for the person, which is to say, it helps those ruled to better flourish. The evidence for rulers' political legitimacy is not a descriptive account of their election but a demonstration of their political wisdom. The latter, however, is less verifiable. How does one define wisdom? Even Socrates demurs.

Modern political thinkers answer this question of legitimacy not by reference to substantive outcomes but to procedures of consent. One need not answer the relatively difficult question of *why* one surrendered their coercive power to the state; one need only point to the fact that one *did* surrender it. Of course, few individuals actually did surrender it. Nonetheless, when pressed, most citizens will argue that they would have done so if given the choice. Others add that they endorse the surrender when they vote to elect public officials. This answer feels especially satisfying because an election is itself a procedure. The legitimacy of the office-holder depends on the outcome of a procedure: counting valid votes. One's eloquent pre-election critiques of a soon-to-be-elected candidate become utterly inadequate to motivate a post-election insurrection. Today, most people acknowledge political power to be legitimate – no matter how grudgingly – when it is united with consent.

What precipitated the practical change from the classical approach to the modern? The Protestant Reformation introduced to Europe profound disagreement over comprehensive doctrines and their consequent conceptions of wisdom. This helped to stoke the sixteenth- and seventeenth-century 'wars of religion,' which after which Europe was ready to consider replacing substantive conceptions of legitimacy with procedural ones. By shifting the question of legitimacy from "why?" to "how?" political thinkers aimed to prevent political conflict. In the realm of theoretical change, the standard story of change begins shortly after Grotius in Thomas Hobbes' state of nature. Hobbes initiates theories of consent as a scientific argument that one concedes one's physical abilities to the state in exchange for security of person. But what if the solution of an all-powerful state is itself a threat? Locke then clarifies that one retains one's first-order possessive rights, and surrenders only the second-order right to punish violations of the first.

Few have thought to explore Grotius as a developer of consent theories, perhaps because he conceals his most direct account in the overlooked theo-political treatise *de Imperio*. A fuller historical genealogy finds in Grotius' pre-Hobbesian corpus both the Hobbesian conception of the state as arising from the consent of the people and the Lockean development of the state as possessing only the powers originally granted it by the people. For this reason, a small but increasing secondary literature (aided by a recent wave of critical primary editions) has identified in Grotius the beginnings of a liberal political theory.[1]

Beyond the quest for historical origins, this move to procedural political legitimacy arouses uneasy philosophical questions. What if we consent to political arrangements without considering the consequences? Is the procedural principle of choice truly self-validating? Have we no obligation to ourselves, others, nature, or God? What if we choose a political order that seems contrary to human flourishing? Might the very need for political society arise from the fact that we often make poor choices? These philosophical challenges further commend a reconsideration of Grotius' consent theory, because it is conscious of such questions.

This chapter argues that Grotius' procedural criterion of consent is only partially intelligible without reference to his lesser-known substantive conception of political wisdom. Grotius does defend consent as procedurally sufficient to authorize a sovereign's status and powers. Strict justice guarantees it. But why should a people create formal governing institutions in the first place? Grotius here outlines a pre-political concept of the human good fundamentally continuous with classical and Christian thought. Prior to politics, justice is already theoretically knowable and practically possible. Yet instituting government may help to make the practical instantiation of justice more likely. One of the best tools of government is the rule of (positive) law, for which Grotius provides a conceptual mooring. He justifies positive law on procedural grounds, as providing organization and order to society. However, he also promotes it on substantive grounds, as it not only gives weight to natural law but also provides the forum in which the formal and universal principles of expletive justice are given content in particular circumstances. This relation between natural and positive law reflects Grotius' twin modalities in God, and establishes a space for Aristotelian practical wisdom.

But this procedure that creates the state and authorizes its consequent mechanisms of positive law does not guarantee political flourishing. If people ignore standards of wider justice in deciding which powers to grant the sovereign, their own poor choice will trap them in a condition worse than pre-civil society. Likewise, if the resulting positive laws are simply decreed without political deliberation, or formulated without reference to a pre-political vision of human flourishing, they will actually make the practical instantiation of justice less likely than in pre-civil society. In other words, the consent that confers the legal validity of rights is only a precondition for teleological considerations of the good. The right of individuals to consent to their political arrangements implies a responsibility to choose their institutions well.

Pre-Civil Society: The State of Natural Right

In the Prolegomena and first chapter of *DJB*, Grotius outlines his philosophical groundwork of justice. With this foundation in place, he then devotes three of the next four chapters to the origins of authority. Yet he does so indirectly. *DJB* is a treatise on international relations, not domestic politics, and Grotius here is interested in the latter only inasmuch as it illuminates the former. What then makes it relevant?

War is the most blatant form of coercion. According to Grotius, to exercise legitimate coercion means to have authority over the subjects of this force. Before one can substantively act justly, one must possess the proper procedural status. This is a special problem in war. After all, few subjects of war have explicitly consented to the use of force against them. But even in civic politics, a consent theory of legitimacy faces challenges. If subjects consented to surrender their right to physical coercion in the creation of the state, they must have possessed that coercive right prior to the creation of the state. Indeed, most are considered to retain this right in cases of emergency even after its creation.[2] Whence arises this right?

Grotius does not have a 'state of nature' theory in the same sense as Hobbes and Locke. Nowhere in his works does he paint a rich portrait of pre-civil society, or speak in detail about the movement into civil society. Yet he takes for granted that the civil rights of individuals (or the governing right of coercive political authorities) are based on natural rights that precede the state. In his initial discussion of justice, Grotius has already told us that the moral faculty of *jus* – "a moral quality of a person, making it possible to have or to do something justly" – exists by nature.[3] The world prior to the institution of government (and continuing outside it) is a normed existence, one that includes some knowledge of natural justice and some possibility of instantiating it. Indeed, the pre-civil condition may even be a social existence; it is not the world of Hobbes' atomized individual.

Grotius' aforementioned natural *jus* includes three sub-categories, all of which may exist prior to the state: ownership, credit, and powers. While ownership and credit refer to rights over objects (such as property), powers refers to authority over other people.[4] The pre-civil presence of this latter sub-category shows that civil authority is only one of several types of authority. This demands an examination of the ways that the latter form of *jus* is justly acquired. According to Grotius, there are three ways in which one may acquire *jus* over persons: generation, consent, and crime.[5]

The 'State of Nature': Paternal and Punishing Authority

The first of these sources of *jus*, generation, is the simplest. When a child is born, he is naturally subject to the authority of the parents to whom he owes his very existence. Grotius further explains that status of subordination also arises from the fact that children are unable to govern themselves through the exercise of reason. (For this reason, the parental *jus* changes once the child comes of age.)

The capacity for reason grants parents the moral right to use coercive force over their children. However, it does not confer a complete freedom of action; parents have a higher obligation to exercise this right responsibly. The paternal *jus* is ordered toward an end beyond the interests or even the good of the parents who hold the right.

Nonetheless, this parental *jus* is not lost through misuse or violation of natural law, even if God will hold the father to account. While the status is ordered to a particular action, unjust action does not invalidate the status. Nor can this paternal *jus* be usurped by others, or by the child himself. Hence, the status of parental authority is unchallengeable even as its exercise is tightly proscribed. This contrast between status and action also applies to the children themselves, but in inverse fashion. Children can have no *jus* over people, but they may have a *jus* over possessions. However, until attaining the age of reason and judgment, they cannot exercise this *jus*. Here the status of authority (albeit one of *dominium* rather than *imperium*) is entirely proscribed, and the parent must act as a trustee over the property of the child. Just as a father's lack of wise parenting does not invalidate his fatherhood, the child's inability to be a wise steward of property does not invalidate his ownership of it. This juxtaposition between status and exercise in the *jus* of both parent and child foreshadows Grotius' conception of political authority (Chapter 5).[6]

The second source of *jus* as a power over persons (i.e., authority) is punishment. As Grotius states in his Prolegomena, "*jus* properly so-called" (which we now recognize as expletive justice) calls for the punishment of acts against natural law. Hence, in a criminal act, the criminal automatically takes on a status as "legitimate subject of coercive force." This means that a corresponding status of punitive *jus* must be simultaneously conferred on a punisher. As with paternal *jus*, punitive *jus* does not require the formal apparatus of law enforcement in civil society. This reveals a crucial point: the subjection of criminals to punishment cannot arise from their prior consent. Rather, the need for punishment – demanded by natural Right – is an independent source of *jus* over another person.

But on whom is this punitive *jus* conferred? In paternal *jus* (and indeed in governing *jus*), there is a clear superior-subordinate relationship that delineates the superior. The authority figure has a perfect right: a right of a specific person against another specific person and/or thing. However, in punitive *jus*, the punisher(s) and the criminal are in a relationship of equality. Hence, the violator confers an imperfect punishing authority on anyone, subject to one condition: their innocence of the same (or similar) crimes against natural Right.[7] This approach is noteworthy, because another alternative is readily available. Grotius could have said, as Locke later appears to say in regard to reparation, that the right to punish is conferred on the specific victim.[8] However, Grotius not only extends the punishing power beyond the victim, but even states that the victim may be prohibited from punishing if he is guilty of that same act toward someone else. This separation of punishment and victimhood is a crucial element of Grotius' political thought, one whose wide-ranging implications we will later explore in Chapter 6. For present purposes, it is sufficient to note two elements.

First, Grotius' origins of authority in punitive *jus* include a necessarily moral component, as the punisher must be innocent. Second, much like the generative source of paternal *jus* arises without the consent of the child, the criminal source of punitive *jus* arises without any explicit consent of the criminal. For this reason, both precede the creation of civil society.

Consent: The Formation of Governing Authority

The third and final source of *jus* is governing authority. It shares with the other two sources the first of these two notable elements: it is inherently moral. However, it differs on the latter element, as it is constituted in an act of explicit consent (or promise) by the future subjects. In pre-civil society, the political status of each individual appears to fall under the category of concessive natural Right. In other words, each individual is free from inherent political subjection, but also free to take on such subjection. In that regard it is no different from any other potential promise. One might remain single or choose to marry; one might remain self-employed or accept a job from an employer. However, once the promise is made, its performance becomes a requirement of natural Right, under the sub-category of human positive Right. It is a voluntary surrender of one's freedom to act, because it allows the superior to compel a singular course of action. In politics, this promise allows the superior to issue and enforce positive laws that go beyond the natural laws already issued and (potentially) enforced outside the state.[9]

Grotius conceives the power of promise to be unusually strong. He shows this in his belief that even *unjust* promises – those impermissible under preceptive natural right – may contain an element of binding force. Consider a contract to kill. In this agreement, both parties make promises that violate natural law. Because the payer's promise to the assassin creates an inducement to kill, it does not morally bind the payer; he can (and should) unilaterally withdraw his promise. However, once the hired gun carries out his evil deed, the debtor's promise no longer serves as a continuing inducement to crime. At this point, the higher standard of preceptive natural law no longer invalidates the payer's promise. Thus, the promisor is now obligated to deliver on his financial promise to the hit man, even though that promise induced a crime. If he fails to pay, the assassin could presumably sue in court – although one imagines that such self-incrimination would dim the assassin's future prospects.[10]

While the promises of marriage or economic services are promises between individuals, promises of political subjection are promises of a "people" or a "nation."[11] That is, the agreement that creates political authority does not also create a people; rather, it presupposes the prior existence of one. Grotius establishes this position indirectly but tellingly when he states, "that sovereign power which is in the king as head, rests still in the people as in the whole."[12] Alexander Hamilton cites this very passage in *Federalist 84* to reassure his readers that union would not cancel the debts due to each of the peoples known as states.[13] Rousseau underscores this point in the *Social Contract*: "according to Grotius, a people is *a people* even before the gift to the king is made."[14] Hence, the members of this social contract are not simply a numerical aggregation of private individuals – or, as Grotius narrows it, heads of families. One thousand heads of households, each making mutual-protection promises with each other, does not constitute a nation. In other words, a "people" seems to differ in essence, and not merely in degree, from the category of "individual."

What signifies the difference between an aggregation of individuals and a people? Grotius states that the latter is constituted by its "single essential character": the "full and perfect union of civic life." Although the matter of the state (the individuals of the nation) may change over the centuries, Grotius argues that its form (the spirit, habit, or disposition of the people) nonetheless remains the same. Here he explicitly rejects the proto-nominalism of Heraclitus' ever-changing river, aligning himself instead with the ontological realism of Plato and Aristotle.[15] Thus, while consent is necessary, it is not sufficient; it must reflect a deeper unity that pre-exists the decision to unite. This formulation suggests a particular shared vision of human flourishing, presumably determined through the unique human capacities for moral reason and foresight. In other words, contra Hobbes, the agreement to create the state does not create politics *ex nihilo*. Rather, a people undertakes the procedure of creating governmental authority as a response to the substantive character its members already share.

Nonetheless, forms are important. Grotius then asserts that the first act or product of a people is the institution of public authority or government. In this original agreement, the people confer on the governing authority a *jus* of governing, or a status that delineates superiority and subordination. Indeed, Grotius describes this "civil power" as "the moral faculty of governing a state," echoing his earlier definition of *jus*.[16] The government is the "bond which binds the state together, that is, the breath of life which so many thousands breathe."[17] Hence, the institutions that are created by the process of consent (and that subsequently outline the processes of government) are an integral element of the political community. Just as the formal character of strict justice points toward the content of wider justice, the process of government goes hand in hand with the substance of politics. Government does not bring politics into being, but it does assist its maturation.

Grotius further reinforces the importance of political consent when he states that governing authority is primarily extended over a people, and only secondarily over territory. In fact, in some cases – such as governing authority over an army – it is only extended over people. Hence, the *sine qua non* of sovereignty is not geographical but personal. This indicates that Grotius' conception of sovereignty is not entirely identical to the territorially contiguous conception of sovereignty today. Governing authority is primarily a concern for the people of the nation, not the resources of the nation.[18] Put another way, government deals first and foremost with subjects, not objects.

Because governing *jus* – unlike paternal and punishing *jus* – is constituted in the consent of its subjects, its subjects – also unlike paternal and punishing *jus* – are able to limit its jurisdiction. When the status of authority arises from generation or crime, its parameters are automatically indefinite. The parent or punisher is limited only by the same preceptive natural Right that limits the actions of all;

it has no further positive restrictions. On the contrary, the subjects of governing authority can impose further formal restrictions on ruling jurisdiction if they so choose. As Grotius says,

> just as, in fact, there are many ways of living, one being better than another, and out of so many ways of living each is free to select that which he prefers, so also a people can select the form of government which it wishes.[19]

It may choose an absolute monarchy (analogous to parental or punishing authority), a limited monarchy, a republic, or any possible variant thereof. Their choice confers formal legitimacy:

> the extent of [the people's] *legal* right [italics mine] in the matter is not to be measured by the superior excellence of this of that form of government, in regard to which different men hold different views, but by its free choice.[20]

As a matter of concessive natural Right, the only restrictions on the people's power of promise are those five elements of strict justice that already exist under preceptive natural Right.

Yet this procedural approach need not be a morally and politically agnostic one; after all, Grotius has just called some arrangements better than others. Hence, the decision to enter civil society is not actually a morally neutral matter of concessive natural Right. Rather, it is a matter morally governed by fitting natural Right. A people is not forced to enter civil society; by declining to do so, it does not violate an obligation of natural law. However, such a refusal would offend against the guidance of attributive justice.

If civil society is morally salutary, why allow a people the option to decline it? Why not demand it as a matter of preceptive natural Right? One possibility is Grotius' sensitivity to the need for situational guidance. If each people has a unique spirit, its most fitting form of government must surely differ from that of every other people. Grotius cannot mandate a single universal form of government. Hence, Grotius cannot place it under the strict and universal dictates of expletive justice. He can state only that the five elements of strict justice be respected. Beyond this, the people must be free to choose their form – and thus to decline to choose any form at all.

However, the freedom of consent is a double-edged sword. A people is free not to make such promises, but it is absolutely compelled in justice to abide by any promises that it does make. Should its members choose a less-than-ideal constitution, they are still bound to obey it. Attributive justice outlines the wisdom of a particular promise but does not constitute a ground for subsequent release, just as a too-late attack of conscience by one who hired a successful assassin does not absolve him of his obligation to pay. After all, a promise is a promise. At that point, one must hope that the governor will exercise his wider-than-appropriate governing authority according to attributive justice. (Fortunately, as Chapter 5 will indicate, subjects may influence the governor to do exactly that.)

Yet if subjects are morally obligated to abide by their poor promises, there are no guarantees that they actually will do so. Grotius points out that a poorly designed constitution is likely to undermine its own foundations. James Madison cites Grotius' sentiments in *Federalist 20*: "It was long ago remarked by Grotius, that nothing but the hatred of his countrymen to the house of Austria kept them from being ruined by the vices of their constitution."[21] In the Dutch case, the design was poor, and only the comparatively greater contempt for the threatening enemy held it together. Grotius surely would have endorsed the political seriousness with which the Framers took their task of constitution-building, a posture both defended and manifested in this appeal to the people of New York. Indeed, he is aware that a lack of political wisdom (which can never be compelled under strict justice) may practically undermine the performance of promises (even if they can theoretically be compelled). The strict right of consent implies a responsibility to wider justice.

Command: The Functions of Governing Authority

Thus far, Grotius' concept of governing authority appears to be an organized civil analogue to punishing authority, one that differs only in the aforementioned limits its subjects may impose. However, governing authority diverges from punishing authority (and coincides with paternal authority) in another way that follows from its superior-subordinate form of *jus*.[22] In any relationship of equatorial *jus*, one may exercise "constraint" against another. For example, Grotius asserts that private citizens can constrain other private citizens to make good on their debts to creditors. After all, debtors have a natural obligation to pay their debts. However, such constraining coercion arises only once the debtor himself exercises his concessive natural Right to take on the financial obligation. Private citizens lack authority to constrain a future debtor's concessive right by directing him to take on the debt in the first place.[23] In other words, while an equal may constrain another person to fulfil a pre-existing obligation of natural law, an equal cannot inaugurate a new obligation. On the contrary, the moral capacity to command belongs only to the superior in a status of superiority-subordination. In pre-civil society, fathers have private command over children, but the only public capacity of command is in God's natural and positive law. Once God forbids murder, everyone is justified in forcibly restraining others from murdering, or in forcibly punishing murderers. However, one with this merely equatorial *jus* can issue no positive commands that add to the pre-existing expletive dictates of preceptive natural Right. At most, an actor in this position can promulgate these commands of God.

This capacity to command (and not simply to promulgate or to enforce) is a prerequisite for government, which Grotius describes in *DJB* as having three essential functions. He begins to outline them by referencing Aristotle's own tripartite taxonomy of functions: consultation about public affairs, appointing magistrates, and making judgments. Without disputing the content, he reorganizes the first two into somewhat different categories: "law-making" and "deliberation." The first, the making and repealing of laws, deals with general or universal interests. This follows Grotius' understanding of law as being that element of mandatory natural Right that applies universally to all within its jurisdiction. The second, deliberation, deals with particular interests of a public nature. Grotius describes this deliberative function as essential for what we might today call executive decisions, which seem to fit wholly into this category.[24] This seems to include Aristotle's category of appointing magistrates, which Grotius describes elsewhere as "allocating permanent functions."[25] However, it also includes presumed matters of consultation about public affairs, such as foreign policy or the administration of laws. However, in this deliberative (rather than law-making) function Grotius also conspicuously mentions contingent domestic issues such as taxation and spending.[26] Hence, Grotius seems to emphasize the importance of deliberation even in some matters that are associated today with the legislative branch of government. Indeed, one wonders whether he is actually limiting the "legislative" function to implementing those matters that do not change, such as the basic elements of strict justice that follow preceptive natural law. This suggests that Grotius' "law-making" function may simply be a task of implementing (that is, promulgating and sanctioning) natural laws that already exist. In this regard, it may correspond more closely to the design of a constitutional charter of rights than to the passage of ordinary statutes. Grotius thus seems to reorient Aristotle's functions of government to more closely align with Aristotle's own distinction between *techne* (or *poiesis*), and *phronesis* (or *praxis*).

What is more, this distinction between law-making and deliberation clearly aligns with Grotius' own distinction between natural law and Divine or human positive law. He has earlier emphasized the immutability of nature (see Chapter 3), as he dwells on its existence outside of time. On the contrary, positive laws (with the exception of those that simply reiterate and implement (*explere*) strict natural law) are inherently mutable: they deal with particular interests that inevitably change and become increasingly obsolete over time. Yet these positive laws need not simply be morally indifferent matters of co-ordination, which require only the mere implementation of an imperative will under concessive natural Right. Rather, many positive laws serve the immutably rational and social purposes of human political existence. As a particular instantiation of universal moral principles, they are an attributive matter of fitting natural Right. These require deliberation and thus follow the rationally indicative mind of the law-maker. These positive laws are thus a second-order sign of a first-order rational will.[27] They are a marriage of reason and will, emulating a God both all-good and all-powerful.

Unlike these first two functions of law-making and politics, Grotius understands the third to echo that of Aristotle: the function of judging. This function attends to particular interests in the private realm. Chapters 6 and 8 will explore this function in more detail, so only two brief points need draw our attention here. First, it is the deliberative branch of government that chooses the magistrates to carry out the judicial function. Second, judges themselves must use a faculty much like deliberation when they judge.[28]

Sovereignty: The (In)divisibility of Governing Authority

While these three functions of governing authority are separate, Grotius does not insist that three separate persons or bodies carry them out; one governing authority may cover them all. Indeed, this authority is indivisible, and cannot be shared between superior and subject.[29] The governor may delegate jurisdiction to an inferior magistrate, but he cannot alienate it.[30] The superior (or the inferior magistrates acting in his name) issue respective commands in general affairs, particular public affairs, and particular private affairs. However, these positive commands cannot be effective unless the subject knows that they are grounded in a supreme power incapable of being overruled by a higher *jus*, or a higher will.[31] Thus, human governing authority reflects the governing authority of God, whose absolute power allows him to issue divine positive laws. The supremacy of the governing will is a prerequisite for the possibility of political action – including the making and altering of positive laws.

Indeed, for this reason, the ruler – at least in his specific function as ruler – is not technically a part of the community. As the one who makes the laws, the commands cannot apply to the ruler *qua* ruler. No one can be simultaneously director and subject, as "no man can lay himself under the obligation of a law, that is, to which he may be subject, as coming from a superior." This reflects Grotius' belief that positive law is grounded in the will of the lawmaker. For this very reason, the (first-order) will of the lawmaker in any given situation can never be subject to his own (second-order) positive command. Rather, Grotius describes the ruler as "the one in whom the power of the body resides."[32]

Grotius' demand for a supreme ruler outside the community appears proto-Hobbesian. This creates the impression that Grotius' governor is a "mortall God" defined purely by its imperative will. Yet Grotius goes on to outline several possible limitations on the supreme ruler. The first is private subjection. Much as one person can carry out the three distinct functions of public government, the same person is divisible into public and private functions. The ruler in his role as governor is outside the community, but the ruler as private citizen is not. The ruler as governor still binds the ruler as private citizen; his laws governing property still bind his personal estate.

The second possible limitation is a jurisdictional limitation that applies to the ruler as governor. What happens when a governor makes a promise, thus conferring a *jus* upon the promisee? Does this not make his own *jus* less than absolute? According to Grotius, it does not. The authority of the absolute governor is not compromised, because he still maintains a sphere of authority in which he is free to act as he wishes. He may have hived off part of his existing sphere of authority, but the remaining smaller sphere of authority is no less supreme. The same is true of a promise made to God. Such a promise also binds the ruler, but does not make him any less absolute as a ruler. Grotius hastens to add that he is not here speaking of adherence to natural law, divine law, or *jus gentium*, the observation of which limits the promises that any ruler can make.[33] Thus, while Grotius emphasizes the importance of sovereignty, he seems to accept divided sovereignty. Although a unity of *jus* within a particular jurisdiction is necessary in order to command with authority, not all areas of public life need be governed by the ruler. In their constituting agreement, the people can decide which areas of *jus* to transfer (absolutely) to the authority, and which to retain. Thus, public life may be divided into separate jurisdictions. Although Grotius says that "sovereignty is a unity, in itself indivisible," he appears to apply this statement only within a particular jurisdiction that presupposes the possible existence of other jurisdictions. The state cannot have two heads that may conflict with each other, but it may have separate heads over each area.[34] Thus, while Grotius insists on the theoretical unity of supreme power, he allows a significant place for what, in practice, appears to be divided sovereignty.

Moreover, Grotius also permits temporary sovereignty. Here the ruler may be unquestionably supreme, but only within a defined time frame. If the original agreement of the people does not stipulate indefinite rule, the ruler must abide by the agreement. However, Grotius adds that the relinquishing of this sovereign authority cannot be at the pleasure of the people; its termination must be stipulated in advance in the original agreement.[35] This also reflects the idea that the people cannot break the promises that they have made in the original constitution of the state.

Hence, while Grotius asserts that governing authority requires a monopoly on the power to punish, he does not seem to assert a Hobbesian or even a Westphalian conception of sovereignty. The status of governing authority is necessary only because it is a prerequisite for issuing political commands. In order for its status to be effective, it requires clearly delineated boundaries within which the superior-subordinate relationship is absolute and thus effective. However, those boundaries need not enclose a particular territory, or preclude other boundaries held by the people, or pretend to master time. Grotius' sovereignty need not be territorial, undivided, or perpetual.

Positive Law: The Purposes of Governing Authority

Grotius has begun his discussion of the origins of political authority by differentiating it from pre-civil punishing authority. He has also emphasized the centrality of consent in instituting the special status of superiority-subordination that replaces the equality of the pre-civil punishing authority. Only this formal procedure of authorizing a sole authority can confer the essential powers of legislation, political deliberation, and judicial determination on the government. The nation that comes to such an agreement ought to choose well, but the *sine qua non* of governing authority is the choice per se.

But why should the people choose to do so in the first place? Grotius has thus far described the "how?" and the "what?" of the state, but not the "why?." And in answering the "how?" question by recourse to consent, he has emphasized that it *is* a choice. The state is not an absolute moral imperative demanded by the necessities of expletive reason. Those who inhabit pre-civil society and show no proclivity for civil society are not guilty of violating strict justice.

If Grotius wished to emphasize the imperative of government without recourse to the necessities of reason, he could have also placed it under the category of natural Right known by history, or what Grotius sometimes calls primitive, or empirical, natural Right. This category does not partake of rational necessity, as (for example) the natural law dictating that protection of life is an obligation of any person at any point in history. Nor, however, is it part of attributive justice, which provides the guidance of wisdom and virtue in particular situations. Rather, it concerns those things that have been practiced since the primitive era of the human race, and have subsequently gained the universal assent of humanity. Notably, this is where Grotius places the institution of property. He does not have a natural theory of property, as in Locke's subsequent labour theory of property. There existed a time in human history in which all goods were held in common. However, Grotius argues that the concept of property has gained universal human assent through time, creating a universal moral obligation to respect the property of others.[36]

However, Grotius conspicuously avoids placing government in this category. In other words, the creation of the state is less necessary even than the institution of private property. Natural law is thick enough to be known and taught outside of civil society. Indeed, by identifying a pre-civil punitive authority, he has suggested that the state is not even a necessary condition for enforcement of natural Right. Grotius' pre-civil society is not Hobbes' "war of all against all"; natural law can be known and even enforced outside of civil society. A minimally moral and social existence does not require the formal civil authorities and legal statutes of government.[37]

Why, then, does Grotius tell us that the "equity and reason given to us by nature declare that so praiseworthy an institution should have the fullest support"?[38] Why does he want us to enter into civil society? We may know the essential functions of government, but what makes them so praiseworthy? A mere value-neutral description of government is insufficient to persuade us of its evaluative merits. Why is the creation of the state a matter of attributive natural Right, one that recommends a particular use of our freedom, rather than a matter of concessive natural Right, which merely safeguards our otherwise value-neutral choices?

Grotius' best answer to this question comes not in *DJB*. Rather, it comes in his treatise of political theology, *de Imperio Summarum Potestatum Circa Sacra* (*On the Governing Authority of the Supreme Powers Concerning Sacred Things*). Here he outlines a five-fold taxonomy of purposes of the state. Each purpose constitutes an implicit justification for the wisdom of entering civil society, each of which is related to the fact that government enables positive law. His first three purposes each involve increasing the likelihood of adherence to natural Right.

The first of these purposes of government, he tells us, is to protect natural Right. The coercive force of punishment creates incentives to adhere to its pre-existing dictates.[39] Natural law, including Grotius' five basic elements of expletive justice, can be known in pre-civil society by unassisted reason. Indeed, this knowledge of natural law is precisely what prompts individuals to take up the pre-civil punitive authority that responds to its violations. However, such authority is clearly an ad hoc authority. It arises in response to particular cases, and it ceases once the punishment has been administered. Lacking any permanent organization, its weight is surely limited. On the contrary, as a permanent institution, the state carries far greater force than any collection of individuals in pre-civil society. Moreover, the state can use its bully pulpit to more clearly promulgate the punishment. This justification aligns with his brief defence of government in *DJB.* In pre-civil society, there is no guarantee that the punishment will be carried out impartially. After all, individuals "too often have only their own interests in view." Although public tribunals do not exist in nature, the creation of such is more conducive to peace and justice.[40] Later, he also suggests that it is better for us to be punished by our nearest relations, rather than by humanity in general, presumably because those who are nearest to us are more likely to punish with our own good in mind.[41] Thus, attributive justice recommends the creation of laws that will protect the natural laws of expletive justice.

Grotius' second and third purposes contribute to the first by adding a positive element: to promote natural Right. He describes the second purpose of government as removing obstacles to adherence to natural law, and providing support to the cause of justice. His third purpose is similar to the second: to remove occasions for temptation.[42] Clearly, his aforementioned first purpose of punishing crime already contributes to these two objectives, by creating disincentives to criminal activity. However, these subsequent two purposes appear to suggest that government can be proactive and not merely reactive. The state may recognize situations that create favourable conditions for vice, such as those in which teenagers may obtain car keys and whiskey. Even though the activities of operating motor vehicles and consuming alcohol are not in themselves contrary to natural law, the state might respond with graduated drivers' licences and age minimums for taverns. Likewise, the state can and ought to provide moral endorsement to just actions. Politics need not merely prevent crime; it might actively promote positive moral goods. For example, the state might give honours to volunteers, or provide tax deductions for religious and charitable causes. (Grotius himself references the Old Testament example in which King Cyrus gave the Hebrews funds with which to rebuild the Temple in Jerusalem.)[43] Where Grotius' first purpose mirrors Augustine's conception of the state as punishing wickedness, these next two purposes appear to follow Aquinas' development of the state as fostering positive natural goods.

All three of these purposes can be described as the mere state addition of sticks and carrots that incentivize the natural laws of which pre-civil society should already be conscious. In other words, they appear to correspond to the earlier law-making function of politics, rather than the deliberative function. They do not discern natural law; they merely add rewards and punishments to natural laws that are already known. The text of the positive law proscription may be taken verbatim from the natural law proposition. For this reason, attributive justice recommends the establishment of these public incentives that will increase adherence to expletive justice.

Grotius' fourth purpose of government, however, is somewhat more intriguing: to promulgate natural Right. Where an official government sanction adds imperative force to the pre-existing indicative weight of natural law (as seen in the first three purposes), Grotius mentions that it also adds additional *indicative* weight to the conscience alone.[44] In other words, government adds not only extrinsic reasons to follow natural law, but also intrinsic reasons. Politics does not simply add punishments and rewards, but also knowledge of moral truths; it is not merely coercive but also educative. For this reason, Grotius later asserts that the law should not simply give specific ordinances. Rather, it should contain preambles that educate subjects on the underlying reasoning that supports its commands or prohibitions. The best way to ensure political harmony is to rely not only on the sword, but also on reason.[45] While individuals in pre-civil society are theoretically capable of understanding natural law through their own reason, not everyone is capable of discerning the myriad of reasons it may adduce in its defence. However, the state can surely draw upon the wisest political thinkers and most skilled rhetoricians to reinforce natural Right. Hence, while the first three purposes protect and promote natural Right, the fourth promulgates it. Attributive justice now recommends a governing function that will make expletive justice better known.

However, natural Right is not exhausted by immutable natural laws of preceptive natural Right that arrive, as it were, already predetermined. Such natural law dictates of expletive justice are only part of the story. There remain other areas of natural Right that are either completely free (concessive) or open to the human guidance around contingent courses of action (attributive).[46] While some dictates of natural law (such as "thou shalt not kill") are relatively easy to understand, many other moral imperatives (such as "promote safety") are less amenable to systematization. Many interpretations of the directive are possible, some of which may superficially appear to contradict the imperative. Hence, the authorities must situationally determine how best to carry out natural Right according to "time, place, manner, and persons."[47] The realm of politics allows for these prudential determinations, in regard to both moral means and ends.

The need for interpretation corresponds to Grotius' fifth purpose: situational determination. Government regulation allows natural Right to be carried out in a decent and ordered fashion.[48] This purpose of situational determination may take two distinct forms, which might respectively be termed "co-ordinative" and "prudential." The prudential determination is more relevant to the unique benefits of civil society, but becomes more intelligible only when contrasted with the co-ordinative determination. This first form deals with co-ordination problems, or moral means rather than moral ends. For example, the natural law obligation to protect life may entail ordered highway traffic, but the natural law is silent about the side of the road on which motorists should drive. Indeed, this determination is amoral. Neither side of the road is inherently morally superior to the other. Hence, the decision is a matter of concessive natural right, as the state is at liberty to choose either one. Unlike the laws following the first three purposes of government, these laws do not concern moral ends in themselves. At most, they are means toward a moral end of promoting safety. They can only have moral value inasmuch as they point toward an underlying natural sense of morality.

For this reason, the moral value of such a co-ordinative law is inherently tied to enforcement; if the state could not or would not enforce it, the people would gain no benefit from it. This contrasts with laws which, for instance, prohibit murder, as those laws indicate an inherent moral reality even if unenforced. However, once that state makes this amoral and perhaps even arbitrary co-ordinative decision, subjects are then morally bound to obey it under human positive Right. The expletive component follows not from a substantive pre-existing precept, but only from the formal pre-existing precept that promises must be kept. Pre-civil society obviously lacks such an authoritative decision-making apparatus to enforce matters of co-ordination. Hence, the benefit of entering civil society is clear. Attributive justice thus counsels the creation of these positive laws that do not require reference to directive expletive justice, but become strictly obligatory once enacted.

However, the second form of determination relates to moral ends and thus requires the virtue of prudence. Here the natural law obligation to protect life may raise the question, for instance, of rationing scarce medical treatments. Should a life-saving treatment be given to an average citizen who has taken careful steps to avoid needing the treatment until this point, or to a beloved public figure who has done little to prevent his illness? Such a question is anything but arbitrary, and the judgment will shape the character of the polity. However, natural law may provide no clear answer. What if the former is already ninety-five years old? What if the latter has disregarded his health out of a superhuman devotion to others?

Thus, this second realm of prudent determination is unlike the first realm of co-ordinative determination, because its decisions are inherently moral. The law does not create a moral obligation by fiat; rather, it testifies to a pre-existing normative reality. However, unlike the fourth purpose of government, its normative content cannot be known in advance by philosophers, through universal and extra- (or even pre-)political formulations of natural law. Rather, the particular formulation of such a normative directive is knowable only through the classical virtue of political prudence. The norm itself is revealed to the community only through its determination in a particular situation. Indeed, these directives will likely differ from one context to another, and for this reason, cannot be distilled into a universal formulation of strict justice. Governments are free – or, more accurately, they are enjoined under attributive natural Right – to make positive laws that fit the situation. However, because situations change, the laws may also need to change over time.

Hence, unlike the concessive realm of amoral co-ordination, here prudence (as part of fitting natural Right) is not simply an interpretive application of a definite natural law. Prudence does not (and cannot) simply deduce a course of action from a formal and propositional imperative of natural law to protect life. Rather, it must draw from a substantive vision of human flourishing, one that transcends the depersonalized formulae of natural law. Yet while it can only be discerned in particular situations, it is not simply relative to situations; rather, the prudent man ascertains a higher nonpropositional truth in a particular situation. As a result, the positive laws that instantiate the guidance of prudence have an ontological existence in the discernment of moral truths, one separate from the indicative knowledge of natural law. Thus, positive law has independent indicative weight.

This fifth purpose of prudential determination contrasts with the first three purposes, in which positive law has imperative but not indicative weight. It also contrasts with the fourth purpose, which promulgates and thus adds to natural law indicative weight. It also contrasts with co-ordinative determination, in which the positive law has indicative weight only inasmuch as it is also imperative. By contrast, in this realm of prudence, the positive law points toward true morality regardless of enforcement – although one certainly hopes that it will be enforced. Hence, it adds both indicative and imperative weight. However, it does not add indicative weight in the same manner as the fourth purpose; rather, one might say that it actually discovers its own indicative weight. It both adds to the moral knowledge that one could have known through pre-political natural laws, and it makes more likely the instantiation of those mores of natural Right. If the first three purposes promote and protect natural Right, and the fourth promulgates it, one might describe the fifth purpose as prudentially producing natural Right.

One might add that because the state is able to draw from a far larger pool of potential magistrates than the small informal networks of pre-civil society, it is much more likely to identify those rare individuals wise enough to make such determinations. Moreover, through the practice of political prudence, those individuals may hone their skills of prudence, which cannot be known apart from experience. Hence, the benefit of politics includes not only a platform for prudence, but also an education in prudence. As with each of the previous four purposes, expletive justice fails to compel the creation of government that will fulfil this fifth purpose. However, much like the previous four purposes, attributive justice certainly recommends the creation of a government that will now foster not only the dictates of expletive justice, but also the prudential virtues of attributive justice.

Hence, Grotius provides a justification for the human positive law whose *sine qua non* is a procedure. After all, positive law cannot exist unless the people consent to create the state. Nor can the state command positive laws without following the legal procedure set out in the original agreement. This can be seen in his first three purposes of government, in which the positive law simply adds imperative weight to the pre-existing natural law. However, it is perhaps even more evident in the positive laws arising from the co-ordinative function of determination. These positive laws fit under concessive natural right, subsequently governed by human positive right. Such laws are not simple implementations of natural law precepts, or even discerned from attributive natural Right. Yet even these co-ordinative positive laws, which require no acknowledgement of a comprehensive doctrine, have a value in Grotius' eyes. A state can (and should) use its realm of pure freedom to pass such seemingly amoral laws simply for the sake of order. In other words, Grotius endows a worth to laws of mere human positive right whose apparent value rests solely in the fact that they have been duly enacted through the proper legal procedure. One ought to follow these laws even if they do not, on their own terms, point to any higher moral content.

This high regard for political institutions (such as positive law) likely helps to account for Grotius' later conservatism regarding the right of rebellion (to be explored in Chapter 5). This will echo Aquinas' counsel that one ought to suffer even unfair laws if civil disobedience would weaken overall respect for the law as a whole. The positive institutions can be shown as worthwhile without referencing any notion of natural Right. Because the purely imperative nature of these co-ordinative laws requires no pre-existing consensus on the content of natural law, they are highly suitable to pluralistic societies. Of course, even these co-ordinative determinations ultimately do serve a principle of natural Right such as "preserve safety" or even more generally "preserve order." Just as the natural law known by atheists exists because of God, the procedural validity of the co-ordinative laws easily agreed upon by pluralistic societies gains its ultimate value by reference to a pre-existing good indicated in natural Right. However, one need not know or even recognize these substantive principles in order to defend the positive law.

The first three purposes of law are slightly more ontologically 'thick,' as they take their lead from natural law. However, while the state here must justify its commands by reference to a pre-existing natural law (even if the rather 'thin' standard of strict justice), the state's action on its own terms merely adds power. While the state's moral authority is purely derivative of pre-existing natural laws, it is still worthwhile. Here the state's positive authority is made meaningful through its participation in natural law. The political order protected through procedural validity ultimately points toward the pre-existing natural moral order that it reinforces. It is suitable for a pluralistic society, but ultimately points toward a substantive (if thin) conception of the person.

The fourth purpose, however, indicates Grotius' hope that the state itself will play a role in cultivating its subjects' knowledge of natural Right. Here the state does not merely add power to a simple dictate of natural law. Rather, it actually seeks to understand, explain, and justify that very dictate. Here the state plays a role as moral educator. Grotius' fifth purpose of prudence only deepens this role. Here the state is not a mere educator of pre-political truths but in fact both the locus and condition of moral discovery. That is, public life actually adds to the knowledge that one may have of natural Right. While the positive laws of governing authority are justifiable in purely formal terms, politics is ultimately meant to play a crucial role in human flourishing.

Conclusion

When Grotius comes to mind, he is often thought of as a social contract thinker. Yet when social contract theories come to mind, observers rarely think of Grotius. If this omission is due to the absence of an explicit state of nature in Grotius, it is understandable yet no less regrettable. Grotius' lack of a radical Hobbesian disjuncture between pre-civil society and governing authority illuminates a crucial point: natural Right exists and is knowable prior to the institution of the state. Moreover, prior to this institution, individuals have the right to enforce natural law through punishment of its violation. Hence, the creation of the state is not a moral imperative of natural law; the choice to remain outside civil law is not an offence against strict justice. It is illegitimate to force one into political society against their will; such would be a procedural violation and hence unjust.

Nonetheless, while both outcomes (the creation of the state or its continued absence) are procedurally legitimated through the choices of individuals, the decision is not an amoral or arbitrary one. Attributive justice cannot make the state morally necessary, but it can point toward the morally salutary nature of the state. The artifice of politics and positive law plays a role that pre-civil society is incapable of performing well – or, in some cases, of performing at all. Grotius outlines this role in his five-fold purposes of government. The first three purposes of human positive law are to provide additional extrinsic motivations to follow strict justice, or preceptive natural Right. Government is capable of incentivizing adherence to natural law in a manner inaccessible to pre-civil society. The fourth is to provide additional intrinsic reasons for adhering to strict justice, further educating subjects in natural law. Here, government adds a mechanism for publicly promulgating the truths of natural law that pre-civil society lacks. The fifth purpose is to reveal (and thus promulgate and enforce) indicative truths of morality that, in their particularity, are not (and cannot) be known through universal natural laws. While pre-civil society, possessing only natural law, lacks this capacity, government adds both an opportunity for prudence and an education in prudence. To sum up, in the first four purposes, attributive justice recommends this greater knowledge and instantiation of expletive justice; in the fifth, attributive justice does the same for itself. Expletive justice cannot demand the conditions in which it is more likely to be fulfilled; it must rely on attributive justice to do this.

In other words, while Grotius' understanding of the creation of the state involves procedures of individual consent, it does not arise from a purely self-interested desire to protect one's life. Rather, this consent institutes a governing authority that will protect, promote, promulgate, and even (metaphorically speaking) produce natural Right. This final ability – discerning natural Right – involves judgments in the moral realm to which expletive justice, owing to its blunt universality, is inadequate. Here politics can promote the higher goods of wider justice, flowing from a conception of human flourishing. In other words, wider justice recommends the creation of a state that will then provide ongoing space in which the attributive judgment of wider justice can operate. Put another way, wider justice recommends the use of formal procedures to establish formal institutions that will point toward substantive virtues.

Why does this justify an elevation of Grotius as a major figure in the social contract tradition? Perhaps it offers a way to enlarge the liberal self-understanding of political authority. It justifies the existence of the state without recourse to thick comprehensive doctrines, while recognizing that choice is not an end in itself. Consent is enriched when understood as an intermediate end that finds its fulfilment in something beyond choice. The positive law of the state arises through valid procedures, but it gains a greater meaning (and justification) when used to enrich the knowledge and promotion of natural Right. A state that comes into being without such purposes is a valid state, but a constitution that fails to promote the highest purposes of government may undermine its own effectiveness. This underscores the imperative of responsibility on the part of every individual in exercising their right to designing the contours of the state, because they will have to live with their decisions. The right of consent points toward the responsibility of exercising the attributive virtue of political judgment.

Indeed, at the very end of Grotius' detailed analysis of sovereignty in *DJB*, he concludes by re-emphasizing the distinction between the possession of the *jus* of supreme authority and the exercise of this *jus*.[49] A legal-positive description of someone as holding valid governing authority is only a starting point for the question of whether they are exercising it according to a higher substantive standard of justice. The fact that the former can be understood on its own does not obviate its need for ultimate fulfilment in the latter. Consent stands on its own as a legitimating principle for valid political institutions, but validity is only an intermediate end. Hence, the deontology that grounds the validity of consent leads to the teleology that guides its content. Indeed, Grotius may insist on the necessity of consent precisely to protect a people's capacity to prudently determine particular political arrangements that fit their time, place, and character.

This, of course, raises obvious questions: what if the valid holder of a position exercises it poorly, in opposition to higher justice? What if the legitimate rulers issue illegitimate commands? Can a subject disobey the command? Can subjects legitimately eject the rulers from their position? To these questions we now turn.

Notes

1 See, for instance, Michel Villey, *La Formation de la Pensee Juridique Moderne* (Paris: Montchretien, 1975); Richard Tuck, *Natural Rights Theories: Their Origin and Development* (Cambridge: Cambridge University Press, 1979); John Finnis, *Natural Law and Natural Rights* (New York: Oxford University Press, 1980), 205–8; Tuck, "Grotius and Selden," in *The Cambridge History of Political Thought 1450–1700*, ed. J. H. Burns (New York: Cambridge University Press, 1991), 506–07, 515–19; Tuck, *Philosophy and Government 1572–1651* (Cambridge: Cambridge University Press, 1993); Stephen Buckle, *Natural Law and the Theory of Property: Grotius to Hume* (New York: Oxford University Press, 1993); Peter Haggenmacher, "Droits subjectifs et systeme juridique chez Grotius," in *Politique, Loi, et Theologie Chez Bodin, Grotius et Hobbes*, ed. Luc Foisneau (Paris: Kime, 1997), and Jerome Schneewind, *The Invention of Autonomy: A History of Modern Moral Philosophy* (New York: Cambridge University Press, 1998).

2 Hugo Grotius, *The Rights of War and Peace*, ed. Richard Tuck, from the Edition by Jean Barbeyrac (hereafter *DJB*) (Indianapolis, IN: Liberty Fund, 2005), 1.2.1, 180–85; 1.3.1, 240–41. Citations from *DJB* are occasionally taken from Hugo Grotius, *De Jure Belli ac Pacis (The Law of War and Peace)*, trans. Francis W. Kelsey, intro. James Brown Scott, Carnegie Classics of International Law, No. 3, Vol. 2 (New York: Bobbs-Merrill, 1925), or from this author's own translations from the Latin.

3 Ibid., 1.1.4, 138.

4 Ibid., 1.1.5, 138–39.

5 Ibid., 2.5.1, 508.

6 Ibid., 2.5.1–6, 508–12.

7 Ibid., 2.20.1.2–3, 949–51; 2.20.3.1–2, 955–6; 2.20.7.2, 963–64.

8 John Locke, *Second Treatise of Government* (Indianapolis, IN: Hackett, 1980), Secs. 10–11, 11.
9 Ibid., 1.3.16, 301; on the right arising from promises, see also 2.11.2–4, 703–10.
10 Ibid., 2.11.9, 715–17.
11 Ibid., 2.5.17, 545.
12 Ibid., 2.9.8, 671.
13 Ibid., 2.9.8–9, 671–3; Alexander Hamilton, *Federalist* No. 84, in *The Federalist*, ed. George W. Carey and James McClellan (Indianapolis, IN: Liberty Fund, 2001), 448–49.
14 Jean-Jacques Rousseau, *The Social Contract*, trans. Maurice Cranston (London: Penguin, 1968), 59. Italics original.
15 Grotius, *DJB* 2.9.3.1, 665–67.
16 Ibid., 1.3.6, 257–59.
17 Ibid., 2.9.3.1, 665–67.
18 Ibid., 2.3.4.1, 487.
19 Ibid., 1.3.8.2, 262.
20 Ibid., 1.3.8.2, 262; 1.3.10.5–11.1, 279–85. This freedom to determine the nature of governing authority reflects the freedom to choose in any other consensual arrangement (such as in property arrangements); the matter in question does not dictate a particular mode of use or possession.
21 James Madison, *Federalist* No. 20, in *The Federalist*, ed. George W. Carey and James McClellan (Indianapolis, IN: Liberty Fund, 2001), 96–97.
22 Grotius, *DJB* 1.1.3.2, 136–37.
23 Of course, the debtor's promise is then guaranteed by the natural law obligation to uphold promises. However, just as nobody can force the debtor to make a promise in the first place, nobody can take out of effect the natural obligation to honour promises. The power to punish arises from a moral horizon that is outside the control of the punisher.
24 Grotius, *DJB* 1.3.6, 257–59.
25 Hugo Grotius, *De Imperio Summarum Potestatum Circa Sacra (On the Power of Sovereigns Concerning Religious Affairs)*, critical edition with introduction, translation and commentary Harm-Jan Van Dam (Boston: Brill, 2001), 8.1, 374–75. Translations are occasionally those of this author.
26 Grotius, *DJB* 1.3.6, 257–59.
27 Grotius, *de Imperio* 6.13–14, 316–21.
28 Grotius, *DJB* 1.3.6, 257–59. The placement of criminal law is somewhat unclear, as Grotius does not mention it in this section. Initially, its element of adjudication would seem to place it in the 'judicial' category. However, its public nature – as seen in its emphasis on crimes against the state – would place it in the 'political' category. Chapters 6 and 8 will deal with this distinction in greater detail.
29 Ibid. See also 1.3.17.1, 305–07. Of course, the people may withhold some elements of jurisdiction from the ruler in the original agreement to create the state.
30 Grotius, *de Imperio* 8.11, 386–87.
31 Grotius, *DJB* 1.3.7.1, 259.
32 Ibid., 2.4.12.1, 500–1; Grotius, *de Imperio* 6.13–14, 316–21.
33 Grotius, *DJB* 1.3.16.1, 300–05.
34 Ibid., 1.3.17, 305–7; 1.3.20, 309–18. See also Knud Haakonssen, "Grotius and the History of Political Thought," *Political Theory*, Vol. 13, No. 2 (May 1985), 244–45.
35 Grotius, *DJB* 1.3.11.2, 280–85.
36 Ibid., 2.2.2.1–4, 420–27.
37 This conception of some form of social organization lends additional weight to Grotius' assertion that a people pre-exists a government.
38 Ibid., 1.3.1.2, 241.
39 Grotius, *de Imperio* 3.11, 222–23. In the ordering of *de Imperio*, this is Grotius' fifth purpose.

40 Grotius, *DJB* 1.3.1.2, 240–1; 2.20.8.4, 968–70.
41 Ibid., 2.20.7.2, 963–64.
42 Grotius, *de Imperio* 3.11, 222–23. In the ordering of *de Imperio*, these are Grotius' first and fourth purposes.
43 Ibid.
44 Ibid. In *de Imperio*, this purpose is number two.
45 Ibid., 6.10, 312–15. See also Grotius, *DJB* Prol.25, 100.
46 Grotius, *de Imperio* 3.12, 224–25.
47 Ibid., 3.4, 208–11.
48 Ibid., 3.11. In *de Imperio*, this purpose is listed third.
49 Grotius, *DJB* 1.3.24, 335.

5 The Bounds of Coercive Authority

Sovereignty and Rebellion

In the final week of May 2007, the White House prepared its standard protocol to receive a foreign head of state. Iraqi President Jalal Talabani would receive an official invitation from the President of the United States. He would enjoy luxurious accommodation at the President's official guest house. Most importantly, he would be granted a private audience with the world's most powerful political leader to discuss foreign policy and advance Iraqi interests. These are rare privileges, chiefly reserved for those who officially represent their country. The Jalal Talabani of 2002 – mere private citizen of Iraq – could have hardly dreamed of such dignified treatment. Membership in the international club of sovereignty has its privileges.

When President Talabani's return flight landed in Baghdad, he was met by armed forces that were anything but ceremonial. They had already swept the area, fenced the perimeter with snipers, and guarded his secret arrival time, before quickly whisking him away to a heavily guarded motorcade. Their concern was justified. Only three months before, assassins had killed ten people while attacking his Vice-President; a year later, others would target his wife. The city itself was cleft into sectarian enclaves, as entire neighbourhoods were no-go areas for religious outsiders. Even within one's own factional stronghold, life could only be described as "solitary, poor, nasty, [and] brutish"; every week the country weathered 1400 violent attacks and suffered 600 civilian deaths.[1] President Talabani's domestic sovereignty only ensured a condition "which is worst of all," one of "continual fear and danger of violent death."[2] While his sovereignty abroad was magnificent, at home it was ugly.

The political theory of sovereignty is often traced back to Thomas Hobbes' development of Jean Bodin. Yet Hobbes' theory was the inverse of this twenty-first century portrait. In Hobbes' account, life outside the state is an anarchic and nonpolitical war of all against all, precisely because it lacks a supreme power to overawe. Each of the actors – that is, sovereigns – remain "in continual jealousies and in the state and posture of gladiators" toward each other. Needless to say, each sovereign is thus insecure abroad. Yet life inside the state is a realm of peace, because its individual constituents have surrendered to the sovereign their gladiatorial weaponry and authorized it to rule them. Inside this area fenced off from anarchy, each sovereign is absolute, secure, and benevolent, leading to peace (that is, to politics). In other words, the sovereign state is a precondition for politics; one might say that the state creates politics *ex nihilo*. Indeed, this supremacy of power both constitutes and defines politics; a state without sovereignty is no state.

The sovereign state and its constitution also enables the modern science of politics, because it presents to scholars a geographical object with precise boundaries and a written document commanding unqualified allegiance. Political scientists can thus define their terms and eliminate multiple variables. While Aristotle studied practices and virtues in his *Politics*, multiple contemporary scholars have written works simply named *The State*. In similar fashion, the ironically christened United Nations does not admit nations; it admits states. The nature of the nation and its regime matters little. For example, the UN General Assembly welcomed President Saddam Hussein in the same capacity of "sovereign" in which it later welcomed President Talabani – and President Bush. Likewise, individual UN member states continued to recognize President Talabani in this role even as his domestic rule progressively ebbed.

Yet for these very reasons, the Hobbesian concept of sovereignty seems to have limits. Its very strength of precision seems to come at the cost of excluding the practice from its definition. Philosophical questions follow. Are all sovereign states functionally equivalent? What does the status of sovereignty mean for a country when its office-holders are constantly changing? What does sovereignty mean to a domestically impotent ruler? Is sovereignty truly the boundary between external war and internal peace? Or might it be the inverse? The conceptual architecture of modern political science seems less than firm. Perhaps a reappraisal is warranted.

This leads us back to the theoretical and practical origins of modern sovereignty. As for the theory, the previous chapter might reassess its genesis not in Hobbes' *Leviathan* of 1651 but in Grotius' works a quarter-century prior. Grotius conceptualizes a single supreme power that holds over subjects a discrete governing *jus*, and he anticipates a world of states – including small ones – that treat each other as diplomatic and legal equals. As for the practice, it is often traced back to the 1648 Treaty of Westphalia. This treaty committed the participants to stay out of each others' domestic affairs, enabling in each state a unitary and absolute sovereign unconstrained by other powers. It brought an end to the Thirty Years' War – an end for which Grotius had laboured so diligently as a diplomat. But if this revised history were the motive for studying Grotius' concept of sovereignty, it would only elide the aforementioned philosophical tensions in the concept. Grotius should interest us because his concept of sovereignty is aware of its own limits and designed to overcome them.

Grotius' *de Imperio* outlines his concepts of governing authority, rebellion, and civil disobedience, and shows that the right (or status) of sovereignty is only a beginning – one that points to a responsibility of action. For example, his understanding of ecclesial and political authority prioritizes unity over doctrine, indicating that human flourishing may begin in assent to deontological natural law propositions but is fulfilled in practicing moral virtues that enable social harmony. Second, while he insists on this monopoly of *jus* as a necessary precondition for the authoritative commands of positive law, this authority and its commands in no way exhaust the political life of the people. The deontological guarantee of supreme power points toward the teleological practice of politics. Third, Grotius builds on his dual naturalist/voluntarist ethics by delineating both indicative and imperative components of authority. This grounds his dual concepts of command and rule, in regard to which the supreme power monopolizes the former but explicitly not the latter. Hence, while only the sovereign governor can formally enact law, the entire community is informally enjoined to participate in political discussion to determine the content of rule. Grotius' supreme ruler is not therefore a voluntaristic creator of law but a personally prudent effector of commands that respond to a prior political reality – one inseparable from a trans-political standard of Good. Finally, if the governor uses his expletive status of lawmaker to enact laws that violate the content of attributive (or even expletive) justice, such laws will be practically ineffective. *Pace* Hobbes, if the people cease to believe in the justice of the sovereign, the sovereign will become impotent. Much like President Talabani in Iraq, the governor will retain the international status (and status-symbols) of sovereignty, but when physically present in his political community, he will largely be ruled over by his own people. The sovereignty meant to enable domestic peace will instead promote civil war. On its own, a purely deontological realm struggles to maintain the support of its adherents. Thus, the right to govern ultimately points to a responsibility to govern well. Otherwise, this expletive status will cease to enable a capacity for action, and it will be reduced to a symbolic value whose tenure will likely be as Hobbes finally described it: short.

Church and State

The first decade of the seventeenth century was a good one for Grotius the prodigy. In 1601, at the age of eighteen, he was selected (over a distinguished Professor) as the official chronicler of Dutch history. *De Jure Praedae* soon followed, establishing his public intellectual credibility while defending a matter of national pride. Soon after, he became the Pensionary of Rotterdam, effectively governing Holland's second-largest city. By the end of the decade, he was the right-hand man of Johann van Oldenbarneveld, Prime Minister of Holland. At the age of twenty-seven, Grotius was approaching the pinnacle of Dutch public life.

The century's second decade would bring stormier waters. Oldenbarnevelt's 'middle way' vision of politics and religion encouraged a broad and theologically pluralist state church. By contrast, the orthodox Calvinist party advocated specific doctrines on predestination and grace (the 'five points of Calvinism') and sought a state-convened synod to define (and enforce) them. In order to ward off such a synod, Grotius penned *De Imperio Summarum Potestatum Circa Sacra (On the Governing Authority of Supreme Powers Concerning Sacred Things)*. To advance this policy, Grotius took on two foundational matters: a defence of state government over religious matters, and an outline of the purposes of governing authority.[3] The former – to which we turn shortly – will establish the relative importance of practical order over theoretical doctrine. This will set up the latter, which presents Grotius' concept of sovereignty, rebellion, and civil disobedience.

Erastian Ecclesiology

Grotius begins the work by defining the term "supreme power" as that which has governing authority (*imperium*), and is subject to no other authority except God (*imperio Dei*).[4] This definition clarifies that even the supreme governing power exists within a moral horizon outside his own realm. Political life does not exist simply to ensure the flourishing of the natural or purely physical realm. Its ultimate (if indirect) purpose is to promote a conception of human flourishing that conduces to God-given ends of existence. Thus, that which is the sole concern of priests – the arranging of divine matters – ought also to be the chief concern of the supreme powers.[5] Authority is "ordained by God, especially on behalf of the safeguard of true religion."[6] Thus, Grotius begins by denying any strict separation between sacred and secular matters: the status or jurisdiction of governor includes both matters.[7]

Nonetheless, he immediately seeks to constrain the governor's exercise of the sacred function, stating that there is less latitude in such matters. The first reason is that a larger share of sacred matters are already defined by divine positive law than are secular matters predetermined by natural law, which "leaves less to human choice." If God has already made a law concerning a particular matter, that matter is not open to the free exercise of governmental deliberation. At most, the governor's role is to add his own command to the already-existing content of God's command, as in the first three functions listed in the previous chapter. Moreover, if the scriptures make plain these laws, there is less need for the fourth purpose, that of promulgation from the throne. The second reason is that mistakes in sacred matters are more disastrous than those in secular affairs. Hence, a governor presumably ought to act on fewer matters and move more slowly when he does. However, while these limitations pertain to the exercise of one's governing *jus*, they do not affect the *jus* itself.[8] As earlier explored in the discussion of sovereignty and promises, the constraints on the governor's action do not derogate from his status.

To buttress his claim that the supreme power should attend to such lofty matters, Grotius employs his characteristic tripartite epistemology, providing evidence from reason, revelation, and historical authorities (both sacred and secular). From reason, he argues from the nature of supreme authority, deducing that it would not actually be supreme if it had no authority over spiritual matters. He also draws the analogy that just as man must be directed by an undivided will, the civil body requires a supreme head. He then refers to revelation, mentioning sources from the Bible, as well as from church history, pointing to the practices of the church over time. Finally, he also cites philosophical authorities in secular history, pointing to Plato's argument in the *Statesman* that the art of politics governs the other arts, and Aristotle's declaration that politics is architectonic because it directs education. Thus, from the beginning, Grotius rejects a strict dichotomy between natural and supernatural, secular and sacred.

The state exists to promote the good life as it relates to the entire person, physical and spiritual.[9]

Grotius will later reaffirm the importance of history when he finally comes to his discussion of synods – the ultimate polemical purpose of this theoretical work. Synods are not commanded by natural or divine law. Indeed, because they do not arise from direct precept, the very origin of the concept must point to historical evolution. This leads Grotius to briefly explore the role of history. He has already told us in *DJB* that history may provide both precepts and examples.[10] Here he clarifies that precept is known through the sacred history that promulgates the laws that God gave at a particular point in time. Precepts are universally binding on those who know them; for instance, the New Testament command to meet regularly for prayer, scripture, and the breaking of bread is mandatory for Christians.[11] In contrast, an example illustrates a precept, and shows what would be prudent "according to circumstances." Its guidance is not universal but situational. For instance, 'default' natural conditions such as the common ownership of things, or the rule that the next of kin is the first inheritor, can be freely altered through prudent human action. Even though examples do not reveal deontological truths, they provide the realm of illustration through which teleology can alone be known. This once again illustrates that the area outside the commands of preceptive natural Right is not merely an amoral realm of arbitrary co-ordinative decisions, but a moral realm whose freedom enjoins its holder to act with attributive justice.[12]

Thus, examples presumably show synods to be salutary in some circumstances, but harmful in others. Without the knowledge-source of history, the church could never have availed itself of the benefits of synods at all; after all, they are not mandated in natural or divine law. However, the governors of the church must also exercise the situational prudence to discern when the convening of a synod would actually be detrimental. Grotius, of course, believes that the synod proposed by the Calvinist party would be imprudent, and that the government should not convene one. Thus, Grotius reaffirms history (whether sacred or secular) as a legitimate source of moral counsel, despite its distinct mode of operation from pure reason.[13]

Practical Order over Theoretical Doctrine

Grotius has now established that the political realm is ultimately ordered toward the higher realm of religion. However, this attention to higher matters also benefits politics. A governor cannot "neglect knowledge of church government" partly because nothing is "more important to the integrity of the state." Citing Augustine, Grotius argues that the devout practice of religion makes people "quiet, obedient, patriotic, and adherents of justice and equity." While the moral precepts and sanctions of religion directly benefit the state, even its doctrines and ceremonies bring indirect benefits, because the turning of the soul toward the divine also helps to cultivate moral virtues. Here Grotius cites Book II of Plato's *Republic*, emphasizing that the necessary virtues correspond to the whole person; they are existential and not merely intellectual. Grotius even implies that religion cultivates the virtues needed for governmental rule, as a ruler needs not only "an understanding of sacred matters but a mind that is really religious." Indeed, Grotius identifies as the two major obstacles to right judgment not only ignorance but also wickedness.[14] Hence, religion is not a threat to the state; it is a benefit. A state full of atheists might be able to discern the basic provisions of strict justice, but Grotius seems to imply it would be less likely both to implement and to live by those basic provisions (let alone wider ones). Peace comes not through eliminating religion, but through emphasizing its basic tenets – a point that Grotius will later reaffirm in his discussion of punitive war (Chapter 7).

Indeed, when Grotius turns to discuss the core of Christianity itself, he prioritizes the moral virtues available to all over the intellectual virtues limited to theologians. Theological doctrines are important only on the most basic level. Fortunately, the essential doctrines of Christianity – much those of like strict justice – are simple and thus relatively understandable to all. Once taught, they are presumably assented to with dispatch. Christianity is unlike metaphysics or linguistics, whose content can only be known by experts. This simplicity of belief is further enabled by a Gospel – God's complete revelation in the person of Christ – known by history rather than pure reason. Because the embodied instantiation of teleology is comprehensible to its non-expert onlookers, its virtues are more likely to be adopted. These matters of action modelled by Christ are as clear and simple as matters of advanced theology are murky and difficult.[15] As a result, the heights of Christianity are not limited to theologians, or attained in the ever-more-precise development of doctrine. Rather, the fullness of the faith is open to all through the practical and experiential manifestation of the Christian moral virtues.[16]

For this reason, the "soul of the church" is most fully manifested in peace and unity among the whole body of Christians, from the sophisticated to the simple. To this harmony Grotius ascribes the noble and admirable character of the early church.[17] Conversely, he traces its decline (and the consequent rise of Islam) to an increasing overemphasis on clerical speculation: "as of old, preferring the tree of knowledge to the tree of life, … nice inquiries were esteemed more than piety, and religion was made an art."[18] In other words, this disunity was abetted by the overemphasis on detailed and obscure – and thus inessential – matters of doctrine. Grotius especially singles out theological constructs and terms not found in Scripture.[19] This further illustrates that virtuous action and piety of the mind, not lifeless rites or assent to complex systems of doctrine, are the essence of Christianity.

Indeed, religious speculation may not simply overshadow piety and unity, but actually weaken it. People may become more devoted to a theological debating point than to the worship of God. What is worse, they may arouse dogmatic controversies that undermine peace and unity and threaten schism.[20] Hence, one of the best ways to foster unity is to abstain from definitions in matters other than "those doctrines necessary or very profitable for salvation."[21] He argues that the historical disagreement of theologians over fine points of doctrine has not harmed the body of faith, at least in cases where this disagreement did not spread to the many faithful.[22] Grotius concludes his apologetic treatise *de Veritate* with a similar exhortation. In order that Christians avoid division, they should be "temperate in wisdom." Rather than rushing into combat with doctrinal opponents, they should "wait till God shall make the hidden truth manifest unto them."[23]

Grotius' emphasis on practice over doctrine may explain his comfort with entrusting church governance to a lay supreme power. On one hand, the governor will likely comprehend the essential doctrines of Christianity, due to their simplicity.[24] On the other, his very lack of further theological erudition will help him to be temperate in wisdom. Unlike the theologians, he will not become attached to specific doctrines on inessential matters, thus avoiding rigid positions. As a result, he is well suited for the paramount task of preventing schism, a task accorded great importance by Christian emperors of history (and treated with indifference by the dishonoured Julian the Apostate). Indeed, Grotius praises Constantine for preventing schisms by cutting off discussion of useless questions, and – in a barely concealed polemic – longs for governors of his day to do the same.[25]

Grotius thus provides an important conceptual separation between the speculative function of theologians (or philosophers) and the unifying function of governors. A governor need not be an expert in religious doctrine or political philosophy. The major threat is not heresy but schism. Hence, his function is to promote an order that is more practical than propositional – one that is manifested in peace and unity. The governor's political skill (not to mention his monopoly on coercive force) makes him well-suited to this distinctly public task. It is more important to maintain a "middle way" that will ensure harmony in a particular polity than it is to insist upon conformity to a detailed written constitution that goes beyond strict justice. Indeed, the "soul of the people" is the internal constitution of the hearts and minds of the people, one that is manifested in their interpersonal interactions. To foster this harmony is the task not of constitutional design but deliberative political rule.

Right of Rebellion

The turn from discussing political theology to civil insurrection might seem abrupt. Yet Grotius' thought provides a natural connection. He has just emphasized that the fullest manifestation of Christianity is unity, peace, and harmony, and its greatest challenge is the threat of schism. The secular analogue is clear: the greatest threat to the state is civil war and secession. Correspondingly, the greatest way to prevent civil insurrection is to ensure that the governor's commanding authority is absolute. His monopoly on commanding authority prevents the rise of an alternative potential authority. Likewise, his power to enforce these commands with the sword militates against civil war.

These twin emphases on the importance of unity and the plenitude of governing authority add up to a clear conclusion: there can be no right of rebellion. If the people could at any time terminate the supremacy of power that gives effect to the commands of the governor, every command would be greeted with doubt over its continued effectiveness. This would quickly enfeeble the governor and paralyse his ability to make laws. Thus, according to Grotius, popular sovereignty would result in the "utmost confusion." Such a right of rebellion would threaten the peace and order that is the very purpose of the state. In this chaos, human society would degenerate into a "non-social horde," such as those of Homer's Cyclopes.[26]

What is more, the judgment of the people may actually be incorrect, owing to the challenge of appropriately evaluating the difficult and messy realm of politics. As he acknowledges, "the moral goodness or badness of [political] action[s], … frequently are obscure, and difficult to analyse." For this reason, the people's own perceived judgment is less important than their binding promise to respect the status of the governor. Coercive force can be legitimate only against those of equal status, not against governors to whom one has made a promise of subordination.[27]

This leads to an uncomfortable question: what if the governing authority misuses its governing right? Grotius remains unmoved: "the exercise of governing authority (*imperium*) is not lost by wrong-doing." The need for supremacy means that the *jus* of political authority cannot be lost through its bad exercise. This follows from a more basic premise: the poor use of a right does not jeopardize its existence. As he says, "nobody may be denied his right because there is a risk of abuse; otherwise nobody's right is safe." Prodigal owners do not forfeit their remaining possessions; unduly harsh judges retain their position. Indeed, if expert judgment were a precondition to possess *jus* of judging, Grotius notes that many honest average civil judges would be put out of work. The opposite is also true. Even if it is best that philosophers become kings, as Plato averred, they are not therefore at liberty to usurp the throne.[28]

If *de Imperio* forbids rebellion, why does *DJB* Book I, Chapter 4 list thirteen circumstances that open the door to it? A closer look shows that its opening is rather narrow. The first case involves "extreme and imminent peril." Rebellion is indeed permissible in situations of unavoidable necessity, which release one from the bounds of ordinary morality. Necessity is an implicit exception in any original agreement to constitute a state, as nobody would willingly agree to any arrangement that threatens their own existence. This promised agreement – even one that confers absolute power – assumes that the governor cannot make himself an enemy of the people. As Grotius says, "the will to govern and the will to destroy cannot coexist in the same person."[29] If the governor seeks to destroy the realm, the original contract that constituted it is null and void. However, even in the case of a rebellion to save the political community, Grotius imposes significant constraints. The rebels must spare the governor's life, and even refrain from propagating malicious falsehoods to besmirch his honour. Moreover, if self-defence against a tyranny would so imperil public order as to result in the deaths of many more, a person is compelled to sacrifice himself for the commonweal.[30]

However, the remaining twelve valid titles to rebellion are all procedural. The first six arise not from the governor's misuse of his governing authority, but his attempt to usurp areas of jurisdiction not originally granted to him. Here, rebelling is analogous to resisting a foreign power unjustly attempting to seize another area of jurisdiction. The remaining six titles to rebellion arise when this analogy becomes a reality, and a foreigner unjustly invades.[31] Hence, while Grotius severely curtails the right of rebellion arising from the governor's substantive unjust action, he grants to subjects wide latitude for insurrection that responds to a governor's procedural violations. Unjust substantive actions may turn a good governor into a bad governor, but he remains a governor. By contrast, procedural violations of jurisdiction turn a governor into no governor at all. If he no longer has valid status as governor, the people's rebellion is in fact no rebellion at all; it is a just war.

Yet even here, Grotius values order so highly that he rescinds the latter six titles to overthrow a foreign conqueror if that usurper governs justly. Indeed, he assumes that even the deposed legitimate governor would prefer the governorship of the usurper to total anarchy. By emphasizing the benefits of order, he further strengthens his attributive encouragement to move from pre-civil society to governing authority. Furthermore, if a usurper comes to possess unmolested *imperium* for a lengthy period, time may eventually confer on him the legitimate *jus* of authority, even if his rule is never explicitly authorized by the people.[32] This implicit theory of tacit consent illustrates Grotius' emphasis on history, as long usage and custom can confer a kind of valid legal right without explicit authorization.

Moreover, after having acknowledged at the beginning of Section 7 that all laws may contain implicit exceptions in cases of equity, Grotius devotes the remainder of this section to counseling against exercising such a right. Indeed, Grotius devotes more space to this counsel in Section 7 than he does to the entirety of sections 8–20, in which he outlined the aforementioned thirteen just titles to rebellion. Grotius' tone and emphasis implies that rebellion is not a perpetual sword of Damocles grazing the neck of the ruler; it is an exception of necessity proving the natural law that forbids rebellion. The dictates of expletive justice are universal and strict; the ordinarily admit no exception.

Civil Disobedience

Status of Authority and Action of Rule

Grotius has now established that the governor's status of sovereignty is unassailable. Yet the governor's power is not absolute. How can this be? The answer lies in the premise established in the previous chapter: that the status of governing authority is not an end in itself. Rather, it is only a precondition for the five purposes of government. We now turn to Grotius' strictures on the exercise of this authority. Here he will tell us that the governor should be carefully watched and judged by the subjects of his rule. Although subjects' negative judgment is no licence to eject the ruler from his status, it does permit them to constrain his exercise of this authority. What Grotius takes away from subjects in forbidding rebellion, he will give back in permitting civil disobedience.

In the first paragraph of *de Imperio*, Grotius begins by distinguishing the possession of authority and the manner of its exercise. He later builds on this distinction in Chapter 5 when he outlines the conceptual foundations of *jus*. In regard to the possession of authority, he states that *jus* corresponds only to legal validity (*actus ratus*). This is Grotius' *justitia specialis*, which corresponds to *imperium*, *dominium*, and servitude.[33] In regard to the exercise of authority, he outlines a different standard: moral rectitude (*actio recte*). Hence, the legal status of *jus* provides only the procedural component of the act; valid possession does not guarantee good use. Appropriately, Grotius will entitle his following chapter "How to rightly use one's governing authority."[34]

He then describes four characteristics of an *actio recte*. First, this moral rectitude requires a well-formed understanding. One must not only possess a *jus* passively bestowed upon oneself, but must also actively seek after the knowledge of moral truth. Second, a morally right act requires an honourable purpose. The rightness of the act is not solely constituted by its tangible, external characteristics that are visible to the world. Rather, it is primarily constituted in the intention that preceded the act. Grotius appears to conceive of the act as a second-order manifestation of the first-order will of the person. (This distinction between act and intention will figure prominently in his later theory of punishment.) Grotius' third characteristic deepens this notion of intention: an *actio recte* requires the virtue of moderation. A right intention obeys the directives of reason rather than the demands of appetite. It is not simply an intellectual matter of theory, but a moral matter of practice. Fourth and finally, in order to act rightly one must consider the circumstances. There is no universal law of reason that can dictate the proper course of action. The inclusion of this criterion suggests that it must transcend strict justice. After all, expletive justice outlines universal dictates that require no further investigation; as the etymology of the term suggests, all that remains is implementation. Yet Grotius here mentions prudential judgment, and not simply as derivative or accidental; it is central to right action.[35]

In sum, to govern rightly, one must have the capacity for wisdom, the correct intention, the ability to subordinate one's desires, and the prudence to discern the action appropriate to a particular situation. The possession of *jus* guaranteed in strict justice is conceptually separable from the virtues that ought to guide its exercise. Grotius will soon widen this distinction between strict and wider justice when he states that "the rules for exercising one's wider duties extend through all the virtues and beyond pure Right." One can have a right without acting according to the virtues of wider justice, but one cannot act rightly without those virtues. Natural rights lead to natural Right.[36]

Types of Rule

We have now examined the holder of the *jus*, showing that one may have *jus* alone, or one may have *jus* along with the knowledge, wisdom, moderation, and prudence to exercise it well. But is it possible to possess the latter virtues without holding the *jus* in the first place? If so, what is the effect of these virtues if one lacks the commanding authority of the state by which to exercise them? What if one is capable of discerning or indicating truth, but lacks imperative commanding force? This leads us to Grotius' concept of rule (*regimen*). This concept of rule appears to be broader than that of *jus*, because it shows how one might have an effect on politics even without possessing the official governing *jus* of coercive force.

Grotius provides a four-fold taxonomy of types of rule, as laid out in Table 5.1. Grotius begins his examination of rule by discerning two fundamental categories of rule: "directive" and "constitutive." The genus of directive rule corresponds to the indicative function of Right. This matches the naturalistic component of metaethics that indicates what is right or good. Grotius then sub-divides directive rule into two species. Grotius terms the first of these species "persuasive" rule. Under persuasive rule, those ruled do not lose their freedom of action. A persuasive ruler influences them through the prestige of his counsel, rather than the force of his command. For instance, physicians, lawyers, and councillors exercise persuasive rule when they dispense general advice.[37] While this type of rule helps the listener to better exercise their freedom, it does not impose on them a strict or direct obligation to carry out a specific act. (Indeed, one is tempted to say that even its indicative weight can never be perfectly binding, because it cannot partake of the certainty of preceptive natural law.) One exercises persuasive rule over matters of fitting (or attributive) natural Right. These are matters in which the subject holds a concessive natural right; he commits no offence against strict justice if he ignores the persuasive rule. However, the matter is not morally arbitrary, because persuasive rule recommends one course of action as attributively superior. The subject is not morally free (in the wider sense) to ignore it.

Table 5.1 Grotius' Categories of Rule

	Directive (Indicative)		*Constitutive (Imperative)*	
	Persuasive	*Declarative*	*Consensual*	*Governmental*
Type of Right	3. Fitting Natural Right	5. Preceptive Natural Right	3. Fitting Natural Right, or 4. Concessive Natural Right, which becomes 2. Human Positive Right (Private)	3. Fitting Natural Right, which becomes 2. Human Positive Right (Political)
Type of Justice	Attributive Justice	Expletive Justice	Attributive Justice, or amoral liberty, then guaranteed by Expletive Justice	Attributive Justice, then guaranteed by Expletive Justice
Type of Relation	Equatorial, or Superior-Subordinate	Equatorial, or Superior-Subordinate	Equatorial	Superior-Subordinate

The other type of directive rule Grotius terms "declarative" rule. Under this category, as well as all remaining categories, those ruled do lose their full freedom of action. This freedom is not lost because declarative rule creates an obligation. Declarative rule is purely indicative and carries no imperative weight on its own. However, declarative rule makes someone aware of a previously existing imperative obligation under preceptive natural Right. It does not merely give advice about better and worse courses of action, as does persuasive rule; rather, it points out the expletive dictates of natural law, which are clear, discrete, unchanging, and perfectly binding. By promulgating the natural law to the subject, it renders effective the pre-existing imperative force of God that applies to all natural law. For example, a physician may declare to a patient that if he does not change his health habits, he will die. Once the patient understands this declaration, he is bound to follow it as a command. However, it is not the physician that binds him; it is God's natural law command to preserve life. Likewise, philosophers exercise declarative rule in moral and political life when they promulgate their knowledge of natural moral law.[38] Both persuasive and declarative rule appear to involve a superior-subordinate relationship. But this need not be so. A patient can exercise such rule by directly pointing out that his physician's smoking habit compromises his health, just as a child can point out that a philosopher's vicious moral conduct belies his sanctimonious pontifications. The subordinate may rule the superior. Needless to say, an equal may also directively rule an equal.

The other genus of rule – constitutive rule – corresponds to the imperative function of Right, and the voluntaristic metaethics that makes obligation imperative. Constitutive rule is also sub-divided into two species: one based on consent, and one based on authority. "Consensual" constitutive rule gains its imperative power from the positive agreement of two or more parties. These two parties begin from a status of equality; neither one is a paternal or political superior. One party then makes a promise to the other. In other words, he confers on the other party (or parties) a (temporary) imperative force through his own positive agreement to transfer this pre-existing *jus* (or freedom of action). In a contract, the receiving party then reciprocates with a corresponding promise. For instance, when a restaurant patron orders a meal, he promises to the server that he will pay a pre-agreed sum, just as the server promises to deliver the corresponding menu item. The matter of the promise arises from the realm of either attributive or concessive natural Right in which the parties each had a previous freedom of action. In the former, a patron seeking to trim his waistline may accept or reject the server's (attributive) persuasive rule about healthy options. In the latter, a customer may choose red or blue cake frosting through his own conscious choice or by randomly flipping a coin. However, by limiting the otherwise various licit possibilities of action, the parties bring the matter into the realm of human positive Right. While the patron is free to choose any menu item, once he chooses he is not free to dine and dash. This type of rule brings into existence an obligation that did not previously exist in natural law, even though the expletive justice governing promises now serves as a guarantor of that obligation.[39] This promise, and the *jus* it confers on the server, is a private one that lacks any inherent import for the public realm. It may also be temporary. Once the server has provided the dish and collected on the bill, the rule ends; the server has no right to impose on the patron any future gastronomic decisions or financial obligations.

The final species of constitutive rule is that of *imperium*, or "governmental" rule. (Grotius inelegantly describes it as "authoritative constitutive rule," as opposed to "consensual constitutive rule.") This governmental rule flows from a superior-subordinate relationship that is ordinarily comprehensive and permanent. In other words, the obligating force of any individual command does not come from the consent that the parties have given to that specific order. Rather, it comes from the consent that the parties originally provided when they authorized a type of rule with a permanent status of superiority and subordination. (As Chapter 4 has shown, attributive justice originally recommended that a people institute of this authority, before expletive justice came to compel them to fulfil their promises to obey it.) This permanent status is the *sine qua non* of governing authority, because it confers the ability to create imperative obligations. As outlined earlier, the governor uses this commanding authority to carry out (or to delegate) the three functions of government: law-making, executive deliberation, and judicial adjudication. There is only one type of authoritative constitutive rule that is not derived from a political superior: that of paternal *jus*.[40] Nonetheless, even the head of the household, in his role as citizen, remains subject to the governing authority of the supreme power.

This four-fold taxonomy reconfirms Grotius' inclusion in natural Right of both intrinsic (indicative) and extrinsic (imperative) factors. Although imperative factors may be the efficient cause of government, indicative factors are the final cause. This further demonstrates Grotius' simultaneous approach to government as both a positive-descriptive reality and as a natural-normative one. Positive legal science may elucidate the jurisdiction and powers of the governor, while normative inquiry evaluates how his actions serve the pre-existing purposes of politics. Just as the existence of the natural realm does not lead Aquinas to discount the existence of the supernatural, the possibility of describing politics in the lower positive sense does not eliminate the existence of the higher normative one. For this reason, the one possessing the formal status of governor may be subject to the normative judgment of others. The governor creates a formal and imperative legal obligation, but cannot create moral obligations *ex nihilo*. Indeed, while moral obligations cannot invalidate the legal position of the right-holder, they may trump legal but immoral obligations. After all, the governor remains subordinate to God, and private citizens may be competent to promulgate the truths of God.

Rule and Judgment

Just as legal status is only a jumping-off point for moral-political justice, the status of constitutive rule is only a precondition for the exercise of judgment. Thus, after outlining the several types of rule, Grotius devotes a chapter to the mode of action – the virtue of judgment – that corresponds to each. He asserts that judgment (and not simply intention) precedes acts. This provides clear evidence of the rationality of the will. He deepens this belief when he clarifies the relation between act and will. In a purely descriptive sense, it may be accurate to say that an act of commanding merely depends upon a prior will. However, in order for this will to be right (*recte*), there must be agreement between that will and reason. This reason, in turn, must agree with the object itself. Thus, while an act itself is dependent simply on will, a good act is dependent upon a reasonable will that corresponds to a reality outside itself. Hence, while Grotius allows for a positivistic concept of the purely voluntarist element of will, he points out that a normative concept of the naturalist-rational will is a fuller concept.[41]

After showing that the will is rational, Grotius later shows that rationality needs will. He does this by refuting the common aphorism that scripture (or the law) is a judge. He begins by acknowledging a simplistic truth in the maxim, because scripture (and law) may serve as a standard. However, such a truth is figurative at best, presumably because a personal will is necessary in order to judge properly.[42] The law cannot interpret itself. Indeed, a positive law is only a manifestation of will at a particular point in time, so it must be interpreted according to that (ongoing) will. This prefigures his emphasis on the importance of equity (Chapter 6).

Grotius fittingly concludes his chapter on judgment with his strongest emphasis on situational prudence. Here, he qualifies all the advice he has given about the proper exercise of one's *jus* of judgment, stating that it is not eternal or even always useful. His theoretical account of a practical virtue can only go so far. As he says, "no precepts for prudence are universal, since prudence includes a knowledge of particular facts." The proper prescription varies with the person, the place, and the time. As a teleological exercise, it cannot be defined, only illustrated. One can only learn so much about judging by reading about its nature; to truly learn judgment, one must find a good judge.

Rule and Command

Because judgment reflects a rational will – a potentially universal human capability – it need not necessarily be limited to the governor. While consensual and governmental rule are confined to specific actors, persuasive and declarative rule are open to anyone with the indicative competence. While the governor has a unique ability and role to make effective public commands, his imperative weight is not the end of the story. Subjects have the right (and indeed the responsibility) to shape the content of those commands. Knowing that a command is forthcoming, they can seek to ensure its conformity to natural law and its harmony with attributive justice. The more effective their reason, the stronger their directive and persuasive rule – no matter their station in life.[43] This rule has no limits on its potential domain.

Grotius particularly emphasizes the directive rule of the church as a counterweight to the governing authorities. Although pastors of the church do not exercise coercive rule over the physical body, they exercise considerable directive authority over the mind. This directive rule includes the preaching of the Gospel and the power of the keys (the ability to apply the promises and threats in the Gospels). Pastors exercise declarative rule by announcing what God has bound and loosed, like a town crier who publicly proclaims the judgments of the ruler.[44] They also exercise significant persuasive rule by counseling attention to sanctification, like a physician encouraging health.[45] While clergy lack the sword, they can speak eloquently to those who do. Like a legislative assistant to a legislator, they can shape the content of those laws.

Thus, despite this indivisibility of governing authority in the public realm, the governor is always subject – to a greater or lesser extent – to the directive rule of others. A subject – or indeed a governor – can be simultaneously ruler and ruled. As an example, Grotius notes the historical coexistence of church and state, arguing that "no judgment among men has more weight (*auctori tate*) than the former, and no judgment among men has more power (*potestate*) than the latter."[46] This distinction between church authority and state power testifies to two different modes of action in politics. The imperative supremacy of the latter does not guarantee directive infallibility, or even above-average directive capability. The governor's subjects may be more aware of indicative truth than he is. If the governor submits to this indicative rule, he will be more just and effective in his own realm of *jus* – that of governing authority. In other words, politics functions best when the governor and his subjects work together to rule each other simultaneously. By submitting to the directive rule of others, the governor will be better able to exercise governmental authority over them.

Rule and Civil Disobedience

What if the governor fails to heed the indicative rule of others, and governs unjustly? What if his commands oppose the indicative dictates of justice? In such cases, the directive rule of subjects does not cease. However, it turns the aforementioned simultaneously overlapping forms of rule into an adversarial relationship. The ruler has an imperative legal right to command obedience to his laws. However, civil society has an indicative moral right to disobey the ruler. As with rule and command, Grotius gives a special place to the church in this struggle.[47] The church can increase the quantity of opposition through its stature. It can also increase the quality of opposition, by showing that the indicative truths of nature carry the imperative force of Divine sanction. After all, God's imperative force that underlines natural law is ultimately greater than the imperative force of the state, as the imperative force of the state cannot eternally imprison the soul.

It should be noted, however, that there are at least three separate types of unjust behaviour that the governor might commit, each of which should inspire divergent responses. The first is wrongful behaviour in the governor's personal life. Such might include impiety, adultery, or things that generally set a poor moral example. Subjects would be free to condemn these actions. However, presumably they would not constrain the governor's functions of making laws unrelated to these acts.

A second type of unjust action is a law, executive command, or judgment that imposes an unfair burden on the particular subject of the command. This would offend against what is fitting, suitable, agreeable, or harmonious (*convenientia*) under attributive justice. For example, arbitrary conscription for forced labour would place an excessive and unjustifiable burden on the individual chosen. Nonetheless, such a person could not exercise declarative rule, because there is nothing inherently wrong with the act of labouring. Thus, Grotius argues that they ought to endure it rather than to refuse to obey. His counsel of obedience adverts to the value of political order, whose presence can lift up the downtrodden individual, but whose absence can ruin even the prosperous one. He also reassures the Christian that such long-suffering will not fail to achieve its (eternal) reward.[48] Yet while the subject many not challenge the imperative rule of the government through a refusal to obey, he is yet enjoined to register his disapproval. Just as attributive justice recommends the creation of governmental rule, it recommends the exercise of persuasive rule.

A third type of unjust action is a governing command that orders subjects to violate natural law or the commands of God. Examples include the worship of political rulers, murder of innocents, or blasphemy against God. Here the governor inflicts an injustice against God rather than the subject. In this case, subjects would exercise declarative rule over the governor, publicly registering their moral opprobrium. Of course, they could not punish the ruler (as they lack such imperative authority), let alone overthrow him. However, they would be required in expletive justice to disobey the governor's command. Subjects cannot make a promise to violate natural law, which means they cannot promise to obey the ruler inasmuch as his commands do the same.[49] Put another way, the depth of the governor's injustice (or inattention to public justice) corresponds to the breadth of individual freedom to self-legislate in accordance with natural law.[50] In regard to the imperative force of the governor's commands, his authority to command is dead on arrival. He will retain it in name, but it will have no effective voice. If he ignores his wise subjects, they will ignore his unwise laws.

Despite his wide latitude for civil disobedience, Grotius devotes surprisingly little explicit attention to it. Perhaps he sees it as obvious enough to be unworthy of extended treatment. Often it is simply implicit in his treatment of other subjects. Take, for instance, his argument that sovereignty is not lost through misrule. He goes on to say that if this means that a manifestly wrong command should not be obeyed, he is simply "saying what is true and is acknowledged among all good men." Occasionally he makes the point more forcefully, arguing that obedience to natural law is "an infallible rule of action, which is written in the hearts of all men."[51]

Hence, while the governor's imperative status is secure, his ability to exercise command is a great responsibility for which he is constantly being held to account. In the words of Oliver O'Donovan, Grotius' supreme power is "unchallengeable from below and perilously exposed to judgment from above."[52] However, only the status is unchallengeable from below; the exercise is exposed to judgment from all sides. This discrepancy between status and exercise highlights the distinction between the institutional and active understandings of the term "government." In the formal and institutional sense, the sovereign's government is secure; in an active sense, it may easily crumble. This familiar distinction between status and action echoes Grotius' later discussion of child kings. In such a case, the child holds the status of sovereign authority. However, because his age prevents him from governing, his exercise of that authority is silent.[53] If an adult governor makes an unjust command to violate natural law, he infantilizes himself.

Grotius and Modern Sovereignty

Grotius' extreme limitations on the right of rebellion appear to herald the Westphalian paradigm, in which political loyalty is unified under a clear sovereign authority that answers to no one. Indeed, his strict justice guarantees the status of the ruler and virtually forbids subjects from rebellion. Yet a wider reading of Grotius' concept of governing authority shows a more nuanced impression. Grotius' wider justice outlines a standard of action to which the ruler himself is subject. He speaks of the term "supreme power" in such a way that implies the pre-existing limits of divine and natural law.[54] Because others may be better aware of these limits, the supreme power is always subject to the rule of others. The supreme authority is supreme only in regard to imperative coercive force; there are other methods of indicative rule in which he may not even rule, let alone rule supremely. The supreme power is supreme in that it is not subject to the *jus* of another, but it is far from absolute in its ability to act. Indeed, Grotius never uses the term "sovereign," favouring instead "supreme power."

By rejecting rebellion yet endorsing civil disobedience, Grotius sketches a nuanced conception of sovereignty that diverges from several elements of the modern concept. The modern approach includes four implicit components, which Stephen Krasner delineates in his *Sovereignty: Organized Hypocrisy*. The first is "international legal sovereignty," which refers to a state's recognition from others as the sole valid legislator for its territory. In this component, Grotius clearly prefigures the modern concept, because he clearly intends for the governing authority to possess it. This status is unassailable, because it is a prerequisite to the governor's ongoing ability to carry out its three functions. It is a binary all-or-nothing status; either a state has it, or it does not. The second component is "interdependence sovereignty," or a state's ability to control movements across its borders. It is not entirely clear that Grotius would have been concerned with this type of sovereignty, especially considering his statement that the state rules primarily over its subjects and only secondarily over its territory. In any case, control over borders was likely less possible in the seventeenth century, and threats of mass movement were much less prevalent. If this second type is less important, the third is more. Entitled "domestic sovereignty," it refers to the effectiveness of the authority structures within a state. Grotius' concept of civil disobedience challenges this claim, a concept grounded in his taxonomy of rule. Here the state has effective domestic sovereignty only inasmuch as it conforms to the dictates of its subjects' indicative rule. While a state's legal sovereignty is secure and unchallengeable, its domestic sovereignty is constantly in flux. Indeed, unlike legal sovereignty, domestic sovereignty exists in time; it waxes and wanes, depending on the actions of the governor. One might almost say that the state's domestic sovereignty is a shared reality constituted by multitudes. The final element of sovereignty is "Westphalian sovereignty," or the right of states to exclude the armies of foreign states.[55] This type of sovereignty will be treated in Chapter 7. At this point it suffices to say that Grotius sees Westphalian sovereignty as closer to the active character of domestic sovereignty than to the static nature of legal sovereignty. In conceding the latter three of these four components of sovereignty to be less than absolute, Grotius' concept of sovereignty is not the modern concept. Indeed, his indicative elements of rule point toward a higher moral order, one grounding a classical conception of sovereignty as responsibility.[56]

Conclusion

At first glance, Grotius' conception of sovereignty appears to be that of modern political science: unitary and systematic. Grotius regularly uses the term "supreme power," he insists on a monopoly on coercive force, and he appears even to reject popular sovereignty. His unity of power marks a shift from the overlapping sovereignties of the medieval world, and allows one to know the exact contours of the state. It includes precisely those who have participated in the original agreement (or are subsequently born into it); it excludes exactly those who have not. Moreover, those who are inside the state have a status of subordination to the governor that is absolute; their promise precludes the possibility of rebellion. Only by granting this assurance can the governor enact the commands (including those of legislation) that differentiate its authority from that of private contractors and fathers. More simply, the governor's plenitude of power grounds the validity of positive law. Without this monopoly, his statutes cannot be effective, enforceable, and noncompeting. In sum, Grotius' unitary status of sovereignty appears to enable a value-neutral and positivistic science of law.

Yet Grotius' apparent methodological positivism is not that of Hans Kelsen, the archetypal legal positivist of the twentieth century. Kelsen argues that law can be understood on its own terms without any reference to the political society that enacted it.[57] His globally value-neutral definition disentangles the concept from contested accounts of nature or political self-understanding. Yet as Kelsen's student Eric Voegelin points out, both statute and case law can only be a static instantiation at a specific moment in time. This static conception of law facilitates its development as a science. Yet this very stasis renders it inadequate (both descriptively and especially prescriptively) to the dynamic human world. Much like a series of still photographs of a runner, applications of the law at particular points in time are bound to miss all of the intermediate 'time-slices' between snapshots.[58] Hence, while some have described Grotius (perhaps accurately) as "the father of the modern science of law,"[59] they have also missed the wider context. Grotius' dynamic concept of *rule* shows that – like Voegelin – he is already aware of the limitations of static concepts such as sovereignty and law.

If he develops a systematized and complete science of the state and its positive law, he does so while denying the same possibility for the very politics that grounds the state – or for the political rule that determines and applies the law.

Grotius, of course, does not reject the importance of status as a precondition for action. The creation and sustenance of the state does, indeed, require a sovereign governing authority. Hence, one can determine exactly where the sovereignty resides (and will continue to reside) in a state. To paraphrase Kelsen, one can understand the *form* of sovereignty without an account of the political community. One's international legal sovereignty, manifested in the privileges of being a foreign head of state abroad, needs reference only to the possession of sovereignty. However, one cannot understand the *content* of sovereignty – that is, the action (or rule) that flows from it – without an account of the political community. While the status of sovereign authority is temporally first, it is not ontologically primary; while it is essential, it is not the point. International legal sovereignty is of little use without the domestic sovereignty that enables one to effectively guide the country. A truly descriptive science of a polity requires more than a static description of sovereignty, because it must also convey the dynamic lived reality of that indicative rule.

Thus, a Grotian political science looks to the interpenetration of indicative and imperative rule and examines the interrelationship between the beliefs of the official *politeuma* and the unofficial *politeia.* While the sovereign's imperative power enables the validity of positive law, its effectiveness relies on its conformity to the indicative belief of the people. If the sovereign accepts the persuasive and declarative rule of civil society, his status of governing authority will enable effective governmental rule. By permitting the indicative rule of civil society, his own imperative rule will be strengthened. However, if these two forms of rule are discordant, the governor's effective rule will begin to wane. He will maintain the same unimpeachable deontological status as before, but the country will move ahead toward a teleological reality far different from what he intends. His people may not force him out of his palace at gunpoint, but they will ignore every order he attempts to make. Without accounting for both types of rule, one is unable to differentiate between Jalal Talabani, sovereign of Iraq, and Saddam Hussein, sovereign of Iraq – except perhaps by Saddam's penchant for Cuban cigars on foreign junkets.

What is more, a prescriptive account of a polity requires not simply discerning its indicative beliefs, but judging their correspondence to the trans-political natural Right from which they take their lead. Only a knowledge of natural Right, likely conveyed from civil society and religious institutions, can reveal to the governor the wider normative horizon within which he must govern. Expletive justice does not simply compel the subjects to keep their initial authority-constituting promise to the governor, but it also compels the governor to uphold and promote the precepts of natural Right. Indeed, the governor's potency to command rests not simply on his ability to protect and preserve property, but his ability to direct his people toward the development of their rational and social nature. The right of governing *jus* leads to the responsibility to exercise it well. Without its good exercise, the *jus* is impotent; all that remains are the empty status symbols, the gratification from which dissipates as quickly as a fading cigar stub.

This responsibility to rule well obviously follows from the purposes of government outlined in the previous chapter. However, in the ecclesiology of *de Imperio*, Grotius deepens this sense of mission by showing that 'secular' government also ought to point toward the (ultimately divine) origins and ends of human existence. While the roles of governing the two realms of state and church are conceptually separable, the purposes are not. Nonetheless, the secular governor need not be an expert in theology. Indeed, his very lack of erudition may assist him in fulfilling this role the best way he can: to ensure that the church is orderly and unified. Through his governing expertise (or at least governing authority), the governor can promote the preconditions under which pastors can be effective. Order is not first and foremost a matter of law-making that discerns basic doctrine, but an active practice of politics that promotes unity.

However, this close church-state relationship is symbiotic; just as the state may foster the preconditions for religious growth, religion may foster the conditions for political success. The development of Christian virtues helps to make people peaceful and orderly. Indeed, the Christian conscious of his eternal destiny is unlikely to insist that the overthrow of a sovereign will hasten the millennium. Hence, religion is not a threat to the peace of the state. Rather, the religious aim of peace is beneficial to the state. Grotius does not aim at peace and unity through the eclipse of religion, but through its very exercise.

Moreover, when the church does its job, it will better enable its members to exercise indicative rule over the state. Thus, while the church is governed by the state in the most obvious (imperative) sense, in a subtler (indicative) sense it may be the one governing the state. The practice of rule is wider than the imperative force of the state, which is why it can be undertaken outside the formal apparatus of the state. Hence, natural law has weight on its own, even if – in contrast to positive law – it lacks the sword of the state or the damning power of God. Rule and law (in the wider sense) are not reducible to coercive force. Rather, by marrying reason and will, they reflect God's twin modalities of naturalistic creator and voluntaristic governor.

Nonetheless, if coercive force is not the essence of government, it is still a component of it. If the governor is heeding the indicative rule of his people and enacting good laws, his particular contribution is simply to add the weight of the state. Indeed, this is a contribution that his subjects cannot make; he alone is capable of using the sword. In other words, the superiority that grants the governor the status to enact positive law also grants him the status to punish its violations. But just as the status to make law invites the question of the purposes of law, the status of punishment requires us to examine the purposes of punishment. What are they? How can one determine the nature and extent of punishment? Does it vary from case to case? Should all lawbreakers go to prison? What is the role of prudence in punishing? Many of the conundrums that Grotius has faced in the formation and content of state sovereignty, and the insights he has developed to address them, are only amplified in his treatment of punishment.

Notes

1 Iraq Body Count, www.iraqbodycount.org/database/, accessed 28 July 2015.
2 Thomas Hobbes, *Leviathan*, ed. C. B. MacPherson (London: Penguin, 1985), Ch. 13, 186–87. See also Ch. 30, 394: Sovereigns are governed in their relations by the law of nature, which is identical to that of individuals in the state of nature that he has described in such dark terms.
3 Strangely enough, this premise was a rare point of agreement between Grotius and his adversaries.
4 Hugo Grotius, *De Imperio Summarum Potestatum Circa Sacra (On the Power of Sovereigns Concerning Religious Affairs)*, critical edition with introduction, translation, and commentary Harm-Jan Van Dam (Boston: Brill, 2001), 1.1, 156–57. Translations from *de Imperio* are occasionally the author's own.
5 Grotius, *de Imperio*, 2.6, 196–99; 5.8, 266–69.
6 Ibid., 5.9, 272–73.
7 Grotius will echo this position in *de Jure Belli*. Already in its first chapter, he writes, "Christian princes may now make laws of the same import with those given by Moses" (Hugo Grotius, *The Rights of War and Peace*, ed. Richard Tuck, from the Edition by Jean Barbeyrac (hereafter *DJB*) (Indianapolis, IN: Liberty Fund, 2005), 1.1.17, 175–79. Later, he writes that the authority to make or repeal laws may extend as well to sacred things (Grotius, *DJB* 1.3.6, 258). Note that while the role of the supreme power is to use his imperative power to ensure unity, it is not to be an indicative expert who discerns doctrine and preaches the Word. While the sovereign calls (or refrains from calling) a synod, he does not determine its canons. Hence, the church as a whole indicatively determines the content of the canons that will then be enforced by the state as essential to the status of church membership. Citations from *DJB* are occasionally taken from Hugo Grotius, *De Jure Belli ac Pacis (The Law of War and Peace)*, trans. Francis W. Kelsey, intro. James Brown Scott, Carnegie Classics of International Law, No. 3, Vol. 2 (New York: Bobbs-Merrill, 1925) or from this author's own translations from the Latin original.
8 Grotius, *de Imperio* 3.15, 230–33.
9 Ibid., 1.3–1.9, 158–73.
10 Grotius, *DJB* Prol.47, 123–24.
11 One is reminded of Grotius' earlier inclusion in the category of "nature" those principles that proceed in a stable and consistent manner out of supernatural foundations.
12 Grotius, *de Imperio* 7.2, 326–31.
13 Ibid.
14 Ibid., 1.13, 174–79; 5.8, 266–69; 6.6, 298–99.
15 Ibid., 6.9, 308–13.
16 Ibid., 5.9, 268–75.
17 Ibid., 6.9, 308–13.
18 Hugo Grotius, *The Truth of the Christian Religion (hereafter de Veritate)*, ed. and intro. Maria Rosa Antognazza, trans. John Clarke (Indianapolis, IN: Liberty Fund, 2012), 6.1, 231–33.
19 Grotius, *de Imperio* 8.6, 380–83. Such terms include "*homoousion*," "Trinity," and "unbegotten."
20 Ibid., 5.9, 268–75.
21 Ibid., 6.9, 308–13. Compare this with Hobbes' insistence in *Leviathan* that one can say nothing without the prior foundation of definitions: they are "but insignificant sounds" (Hobbes, *Leviathan*, Ch. 4, 108).
22 Ibid. For instance, he argues that the church resolved the Pelagian controversy without addressing issues of free will and predestination.
23 Grotius, *de Veritate* 6.11, 246–47.
24 Grotius, *de Imperio* 5.9, 268–75. Grotius does admit the possibility that the governor may rule badly on these matters. However, all men are fallible; passing this role on to

someone else is no guarantee of good government. He adds that Divine Providence is able to work through bad governors as well as good ones. After citing Augustine, he says, "sometimes calm weather is more useful to the church, sometimes a storm" (Ibid., 8.2, 374–77).

25 Ibid., 5.9, 268–75; 6.9, 308–13; 8.6, 380–83.

26 Grotius, *DJB* 1.3.9.2, 276–77; Grotius, *de Imperio* 5.14, 284–87.

27 Grotius, *DJB* 1.3.8.13–1.3.9.2, 260–77; 1.4.2.1, 338–43; Grotius, *de Imperio* 3.14, 226–31. To use the anachronistic framework of the social contract, one might be tempted to say that in the former case, the contract is between the people and the governor (as in Locke), but in the latter case, it is only between the people (as in Hobbes). Such an interpretation, however, would obscure the fact that Grotius uses the framework of promise, not of contract. In the case of unrestricted governmental authority, the people still involve the governor in their promise, because the governor is the recipient of the promise. A promise is like a contract in that it involves at least two parties; however, it is unlike a contract in that it may oblige only one party. This promise to the governor itself constitutes the governing authority of the governor, even if the governor is only a recipient of the promise. This differs from Hobbes' covenant, in which the people covenant amongst themselves, and the creation of the Leviathan is a by-product – even if inevitable – of this covenant.

28 Grotius, *DJB* 2.1.9.2, 404–05; Grotius, *de Imperio* 5.11–12, 274–83; 8.2, 375.

29 Grotius, *DJB* 1.4.11, 375–76. This concept of necessity is not simply a *deus ex machina*; it appears elsewhere in *DJB*. For example, in *DJB* 2.2.6, 433–35 he argues in detail that one may use the property of others in cases of absolute necessity. *DJB* 2.6.5, 569–70 hints at a possible theoretical justification for such an exception. Here he argues that necessity does not contradict natural law, but simply reduces the naturality of law to the bare sense of animal nature referenced in the early Prolegomena. While this sense of nature is lower, it is nonetheless still part of nature.

30 Ibid., 1.4.7.2–7, 356–72.

31 For the first six, see Ibid., 1.4.8–10, 372–75 and 1.4.12–14, 376–77; for the latter six, see 1.4.15–20, 377–83.

32 Ibid., 1.4.15–20, 377–83.

33 Grotius, *de Imperio* 5.11, 274–77. As Oliver O'Donovan points out, Grotius curiously abandons this phrase after *de Imperio*; it is not used in *DJB*. However, the distinction between "strict" and "wider" justice that it appears to represent is present throughout *DJB*. See Oliver O'Donovan, "Review: *De Imperio Summarum Potestatum Circa Sacra*," *Theological Studies*, Vol. 64, No. 3 (September, 2003), 627–30.

34 Ibid., 6.1, 292–93.

35 Ibid., 5.11, 274–77.

36 Ibid., 6.13, 316–19.

37 Ibid., 4.6, 246–49.

38 Ibid.

39 Ibid.

40 Ibid.

41 Ibid., 5.1, 262–63.

42 Ibid., 5.6, 266–67.

43 Ibid., 4.12, 256–59.

44 Ibid., 9.2, 394–97; 9.6–8, 400–07.

45 Ibid. Grotius addresses the practice of withholding the Eucharist as a liberty, much like a doctor may refuse a cup of water to a patient if it is inappropriate for the patient. Because it does not exercise force over the recipient, it is not a (governing) act of jurisdiction.

46 Ibid., 5.7, 266–67.

47 Ibid., 3.14, 226–31.

48 Grotius, *DJB* 1.4.1.3, 337–38; 1.4.4.2–4, 345–49; Grotius, *de Imperio* 3.14, 226–31; 5.2, 262–63; 5.12, 276–83; 6.14, 318–21. Grotius argues that one may flee the

country, but the Christian resorts to such an option at his own peril, as Christianity requires submission to governors, even unto death.

49 Grotius, *DJB* 1.3.8.16, 272–76; Grotius, *de Imperio* 3.14, 226–31; 5.2, 262–63; 5.12, 276–83; 6.14, 318–21; 8.2, 374–77. Regarding the governor, the latter reads, "a stern judgment awaits him from the King of the church, who will not let the church be unavenged."

50 Grotius, *DJB* 1.4.1.3, 337–38.

51 Ibid., 1.3.9.1, 276–77; 1.4.1.3, 337–38.

52 O'Donovan, "Review," 629.

53 Grotius, *DJB* 1.3.15, 297–300.

54 Grotius, *de Imperio*, 3.13, 226–27; 4.13, 258–59.

55 Stephen Krasner, *Sovereignty: Organized Hypocrisy* (Princeton, NJ: Princeton University Press, 1999), 3–25.

56 For a fuller discussion of pre-modern and modern sovereignty, see James Turner Johnson, *Sovereignty: Moral and Historical Perspectives* (Washington, DC: Georgetown University Press, 2014).

57 See Hans Kelsen, *General Theory of Law and State*, trans. A. Wedberg (New York: Russell and Russell, 1961).

58 Eric Voegelin, *The Nature of the Law and Related Legal Writings* (Collected Works of Eric Voegelin, Vol. 27), ed. Robert Anthony Pascal *et al.* (Baton Rouge, LA: Louisiana State University Press, 1991), 16–17, 33–35.

59 Hamilton Vreeland, *Hugo Grotius: The Father of the Modern Science of Natural Law* (New York: Oxford University Press, 1917), 39–40.

6 Rights and the Responsibility (Not) to Punish

Bernie Ecclestone is a wealthy and famous man. He has amassed a multi-billion-dollar fortune as the worldwide head of Formula One racing, while gaining public notoriety through his distasteful public comments. In 2014, a German prosecutor concluded he had also acquired a portion of his fortune in unsavoury fashion, and charged Mr Ecclestone for the crime of paying a $44M bribe to a German banker. While a conviction would have called for a prison sentence of up to ten years, the case ended suddenly in mid-trial. Under a provision of German law, prosecutors offered a deal amenable to Mr Ecclestone: the case would be dismissed in exchange for a $100M payment to the German treasury.[1]

For critics of this plea bargain, the irony is particularly hard to swallow: Mr Ecclestone effectively bribes the state to avoid punishment for bribing a sports official. But defenders argue that this is exactly the point. The cost of his bribe to the state exceeds the benefit from his bribe to the banker, rendering any future bribes a poor business proposition. The state need not concern itself with Mr Ecclestone's character, whose continuing propensity toward bribery it may have only fuelled. Nor need it assign a criminal record as a mark of supposed immorality. Rather, it should enforce legal incentives to align Mr Ecclestone's self-interest with fair and honest non-bribe-paying procedures – the definition of the common good.

This approach to criminal law was not simply the whim of a German prosecutor who had lost the plot. Richard Posner, one of the progenitors of the ascendant "law and economics" movement, has famously argued that white-collar crime is best punished not through prison time but financial penalties. In his account, the disutility of pecuniary punishment is interchangeable with the deterrent effect of prison as well as the stigma associated with a criminal record. Such stigmas are in fact inefficient, as the disutility of the stigma to the criminal has no corresponding utility to society.[2] The law aims not to shape character according to a morality that transcends it.

The law and economics movement is built on rational choice theory, which in turn arises from the modern liberal innovations of Thomas Hobbes. Hobbes proposed to seek security of person not by cultivating political virtue but by realigning incentives. He saw the existing classical approach as incoherent because one could not ascertain rational intentions; one could only examine actions.[3] That approach was also irrelevant, as the liberal objective to protect life rendered any account of the inner life of citizens moot (and perhaps even dangerous).[4] Indeed, Hobbes argues that obligation arises only in the act of consent; acts are amoral until one has promised to undertake or avoid them. This approach purports to bring clear benefits: it requires no adherence to comprehensive doctrines, and it eliminates the possibility of thought-crimes.

Yet this liberal focus on outcomes rather than intentions struggles to justify criminal law, "the domain *par excellence* of moral … thinking in law."[5] It may claim criminal law as a deterrent, but this only works for the poor who – unlike Mr Ecclestone – have little to lose.[6] Moreover, such an outcome-based foundation would seem to license criminal sentences for civil violations: for example, the threat of prison time would surely control speeding motorists. Regardless of outcome, can it truly be just to imprison an ordinary motorist who accelerated negligently – while freeing a Formula One racing boss who bribed intentionally? Doesn't the former mistakenly assign a criminal penalty to a civil liability, and the latter a civil penalty to a crime? Ignoring moral intent seems to blur the lines of civil and criminal law.[7]

A liberal theory of punishment might look more profitably not to Hobbes (or even Locke[8]) but to the Grotius who preceded both. Legal historians have identified in Grotius "the first modern theory of criminal jurisprudence."[9] But if historical lineage suggests a return to Grotius, the aforementioned philosophical conundrum urges it. Grotius' theory of punishment establishes a foundation for a liberal contractarian civil law that is independent of intention, but it does so in full awareness its own limits. For this reason, Grotius also establishes a robust theory of an ontologically higher – and fundamentally moral – criminal law that transcends the limitations of civil law.

Cornelius Van Vollenhoven, an influential early twentieth-century reader, assesses Grotius' hefty chapter on punishment in *De Jure Belli (DJB)* as "the zenith of [his] argument."[10] But Grotius explores the interplay of civil and criminal law even further in his often-overlooked Book III of *DJB*, his virtually unknown *de Satisfactione Christi (The Satisfaction of Christ)*, and his untranslated work *de Aequitate, Indungentia, et Facilitate (On Equity, Indulgence, and Liberality).* His treatment therein reveals several important themes. First is the fact that the expletive justice of civil law provides an inadequate framework for the whole of law, because of its inability to shape internal intention. This deontological rights-based protection of objects must coexist alongside a teleological attributive conception of punishment for subjects. Politics does not simply govern actions and their results, but considers the character of persons who intend them. More broadly, this criminal law theory further suggests that Grotius' ostensibly amoral social contract theory actually points toward a wider moral framework, because a theory of civil law alone would suffice for a contractarian politics protecting property. Second, expletive justice grants the state a necessary right to punish, but a right whose silence about its subsequent content licenses any punishment, no matter how inhumane. The expletive right to punish thus bestows an attributive responsibility to discern the most fitting punishment for a particular person at a particular time. Hence, Grotius' rights are not simply possessive rights, but duties. Third, the multiple interrelated purposes of punishment require prudence to discern and apply. Unlike the rights-based remedies of civil law, they cannot rely on deontological reason, but must take their lead from a teleological orienting point. Fourth, criminal law is not a private matter between self-interested individuals, but a public matter of fostering harmony among the entire polity. Hence, Grotius' politics is not an aggregation of individual property claims but an interpersonal practice. Fifth, Grotius' concept of equity shows that justice requires a judge to transcend the letter of the law. This higher spirit of the law reveals the limits of pure reason. Sixth, his concept of pardon shows that even some equitable legal convictions call for the governor to pardon a criminal out of fidelity to a wider political good. A strict adherence to legal justice may lead to sub-optimal punishments, undermining political trust and enervating the order that protects the very governmental right to punish. Teleological politics transcends deontological law. The right to punish is in fact the responsibility to punish – and to punish well.

Definition of Punishment: Symbolic Reasoning

Grotius begins the Prolegomena to *DJB* by enumerating his five fundamental elements of justice: protection of our *jus*, returning unjust gains, keeping promises, restitution, and punishment. These five titles – and these alone – confer a true *jus* on the holder, one that is justiciable in a court of law.[11] In Book II he then shows how these five titles alone constitute potentially just causes for war. The final title, that of punishment, takes up only one chapter. However, Grotius makes it the largest of the fifty-five that comprise *DJB*, taking up 100 pages in the annotated Tuck edition.

Grotius begins this chapter just as he began Book I (on justice) and Book II (on war): with a definition. Punishment is "an evil (*malum*) of suffering which is inflicted because of an evil of action." These sufferings, when understood in a literal, descriptive sense, may be identical to those brought on by misfortune or disease. Yet to describe the latter as punishment would be to misuse the term.[12] A true definition of punishment connects an imposed suffering to a prior wrong and its moral condemnation. The external act of punishment is only a means to another end, and requires the symbolic imagination to connect the two.[13] If law enforcement officials fail to inform the criminal of this connection, their hard treatment fails as punishment, even if they carry out the exact physical instructions. Hence, while Grotius begins with a clear, discrete, and value-neutral definition, he immediately recognizes the limitations of this approach. Punishment can only be understood by reference to its teleological purposes.

After defining punishment, Grotius then asks a question: is it a matter of expletive or attributive justice? His uncertainty surprises the reader, because his treatment of the previous four titles to *jus* was clear: they each belong to expletive justice. For instance, in regard to the title of restitution, he states, "But from a mere aptitude or fitness, which ... belongs to attributive justice, arises no true property right (*dominium*), and consequently no obligation to make restitution."[14] Arriving at the fifth justiciable title, that of punishment, why should he now introduce the question? The answer is that Grotius' first four titles have all fallen under the realm of civil law. Civil law has seven characteristics, each of which fits neatly into expletive justice. Each characteristic also forms an axis of contrast with the elements of criminal law – the realm which will underlie his fifth title of punishment. Through this contrast, we can understand why criminal punishment is not so easily placed under expletive justice, and thus why Grotius must raise the question.

Realm of Property: Civil Redress

In order to best explore criminal and civil law, we must turn to *de Satisfactione*. Grotius here presents his Atonement theology, whose details and implications are interesting and important enough to merit their own subsequent chapter (see Chapter 8). For present purposes, however, we may fruitfully explore in isolation the legal theory he presents therein. He begins *de Satisfactione* by setting out distinctions between two types of legal obligation: payment of debt and punishment. The obligation to repay a debt is the realm of private law. A debt may arise when an individual voluntarily exercises his concessive natural Right to incur a financial obligation in exchange for a good or service. This is the realm of contract law, or Aristotle's 'voluntary transactions.' However, a debt may also arise when an individual nonmaliciously obtains from a rightful owner an object without his consent. This is the realm of torts in common law (or "delict" in civil law systems), or Aristotle's 'involuntary transactions.'[15] Torts violate either mandatory natural Right or human positive Right (which is subsequently guaranteed by mandatory natural Right). As Grotius will clarify below, torts are not crimes of theft. In order to remedy a debt arising from contracts or torts, one would petition not a criminal court but a civil (private) law court.

Debt repayment involves several components that mirror the examination of expletive justice in Chapter 3. The first is its exclusive concern with external possessions rather than internal qualities of character. In Grotius' formulation, debt is the realm of "material equality." It is a commodity that exists in the material world and is measurable in tangible terms. Its nature is simple and unambiguous, and its legal description conceals no deeper hidden meaning.[16] Likewise, the purpose of private law is not to address the internal state of either owner but to ensure justice among possessions. The plaintiff seeks not the punishment of the defendant but the return of the object in question. He is unconcerned over any potential suffering of the defendant. Should a third person come along to pay the debt, justice is untroubled.

What is more, in private law, the intention of the defendant is immaterial. His lingering intention to incur future torts is irrelevant to the repayment of the liability in question and the rectification of the debt-related injustice. As Grotius writes, "the primary and essential cause of the debt-in-nature is not the wrongness of what was done but the deprivation I suffer from it."[17] The justice concerns the object, not the persons; the persons are relevant only inasmuch as a person has possession of the object.[18]

For this reason, one need not know the plaintiff's intention for the money repaid. His subsequent act of spending it on humanitarian relief (or on poker chips) is irrelevant to his possession of the repaid funds. If the judge determines that the money is his legitimate possession, either subsequent action is permissible in justice. Nor does it matter whether the defendant recognizes his wrong and cheerfully pays the debt, or grudgingly satisfies the obligation only upon pain of physical coercion. The two acts are identical, as either one changes the status of ownership over the sum in question.

Second, debt repayment requires only a calculative rationality. Because the subject matter of justice consists in physical factors, it can be comprehensively known. Indeed, it is often reduced to a monetary consideration, which involves only the single ontological dimension of quantity. Because its numerical language (that of Aristotle's 'arithmetic justice') is purely formal, there is no need for interpretation.[19] Hence, a civil obligation is essentially predetermined by the external facts of the case. The "material equality" of justice means that if the unreturned object was 10,000 dollars, the debt to be legally enforced is the same. The determination of liability already contains within itself the remedy.

This leads to the third implication: much like the dictates of mathematics, the prescriptions are universal. The determination of the nature and extent of the debt is, at least in theory, clear to all.[20] Moreover, one person's debt of 10,000 dollars is identical to another's debt of the same. Consequently, all debts of that amount are satisfied in exactly the same way. There is little need to consider particular personal or situational factors. The course of justice is simple: justice is served when the object in question is returned to its rightful possessor.

The fourth element of civil law is that it looks backward. The remedy in civil justice is to reverse the original injustice: the rightful owner must be paid 10,000 dollars. Once this happens, the defendant and the plaintiff are in the same position (in terms of possessions) as before the offence. It is as if the tort had never occurred; the act is undone. Justice seeks to restore a prior condition that has been disrupted.

This idea of restoring a condition points to the fifth element: justice is simply a forensic status. Justice occurs in the instant that the 10,000 dollars switches status from being the possession of the defendant to that of the plaintiff. This radical change in status is possible because the relation between possession and possessor is unambiguous. Use of (or interaction with) such objects can be excluded from all others. To use Descartes' phrase, the owner has complete "mastery and possession" of the object.[21] Hence, the status of ownership is binary. If the defendant owns it, the plaintiff does not, and vice versa.

This focus on atemporal status over action points to a sixth element: in debt repayment, justice can be fully accomplished. The judge's decision completely and perfectly determines the course and content of justice; the intellectual case is closed. All that remains is to implement it (as the term *explere* would suggest). When the defendant transfers currency to the plaintiff, the possession of those bills changes from perfectly unjust to perfectly just. In the act of making the creditor whole, justice is unreservedly accomplished; there no longer remains any breach of private justice or any ongoing harm.

The seventh element of private law is that the position of creditor is extrinsically desirable. If a plaintiff obtains a successful judgment, he gains a claim-right. The just resolution of this right entitles him to tangible benefits. Relative to his status prior to the commission of the tort, he is made whole; relative to his status after the commission, he gains a windfall. The judge's decision in favour of the plaintiff leads to the same result as a lottery that draws the numbers of a ticket-holder. Private law serves the plaintiff's self-interest.

It should now be clear why Grotius declined to speak of attributive justice in his treatment of restitution. It hardly bears repeating that these seven characteristics of debt repayment correspond almost precisely to the seven characteristics of expletive justice outlined earlier. Civil law is concerned with external states of affairs, rather than considering active internal intention; it uses calculative rationality rather than prudence; it need not consider particulars of time and place; it is perfectly fulfillable; it concerns the status of possession over things rather than action in time; it looks backward rather than forward; and it entitles individuals to self-interested claim-rights.

Nonetheless, civil law also involves an important eighth element that does not overlap neatly with expletive justice: its realm is private, not public. The plaintiff demands his money from the defendant, not the state. Overall, the dispute is a matter between two parties, not between a party and a state. The state enters the conflict as neutral referee, simply to enforce the right of the plaintiff. Should the defendant have a change of heart and voluntarily choose to repay the debt, the state need do nothing more.

Realm of Persons: Criminal Punishment

Because Grotius' first four justiciable elements of justice fit into civil law, they primarily involve expletive justice. However, his fifth element of punishment fits not into civil law but into criminal law, and thus cannot (like the others) automatically be assigned to expletive justice. Rather, he must carefully investigate which category of justice applies to punishment. Grotius first gives reasons why punishment might plausibly fit into expletive justice. In order to punish, one must first possess the expletive *jus* of punishing. Just as this status distinguishes between creditor and debtor in civil law, it delineates punisher and criminal in criminal law. This should not surprise us; after all, the purpose of Book II is to discern who may have the legitimate (expletive) status as war-maker, and punishment is one such title. By committing a crime, the criminal confers a right on the punisher and the desert of punishment upon himself.[22] Hence, the holding of an expletive status (the fifth element of civil law) also has some applicability to criminal law.

Furthermore, this status suggests that punishment is due to someone. This language of "what is due" calls to mind the traditional formulation of justice, which Grotius has fully incorporated into expletive justice. Likewise, Grotius references Aristotle's idea of geometric proportion, which holds that greater offenders ought to be punished more severely. Although this proportion is part of Aristotle's distributive justice, Grotius has also told us that its mathematical nature places it within his own expletive justice. Indeed, Grotius suggests that the proportion is between the offence and the punishment, which suggests

Aristotle's even more simple mathematical category of arithmetic. Hence, on first glance, the second expletive element of civil law – calculative reason – also appears to apply to punishment.

Moreover, before one can be charged with a crime, one must have committed an unlawful act. In a certain sense, this follows the first element of civil law: the focus on external physical damage. In order to bring a criminal charge, one must identify a tangible – even if now perhaps indirect – harm. Purely internal offences cannot confer a true *jus* of punishment; these must be left to God. Citing Seneca, Grotius argues that "if every man of a corrupt nature were to be punished, no man would go unpunished." Such are to be "connived at," presumably through social disapprobation, rather than punished. In other words, there must be an offence against expletive justice, such as an external injury, in order to give rise to a right to punish.[23] Nor can one punish for a failure to carry out the positive virtues of attributive justice.[24] Hence, expletive justice also limits the possibilities of punishment; there must be an (expletive) visible act before one can punish an (attributive) internal intention. Expletive justice must play some role in criminal law.

Yet despite these apparent grounds for situating punishment within expletive justice, there are also many compelling reasons by which to situate punishment within attributive justice. This is evident when we contrast the eight elements of civil law with criminal law, beginning with the first axis. First, in civil law, the damage is the only relevant matter. By contrast, in criminal law, the damage is only an indicator of the truly important element: the intention of the offender. Establishing the act makes it possible to investigate the intention.[25] As Grotius states, punishment aims not at external acts but at the will that precedes them.[26] While expletive justice is temporally first, it finds its completion in attributive justice.

This ultimate focus on intention is an obvious contrast with civil law, which seeks to ensure the justice of objects by returning them to the plaintiff. However, if the injustice of objects was carried out deliberately, civil law does nothing to change the malicious intention of the defendant. Indeed, criminal charges are possible even when the criminal intention does not culminate in its intended act. For example, an attempted murder may be prosecuted in criminal law, even though such an attempt could not give rise to a civil lawsuit without evidence of physical damage.[27] In other words, while debt exists by reference to the external object, punishment exists by reference to the internal condition of the perpetrator.[28]

The first axis of comparison leads to the second. To determine a civil liability a judge examines only empirical and calculable factors, but to determine both guilt and punishment a judge must consider nonempirical and non-quantifiable factors. Although Grotius has earlier referenced a mathematical proportion between the crime and punishment, the empirical facts of the crime are anything but clear; a mere physical description of the allegedly criminal act is insufficient.[29] This is because one is not ultimately punishing an act, but a person who chose to commit an act. Hence, Grotius states that determining this proportion requires "much prudence." One must discern the internal intention of the perpetrator – an intuitive reality to which the physical description of the act is only a beginning. The role of intention explains the difference between the criminal charges of first-degree murder, third-degree murder, and manslaughter, even if the victim is equally dead in all three.[30] What is more, criminal trials must discern not only the intention at the time of the crime, but the fundamental character from which it sprang.[31] For this reason, character witnesses are common in criminal trials but narrowly restricted (if not entirely prohibited) in civil suits.

This focus on nonempirical intention reflects Grotius' initial recognition that empirical definitions of punishment are insufficient. There he had noted that the suffering of punishment may look empirically identical to the suffering of a diseased person (or the suffering of restitution). Yet punishment is unlike the suffering of disease and restitution, because it also (indeed, primarily) brings a suffering through the moral opprobrium that its empirical harms are meant to represent. As he points out, there is nothing inherently good in the sufferings of punishment per se; one should punish only inasmuch as it leads to some other good.[32] This concept of representation in punishment is deepened through a further contrast with civil law. In restitution, the empirical deprivation of the defendant is exactly the empirical gain of the plaintiff; the plaintiff's right specifies the content of the defendant's deprivation. But in punishment, no specific empirical deprivation is ever essential, because the punisher's right to punish never specifies the content of the punishment. This contrast can also be explained the other way around: the suffering of the civil law defendant corresponds to the right of the plaintiff, but the suffering of the criminal offender corresponds to his own wrongdoing.

Thus, although the effects of restitution and punishment may appear the same when examining external consequences (such as the transfer of property), punishment actually involves a higher-order reality, because the property now represents something beyond itself. Restitution involves only scientific language that represents only one dimension of meaning, and takes for granted that the language involved is fully adequate to the essence of the matter. On the contrary, punishment involves representational and symbolic elements that point toward to the underlying purposes of the act, thus requiring imaginative (and in fact teleological) reasoning in order to discern their higher-order meaning.

The third distinction also involves noncalculative reason: unlike civil debts, no two crimes are ever identical. In civil law, any defendant who incurs a debt of 10,000 dollars will face an identical judgment: repay 10,000 dollars. It is merely a matter of implementing justice (as the term *explere* suggests). However, in criminal punishment, two actions may have different meanings based on the time, place, and especially motive. Hence, one must prudently consider the contingent circumstances surrounding the criminal act. For instance, Grotius points out that a greedy rich thief and a needy poor thief do not deserve the same punishment.[33]

One might protest that punishment does have some universal elements: in particular, every person punished must first have the status of "criminal." However, universal reason is inadequate to determine punishments that will be appropriate for unique individuals. Because it is binary, it has no sense of proportion. This is not a problem in civil law, because the verdict contains within itself the remedy. The remedy is a right to an object, and there is no problem with a creditor taking repayment of the entire debt. Prudence is unnecessary. However, such an "unlimited right" to punish a criminal permits punishment without restraint. Even the slightest injury ("a box on the ear") would be punishable by death.[34] To be sure, calculative reason could then determine that the now-deceased punishee is no longer "criminal," but any pronouncements about serving justice would surely ring hollow. For this reason, one must be "judicious and prudent" in punishing.[35] Expletive justice must give way to attributive justice. Lawmakers often recognize this fact by outlining a range of potential punishments for each crime. Even still, a judge or jury must exercise careful deliberation to determine the appropriate sentence for the particular person within the range provided. As Grotius adverts, the determination of how to exercise punishment is a "difficult and obscure" topic, one we will revisit later in the chapter.[36]

This inability to determine punishment in advance of a crime leads to the fourth axis of comparison: while civil law looks backward, criminal punishment looks forward. Where civil law seeks to restore the victim to a past condition, criminal law looks to dissuade the perpetrator (and perhaps others like him) from reoffending.[37] Punishment cannot simply be an equal and opposite reaction that cancels out the effect of the original unjust act.[38] Quoting Seneca, Grotius writes that "what is once done cannot be recalled, but what is to come may be prevented ... therefore all punishments have regard to the future."[39] While an object can be restored, a deed can never be undone. Imagine a judge permitting a victim of burglary to reciprocate by burglarizing the perpetrator. The absurdity is obvious. While reciprocal actions are the very essence of civil justice, they diametrically oppose the spirit of criminal justice. Hence, justice is not entirely accomplished in the act of punishment; rather, it is instantiated inasmuch as the punishment helps to meet the higher-order purposes of the act.

This points to the fifth characteristic of punishment: justice consists not in the shifting of a status, but in the carrying out of actions. In civil law, the shifting of a binary status of monetary possession is the end; in criminal punishment, the establishment of a binary status of "punisher" and "criminal" is only the beginning. Every criminal would be happy to be released with only the sanction of a criminal record. But that would make a mockery of punishment, which requires interaction between the punisher and the criminal. Moreover, the purposes of punishment can never be achieved instantaneously. They can only be attained in the criminal's subsequent law-abiding actions. The binary status of expletive justice cannot provide a remedy in criminal law, or a way to move from injustice toward true justice. Rather, the goals of punishment are more of an orientation point to which we strive in dynamic fashion.

The sixth element of punishment follows naturally: unlike civil remedies, punishment can never be perfectly fulfilled. Of course, law enforcement officials can carry out the precise punishment outlined in the sentence. However, because the criminal act cannot be undone, the punishment can never exactly make up for the crime. The words "justice has been done" always ring somewhat hollow.

Of course, wisely chosen punishments should – on the whole – increase the likelihood of respect for the law, thus helping to instantiate the aims of punishment. Nonetheless, no punishment can ever completely guarantee future law-abiding actions in the same way that the restitution of property completely resolves the property-related injustice. The criminal, possessing free will even behind bars, holds the ultimate choice whether or not to reoffend, or even whether or not to apologize for his original crime.[40] The language of perfection is inadequate to the practice of punishment – a point that will become even clearer in Chapter 8.

The seventh characteristic of punishment is particularly important. Unlike civil law, the punisher in criminal law does not seek a tangible possession. In civil law, the plaintiff initiates a self-interested claim, and if the judge rules against the defendant, the plaintiff then gains a claim-right. In criminal law, one would hardly say that a criminal has a right to be punished, given that this claim is not sought after and seldom brings any joy to the recipient. Rather, according to Grotius, it is more appropriate to say that it is fit that someone be punished, or that the subject is worthy of punishment. These terms of fitness or worthiness obviously connote attributive justice. Indeed, inasmuch as anybody holds a criminal right, it is the punisher. However, unlike the status of "ownership" or "credit" in civil law, nor does the expletive status of "power" (to punish) overlap with any personal advantage or self-interest of the holder. This status brings no joy, but only a difficult duty. (Indeed, any sensitive parent or public official knows well that punishing is a burden.) Thus, punishment fundamentally differs from restitution, because it does not confer external benefits, and it may indeed increase the obligations of the person holding the right to punish.[41] The implication is critical: Grotius' concept of a right transcends an individual claim on a possession whose pursuit requires no virtue. By using the language of rights in punishment, he indicates that his rights framework is not simply a self-interested scramble for scarce resources or a lowering of moral standards through a wide realm of morally indifferent permissions. Rather, the right to punish compels its holder to exercise a virtue that Grotius calls *antapodotike*: the prudent ability to discern a fitting punishment.[42] Rights lead to responsibilities.

Thus, while expletive justice is necessary as a precondition for punishment, it is clear that attributive justice plays the principal role in punishment. In order to determine guilt and carry out punishment in any meaningful sense, one must exercise attributive justice. Grotius' seven axes of comparison make this clear: the focus on the damage is quickly superseded by a focus on intention; the mathematical reason quickly gives way to prudence; each crime has an individual character; punishment looks forward; status quickly gives way to action; the punishment can never be perfectly fulfilled; and the right involved in punishment is nonpossessive. Each of these components of criminal punishment differs from the expletive justice of civil law.[43]

As a postscript, we might again recall Grotius' earlier statement that expletive and attributive justice are coextensive with the public and private realms. Hence, the crucial role of attributive justice does not on its own necessarily indicate that criminal law is public. However, there is an additional eighth axis of comparison with civil law that does not entirely align with attributive justice – one that will, in fact, vindicate the public nature of punishment. In criminal law, the antagonism is not between an individual defendant and an individual plaintiff, but between the accused and the prosecutor. Yet this antagonism with the prosecutor represents an antagonism with the community, as the prosecutor charges in the name of the "the people" or "the crown." Put the opposite way, the original criminal offence was not ultimately directed at the victim, but at the community as a whole. In breaking the rules of the community, the criminal damages the common good of the community – that is, its sense of trust and respect for authority. The need to ascertain the direct and indirect effects on human society further adds to the challenge of discerning an appropriate punishment. Because wider justice is needed to determine punishment, it cannot simply be relegated to the non-political realm of private charity or Christian virtue. It is essential to politics.

Likewise, because punishment concerns the community as a whole, it must be delivered in the name of the governor who has been entrusted with the care of the community. For this reason, the role of the state is not a neutral referee (as in civil law) but an interested party with a metaphorical right of its own. It carries out punishment for the sake of the entire community, not for the victim (who in fact gains no tangible benefit in criminal law).[44] In fact, the state may press charges even if the victim opposes them. Even if the victim forgives the offender, public justice must still be carried out. Hence, while individuals are the agents who can carry out attributive justice in civil law (if it is carried out at all), the government is the agent that can (and must) carry out attributive justice in criminal law. Punishment is fundamentally public.

This place for public punishment counters the appearance of methodological individualism in Grotius' earlier pronouncements. In the beginning of *DJB*, Grotius might appear to de-emphasize the public realm by departing from the scholastic practice of making the private-public distinction the first and most fundamental one in cataloguing justice. However, Grotius does so not to minimize the importance of the common good, but to play up the difference between the strictness of legal justice and the wider sense of virtue. Indeed, Grotius' seminal role in developing a philosophy of punishment testifies to the importance of the public good in his thought, even if he lacks a specific category of justice corresponding to the public realm. Just as punishment is qualitatively different from restitution, the public good qualitatively transcends the aggregation of private individual claim-rights. *Pace* Tuck, Grotius' politics is not the mere self-interested pursuit of claim-rights, nor is his liberty reducible to property. Grotius' a priori rights are only a beginning; they point to the classical political virtue of prudence.

Criminal and Civil Jurisdiction: The "Doer" and The "Deed"

Grotius has now outlined the difference between civil and criminal law. Civil law fits comfortably into expletive justice. On the other hand, expletive justice provides only a beginning point for punishment before giving way to attributive justice. Yet despite clearly distinguishing civil and criminal law in theory, the distinction is not always easy to draw in practice. After all, the unjust status of civil law and the unjust intention of criminal law are both in some way connected to the act of the defendant/accused. Suppose a person has unjustly come to possess the property of another. Should the state indict the person before a criminal court, or leave it to the plaintiff to bring a civil suit? What is the dividing line between a crime and a tort?

In order to determine whether the act calls for criminal punishment or civil liability, Grotius begins in a familiar place: with Aristotle's *Rhetoric*. Here Aristotle distinguishes between doing unjustly (or "acting wrongly" (*adikein*)), and doing that which is unjust (*adikon prattein*). The former corresponds to the internally unjust intention of the person who carries out the action. In contrast, the latter indicates an external state of injustice arising from the result of the action in the world. For further simplicity, Grotius aligns these two types of injustice with their relevant subject (the "doer") or object (the "deed"). The doer does unjustly, while the deed indicates that someone has done that which is unjust. A doer can only *be* unjust (i.e., "act wrongly") if he consciously knows that he is committing an injustice. Without such intention, he has no (internal) guilt. Yet he may unknowingly commit an unjust deed, breaching strict justice and violating the letter of the law. His act was done without (external) *jus*. The party who has suffered as a result of this deed is entitled to redress the deed in a civil court, but the state ought not to indict the doer.[45]

This distinction between "doer" and "deed" maps onto two types of legal injustice: "wrongs" and "faults." Grotius here draws not only on Aristotle's *Rhetoric* but also his *Nicomachean Ethics*. In fact, Grotius so emphasizes the latter that he provides a complete Latin translation of Book V.8 in the midst of his own work – an odd labour for a supposedly anti-Aristotelian thinker. This "truly notable" passage outlines three possible situations that may arise in a court of law, of which two – "wrongs" and "faults" – are relevant for our purposes.[46]

A wrong (*injuria*, or the opposite of *jus*) is premeditated and carried out deliberately. In committing a wrong, the injustice attaches to the doer himself. Aristotle's *Rhetoric* explains that

> the intention of the mind is the main point, and not the external act: it is this intention that constitutes the whole turpitude and injustice of the act, and which is therefore always implied in the word denoting the crime.[47]

In this case, the wrong is active, and Grotius identifies its doer as "truly wicked and unjust." The prince is praised for punishing these doers severely for their wrongs.[48]

On the other hand, a "fault" (*culpa*) is carried out without full deliberation. Faults correspond to common law torts, or "delict" in code law systems (a term derived from a Latin synonym for "*culpa*.")[49] In a fault, the offender is conscious of his act but lacks an actively evil intent. Rather, his ephemeral animal passions occlude his capacity to foresee how his act will cause unintended damage. As Grotius translates Aristotle: "he designed to pinch, not to wound, either not this person, or not in that manner." Grotius cites the example of a deer-hunter who instead happens to kill a man. The hunter ought to be held accountable for the ignorance that led to the unjust damage, but not for a premeditated intent to kill. His lack of deliberation is not an active failure to intend rightly, but a passive failure to intend at all. He commits an unjust deed, or a fault, but is not a wrongful unjust doer. Justice requires the hunter to provide restitution to the victim's estate for this deed. However, it does not call for punishing the defendant as a doer – unless the principles he ignorantly violated are absolutely foundational to human society.[50] (We will further explore the limits of criminal immunity for ignorance in Chapter 8.)

This distinction between doer and deed resurfaces in Grotius' subsequent chapter on inheriting liabilities and punishments. When a father dies before paying a civil liability, his heirs must continue to pay off the debt. In civil law, the matter at hand is the deed, which creates a debt that can be satisfied by his children. However, when a father dies before fully undertaking his punishment, his children cannot be punished or kept in penal servitude for his crimes.[51] In criminal law, the matter at hand is the doer, an internal condition that is not transferable from father to child. Indeed, in Grotius' drama *Sophompaneas*, his main character Joseph (of Genesis) decrees that he will not transfer a man's guilt to his family, discontinuing the pathological custom that causes "five families [to] wrap in like contagion."[52]

By separating the doer of the wrong from the deed producing a fault, Grotius provides an independent grounding for civil law. Two people cannot actually hold the same right, such as a piece of property (or indeed political sovereignty), but two people can innocently pursue that right. When the judge determines that the current possessor lacks the true right to property, he does not indict the defendant for holding it; he only asks the defendant to return it. The fault does not imply a crime; objective injustice need not confer subjective guilt. Indeed, if every injustice of deeds (such as a civil liability) led to a determination of guilt, the polity would be highly criminalized and illiberal. It would be comparable to the courts of ancient Greece, in which an unsuccessful prosecution could result in the punishment of the accuser.

Benjamin Constant famously described ancient democracy as the freedom to directly participate in government without the security of rights. He described modern democracy as the inverse: the protection of rights through indirect representation.[53] Grotius appears to develop the latter by providing a legal remedy outside of criminal law by which to pursue one's right. The frequent inevitable violations of right in any complex society need not result in a highly criminalized society. One might say that Grotius provides a right not to worry that one's unintended damages will lead one to prison.

Grotius' concept of a civil law concerned with mere unjust deeds rather than criminal doers coheres with many of his other political and philosophical themes. For instance, his initial category of concessive natural Right already suggests that his world is not one of pure guilt and pure virtue. Outside of the commands and prohibitions of preceptive natural Right exists a realm of moral innocence. He builds on this concept of innocence (rather than active virtue or vice) in his definition of *jus* as "that which is not unjust." Chapter 7 will also flesh out his distinction between moral innocence and mere legal immunity from punishment, and build on his hesitancy to punish 'victimless' crimes.[54] Grotius outlines areas of moral neutrality that coexist with realms of moral obligation; the latter need not preclude the former.

Early in the Prolegomena of *DJB*, Grotius distinguished humans from animals by reference to the capacity for reason – and more specifically of foresight. It is appropriate that he now seems to envision deliberation as lifting one out of the realm of passive necessity and into the realm of active personhood. Failing to act according to the higher guidance of attributive justice is a sort of passive fault; a fault of omission. It is not a misuse of will; it is an absence of free will befitting an animal. Fulfilling attributive justice would call for action, which is why it cannot be demanded in expletive justice. To be truly human, one must go beyond expletive justice (a theme we will further explore in Grotius' concept of glorification in Chapter 8). Yet when one acquires an expletive right, one gains the very opportunity to become a doer of intentional virtue: having acquired the property deed, one may then use it generously. In sum, just as moral immunities coexist with moral imperatives, the deontological rights of strict justice coexist with the teleological virtues of wider justice.

Purposes of Punishment: Correction, Example, and Satisfaction

Armed with the distinction between civil and criminal law, we can now distinguish injustices demanding only restitution from those (also) calling for punishment. Yet in the latter case, we know that punishment is not merely a matter of implementation; it requires prudence to determine. We have read this in Grotius from the beginning, when he pointed out the purposive nature of punishment. If we must discern a particular punishment by reference to the purposes of punishment, what are those purposes?

Grotius begins to examine this question by ruling out two pseudo-purposes. The first is revenge. Revenge fails because it flows from the anger of the punisher, rather than the reason that discerns the good of the one punished.[55] Hence, revenge gratifies the beastly instinct of the appetites, and departs from the uniquely human capacity to rationally determine the (social) good. In fact, revenge and reason are inverse correlates: according to Grotius, "the weaker anyone's reason is, the more prone he will be to revenge." For example, the irrationality of revenge often leads the agent to mistake its target. Grotius perceptively compares the vengeful person to "a dog [that] bites the stone that is thrown at it." Citing Plutarch, he concludes that revenge is "medicine only to a sick and inflamed mind."[56]

The second pseudo-purpose is retribution. Grotius has earlier defined punishment as purposive, which means its harms are intelligible only inasmuch as they prevent subsequent evils.[57] That is, one cannot punish simply for punishment's sake; one must punish for an end outside of punishment. Retribution fails to do so, because it looks backward rather than forward. It is comparable to civil law, in which the remedy – the returning of property – is an end in itself. Much like civil law, retribution would require only calculative reason, seeking to impose on the offender a penalty precisely equal to that of the offence. Putting these factors together, the simple retributive calculation instructing the state to take "an eye for an eye" would fail to point beyond the punishment itself. Rather, in the memorable words of Tevye in *Fiddler on the Roof*, it would merely leave everyone blind and toothless.

A critic might object that Grotius permits capital punishment (albeit very cautiously). He licenses it for "men with incurable natures," where it is certain "that by living they will grow worse." This ultimate sanction seems to violate Grotius' forward-looking orientation; indeed, it appears rather retributive. Yet Grotius' reasoning is consistent: he cites Seneca's argument that in such cases, it is to the advantage of such men that they should die.[58] Their own future is best served by bringing their earthly moral wretchedness to an end. Such a conception of self-interest is surely not what most observers have in mind when they frame Grotius as a possessive individualist. In this case, protection of one's most treasured 'possession' (namely, life itself) must be contrary to a higher 'self-interest': that of the soul. Hence, his limited endorsement of capital punishment is not retributive.

Grotius notes only one true justification for retribution, in which the punishment needs no end beyond itself. This is when the punisher is God. For one thing, God is an end in himself. More importantly, however, God is outside of time. After God's final judgment, there is no place or hope of amendment.[59] In other words, the only exception to the forward-looking requirement of punishment is when time has come to an end. Indeed, one could say that retribution already exists outside of time, because it follows from strict and abstract reason and admits of no exception. As an element of expletive justice, it flows from a deontological order of right rather than a teleological realm of good to which humans ever strive. This makes it inappropriate for government. Government can only exist in time as a forward-looking institution, just as God manifests his governmental modality by entering into time. Hence, human society cannot punish on retributive grounds.[60]

What, then, are the true purposes of punishment? Grotius outlines three: correction, example, and satisfaction.[61] Each purpose is ostensibly directed toward a different party: correction to the perpetrator, example to society at large, and satisfaction to the victim.[62] However, a deeper inquiry shows that all three purposes relate to the public good.

The first purpose, that of correction (or "reformation"), looks to heal the internal constitution of the offender. Grotius first uses a medical image, citing Plutarch's description of punishment as "surgery for the soul." His second citation is clearer about the goal: in Plato's words, correction is "the pain that teaches us prudence." This painful deterrent aims to change the internal will that preceded the criminal act, turning a vicious soul into a virtuous one.[63] Correction may also call for removing the offender from society, thereby eliminating the opportunity for reoffending. While both elements of correction deal most immediately with the individual, they ultimately benefit the community by preventing a recurrence of the crime.

What, then, is an appropriate correction? Expletive justice provides the initial parameters. It states that the maximum punishment is the intrinsic desert that mathematically corresponds to the criminal act.[64] To calculate this outer bound, one need only know the (internal) criminal intention and its (external) circumstances. However, expletive justice cannot determine these two things, because they both require prudent determination. Only attributive justice can address this "difficult and obscure" topic. How does attributive justice do so? One must prudently consider four elements ranging respectively from external to internal: first, mitigating reasons; second, freedom of judgment; third, desires; and fourth, character.[65] First, one must consider the place, the time, the opportunity of wrongdoing, and the other person(s) involved. A criminal who broke the law in order to avoid "death, imprisonment, pain, or extreme poverty" should generally be judged in light of these extenuating circumstances.[66] Second, one must evaluate the perpetrator's freedom of judgment, especially when the conditions circumvented his capacity to reason. For instance, the person may have feared an imminent evil or been angered by a recent injury. If such momentary passions overwhelmed the doer's active intention, he may be cleared of criminal charges and subject only to civil penalties. Beyond the circumstantial capacities, one must also consider the person's natural capacities of physical strength, age, education, or intelligence, all of which affect freedom of judgment. The third element to consider is desire, as one must distinguish between severity of the law broken and the manner in which it was broken. Establishing a legal violation is only a starting point for the trial, as conviction and sentencing then call for examining the criminal desire. Fourth and finally, one ought to consider a person's past and present character. Some types of personalities may be more or less prone to reoffend in certain ways: the choleric may be prone to anger, the sanguine to lust.[67] Moreover, character affects the punitive effect: an honourable man will be dissuaded by a small punitive dishonour, while a dishonourable one may be unmoved by the greatest of dishonours.[68] In sum, Grotius begins to discuss correction by talking about the expletive demand for a mathematical proportion between the offence and the crime, but goes on to identify many contingent attributive factors that determine such a proportion. The expletive beginning is simple, the attributive process complex.

Grotius' emphasis on desires and character implicitly disclose a philosophical anthropology. Elsewhere in the chapter, he will reveal it more directly. There he will begin – once again – with Aristotle, distinguishing between virtue and continence. However, this time he questions Aristotle's category of vice, saying that "if any one delights in wickedness for its own sake he is beyond the pale of humanity." Rather, most moral failings are a result of incontinence, which leads the agent astray by desire. Here Grotius de-emphasizes the ancient bogeyman of ignorance (central to vice) and accentuates the Christian concern with weakness of will (central to incontinence). He also sees various gradations of will. For example, lust is more voluntary than cowardice, because lust actively pursues a positive pleasure while cowardice only seeks to avoid a negative harm. Because lust proceeds from a more definite and voluntary will, it ought to be punished more severely than cowardice. Finally, some unjust desires immoderately pursue legitimate material goods, while others pursue inherently unjust objects. For instance, the desire for pleasure or profit, which Grotius calls real goods, is somewhat excusable. On the other hand, the desire for revenge, power, or vain-glory, which Grotius calls imaginary goods, is more blameworthy, and thus calls for stronger punishment.[69] This emphasis on the potential goodness of material desires demonstrates an incarnational Christian perspective, one that gives pause to a reading of Grotius as a modern Stoic.[70] The importance of correcting wills rather than acts shows that the determination of desert requires more than the pure reason of objective calculation; one must have the practical virtues of subjective insight into character.

Grotius' second purpose of punishment is example, which has a more obvious public aim than does correction. It punishes the criminal to send a message to other potential criminals: "to strike terror into many." In this sense, it incorporates some elements of contemporary deterrence. For instance, Grotius calls for heavier penalties for crimes that are difficult to deter (such as stealing from a field) than for more easily policeable crimes (such as stealing from a house) – a principle that modern-day economists could endorse.[71] However, these exemplary penalties aim at more than simply deterrence; they also aim to reform the criminal and to provide satisfaction. Indeed, deterrence is not really an aim but a by-product. If deterrence were the true aim, one could punish even those who needed no correction or owed no satisfaction. The exemplary nature of punishment is particularly important to Grotius because the crime itself is always public; it is not ultimately aimed at the victim but the entire polity. Grotius adds that the worst crimes are those that directly affect public order, which is why treason is punished more severely than petty theft. Thus, example is directed toward the benefit of the community as a whole, seeking to ensure its future adherence to the law.[72]

Grotius' third purpose of satisfaction requires more unpacking than the previous two. He states that satisfaction is most directly addressed to the immediate victim of the crime. Its purpose is to prevent him from being similarly maltreated by others. This definition is conspicuous for what it omits. Notably, Grotius makes no reference to transferring goods – or even to undoing the immediate harm to the victim. Satisfaction in punishment is not compensatory. Because it has nothing to do with punitive damages or reimbursing costs, it fundamentally differs from satisfaction of a debt, which seeks to undo the damage to the plaintiff. Nor does satisfaction involve revenge or even retribution, which Grotius had earlier ruled out.[73] Rather, satisfaction is undertaken by reference to the future prevention of crime.

If this is the case, how does it differ from mere deterrence? One very plausible interpretation is that satisfaction restores to the victim(s) the dignity or integrity damaged by the criminal act. Criminality is not, like civil law, a matter of transferring goods (or of Aristotelian 'shares'); it is fundamentally an interaction between people. At minimum, the criminal act subjects the victim to the disordered intention of the criminal. How can satisfaction address the damage effected by this intention? The answer is not obvious. Satisfaction is not a mathematically equal and opposite reaction to the original crime, as in debt repayment, revenge, or retribution. At most, it is an equal and opposite reaction to the harm to the dignity and stature of the victim. However, dignity and stature are intangible qualities. For this reason, the expletive demand for satisfactory redress could be determined only through the symbolic reasoning of attributive judgment.

However, the estimation of damage becomes even more indeterminate once we reconsider who is actually the victim of the crime. In civil law, the victim is the one who lacks possession of his right. He brings a lawsuit in order to rectify his shortage. However, in criminal law, the offended party is not the immediate victim; it is the polity as a whole. It is the state that presses the criminal charges, not the immediate target (who may seek redress only as civil plaintiff). This conjecture of 'polity as true victim' is further buttressed when we revisit Grotius' concept of pre-civil society. In that condition, the power to punish crime arises not from being immediately targeted by crime, but from the moral authority conferred by innocence of that very crime. Punishers act on behalf of a wider injury. Indeed, immediate targets of crime who have also committed the same (or even merely similar) crimes are actually prohibited from punishing. Despite the fact that Grotius discusses satisfaction by reference to "him who suffers by the offence," these two premises seem to suggest that the real victim is the community itself. Thus, satisfaction must address not the immediate target of crime but the entire polity, and must seek to restore its reputation, integrity, and honour. In particular, satisfaction should restore the dignity of public law – which is to say, of the governor in whose will the law ultimately rests. Grotius seems to confirm this conjecture when he later says that the public good requires the same things as the injured party.[74]

However, these measures to restore the dignity of the law and its governor are not ends in themselves. After all, attributive justice does not endorse the creation of government in order to enable the Machiavellian glory of the ruler. Rather, it recommends the institution of public authority as a means to protect, promote, promulgate, and discover natural Right. The glory of the state is only a means to these trans-political ends. Thus, satisfaction does not consist in restoring state dignity per se, but only restoring state dignity as a means to promoting public virtue. It must have ongoing effects.[75] Unlike the full repayment of a debt obligation, punitive satisfaction does not happen in an instant, like the switching of a binary status. It points toward a further ongoing and dynamic practice of restoration. Grotius' concept of satisfaction in punishment is much more complex than the meaning of satisfaction in civil law; it looks forward and outward rather than backward and inward.

These latter two purposes of example and satisfaction particularly demonstrate that punishment cannot simply be undertaken by reference to the offender himself. The punisher must prudently consider how the exemplary and satisfactory component will affect the general public good. This further illustrates Grotius' recognition that criminal law is a fundamentally public exercise, and that the criminality is a matter of the common good. Punishment does not simply arise as the contractarian choice of individuals to protect their private property claims. Rather, it inherently deals with persons, aiming to protect the fundamentally social and moral purposes of human existence. This aim may be mandated by expletive justice, but it can only be realized through attributive justice. Grotius will only underscore these points in his theology of the Atonement (Chapter 8).

The Responsibility (Not) To Punish?

This exploration of Grotian punishment has now covered the question of whether punishment is applicable, and if it is, of what nature and to what extent. An unjust doer may be punished less severely due to extenuating circumstances, and an innocent doer should face only a civil liability for his unjust deed. Nonetheless, whether the doer commits a wrong (as in the first case) or only a fault (as in the second), there is a clear injustice calling for a remedy. But a third situation is also possible. What if one causes legal damage not maliciously, nor in the mistaken pursuit of what is believed to be one's own, but rather in the just pursuit of what is legitimately one's own? What if one causes a result legally classified as a harm, but one that seems perfectly justified to a reasonable observer – or to the governor? In other words, what if the problem is not a criminal intention or an ignorant fault, but the law itself? Might justice call for a standard beyond the positive law? Grotius is aware of these questions. They lead him to explore (and advance) the concepts of equity and pardon, and to produce an implicit theory of constitutional law.

Equity enters the legal arena precisely in order to oppose the prescription set out by the law. A cursory reader of Grotius will likely be surprised to learn that he defends it. Grotius has been dubbed the "father of the modern science of law" because of his systematic approach. This makes it possible to see the law as a tight-knit, self-contained system not requiring reference to anything outside itself. One need examine not natural law but only positive statutes. Indeed, the very internal logic of written law aims to minimize or eliminate the need for discretion or judgment beyond the language of the statutes. The effectiveness of the system is not supposed to depend on the classical political wisdom of judges but rather their modern technical expertise. It is not really a judge who judges; it is the law. Once equity enters, the tight-knit system begins to unravel.[76] Yet Grotius' system of law is only the beginning of his thought, because it points toward equity.

The concept of equity goes back to the Ancient Greeks, as detailed in Chapter 2. It testifies to a spirit of the law that transcends the letter; to a natural Right that transcends positive law. However, *aequitas* undergoes an alteration in the Augustinian thought of the Protestant Reformers. These thinkers were charged with a great sense of the sinful nature of even the best magistrates. They saw the judge himself as a criminal in the eyes of God (the ultimate righteous judge), and thus de-emphasized the moral hierarchy between judge and criminal. This led them to reconceptualize equity. Equity had always been meant to transcend the law and to give the person their true desert, rather than the outcome demanded by the strict law. It generally led to a reduction or elimination of the sentence. However, according to the sixteenth- and seventeenth-century

Reformers, every person truly deserved eternal damnation before God. Fortunately, God met this situation with unmerited mercy. The sinner was condemned under law but set free by the 'equity' of the divine judge. Hence, equity was now a gift rather than a desert. Its meaning was transformed from a merited justice transcending law to an unmerited mercy transcending justice.[77]

Which of the two concepts does Grotius employ? The classical or the Reformed Christian? One might just as well ask whether Grotius espouses expletive or attributive justice. The answer is both – simultaneously. Grotius provides this answer in his *de Aequitate, Indulgentia, et Facilitate*. This short work was published only after his death, and today remains untranslated and virtually unreferenced in the English literature. Grotius pens this brief tract in recognition that strict justice demands observation of the laws. If equity contests the law, how can it be just? Grotius defends equity by reference to its classical roots. However, he also discusses it in conjunction with the higher concept of pardon, which adds a distinctively Christian element.

On Equity

Early in his treatise, Grotius asserts that equity, indulgence (or pardon), and liberality are all virtues of the will. In other words, these three topics are a matter of more than theoretical reason, or even practical reason; practical knowledge points to practical action. Thus, Grotius reaffirms his emphasis on the primacy of the will, and the insufficiency of theoretical knowledge. In doing so, he deepens his emphasis in *de Imperio* on ethics over metaphysical dogma.[78]

Grotius quickly turns to equity in particular. He begins with his standard descriptive methodology: examining received definitions of equity. Some of these take equity to be the whole of justice; others see it as the discretionary action of a judge in filling a gap in the law. Grotius sides with the latter. He defines equity as "correcting the law where it fails on account of its universality." Positive laws are necessarily finite. However, they profess to govern human situations that are potentially infinite.[79] Their very universal purport makes them insufficient. Laws – indeed, words – are inadequate to the fullest meaning of justice.

As a result, a strict adherence to the law sometimes produces a judgment contrary to the original intention of the lawmaker. For instance, governors decree laws against theft that compel a person to return a borrowed object when the owner requests it back. However, lawmakers surely do not intend for borrowers to return a sword to an original owner who has since become insane. Thus, the spirit of the law supersedes its textual formulation.[80] This approach recalls Grotius' understanding of imperative rule: positive law binds not through its words but through the intention and will of the lawmaker in enacting the law. One cannot simply read the legal code; one must interpret the intention of its designer. This is the province of equity.[81] By focusing on intention, Grotius reaffirms the place of the rational will in his philosophical anthropology.[82]

Thus, equity arises when laws appear to conflict with one another, and it resolves the tension by referencing the first principles of nature.[83] In doing so, it does not remove the obligation of the law. Rather, it advocates that the law does not oblige in a particular fashion in a particular case. Grotius gives the example of one who kills another in self-defence. The law forbids murder. Yet the rightness of defending oneself is one of the basic principles of nature. Hence, the person should be pronounced as not guilty – not because the law proscribing murder ceases to apply, but because the action cannot be considered as murder.[84] Equity does not remove the force of the law; rather, it determines which cases should be governed by that force.

Grotius does mention one kind of positive law immune to equity: namely, those laws which simply reiterate the first principles of nature. Grotius offers several examples, beginning with the general commandment of virtue and the prohibition of vice, and proceeding to specific laws such as loving and serving God, refraining from adultery, refraining from theft, and living holily, honestly, and soberly. Unlike laws subject to interpretation, these basic laws of preceptive natural Right are not defective as a result of their universality.[85] Again, Grotius reaffirms a small realm of expletive natural law in which propositional laws are supreme and absolute, coexisting with a wider realm of positive law in which equity can and should operate. This distinction follows from Grotius' twin modalities of God as creator and governor, which respectively ground unchanging nature and personal will. Natural laws cannot be subject to equity, because they exist before (and outside of) time. However, positive laws are inherently subject to equity, because they are only a sign of the lawmaker's will.[86] This may explain why Grotius rejects Aristotle's concept of equity as the whole of justice. Grotius immediately (and appropriately) applies this concept of equitable interpretation to divine revelation. The first principles of natural law (i.e., creation) are inherent in God, and cannot be subject to equity. Remarkably, however, those positive commands of God in time *can* be subject to equity. One would overrule the commands of God the governor by recourse to the overarching principles of nature which God the creator has implanted in humanity.[87]

After exploring the important role of equity in establishing guilt or innocence, Grotius then mentions that it may also help to determine punishment. Hence, our aforementioned discussion of how to exercise the right to punish has implicitly been a treatment of equity, and Grotius adds little here that is new. However, he notably reasserts his surprising idea that equity may actually call for a harsher sentence than that prescribed in law. For example, one who murders his own father deserves a more severe punishment than one who murders a stranger.[88] Here Grotius again combats the idea that equity is simply a reduction of the law, as though it were a simple halfway point between the extremes of full punishment and complete exoneration. Equity does not exist within the wider horizon of law. Rather, the opposite is true: equity forms the wider horizon within which much of the law exists.[89]

Grotius argues that equity is task of the judge.[90] Expletive justice assigns it to his jurisdiction, and thus compels him to employ equity – just as it compels a governor to punish. Yet the actual exercise of equity cannot follow the deductive methods of strict justice. Thus, equity must employ the imaginative reason of attributive justice in order to ascertain the spirit of the law. While expletive justice creates the formal opportunity for equity, attributive justice governs its substantive exercise.

Thus, Grotius' concept of equity seems to build on the classical approach to equity most fully outlined in Aristotle's *Rhetoric*. According to Aristotle, equity plays a central role in properly distinguishing between wrongs and faults, and in exonerating entirely. Indeed, equity represents "not the deaf insensible law, but the living, merciful lawgiver." This allows a stronger emphasis on intention relative to words, both in regard to the legislator creating the law and the defendant apparently violating it. In determining intention, equity also looks to the character of the person, presumably to determine whether the intention arose from a momentary passion or from the virtue or vice of the defendant's settled character. However, Grotius sees the judge in a less technical capacity than Aristotle, who constrains the judge to the letter of the law. Grotius permits equity not simply to the arbitrator (as does Aristotle) but also to the judge.[91] More substantially, Grotius differs from Aristotle by distinguishing between the verdict of "not guilty" and the pardon of the guilty criminal, and criticizes other contemporaries for failing to do so.[92] In the following section, Grotius will outline the differences between the two.

On Pardon

In his second chapter of *de Aequitate*, Grotius covers indulgence, or pardon. Thus far, he has shown how equity dictates that a particular legal obligation does not apply in a particular fashion to a particular case. In contrast, indulgence cancels the obligation of the law in the case.[93] Unlike equity, it does not arise when laws conflict, owing to the insufficiency of words to capture the will of the lawmaker. Rather, it arises where a law is good law, not superseded by another law, and yet is unjust in a particular circumstance.[94] In other words, it seems to arise when a subject acts against the original will of the lawmaker, and yet the maker recognizes a higher standard – one that transcends not simply his words but even his will at the time of making the law.

Grotius' own example is a law mandating a minimum age of twenty-five for public magistrates. This is a good law, because most adults under twenty-five lack the requisite ability to be good magistrates. However, in exceptional cases, a younger person may demonstrate sufficient prudence to carry out the position well. This does not mean that the law is overturned, as it would be highly imprudent for rulers to spend their time examining every under-twenty-five aspirant to office. Nor does it mean, as in equity, that the judge deems the precocious young man to be over twenty-five years of age and his prohibition contrary to the intention of the lawmaker. Rather, in such a case, the ruler may remove the force of the law which bars those under twenty-five from office. However, Grotius hastens to add that the obligation of this law can be removed only in a case where justice and public utility will not be injured.[95] Such a dispensation is null and void if it violates natural or divine Right.[96] Thus, the freedom of action associated with pardon is necessarily subject to the guidance of natural justice.

As with equity, no pardon can be granted to those who transgress civil laws that merely repeat the injunctions of preceptive natural Right.[97] For example, Grotius argues that murderers cannot escape capital punishment – presumably because the statutes prohibiting murder merely restate a fundamental principle of nature.[98] In contrast, indulgence can reduce the punishment for other acts that violate natural Right but not a specific first principle of natural law. However, these punishments cannot be waived entirely, because it is an (expletive) first principle of nature that crimes must be punished (a principle that will be central to Grotius' critique of Socinian Atonement theology in Chapter 8). Finally, pardon can completely waive punishment only for violations of laws that are purely co-ordinative, such as traffic laws.[99]

Another difference between equity and indulgence involves the jurisdiction that employs each. Equity ascertains the spirit of the law in order to determine whether an accused is guilty or not guilty of transgressing it. If equity recommends a verdict of "not guilty," it is because the accused professes his innocence truly. The determination of equity is thus the role of the judge. Expletive justice demands equity even if it cannot guide its determination. By contrast, pardon can be granted only once a criminal has been determined as guilty. In indulgence, the accused should be fully aware of their legal violation, but plead a standard beyond the law. For this reason, a judge cannot pardon a criminal; the determination of pardon is the role of the governor of the community.[100] It is not a legal action but a political one. Because indulgence is always discretionary, expletive justice can never demand that the ruler exercise pardon. Only attributive justice can enjoin – and then govern – the exercise of pardon.

Not surprisingly, Grotius immediately points out a theological analogue. Just as a good ruler partially or fully pardons violations of positive laws when appropriate, so God grants indulgence to his purely positive commands of time and place. God does this partially in the case of the Fall, fully in the case of the temple regulations given only to the Hebrews. Grotius then identifies a theological distinctive. Just as a ruler cannot pardon violations of positive laws decreed by rulers of other jurisdictions, he cannot pardon violations of the positive commands of God.[101] This distinctive is a conspicuous contrast with the theological analogue of equity. Grotius earlier argued that people are free (and encouraged) to subject the commands of God to equity, interpreting the letter of God's commands by reference to the spirit of God's character. This permits them to carry out an act that opposes the plain meaning of a particular Divine command but conforms to its wider spirit. However, people cannot pardon violations of the spirit of God's law by reference to a higher standard, because there is no standard beyond the spirit of God. In other words, the people can act as God's equitable magistrates; as legal officials, magistrates are in a subordinate position to God. However, the people cannot usurp God's role as pardoning sovereign; God's political position is unavailable to humanity. Only God can forgive sin.

This reference to theology is appropriate. The very concept of indulgence transcends not only the written law, but even the spirit of the law that constitutes justice. It bestows mercy on a person who violates justice, in order to better promote the flourishing – the *telos* – of politics. This mirrors the Reformation transformation of equity into a mercy that can never be demanded in justice. Thus, Grotius makes room for an Augustinian sense of indulgence that recognizes the fallenness of humanity and follows the mercy of God. However, he does so without jettisoning the classical concept of equity, or the underlying belief that at least a limited justice on earth is possible. Even sinners deserve an equitable evaluation, one that conforms to the spirit of justice. Yet while Grotius makes room for these two concepts to coexist, he does not see them as equal. A judge cannot equitably rescind a governor's pardon, but a governor can pardon a criminal who has been equitably judged as still guilty. Indulgence can trump equity, but the reverse is not also true. The governor may find reasons transcending strict justice that substantiate a pardon from just punishment. Justice is valuable, but it is incomplete in light of the need for divine-inspired grace.

Grotius' third concept in this treatise is called *facilitate*, which translates somewhat imperfectly as "good-naturedness" or "ease." A more equitable translation might render it as "liberality." The connotes ease, affability, or friendliness, and applies to those who are not rigorously attached to their interests. They relax their right out of their good will or for the sake of peace.[102] Grotius' brevity in treating the topic leaves something to be desired. However, it seems clear enough that liberality applies not to judges or governors but to private individuals; it is not a legal or political action. In liberality, individuals possess a right, but choose not to exercise it, perhaps out of consideration for a greater good. Grotius suggests that one finds liberality most often when laws are most contrary to natural equity.[103] However, he is unclear as to whether such liberality is an obligation demanded in the equitable spirit of the law, a free gift enjoined by a standard transcending the spirit of the law, or a potentially arbitrary choice of morally indifferent individual whim. The last of these would confer on liberality its most distinct meaning, as the first is already covered by equity and the second by charity (and perhaps indulgence). At most, *facilitate* might describe Aristotle's magnanimous man, who is liberal with his possessions in order to show that they do not have a strong hold on him. He ultimately gives gifts not for the good of others but for the honour that accrues to himself; any benefit to the other is a mere by-product.

Grotius concludes the discourse with the statement that none of these three virtues are contrary to justice. Equity is not unjust because justice obeys not the terms or limits of the law, but the intention of the legislator. Indulgence is not unjust because the obligation of the law, emanating from the will of the legislator, ceases when the legislator wills so. Liberality is not unjust because the law does not force us to exercise our rights.[104] Under these formulations, the exercise of indulgence and liberality may appear potentially arbitrary. Indeed, under expletive (or strict) justice, any act that is "not unjust" is permissible. Yet the meaning of pardon – like that of punishment – is unintelligible if done arbitrarily and without attributive justice; the governor would fail to govern purposefully and thus would undermine his own governance. By contrast, liberality is intelligible even if exercised arbitrarily. Yet even here, this liberty still leaves open the possibility of allocating one's private goods according to a higher standard.

These three concepts help to illuminate Grotius' other texts. When he treats the obligations arising from promises in *DJB*, he cites Maimonides' uncovering of a tripartite distinction among the Hebrews. First is that which is due under strict *jus*, which Grotius translates as *judicium* (the dictate of the judge). The second is translated as *justitiam*: that which is due in accordance with equity. Finally, there is that which is beyond all requirements of what is due, which characterize someone "overflowing with good things." These are things given out of pure generosity.[105] These seem to correspond to Grotius' categories of strict law, equity, and indulgence.

Prudence and Charity: Reasons (Not) to Pardon?

Grotius' theoretical exposition of equity and indulgence in *de Aequitate* allows us to return to his treatment in *DJB* with additional insight. His chapter there on punishment addresses indulgence first by defending its legitimacy. The Stoics had alleged that punishment was deserved and thus could not be remitted. However, Grotius counters that punishment is permitted and can be pardoned.[106] His expletive justice does not compel an exact punishment according to natural law, but only confers a right to punish the criminal. Because this right grants a (concessive) freedom rather than (preceptively) dictating the punishment, the ruler may exercise higher wisdom in remitting the punishment. Grotius' very portrayal of punishment as a right – which may seem unusual to contemporary ears – is precisely what permits the possibility of pardon.

However, indulgence is not arbitrary; it ought to flow from "regard for others or rectoral justice." It is particularly laudable in two types of situations. In the first, the criminal faces a lawful punishment that is severe relative to his crime. This provides an "intrinsic cause" for pardon that refers only to the individual. In the second, a wider imperative provides an "extrinsic cause" for pardon that refers to the overall public good. For instance, in a crime known to few people, public prosecution may be unnecessary or even harmful to the public. Likewise, if the offender has been corrected and has offered satisfaction to the victim, there may be no need of punishment. It would seem that if the criminal can be reformed, deterred, and offer satisfaction outside the full lawfully specified punishment, then wider justice would counsel pardon.[107]

Grotius' treatment of punishment in *DJB* also builds on his theological analogues in *de Aequitate*. Here he states that any ruler ought to exercise his right to punish according to the higher standard of attributive rectoral justice, which may counsel indulgence. Yet the Christian ruler must act by an even higher standard. The Christian is aware of a higher judge before whom even he stands condemned in justice. Hence, the ruler is always somewhat hypocritical in punishing the injustices of others while standing condemned as sinful under God's just judgment. Hence, he ought to act according to Christian charity, which enjoins further clemency. Elsewhere, Grotius notes that "all punishment … has something in itself that is repugnant, not indeed to justice, but charity."[108] This gracious pardon is the role of the governor who – not being subject to the law – is free to act outside it.[109] The distinction between strict justice and charitable grace again reflects Grotius' dual modalities of God the creator and God the governor. We see an implicit distinction between the inflexibility of the nature that demands the strict justice of the law, and the personal and freely willed virtue of the governor that exercises pardon.

This right to pardon does not, however, confer a radical freedom to pardon – even for the Christian. Wider justice does not merely oppose a simple conception of punishment with a simple, one-dimensional conception of pardon; it does not simply offer a binary choice between absolutes. Indulgence must be applied carefully and with "worthy reasons" rather than caprice. Even Christian charity must be paired with "rectoral justice," which may counsel against pardon.[110] For example, clemency would be imprudent – indeed, uncharitable – if the governor expected the criminal to continue actions destructive of the community. It would also be imprudent and uncharitable if its extensive use undermined the dignity and integrity of the positive law itself, thus emboldening additional crimes. Charity does not overturn prudence; the two must work together. Prudence guides charity by recommending punishment, pardon, or a judicious combination of both. This balance between charity and governmental prudence further foreshadows Grotius' Atonement theory.[111]

Conclusion

The standard reading of Grotius outlines a thinker who reduces politics to the protection of property rights (that is, civil obligations).[112] In the words of Richard Tuck, Grotius was "willing to explain relationships in terms of the transfer of *dominium*, and to treat liberty as a piece of property."[113] This signifies a radical break with the traditional Aristotelian conception of politics as an interpersonal and moral practice. Yet a closer examination of Grotius' wider writings on punishment suggests otherwise. Grotius' justification of criminal law by reference to intent and character shows that his rights-based society is not merely a contractarian one that follows from the deontological keeping of promises. If it were, he would need only civil law. An organized judiciary is not simply the self-interested creation of individuals ascertaining the most efficient way to secure their lives and liberties. The sanctions of the law are not a pill prescribed to cover up – however perfectly – the symptoms of a diseased character, or a set of economic incentives that check – however universally – the demonic urges of rational predators. Prison sentences cannot simply become fines (or, more accurately, fees), with the price floor set so high as to make the market in crime prohibitively inefficient. Such actions might meet the aims of a liberal society conceived not as naturally just but as Glaucon's (or Hobbes') contract among the many self-interested weak. But Grotius' liberalism is a deeper one. The essential place he accords to criminal law testifies to a politics that seeks not to channel interests so much as to cultivate interpersonal trust. Reformation of the character, guided by a teleology of the person, is a central element of the purposes of punishment. Another element, satisfaction, does not simply require one to complete a legal sentence; it directs one to actively restore and uphold the integrity of the legal and political order that one has damaged. By focusing on 'positive' elements of personal character and interpersonal trust, Grotius' liberalism transcends the mere protection of 'negative' rights to person and property.

The inescapably public purposes of punishment point to the need for the virtue of prudence in those who exercise coercive force. First, the attorney-general must determine whether or not the damage flows from a criminal intention or merely constitutes a civil liability. Next, if the court finds an intentional act against the law, it may yet need the prudential virtue of equity to judge whether the text of the law itself obstructs the foundational purposes for which the law was intended. If the law is sound and the act calls for the expletive status of "criminal," attributive justice is still necessary if the subsequent punishment is to achieve the reasons for which it was instituted. On its own, the law – and the technical skills of the legal class that interprets it – are inadequate to the task. One needs the situational reason to discern an individual's intention and thus the culpability to be addressed in punishment. One also needs the experiential knowledge to understand how the unique factors around the crime influenced the act. Even in Grotius' third purpose of deterrence (which he consequentially renames "example"), one needs the imagination to discern what kind of punishment will best serve as an example to others. Finally, Grotius' pregnant concept of indulgence suggests that even when a criminal is rightly judged and administered an attributively prudent punishment, a still-higher counsel may enjoin pardon from the governor. This consistent emphasis on virtue fits closely with Grotius' conception of positive law – divine or human – as resting on the will of the governor, which places a high responsibility on the governor (or on the one who carries out the punishment on his behalf). Law points to politics. With the exception of the basic elements of natural law, the punisher cannot simply claim that the law forces him to act a certain way. The right to punish contains an inherent responsibility to punish well.

A ruler who exercises his or her expletive right to punish without the guidance of such attributive virtues will still confer a valid punishment. However, while it will be just in the strict procedural sense of legal validity, it will fail to follow the purposes of wider justice. Indeed, punishments that are publicly perceived as merely legally valid might actually compromise the very political order that secures the ruler's right to punish. Hence, the effective maintenance of the expletive right to punish may depend on the exercise of attributive virtues. A deontological legal order works best when it points toward a teleological moral vision.

Grotius' inherently normative conception of punishment shows it is not simply a human invention that arises only after we have legally authorized it. To be sure, it is best carried out in the artifice of a state that takes its lead from natural teleology. For this reason, attributive justice recommends the creation of the state to whom individuals surrender their pre-civil punishing authority to the state, creating a relationship of superiority and subordination. Yet the surrender of punishing authority applies only inside the state; neither individuals nor the governing authority they have constituted have surrendered any right to punish those outside the state. They remain in an equalitarian relationship to other states. And justice has not gone away. How then should they respond when other states commit injustices? Do such acts not confer on them an expletive right to punish? Does the natural right to punish lead to a just punitive war? To these questions we now turn.

Notes

1 *Guardian*, 5 August 2014, www.theguardian.com/sport/2014/aug/05/f1-boss-bernie-ecclestone-offers-60m-settlement-bribery-trial, accessed 18 November 2016.

2 Richard A. Posner, "Optimal Sentences for White-Collar Criminals," *American Criminal Law Review*, Vol. 17, No. 4 (1980), 409, 416–17.

3

> In deliberation, the last appetite, or aversion, immediately adhering to the action, or to the omission thereof, is that wee call the will; the act, (not the faculty,) of willing.... The definition of the will, given commonly by the schools, that it is a rationall appetite, is not good.
>
> Thomas Hobbes, *Leviathan*, ed. C. B. MacPherson (London: Penguin, 1968), Ch. 6, 127–28

4 The danger arises from the fact that a focus on intentions might lead to comprehensive doctrines or teleologies of the person that could cause one to question the authority of the Leviathan, or inspire one to sacrifice their life on behalf of a law higher than that of the Leviathan.

5 Richard Posner, "An Economic Theory of the Criminal Law," *Columbia Law Review*, Vol. 85, No. 6 (1985), 1193, 1230.

6 Indeed, Posner argues that "criminal law is designed primarily for the nonaffluent" (Ibid., 1195, 1204–05.)

7 Moreover, ignoring moral intent seems to render criminal law unintelligible: faced with a knife, fingerprints, and a dead victim, how could a judge differentiate first-degree murder from manslaughter – or from unsuccessful surgery?

8 Lee Ward points out that Locke's conception of criminal law is effectively one of punitive damages. See Lee Ward, "Locke on Punishment, Property and Moral Knowledge," *Journal of Moral Philosophy*, Vol. 6, No. 2 (2009), 227–28.

9 J. M. Kelly, *A Short History of Western Legal Theory* (Oxford: Clarendon Press, 1992), 238.

10 Cornelius Van Vollenhoven, *The Framework of Grotius' Book* de Iure Belli ac Pacis (Amsterdam: Uitgave van de N. V. Noord-Hollandsche Uitgeversmaatschappij, 1931), 16.

11 This includes both the positive law courts of the state and the 'natural law courts' of God.

12 Hugo Grotius, *The Rights of War and Peace*, ed. Richard Tuck, from the edition by Jean Barbeyrac (hereafter *DJB*) (Indianapolis, IN: Liberty Fund, 2005), 2.20.1.1, 949. Citations from *DJB* are occasionally taken from Hugo Grotius, *De Jure Belli ac Pacis (The Law of War and Peace)*, trans. Francis W. Kelsey, intro. James Brown Scott, Carnegie Classics of International Law, No. 3, Vol. 2 (New York: Bobbs-Merrill, 1925), or from this author's own translations from the Latin.

13 This is particularly true in light of Grotius' insistence on the forward-looking nature of punishment, and his rejection of pure retribution.

14 Grotius, *DJB* 2.17.3.1, 886.

15 Aristotle, *Nicomachean Ethics* 5.2, trans. Martin Ostwald (Upper Saddle River, NJ: Prentice Hall, 1999), 117 (1131a1–10).

16 Hugo Grotius, *The Satisfaction of Christ* (hereafter *SC*), trans. Oliver O'Donovan and Joan Lockwood O'Donovan, in *From Irenaeus to Grotius: A Sourcebook in Christian Political Thought* (Grand Rapids, MI: Eerdmans, 1999), 2.9, 818. Quotations from *SC* Chapters 1 and 3–10 are taken from Hugo Grotius, *Defensio fidei*

Catholicae de satisfactione Christi adversus Faustum Socinium, ed. Edwin Rabbie, trans. Hotze Mulder (Assen, NL: Van Gorcum, 1990).

17 Grotius, *SC* 2.10, 819.

18 Judges in private courts today occasionally assess punitive damages to defendants, in addition to ordering the return of the object to the plaintiff. However, to do so is to import punitive measures into private law. For this reason, the practice is somewhat controversial.

19 *SC* 2.9, 818.

20 Ibid.

21 Ibid.

22 Grotius, *DJB* 2.20.2.2–3, 952–54.

23 Ibid., 2.20.18–19.1, 991–94.

24 Ibid., 2.20.20.1–2, 995.

25 Ibid., 2.20.18, 991–92.

26 Ibid., 2.20.39.2, 1019–20.

27 As Grotius will later clarify, criminal charges still require an act that violates a legal statute. However, the act of an unsuccessful murder or even a conspiracy may violate the security of person protected by law even if the intended victim is not physically harmed.

28 Grotius, *SC* 2.10–11, 819. This attests to Grotius' classical anthropology, including the concept of a rational will. See Jeremy Seth Geddert, "Hugo Grotius' Modern Translation of Aristotle," in *Concepts of Nature: Ancient and Modern*, ed. Steven F. McGuire and R. J. Snell (Lanham, MD: Lexington, 2016).

29 Ibid., 2.10, 819.

30 Grotius, *DJB* 2.20.46.1, 1035.

31 Ibid., 2.20.9.4, 974–75.

32 Ibid., 2.20.5.1, 959.

33 Ibid., 2.20.29.1–2, 1003–04.

34 Ibid., 2.1.10.1, 406–07.

35 Ibid., 2.20.7.2, 963.

36 Ibid., 2.20.37, 1017–18.

37 Grotius, *SC* 2.16, 820. See also *SC* 6, 143; *SC* 8, 185. This shows that Grotius' public conception of satisfaction is also forward-looking. The purpose of restoring the dignity of God's moral government is chiefly to promote virtue, thus preparing believers for the hereafter.

38 Ibid., 2.10, 819.

39 Grotius, *DJB* 2.20.4.1, 956.

40 For a discussion of how satisfaction (punishment) fails to guarantee internal repentance, see Grotius, *SC* 6.13–16, 194–97.

41 Grotius, *DJB* 2.20.2.2, 952–53.

42 Grotius, *SC* 6.18, 196–99.

43 For further discussion, see Oliver O'Donovan, "The Justice of Assignment and Subjective Rights in Grotius," in *Bonds of Imperfection: Christian Politics, Past and Present*, ed. Oliver O'Donovan and Joan Lockwood O'Donovan (Grand Rapids, MI: Eerdmans, 2004), 184–86.

44 Grotius, *SC* 2.16, 820.

45 Grotius, *DJB* 2.23.13.1–3, 1130–31.

46 Grotius, *DJB* 3.11.4.2–5, 1425–27. The third circumstance, known as "misfortune" (*infortunia*), concerns those acts committed in completely invincible ignorance, in which the outcome could in no way have been foreknown even if one fully exercised their faculty of foresight. Here, there may not even be an obligation to restitution. Contemporary legal systems that employ a strict liability conception of tort law would demand an obligation to restitution; those that employ a negligence standard would limit tortious restitution to cases of fault rather than misfortune.

47 Aristotle, *Rhetoric* 1.13, trans. John Gillies (London: Printed for T. Cadell, and W. Blackwood, 1823), 235.
48 Grotius, *DJB* 3.11.2–8, 1425–31.
49 Ibid. In contemporary parlance, these faults correspond to common law torts. A fault might correspond to an intentional or negligent tort, where the tortfeasor commits an act with some knowledge of consequences, but without fully intending the plaintiff's loss of goods. A misfortune corresponds to a loss of goods visited upon a plaintiff without any conscious knowledge by the defendant.
50 Ibid.
51 Ibid., 2.21.19, 1093–94.
52 Hugo Grotius, *Sophompaneas, or Joseph: A Tragedy*, trans. Francis Goldsmith (London, Francis Goldsmith, 1652), 13.
53 Benjamin Constant, "The Liberty of the Ancients Compared With That of the Moderns," in *Political Writings*, trans. Biancamaria Fontana (Cambridge: Cambridge University Press, 1988), 308–28.
54 Grotius, *DJB* 2.20.20.1, 995.
55 Ibid., 2.20.4.1, 956.
56 Ibid., 2.20.5.1–3, 959–61.
57 Ibid., 2.20.4.1, 956.
58 Ibid., 2.20.7.2–3, 963–65.
59 Ibid., 2.20.4.2, 958.
60 Government does, however, direct its forward-looking gaze toward this ultimate end of God's final judgment – one that is outside of history.
61 Grotius, *DJB*, 2.20.6.1, 963.
62 Ibid., 2.20.7–9, 963–76.
63 Ibid., 2.20.7, 963–65.
64 Ibid., 2.20.32, 1010–12.
65 Ibid., 2.20.37, 1017–18.
66 Ibid., 2.20.29.1, 1003.
67 Ibid., 2.20.31.1–2, 1009–10; 2.20.46.1, 1035.
68 Ibid., 2.20.33, 1013.
69 Ibid., 2.20.29.1–3, 1003–05. As will be further explored later, this may account for Grotius' refusal to include even in strict justice the societal honours that Aristotle would have included in his distributive justice. Such discretionary honours can never be claimed or pursued by the potential recipient as "that which is due."
70 See *Grotius and the Stoa*, ed. Laurens Winkel (Assen, NL: Van Gorcum, 2005).
71 Ibid., 2.20.35, 1013–15.
72 Ibid., 2.20.8–9, 966–76.
73 Ibid., 2.20.5.1, 959–60; 2.20.10.2–7, 977–83.
74 Ibid., 2.20.8.1, 966; 2.20.9.1, 972.
75 Ibid., 2.20.5.4, 961; see also *SC* 6.16, ed. Rabbie, 196–97.
76 It should be noted that in contemporary usage, the term "equity" is often taken to connote "equality." While equality is one possible way to conceptualize equity, it is only one of many. Indeed, conceptualizing equity as a mathematically universalizable principle may not be the optimum way to express a principle that responds to the inadequacy of universal formulations.
77 See Oliver O'Donovan, "Law, Moderation and Forgiveness," in *Church as Politeia: The Political Self-Understanding of Christianity*, ed. Christoph Stumpf and Holger Zaborowski (New York: de Gruyter, 2004), 3–12.
78 Hugo Grotius, *De Aequitate, Indulgentia & Facilitate (Traité de l'equité, de l'indulgence, et de la facilité)*, in Hugo Grotius, *Le Droit de la Guerre et de La Paix*, trans. Antoine de Courtin (The Hague: Adrian Moetjens, 1703), Vol. 3, 1.4, 490–91. Translations are occasionally from the original Latin.
79 Ibid., 1.4–5, 490–91.
80 Ibid., 1.5–6, 491–92.

81 Ibid., 1.9, 492–93.
82 Ibid., 1.13, 495–96.
83 Ibid., 1.12, 494–95.
84 Ibid., 2.5, 497–99.
85 Ibid., 1.8, 492. One notes here a rather thicker concept than what Grotius earlier outlined in his five basic elements of expletive justice.
86 The only exception is this: God can act outside of natural laws (as in miracles), because he is the creator of nature.
87 Ibid., 1.7, 492. One notes once again the consistency between Grotius' natural philosophy and his theology.
88 Ibid., 1.10, 493.
89 This mirrors Grotius' earlier rejection of Aristotle's virtue as a mean bounded by definite extremes of vice. He counters that one can never be too extreme in virtue, because its standard is infinite. Here Grotius seems more inspired by Plato's fourfold hierarchy of knowledge in the analogy of the divided line, which locates existential virtue (*noesis*) in a different and higher dimension than law (*dianoia*).
90 Grotius, *DJB* 2.10.9.2, 697.
91 Aristotle, *Rhetoric* 1.13, 236–27.
92 Grotius, *DJB* 2.20.27, 1002.
93 Grotius, *de Aequitate*, 2.4, 497.
94 Ibid., 2.1–5, 497–99.
95 Ibid.
96 Ibid., 2.13, 500–01.
97 Ibid., 2.15, 501–02.
98 This statement seems somewhat inconsistent with his earlier treatment of the topic, in which he asserted that capital punishment was legitimate only in the case of incurable criminals.
99 Ibid., 2.14, 501.
100 Grotius, *SC* 2.3, 816. As the source indicates, this principle is central to his Atonement theology.
101 Grotius, *de Aequitate*, 2.11, 500.
102 Ibid., 3.1–3, 502–03.
103 Ibid., 3.2, 502–03.
104 Ibid., 3.4, 503.
105 Grotius, *DJB* 2.14.6.1, 807–09.
106 Ibid., 2.20.21, 996. A few paragraphs later, he further criticizes the Stoics for wasting time with endless discussions about terms, which is unbecoming of philosophers (2.20.23, 998).
107 Ibid., 2.20.4.1, 956; 2.20.22.1, 996–97; 2.20.25–27, 1000–02.
108 Ibid., 2.20.16, 989–90; 2.20.22.2, 997–98; 2.20.36.2, 1016–17.
109 Ibid., 2.20.22.2, 997–98; 2.20.24.1, 998–99.
110 Ibid., 2.20.27, 1002.
111 Ibid., 2.20.23–24, 998–1000; 2.20.36, 1015–17. Indeed, this calls to mind Grotius' own recognition in *de Imperio* that there are limits to treating the subject of practical reason in a book. None of the theoretical guidelines he lays out here for practical virtue can be "eternal or even always useful"; as he adds, "no precepts for prudence are universal." See Grotius, *de Imperio* 6.13, 317.
112 Michel Villey, *La Formation de la Pensée Juridique Moderne*, 4th ed. (Paris: Montchretien, 1975), 620–21, 630–32.
113 Richard Tuck, *Natural Rights Theories: Their Origin and Development* (Cambridge: Cambridge University Press, 1979), 60.

7 Punitive War and International Responsibility

The term "Trial of the Century" tends to be used carelessly in today's round-the-clock news cycle. However, onlookers at the Ichigaya Court on 4 November 1948 could have legitimately applied the label. That morning, the International Military Tribunal for the Far East (IMTFE) would pronounce its judgment on twenty-eight Imperial Japanese political and military leaders. The roots of the verdict went back several years. In July 1945, the United States, Britain, and China had declared at Potsdam their aim that "stern justice shall be meted out to all war criminals." Their subsequent victory in this punitive war had enabled them to convene a twelve-member panel drawn from eleven nations (including China, India, and the Philippines). The IMTFE judges had considered ample evidence of atrocities committed inside Japanese borders and outside. That morning, before an eager audience, they pronounced judgments of guilt on all twenty-eight Japanese political and military leaders before them.

Yet the verdict included a notable dissent. Indian judge Radhabinod Pal did not dispute the overwhelming findings of fact. However, he argued that the tribunal itself was illegitimate because it lacked judges from Japan. Its legal incompetence rendered its verdict nothing but a victors' justice. Pal also argued that Western colonialism was a war crime, leaving the unmistakable innuendo that the tribunal itself – operating in the shadow of American nuclear hegemony – was one more manifestation of the same. Punitive war was but a pretext for imperialism.

Ralph Waldo Emerson wrote that "one man's justice is another's injustice." In the domestic courts of decently ordered societies, one can at least argue that the standards of justice are generally endorsed by that nation, lending them a legal validity. But the Japanese people did not endorse the IMTFE. Could outsiders legitimately punish them for crimes against humanity, some of which were committed inside their own borders?[1] The previous chapter has established Grotius' belief that a criminal conviction requires not only an injurious act but a reprehensible intention: the perpetrator must know that he has violated justice. What if the Japanese perpetrators held in their minds a different conception of justice, and undertook the allegedly criminal acts according to the dictates of conscience? Is judgment possible when the prosecutor and defendant claim different standards? Should the defendant's claim not exonerate him? Or are some acts, like those ordered by the commanders of Imperial Japan, universally indefensible?

This debate indicated the beginning of doubt over the Westphalian paradigm – then regnant for exactly 300 years – that Judge Pal was attempting to reassert. The Westphalian principles of sovereignty and nonintervention implied that no state could invoke a standard higher than consent by which to judge, make war against, and punish the internal behaviour of another. War could be justified only in the name of self-defence (or, in practice, *raison d'état*). Yet the justification for the Tokyo Trials rested on an implicit departure from this noninterventionist paradigm. Indeed, the Tokyo and Nuremberg trials were only the first of many challenges to Westphalian agnosticism; another was the 2013 push to punish Syrian leader Bashar al-Assad for allegedly using chemical weapons on his own people.

The reopening of the debate over nonintervention directs us back to the historical and intellectual origins of the Westphalian order. Most identify the principle of nonintervention with the 1648 Peace of Westphalia that concluded the Thirty Years' War. However, some have identified an earlier historical genesis in Grotius.[2] His 1625 *de Jure Belli (DJB)* would be reprinted a dozen times by the war's end, and from 1634 to 1645 he himself would work to end war as the Swedish ambassador to France. This historical reassessment implies a philosophic interpretation of Grotius, which sees him as a secularist seeking to prevent future wars of religion by eliminating any political reference to trans-political standards. But if this were the reason for returning to Grotius, it would only re-close the door on the question of punishment by reaffirming the mutual exclusivity of sovereignty and punitive military intervention. Rather, we should be interested in Grotius' international theory because he in fact establishes sovereignty in light of this conundrum – and because he shows a way to overcome it.

A closer look at Grotius' writings on punitive war in *DJB* – including the overlooked Book III – in fact reveals a nuanced justification for punitive war that unites his conceptions of sovereignty (Chapter 5) and punishment (Chapter 6). This framework fits within the just war tradition that permits coercive force in the name of international justice. His concept of just cause for war goes beyond the civil law analogue of defensive war to the criminal law analogue of punitive war. This permits the punishment of territorially aggressive sovereigns. What is more, Grotius also outlines a theory of crimes against humanity that justifies punishment of abusive leaders for crimes ostensibly committed against their own people. Yet Grotius' just war theory still anticipates a world of sovereign states, and shares the Westphalian sensitivity to the potential conflict that comprehensive doctrines may arouse in a pluralistic world. For this reason, he permits intervention not on a thick basis of particularistic teleological doctrines but on a thin set of basic international norms whose deontological foundations are philosophically available to all peoples. In other words, he builds on his conception of intention in criminal culpability by holding international abusers to account if – and only if – their consciences could not but have already judged them guilty. This secular basis compels adherence only to a basic set of negative liberties, but adds a few positive liberties necessary to the protection of the former. Intriguingly, it makes room for natural law and even natural religion. Grotius thus extends the justified coercive force of the sovereign outside its own borders; the pre-existing moral horizon of pre-civil society that grants the original right to punish is the continuing normative horizon between civil societies.

However, once expletive justice has established the right to international punishment, it is again silent about the content of this punishment, including the war waged in its prosecution. This results in a world whose rule by law is distinctively human, but whose punishments of lawbreakers are recognizably inhumane. Only the subsequent exercise of attributive and Christian virtues can bring restraints. What is more, as in pre-civil society, expletive justice tasks no specific authority with the responsibility to punish; it is an uncoercible imperfect duty. While expletive justice grants nations the right to punish, it is unlikely to motivate them to take up this responsibility of apprehending international criminals. Deontology needs the historical-teleological example of personal individuals who alone can inspire. Hence, while Grotius demands only expletive justice of international society, even this basic standard is unlikely to be realized without the virtues of wider justice. The right to noninterference deteriorates in practice if states are not responsible in enforcing it.

International Relations and the 'State of Nature'

Grotius begins *de Jure Belli* by repeatedly emphasizing the place of natural justice even in war. His title adverts to natural justice, his Prolegomena defends it to sceptics, and his second chapter champions it to pacifists. His third chapter then turns to a topic that seems both surprising and odd: private war.[3] A contextualist hermeneutic might ascribe this to a desire to defend Dutch naval expansion through the East India Company. But a closer philosophical analysis shows this chapter to further develop Grotius' commitment to natural justice. Private war illustrates natural justice through a deceptively simple connecting premise: if there is an individual natural right to punish in pre-civil society, that right to punish must continue in the extra-civil society of international relations.

Individuals hold a right to punish in natural justice, and they concede it only through the criminal breaking of law or the noncriminal transfer to a governing authority. However, the noncriminal concede to the ruler only their right to punish others in the same agreement. (In fact, they even retain this right in cases of necessity with insufficient time for recourse to police or judges, in which they may forcibly defend themselves.) No individual surrenders the right to punish others outside the state. The rulers also retain a right to punish outside the state, as they have made no agreement to limit their right. In other words, the world before government remains the world outside government. The natural Right that confers the original right to punish remains unchanged as the overarching moral framework of international relations.[4]

Grotius does prefer that wars be undertaken by (public) states rather than private individuals. Only wars undertaken by states can qualify as 'formal' wars, much like a legal marriage has a formality that a marriage between slaves lacks.[5] But either may be just. In contemporary international law, this licence to punish foreign crimes is known as the doctrine of "universal jurisdiction." Nonetheless, a public or private war-maker must do so justly. Even in the absence of international positive law, an actor must justify his actions through diplomacy and by reference to natural law. Moreover, just as pre-civil society includes the historically developed institution of property, Grotius argues that international relations has developed international customs, or *jus gentium* (the so-called 'law of nations'). Even outside of formal government and human positive law, human society can exist.[6] Hence, war – no less than government – must take its lead from the contours of strict and wider justice.

Defensive War: The International Civil Law Analogue

The just war tradition begins with Augustine, who argues that war is but large-scale robbery unless guided by a higher sense of justice. His foundation for just war is Christ's statement (and demonstration) that the greatest love is to lay down one's life for one's neighbour. The Christian may emulate this other-oriented charity by risking his own life in war to defend his unjustly attacked compatriots. However, the Christian has a harder time justifying violent defence of himself, because it is not motivated by love of another; rather, he ought to consider laying down his own life. In other words, Augustine licenses wars in defence of one's own country, not as an extension of self-defence, but as an extension of other-oriented charity.[7]

In the middle ages, Aquinas echoes this approach of justifying war through Christian charity. He locates his treatment of war in his theological discussion of charity, not his philosophical examination of justice. Nonetheless, his secular philosophy substantiates politics (and life itself) as a natural good, which provides a latent justification for wars to defend one's own political territory and life. In this same era, medieval canonists would revive Roman law, providing a more robust parallel emphasis on the defence of one's life and even personal property. Later, the neo-scholastic Franciscus de Vitoria would build on these foundations by asserting a natural right to self-defence.[8] For instance, American Indians have the right to wage war to defend their property and lives against unjust invasion, even if they are not motivated by Christian charity. Vitoria adds that just wars may defend against material harm rather than spiritual harm, further licensing defence of one's physical person and property.[9] In sum, defensive war has some grounding in the just war tradition, although prominent earlier just war thinkers are conspicuously equivocal in defending it.

Grotius echoes this possibility of licensing wars for defence, and systematically outlines the just causes for such wars in Book II of *DJB*. These follow from his five basic elements of expletive justice. He states, "as many sources as there are of judicial actions" – by which he means five – "so many causes may there be of war. For where the judicial process ceases, war begins."[10] The first cause is that of defending our basic rights, which Grotius will explore in the remainder of Chapter 1. Next he lists the recovery of what is owed. This incorporates the second through fourth elements of expletive justice: recovery of property (Chs. 2–10), the obtaining of what we are owed through promise (Chs. 11–16), and restitution (Ch. 17). The final element will be a title to punitive rather than defensive war (the weighty Chapter 20).

The first cause, defence of our rights, clearly includes war to defend oneself. Grotius justifies defensive war on the same premise with which he justifies individual resistance to an armed robber in domestic politics: the exercise of one's right to self-defence. Grotius further clarifies that the right to defend oneself does not follow from the guilt of the assailant. He proceeds to establish this deontological principle by examining a hard case: when fleeing an assailant, and finding one's only escape route accidentally blocked by an innocent person, can one justifiably slay the person? Strict justice answers in the affirmative. As an element of expletive justice, this right is not conditional or proportional. Hence, both a person and a state may justly exercise violent force to defend themselves against threatening outsiders. Indeed, the defence of one's own *jus* includes not only defence of life but also limb or chastity. Indeed, if only expletive justice is considered, one may kill even in defence of property, provided it is of substantial value. Grotius' only qualification is that the danger must be immediate and certain; a pre-emptive war brought on by fear is illegitimate.[11] Thus, it appears that the right to kill another person in self-defence is analogous to the right of a plaintiff in private law. One maintains a right even if the other party is innocent of any criminal wrongdoing.[12]

Next, Grotius outlines the second through fourth just causes of war, also related to defensive war: recovery of property, claims of promise, and restitution. These wars essentially seek to retroactively defend (i.e., reclaim) that which could not initially be defended. Grotius' discussion is long and shows his great legal erudition, the details of which need not concern us here. But we might note the tripartite epistemology by which he makes his claims. First, Chapters 2–17 explore those elements of property, promise, and restitution claimable in reason. Obviously, there are many. Second, Chapters 18 and 19 then examine the claims arising from *jus gentium*. Such claims may appear to arise from positive natural Right, but this is a misperception. Such claims could only arise in laws explicitly commanded by an (international) sovereign authority. Rather, they are elements of preceptive natural Right arising not from pure reason but from historical reason. Time has revealed a consensus among healthy nations that instantiates in history a pre-existing preceptive natural Right. This shows that Grotius' concept of international law is not a merely positivist conception. Rather, international law builds on a pre-legal consensus that actually reveals preceptive truths in history. Third and finally, Grotius also inserts references to those Biblical just causes inspired by his third source of moral knowledge, that of direct divine revelation. However, Grotius sees no such instances of divine fiat in the common era. In an Augustinian spirit, he argues that Christian charity generally limits – rather than expands – the titles to defensive war.[13]

Such a defensive war is analogous to repayment of debt in private law. It corresponds to the seven elements of civil law we have explored in the preceding chapter. Civil courts are concerned with property, whether arising from contracts or according to tort law. This appears to correspond to Grotius' original "ownership" and "credit" sub-categories of expletive justice. In defensive war, the concern is a possession – namely, territory. The unjustly captured territory can easily be measured through calculative reason. The remedy is universal: the territory must be returned. Justice involves looking backward to undo the acquisitive act of the aggressor, restoring the status of the territory to its original holder. When this is done, justice is accomplished. Having been invaded, the defending nation has a perfect claim-right on its territory. Hence, a nation with a just title to defensive or restitutionary war has a claim on a liability, rather than a title to punish.

Defensive (or restitutionary) war is well established today in the United Nations Charter, which effectively permits war only when a state has been attacked. In other words, war can only be undertaken in the name of self-defence, in order to protect the inviolability of state sovereignty and the corresponding Westphalian norm of nonintervention. In such a case, the invaded state is entitled to defend against the aggression, and to ensure restitution by recapturing the territory unjustly annexed by the aggressor. In legal terms, the aggressor incurs a debt to the offended state, which can only be repaid by returning the conquered territory to its pre-war status.

However, this limited conception of war ignores the possibility of criminal intent. It does little to change the aggressor's acquisitive desires or restrain the aggressor from future offences. Nor does it allay its neighbours' fear and mistrust. Only the possession of territory has been altered; personal character and social trust remain unreformed. Thus, much like with a robber, it is necessary to invoke the criminal law paradigm; the aggressor must also be punished.

Punitive War: The International Criminal Law Analogue

While the Just War tradition cautiously permits defence as a valid title to war, since its Augustinian beginnings it has firmly emphasized punishment as a just cause.[14] This follows from Augustine's conception of political coercion. He justifies it not in service to the glory of the state but to a trans-political divine standard. This standard holds up peace as a good, and enjoins worldly rulers to foster (however imperfectly) such peace in the world. Yet Augustine's peace does not imply pacifism; rather, it is "the absence of strife that comes into being ... when a just order is maintained."[15] Augustine thus recommends a "benevolent severity" in order to "terrify sinners" into acting justly. This principle can be carried outside one's borders, as Augustine extends the domestic power to punish into punitive war; most just wars are in fact punitive.[16] It is cowardly to "live, subjugated, in peace," and to die in the service of justice is no tragedy.[17] (A defender of Westphalia might thus argue that Augustine privileges justice over peace.) Later just war thinkers echo this emphasis. Aquinas outlines just causes for war by merely quoting Augustine: just wars "avenge injuries, ... punish wrongs, ... and restore what has been unjustly taken."[18] Hence, he leaves punishment firmly ensconced as the primary justification for war.

Vitoria further defends punitive war for offences against natural law, and gives examples of just punitive wars against peoples who practice cannibalism or human sacrifice.[19] However, in at least one of his works he narrows the opening for punishment somewhat, because he licenses punishment not because of the inherent wrongness of the act of cannibalism, but because that act harms others. This punishment is thus a response to an external wrong rather than an internal intention; it merely seeks to prevent a repeat of the act.[20] However, this would certainly license punishment for international aggression, an act that states can punish by appeal both to history and to natural law.[21] Francisco Suarez is the first major figure in the tradition to unequivocally reject punitive war for offences against natural law. Moreover, as a forerunner of consent theory, he argues – notably unlike Grotius – that the right to punish arises only from consent. This obviously makes it difficult to justify punitive war, whose targets have rarely consented to the military incursion.[22] In sum, punitive war has a strong heritage in the just war tradition, and only its later thinkers with proto-modern tendencies express any reservations about the practice.

After outlining the titles to defensive war, Grotius then establishes the other major cause for war: to address uncorrected wrongs.[23] He thus follows squarely in the classic tradition of just war theory – and does so self-consciously, by explicitly citing Augustine. This endorsement of punitive war should not surprise us, considering the careful attention he devoted to the philosophy of punishment in the first thirty-seven sections of *DJB* Chapter 20. With this framework in place, Grotius now devotes a further fourteen sections in Chapter 20 to punitive war. International punishment follows from the natural punishment of pre-civil society, so many of its applications are straightforward. Much like the expletive right to defensive war arises when another unjustly attempts to take one's territory, the expletive right to punish arises when another country commits an act – not simply an intention – that offends against expletive justice. These include acts that violate the natural laws of preceptive natural Right as well as those that break promises in human positive right. However, those who have merely failed to instantiate attributive justice confer no rightful title to punitive war.

Grotius conceptually separates the defensive and punitive aims of war even in cases where both are applicable, as the "two qualities [give rise to] two different obligations."[24] We should not be surprised that punitive war goes on to differ from defensive war according to the same seven elements by which criminal law differs from civil law. First, punitive wars punish offences that ultimately rest in the intention of the offending nation, rather than in the act itself; they cannot punish invincible ignorance (a category he will soon explore in detail). Second, punitive wars call for prudence in determining the appropriateness and context of punishment. Unlike defensive war, a punishing nation's initial determination of injustice does not automatically dictate a remedy. Third, punitive wars have no standard and uniform aims – a contrast to defensive wars, which uniformly seek to return the invading army to its prior position. Fourth, punitive war is not merely an equal and opposite reaction to the unjustified military aggression. Unlike defensive war, which can 'undo' the unjust capture of territory, punitive war must imaginatively look forward to prevent future crimes. Fifth, punitive war is not the shifting of the status of a possession; the return of territory is insufficient. Indeed, the original offence may have nothing to do with the taking of territory. Sixth, punitive wars can never claim to deliver perfect justice, unlike defensive wars that can completely redress the initial injustice.

The seventh distinctive element in punitive war is particularly noteworthy. Like domestic punishment, the 'right' of the punishing nation is not a self-interested claim-right. Rather, it confers an unpleasant and costly duty. Punishment does bring deprivation to the offending nation, but – unlike defensive war – there is no reciprocal benefit to the one that punishes. Finally, the eighth component of punishment also applies to punitive war: it is not necessarily carried out by the victim. Punitive war seeks redress not for an offence against oneself, but an offence against a wider public realm, which in this case is humanity as a whole. In other words, it punishes crimes ultimately committed against the natural law that governs both international and domestic societies. Like punishment in pre-civil society, the right is naturally bestowed on those who are innocent of the same crimes. Also like pre-civil society, this right has not been delegated to governing authorities, meaning that no specific institution has a perfect duty to apprehend international criminals. This creates a unique challenge which will be explored below. In sum, the existence of punitive war further reaffirms the public nature of Grotius' political thought. Coercive force does not simply exist to protect one's own property, but to protect the moral integrity of the broader human world.

Crimes Against Humanity

Grotius has established that punishment requires not only a damaging act but a wrongful intention.[25] A violation of a promise made in ratifying international law would surely qualify. However, Grotius' day sees no official international law, and certainly no international sovereign whose positive laws states have agreed to obey. Hence, Grotius must primarily be speaking of offences against natural law. There is at least one such clear offence: the taking of another state's territory. But is there anything more? Is he targeting only militarily aggressive acts that harm other countries, or is he also targeting 'victimless' crimes that do not affect another international individual? If the former is true, he might be a precursor to Michael Walzer's "legalist paradigm" in his celebrated *Just and Unjust Wars*. Walzer's framework conceptualizes states in international relations as individuals in liberal domestic societies, who can be punished only for crimes against property and person.[26] Indeed, if the improper acquisition of territory is conceived as a tort, and punitive war is simply aimed at preventing such future incursions, one might theoretically conceptualize the punishment as mere punitive damages in civil law.[27] At this point, Grotius might still fit the standard 'possessive individualist' portrayal so often ascribed to him.

However, Grotius goes beyond this legalist paradigm. A nation can punish even after territory is returned and reparations are exacted for the costs of doing so. Furthermore, it may punish even in the absence of territorial violations. That is, a nation may punish acts that simply violate natural law, which is to say that they violate human nature and thus humanity. Grotius' conception of such crimes against humanity shows that his punishment intends not simply to prevent physical damage to another, but also the internal intention that motivated it.

Grotius lists three important examples of crimes against humanity.[28] The first is piracy. Piracy typically involves the unjust taking of possessions. One might point out that the same is true of petty theft, which nobody would consider a crime against humanity. However, unlike theft, piracy is also an outlaw activity, one that displays a fundamental contempt for the very idea of law in the first place. Grotius' second example is cannibalism. Cannibalism typically involves the taking of life. Again, in this sense, it is no different from murder – a serious enough crime, to be sure, but not a specific crime against humanity. However, the subsequent and separate act of devouring the dead person is a fundamentally beastly act, one that shows a specific dishonour not only to the victim but also to the dignity of human nature that transcends animal existence. Grotius' third example is contempt for parents. This example likely strikes us as quaint, especially when mentioned in the same sentence as piracy and cannibalism. Yet like the thieving component of piracy and the murderous component of cannibalism, it also shows a contempt for physical well-being that violates one of the ten commandments (in this case, the fifth). Far more important, however, is the fact that this particular contempt is not simply a passive disregard for the physical well-being of another person of equal status (which might seem merely a noncriminal violation of attributive justice), but in fact a disregard of the one strict duty of subordination to paternal *jus* that remains in effect even after the child reaches the age of reason. The neglect of parents is a specific dishonour to the dignity of the parent and thus toward the very concept of parental government. Indeed, we might recall that a crime against the state fundamentally consists not in the superficial damage to the apparent victim but in its offence against the dignity and integrity of the governing *jus*.[29] Hence, contempt for one's parents is a crime against humanity, even if not outlawed in the criminal code. In sum, none of these three acts are crimes against humanity because of their damage to the property or external possessions of another. Rather, they are crimes against humanity because they display a respective contempt for law, for human dignity, and for the dignity of government, each of which are integral to human flourishing. They call not for punitive damages to the victim but for public satisfaction of the crime against humanity.

Each of these three examples emphasizes the effect of crime on a wider moral-political order – especially the third, in which there may not even be any private damage or civil liability. Grotius will then identify a fourth crime against humanity that reveals not only his concept of punishment but his metaethics and political theology, while being even more likely than the third to repulse the contemporary reader. This crime against humanity is the act of publicly dishonouring God. The criminal nature of this act follows logically from his earlier implied reasoning. In *de Imperio*, Grotius had described the many positive effects of Christian doctrine and practice on public order.[30] In *DJB*, he now outlines in several sections the negative – if indirect – consequences of religious impiety on public morality and order.[31] Here he cites a welter of authorities, some testifying that religion is the "cement of all society," and others reciprocally asserting that impiety is "the first cause of crime for weak men." Grotius builds on this reasoning by arguing in his own words that religion is the "foundation of an oath."

After all, the state can never perfectly enforce all promises.[32] Only a belief in divine punishments and rewards can guarantee the widespread fulfilment of contracts – the most basic (and purely procedural) element of expletive justice. Hence, these basic premises of religion are the foundation of human society; they are the very preconditions for the possibility of political order. This is especially true of international relations, which – unlike domestic society – has few laws, and depends for any enforcement on the fear of God.[33] For these reasons, Grotius concludes that "those who first attempt to destroy these notions ought to be restrained, on account of the general human society which they unjustly harm."[34] Widespread impiety undermines the possibility of law and order, rendering it not simply a crime against God but also a crime against the idea of government, and for that reason a crime against humanity.

Grotius' (international) punishment of crimes against God shows that he rejects a clear dichotomy between crimes against others and 'victimless' crimes. A crime against humanity causes harm to human society even if there is no immediate civil damage. Grotius adduces as evidence the fact that domestic societies punish such nominally 'victimless' crimes as bestiality and suicide. The former is an indignity to human nature similar to cannibalism, the latter a taking away of what God has made.[35] This should not be surprising. As Grotius has established earlier in his treatise on punishment, a crime is fundamentally directed toward the public realm and the one who governs it. Hence, there can be no such thing as a 'victimless crime.' Any crime against natural law shows a disdain for law and Right, and thus is automatically a crime against the common good. The matter is not simply between the offender and God; it is between the offender and the entire moral-political universe created and governed by God, the author of natural Right. As will become even more apparent in Grotius' treatment of the Atonement, no man is an island – even outside civil society.

Eurocentrism, Pagan Religion, and Invincible Ignorance

To modern ears, this justification for punishment may appear rather retrograde. Unsurprisingly, some have suggested that Grotius is a de facto apologist for religiously motivated colonial oppression. For instance, Richard Tuck argues that this idea of punitive war "neatly legitimated a great deal of European action against native peoples around the world," with "often brutal implications." He concludes that Grotius was not an heir to the tradition of Vitoria and Suarez, but in fact carried forth the tradition they set out to oppose.[36]

Yet when we look closer, we see that there is more to the story. Grotius adds subsequent qualifications that actually demonstrate an inversion to the supposed colonialist mentality. First, he argues that other peoples cannot be punished through military conquest for failing to convert to Christianity. Nor can other Christian nations be punished for espousing diverging or supposedly heretical interpretations of Christianity. Holy wars are impermissible against Christians and non-Christians alike.[37] Second, Grotius earlier established the essential role of religion in public order by citing barely one Christian authority – but almost a dozen pagan writers, many of whom wrote before the birth of Christ.[38] Third,

Grotius does not insist that political order requires a belief in the *Christian* God. Rather, he observes that true religion depends on a set of principles shared by multiple religions. These principles include the existence of an unseen Creator-God, his active oversight and care for the world, and his righteous rewards and punishments. The latter two principles are the ones that he earlier described as essential to the keeping of promises and the maintenance of human society. Hence, it is only natural religion that necessarily licenses punishment on its enemies. For this reason, soon after rejecting war for Christian conversion, Grotius remarkably states that pagan peoples can be punished for showing impiety toward their *own* gods.[39] In Grotius' mind, paganism is less problematic than blasphemy; the belief in lesser religion is better than impiety toward lesser religion. In fact, he praises the zeal even for false religion: it is good that others "apply themselves to the principal duty of man, if not by a true practice, at least with a good intention."[40] If Grotius really wants to be a Christian imperialist, he might start by showing less tolerance and even-handedness toward non-Christian religions.

If these principles are common to all true religion, it is clear that they must not arise from supernatural revelations that are communicated through the history of a particular people or civilization. Rather, they must be available through pure reason. Their epistemological categorization into (universal) reason instead of (particular) history determines that they can be demanded of all people. A right to punish cannot arise from an offence against supernaturally revealed religion – but it can arise from one that violates natural law, which we now know to include natural religion. This approach is highly consistent with Grotius' overall method in *DJB*, in which he carefully distinguishes the content of Christian revelation (which is ultimately knowable through history) from the dictates of natural reason. For this reason, he cautions his (largely Christian) audience not to confuse a divine positive law with a law of nature. Likewise, one must be sure not to conflate standards arising from one's own civil customs with those of the law of nature.[41] Grotius thus makes a great effort to combat the very Eurocentrism of which he has recently been accused.

Grotius adds that a nation cannot punish another to promote the goods of attributive justice; they can only punish violations of expletive justice. Even if such punishment would produce a better outcome in the target nation, it cannot be imposed; attributive goods must be freely chosen. As he says, "For those who have the use of their reason ought to have the free choice of what is advantageous or not advantageous, unless another has acquired a certain right over them." A nation cannot wage war in order to collect something owed from generosity, gratitude, pity or charity, any more than an individual could claim such in a court of law.[42] Once again, he re-emphasizes that virtuous actions cease to be so when they are coerced instead of chosen freely.

If universal natural reason grounds the basic provisions of natural religion, one might expect some empirical confirmation that they can be found across societies. Grotius is highly sensitive to this standard of verification. Early in his treatment of punitive war, Grotius states that a punisher should determine that the offender has not only violated a true principle, but one that is *demonstrably* true. Here he even draws an analogy with mathematics, in which some principles are true but not evident to all, while others are "immediately both understood and assented to."[43] The former include notions such as the unity and the invisibility of God; the latter include God's care for human affairs and his judgment of virtue and vice. All of these notions are elements of the natural religion that he demands in strict justice, yet he seems to excuse from punishment those who reject the less obvious former elements. Likely for this reason, he distinguishes between "the notions themselves" and "the manner of rejecting them."[44] Pagans who worship virtuous ancestors mistake created things for the creator to whom worship is ultimately due, but nonetheless recognize qualities of the true God in their false religion. Grotius thus seems to argue that ignorance excuses all crimes of religion save for the two propositions that have universal assent: God's care for the world and his righteous judgment. (For this reason, pagans who worship wicked ancestors are culpable.) Yet while (some) ignorance is invincible, impiety is not. While the content of religion varies from place to place, the worship of the divine is empirically universal. Nobody is responsible to respond to truths that they do not know, but everyone is responsible to respond to the truth that they cannot help but know.[45]

Throughout this discussion, Grotius' tone and emphasis also caution the reader against the overbroad use of even a legitimate right to punish. He immediately states that "[punitive] wars are not to be entered into upon the account of every offence," but only when the crimes are "very heinous and manifest." This international approach follows from the liberal domestic principle by which states do not criminalize all offences even though they are morally free to do so.[46] What is more, attributive justice counsels an international punisher to prudently weigh situational considerations and their implications for "the good of mankind in general," or what Grotius refers to as "that greater society" of all humanity.[47] This may suggest clemency in punishing, which – although never demanded in strict justice – may be fitting to goodness (*bonitati*), to moderation (*modestiae*), and to a lofty soul (*animo excelso*).[48] In fact, after establishing the grounds for just war, Grotius spends a full chapter encouraging rulers to think twice about exercising it. No one should think that simply because "a right has been adequately established," that "either war should be waged forthwith, or even that war is permissible in all cases."[49] The right to punish implies a responsibility to use it (or refrain from using it) wisely.

By reducing or eliminating punishment for those who are partially or fully innocent of internal guilt, Grotius builds on his earlier distinction between the "doer" and the "deed." Criminal law concerns not the deed but the intention of the doer. More specifically, the obligatory force of the law rests on the relationship between accountability and knowability. People cannot be held accountable for their failure to uphold a standard of which they were not aware. Indeed, Grotius' widespread use of the distinction between being (internally) unjust and carrying out an (external) injustice allows him to provide punitive (if not necessarily restitutionary) immunity for those who, through their own ignorance, merely *acted* unjustly (rather than *being* unjust).[50] Indeed, immediately before treating natural religion, Grotius says "it is reasonable that they should be excused who, either through weakness of their judgment, or their ill education, violate those [natural] laws."[51]

This emphasis on the possibility of subjective innocence for an objective wrong brings a further – and surprising – implication for war. Indeed, Grotius first raised his earlier treatment of "doer" and "deed" in conjunction with the following "much controverted" question: whether or not a war can be just on both sides. He concludes that in the objective sense of deeds, both sides cannot be just; at best, only one side can have a just cause. However, if the other side prosecutes in good faith a cause which they mistakenly believe to be just, they incur no guilt. Thus, it is possible for a nation to wage a war that is objectively unjust without being judged as an unjust doer.[52]

Grotius' earlier endorsement of punitive war for dishonour to God led some observers to read in him a "brutally" expansive catalogue of just causes for war. Yet this endorsement of what is often called "simultaneous ostensible justice" has led James Turner Johnson, perhaps the foremost expert on the just war tradition, to the polar opposite evaluation of Grotius' legacy. Johnson argues that Grotius' development of this concept leads (perhaps unwittingly) to the Westphalian concept of nonintervention that not only eliminates punitive war, but indeed *any* account of justice as a cause for war.[53] After all, if objectively unjust aggressors can be exonerated, why even discuss justice before resorting to war? This paradigm thus focuses more on the justice of carrying out war (*jus in bello*), while remaining agnostic about its cause (*jus ad bellum*). Yet if this is the result of Grotius' approach, it does not seem to be the intent of a work that devotes 800 pages in Book II to *jus ad bellum*. Perhaps it is more attributable to the careless post-Grotian widening of an opening that was intended to emphasize the internal intention of the person rather than the physical results of behaviour.[54] If this deeper understanding of the unique human capacity of free will makes possible an unintended agnosticism about justice, it is a price Grotius deems worth paying. After all, few would lament the rise from animal to human existence, even if the uniquely human capacity for free will enables not only greater good but also greater evil.

Ultimately, Grotius puts forward both a wide conception of nature and a rich conception of the subject. In his wide-ranging concept of nature – perhaps uncomfortably rich in its religious implications for many contemporary readers – he sets out a high standard to which the diverse constituents of international society can be held. Yet in his careful treatment of intention, he emphasizes personal responsibility and demonstrates a sensitivity to the frailty of human wisdom in ascertaining natural law, one that exonerates many offences. By overemphasizing either of these elements at the expense of the other, it is possible for such erudite scholars as Tuck and Johnson to see a Grotius who is either unduly punitive or irresponsibly lenient. However, it is equally plausible to see a Grotius navigating the tension between the classical emphasis on objective truth and the ostensibly modern emphasis on subjective responsibility.

Third-Party Judges and the (Imperfect) Responsibility to Punish

One of the most important elements of punitive war is the nonpossessive quality of the punisher's right, which confers not a claim-right but a difficult duty. This nonpossessive quality of the right to punitive war stands out especially when contrasted with wars for defence and restitution. Restitutionary wars often arise when a nation has an expletive right to collect on an obligation from another nation's ruler. This claim-right is so absolute that the creditor nation may even forcibly claim the property of the debtor ruler's subjects, if the ruler himself cannot pay.[55] This wide prerogative reflects Grotius' earlier permission to collect the debt of a deceased father from his son. In both cases, the creditor's satisfaction is more important than the need to ensure that the payment comes from the one liable.[56] In war, as in peace, restitution is justified primarily by reference to the one party holding the claim-right.

In contrast, punitive wars follow not from the right of the punisher but the guilt of the criminal. Hence, unlike restitutionary war, a nation cannot punish a ruler by taking property from that ruler's subjects. This echoes Grotius' earlier idea that punishment cannot be meted out to a descendant. A nation waging restitutionary war can take from foreign subjects property *qua* property for the restitution owed by rulers, but a punishing nation cannot take property *as punishment* of those rulers.[57] In other words, when property represents something beyond itself, it is nontransferable. This argument can also be put the other way around. In defensive war (debt repayment), the *jus* of the creditor (arising from his injury) trumps the innocence of the person connected to the debtor. By contrast, in punitive war, the innocence of the person connected to the offender trumps the *jus* of the punisher. Hence, in war, as in peace, punishment is justified not by reference to the punisher(s) who hold the right but the one criminal whose guilt demands a response.

The character of punitive war as a duty is reinforced by a further distinctive of punitive war: its fundamentally public character. Unlike defensive and restitutionary war, punitive war responds to an offence committed not against one's individual nation as a victim, but against a wider moral-political realm. For this reason, no specific person (or nation) is assigned to punish. As in pre-civil society, any person or nation innocent of the crime is competent to punish. That is, the punishers are many but the subject of punishment is only one. This is a direct contrast with restitution, in which the plaintiff is one but the potential satisfiers are many. In other words, punishment begins with the wrongness of the guilty party, not with the punitive right of the punisher, and it subsequently seeks to 'find' a party that can plausibly deliver the punishment. This contrasts with debt repayment, which begins with the claim-right of the creditor, not the debt of the debtor, and seeks to find someone who can plausibly deliver on that claim. Because punitive war features multiple potential punishers, we can see that the punisher acts on behalf of the common good, rather than in pursuit of his own private *jus*.

In civil society, it is not hard to 'find' a punisher: the state hires law enforcement officials, and compensates them for their labours. By contrast, in international relations, the word "find" is not merely metaphorical. No particular nation has a specific (or perfect) expletive duty to punish crimes against natural law, even if they have an expletive right to do so. After all, none has made a promise to do so, one whose nonperformance would constitute a violation of duty. Moreover, most nations are unlikely to volunteer for such a task, given the cost in blood and treasure.

Yet while no specific nation has this perfect duty, there remains an injustice in the moral universe if none punishes the wrong. Thus, a wider sense of injustice persists even if no nation has violated right by not punishing.[58] Right must thus transcend perfect rights and duties. Nations can have wider attributive duties that are nonjusticiable in expletive justice. They are free in expletive justice not to act, but that does not place them outside a moral horizon. Hence, a nation (or nations) must be inspired by attributive justice to undertake the virtuous sacrifices necessary to bring about just punishment. It is not a matter of concessive natural Right but fitting natural Right. The *jus* of punishment is not a claim-right on possessions but in fact a duty to put them on the line.[59]

Grotius points out the parallel with his civic politics (the argument of Chapter 4), in which expletive justice does not compel the entry into civil society, but attributive justice enjoins it. He observes there that the punitive task of shedding blood is unpleasant, and few in pre-civil society desire to carry it out. Who will take it up? This conundrum recommends the creation of the state, which remunerates enforcers and thus guarantees offers to undertake this chore. Once the state has hired magistrates, the imperfect punitive duty of humanity now becomes the perfect duty of those officials.[60]

However, this option is unavailable to international relations, which remains a pre-civil society; the punitive task must be taken on voluntarily. The need for volunteers thus requires the virtue of self-sacrifice for the common good. However, the subsequent exercise of punishment also calls for good character. If the punishing nation is to promote virtue in the offending state, it must demonstrate that virtue in how it punishes. A punisher must not punish in vengeance or injured pride, as this would be to act on desires ungoverned by reason. Rather, the punisher should seek the good of the subject of punishment, and more broadly of "human society."[61]

As a result, Grotius recommends that a third-party state carry out the punitive war. Such a nation is more likely to punish appropriately and without prejudice, because it is not partial to the case. However, such a nation also acts more honourably and sacrificially when it does so, because it volunteers to punish a wrong from which it has suffered no direct damage itself. Grotius' endorsement of third-party punishment reaffirms that the valid title to punish has no necessary connection with direct victimization, but instead arises from the imperative to maintain the wider moral-political order.[62] Indeed, if direct victimhood were a requirement for punishment in the same way as restitution, then third-party states could never undertake punitive war. Grotius rejects this implication because its parallel implementation in domestic politics would eliminate third-party judges in criminal cases, thus undermining one of the very benefits of entering into civil society.[63] Indeed, this principle would permit the prosecution of domestic crimes only by the immediate targets of those crimes – a task most obviously problematic for murder victims.

Grotius defends this position to contemporaries who disagree. International thinkers such as Vazquez, Azor, and Molina require that a punisher either possess a right of jurisdiction (which reduces punishment to domestic politics), or that the punishing state itself be injured. However, such a view either limits punishment to positive law, or views it through a private law framework of punitive damages. Under the former, punishment is contractarian; under the latter, it protects only possessive individualism. In contrast, Grotius understands punishment to exist prior to consent and by reference to crimes beyond property violations. This puts forward a richer conception of human consociality, and even a natural public realm, outside domestic politics.[64]

Jus in Bello*: Carrying out Punitive War*

Thus far, Grotius has dealt with the criteria that justify embarking upon a punitive war. However, this is only half of the story. Just war theory has traditionally been divided into two components: *jus ad bellum* (the justice of the decision to go to war), and *jus in bello* (the justice of carrying out the war). Grotius organizes *DJB* along these very lines: Book II deals with *jus ad bellum*, while Book III explores *jus in bello*. In other words, *DJB* itself is organized according to the distinction between (expletive) status (Book II) and (largely attributive) action (Book III). Yet the literature shows little observation of this organizing principle and even less attention to the latter Book, which may further account for its overall inattention to attributive justice.[65] Here, once again, the status conferred by expletive justice points toward the exercise of attributive justice. Just as prudence and clemency ought to guide the decision to resort to war, they ought also to guide the prosecution of that war.

Grotius begins Book III with a chapter exploring the expletive restraints of pure reason on waging war. There are few. If the ends of the war are just, virtually any means are legitimate. For example, if the international criminals are hiding under the protection of women and children, the strict law of nature permits one to kill these civilian protectors in search of the criminal. This seems a shockingly lax *jus in bello* for someone who has just spent several hundred pages outlining *jus ad bellum* restraints. However, it is consistent with his expletive theoretical framework. Expletive justice allows a civilian fleeing an assailant to kill an innocent person who accidentally impedes his flight path; the right to kill arises not from the wrong of the blocker but from the runner's own self-defence.[66] The same principle appears to hold true for an international manhunt. While the decision to undertake the punitive war arises from the wrong of the criminal, the licence to kill once the punitive war has begun arises from one's own right to self-defence. This expletive right is absolute; it is not limited by considerations of proportion or public good.

Yet if pure reason outlines one meagre chapter worth of preceptive natural Right restraints, there are still three other possible sources of restraint: historical natural Right, fitting (or attributive) natural Right, and divine positive Right.

These sources will provide another twenty-five chapters worth of *jus in bello* restraints. Grotius explores restraints of human positive right in Chapters 4 through 9, each of which address a particular area of war: killing, despoiling, pillaging, taking prisoners of war, postliminy, and acquiring *imperium* over a conquered people. However, this enumeration of restraints known by (and to) history as *jus gentium* still hardly reassures the reader. For instance, Grotius interprets this standard to permit unlimited pillage, even of sacred property, and to retain the natural law permission to kill women and children.[67] History seems to add few additional restraints to preceptive natural Right.

Yet Grotius is fully aware of the harshness of this description. At the end of this entire section on expletive justice and *jus gentium*, he adds a final cautionary chapter (Chapter 10) that sheds a dramatically new light on these prior permissions. He entitles his chapter with the heading, "In what way honour may be said to forbid that which law permits." He opens it by saying, "I must retrace my steps, and must deprive those who wage war of nearly all the privileges which I seemed to grant, yet did not grant to them." This caveat arises from his re-invocation of the crucial distinction between that which can be done with impunity under law (whether mandatory natural law or human positive law), and that which corresponds to a higher normative order. The *jus gentium* of his previous chapters merely describes what is permitted with impunity among nations, or among international tribunals that exercise compulsive force.[68] As with his earlier definitions of justice, war, and punishment, he again distinguishes between the descriptive and purposive definitions of the word "permitted." Simply because an action is legally permitted under *jus gentium* does not mean it is morally permitted. Many of these legally licit actions are not praised by good and honourable men and ought to be avoided on higher grounds. They deviate from natural Right (*recto regula*), which includes not only strict *jus* but also that which is enjoined by the higher virtues. Grotius identifies this as the distinction between (strict) *jus* and (higher) *justitia*.[69]

Thus, upon arrival at Chapter 11, Grotius enters the realm in which the permissions of strict justice are no longer sufficient. Rather, he is now in a realm where the virtues associated with the higher standard of attributive justice (and occasionally the even higher dictates of Christian charity) must guide the exercise of one's wide right to carry out the war. Accordingly, he begins to employ a distinction between "external" (strict) and "internal" (wider) justice that will continue throughout the remainder of Book III. He will regularly speak of the virtue of moderation or "humanity." This calls to mind his earlier distinction between wrong and fault, guilt and liability, and the doer versus the deed. While the immutable legal propositions of natural and positive law permit a wide array of external acts, the higher virtues of character narrow this right.

What, then, are the true guidelines for war, according to this higher standard of internal justice? Chapters 11 through 16 systematically re-examine the aforementioned six areas of war through the lofty virtue of humanity rather than the lenient merely human laws of *jus gentium*. For example, both expletive justice and *jus gentium* had licensed the retention of sovereignty over a defeated country that waged war unjustly. After all, the right of punishment is absolute and unconstrained by matters of proportion. However, internal justice suggests that one should continue to occupy the country only insofar as the other nation's degree of wrongdoing merits this punishment. Moreover, even if this condition is met and calls for occupation, one should govern the conquered people mercifully, and even share the fruits of victory with them. Internal justice takes its lead from purposes that point toward a peaceful conception of human flourishing.[70]

Because this teleological vision cannot be defined but only illustrated, Grotius cites copious examples from antiquity. However, he cannot universally and coercively demand fidelity to these virtuous restraints, because they cannot be deduced through pure reason. Indeed, until Grotius (or someone else) promulgates these examples, the uninitiated cannot even know of these higher counsels. Fortunately, there are no inherent theoretical limitations on promulgating them to all peoples. The virtues they disclose are not simply supernatural Christian virtues, possessed only by Christians enabled by the example of Christ and the grace of God. Rather, they are also virtues displayed by the best of the pagan Greeks and Romans – examples that Grotius is all too happy to cite.[71]

This mode of enjoining virtues rather than commanding acts also testifies to the voluntary nature of Grotius' counsel, one that preserves human free will. Grotius shows this when he contrasts the virtue of humanity with the practice of equity. When he treats the matter of retaining sovereignty over a captured people, he begins his prescriptions by distinguishing between "the equity which is required, or the humanity which is praised." This echoes his treatment of equity and pardon in *de Aequitate.* Like punishment, equity is demanded in expletive justice, even if its exercise ought to be guided by attributive justice.[72] In contrast, like pardon, exercising the virtue of humanity cannot be demanded in expletive justice, but only enjoined by a higher standard. This emphasizes its truly voluntary nature. The right not to exercise it renders its exercise truly virtuous. Reciprocally, the subjects of an offending nation can never demand moderation in justice, just as a convicted criminal can never claim a right to clemency. (Indeed, if anything, the opposite would be true, as their punishment is deserved.) Crude and harsh punishments, to be sure, would be contrary to the good of the subjects, and to the good of the situation. The unfortunate subjects of punishment could not, however, claim any violation of strict rights-based justice. It is virtue, not justice, that beckons the punisher toward a higher path of restraint.

Nonetheless, this exercise of moderation is not simply the arbitrary concession of the right to punish. Indeed, because the just title to war often arises from the acquisitive nature of the aggressor, public safety and lasting peace – for which a punishing nation is responsible – may demand, for example, that sovereignty *not* be returned to the offending nation. In other cases, prudence might call for compromises, such as leaving troops in the country or demanding occasional tribute.[73] Thus, the exercise of the virtue of moderation and humanity still ought to be governed by prudence. Moderation does not oppose the absolute and simple punishments of expletive justice with a quantitatively equal and opposite release from punishment. Rather, it exercises the static and deontological right of expletive justice with a qualitative and teleological judgment about punishment.

Thus, the restraints arising from this higher justice are more reassuring to contemporary readers, and undoubtedly to his own as well. Where natural law and *jus gentium* permit virtually any means in pursuit of the ends of a just war, the higher moderating virtues of attributive justice (not to mention Grotius' Christian counsels of charity) enjoin a much different path. Grotius cites Quintilian the Father's instruction to "consider rights (*jura*) to be one thing, and justice another."[74] Here is Grotius' clearest proclamation that justice – and not simply a more ethereal sense of honour – goes beyond one's rights. As O'Donovan concludes, "there is an extensive and more important role for the idea of Right ... than can ever be conveyed by the idea of 'rights.' "[75]

In other words, mere rights do not result in a humane world. One cannot merely exercise expletive rights and count on an invisible hand to direct them toward the best of all possible outcomes. If one truly wants to be treated with humanity, one must appeal to the 'better self' of those exercising their rightful authority. When the ruler or punisher submits himself to a higher authority, the outcome will be better for both parties than the adversarial insistence on getting one's due.

In sum, according to strict natural law, very little is impermissible in war. If justice endorses the cause, it places few restrictions on pursuing that end. This strongly testifies to the limits of strict justice. Expletive justice alone results in a recognizably human world ruled by justice (however basic and blunt) rather than pure force. It is perfectly adequate as long as one maintains the perfect status of "noncriminal" (or "not unjust"). However, the deontological nature of its right-based (and status-based) approach follows only from the distinctive faculties of the human being, not the fullest expression of their development toward a teleologically human (and thus humane) end. For this reason, its harsh and blunt punishments struggle to guide the character of a person (or polity) that is never perfectly "not unjust," especially in international relations. The gradual and progressive movement toward wider justice requires a vision of human flourishing that can never be captured in the impersonal formulas or dictates of expletive justice. Deontology gains universal intelligibility at the cost of moral richness. The nonteleological approach that is most achievable in international relations is also least adequate to its needs.

Conclusion

To twist a Canadian phrase, on 2 May 2011 the Marines finally got their man. President Barack Obama proudly announced to a surprised and jubilant audience that the US Navy had killed Osama bin Laden in a daring precision raid. This was primarily an act of punishment rather than defence. Bin Laden had violated the peaceful principles of international society by operating an outlaw organization; he had committed specific crimes against humanity by targeting and killing thousands of civilians in America, Kenya, and Tanzania; and he had since relinquished active control of al-Qaeda, thus posing a much-reduced direct threat to America.

The second-greatest surprise of the evening was the revelation that for several years bin Laden had comfortably lived a stone's throw from the Pakistani military academy. Yet the Pakistani government had made no effort to apprehend this international war criminal. They had no strict duty to punish an Afghan citizen who carried out high-profile crimes far from Pakistan. Indeed, to do so would have brought on significant financial, military, and political costs. Instead, it was America who chose to bear the decade-long costs of finding and apprehending a man at war not only with the United States but with the very idea of nations.

Yet the United States' costly venture on behalf of international society brought it criticism in some quarters. After all, the Westphalian paradigm forbids outsiders from waging punitive war; only nationals can punish their own. Observers have levelled the same criticism at punishers of the Hutu Interahamwe in Eastern Congo, punishers of pirates in the Gulf of Aden, and punishers of the killers of US Ambassador Christopher Stevens in the Sahara desert. It is difficult to justify the capture and punishment of these international offenders without reference to a pre-Westphalian concept of natural law (and consequent natural punishing authority). Positive international law may adapt to surmount these Westphalian constraints by creating an International Criminal Court (ICC), but it still relies on nations (often third-party ones) to pursue and arrest its targets. In an international discourse lacking reference to natural justice, countries generally remain unmotivated to apprehend these fugitives. As of August 2013, almost three-quarters of war criminals indicted by the ICC remained on the run (or, in one case, comfortably ensconced as the sovereign occupant of the lavish Sudanese presidential palace).

Grotius is often seen as a progenitor of the doctrine of nonintervention that accompanies the Westphalian order and rules out punitive war. Yet while he anticipates a world of sovereign nation-states, even his sovereign remains accountable (like everyone else) to natural law. If the ruler offends against natural law, all but his own subjects retain the right to punish him.[76] Grotius' doctrine of universal jurisdiction threatens the unjust exercise of sovereignty and emboldens its just exercise. Grotius conceives coercive force as emanating from natural justice, and thus reaffirms the classical formulation that legitimate force originates not in consent but in wisdom.[77] His willingness to countenance punitive war places him in substantial continuity with the just war tradition of Augustine, Gratian, and Aquinas.

Moreover, Grotius' concept of crimes against humanity reinforces his earlier conception that punishment is not simply a Posnerite quest to efficiently preserve the integrity of property rights. There exist crimes beyond the international 'property crime' of territorial aggression. A nation carries out punitive war not as a plaintiff pursuing restitution of territory, but on behalf of human society. In so doing, it aims to uphold the dignity and integrity of a wider moral-political order that transcends the artifice of geographical delineations. Grotius can thus punish crimes against humanity because they undercut the foundations of international society. This premise undergirds his justification for punishing crimes that undermine belief in a God who rewards and punishes in the afterlife. Such belief is the only way to guarantee the most basic element of expletive justice, one that does not even require pre-existing moral obligations: the fulfilment of promises. Hence, the punishment is not to restore God's honour per se, but to preserve the very possibility of human society – a theme just as central to his Atonement theory (Chapter 8).

Yet while Grotius' emphasis on punishment licenses a seemingly wide range of justifications for war, it also exonerates the unjust acts of many violators who acted in good conscience. Nations can be punished only for actions that they could not but have known to be crimes. The universally knowable (and thus binding) standards include only those basic elements of natural law (or natural religion) that are plain to natural reason. Grotius thus preserves the classical just war tradition on grounds that are fair to the non-Christian peoples of a pluralistic world. Grotius certainly believes in further truths of divine revelation, but he acknowledges that these highest examples (such as that of the divine Christ) can be known only through sacred history. For that reason, he does not hold Amerindians to a standard that their own consciences could not possibly have known, and thus been bound to. Likewise, he offers the same clemency to nations who conducted an objectively unjust war while believing it to be just. His resultant simultaneous ostensible justice flows not from an incurious despair over the difficulty of ascertaining truth in a world of competing claims, but from a fundamentally Christian sensitivity to individual conscience. Grotius' supposedly modern emphasis on subjective responsibility exists within a classical and medieval framework of natural Right.

One might also invert that last phrase and its emphasis. For all of Grotius' seemingly pre-modern talk of public religion, he does not expect that modern international society will have the same thick vision of human flourishing shared by medieval Christendom. One might hope for a Christian standard between Christian nations, but one can hold global society responsible to no more than the basic nonteleological standard of expletive justice.[78] Nor can one punish violations of anything beyond this minimum standard. But Grotius' consequent doctrine of universal jurisdiction licenses *anyone* to punish this – that is, anyone can punish a violation of any universal human right. Perhaps this explains why he limits such universal human rights to the basic 'negative' protection of territory, property, and promises.[79] If expletive justice were to confer a strict universal right to positive goods such as information or a healthy environment, South African buttoned lips or litterers might face the long arms of the United States Marines.

When states undertake punitive war to enforce human rights, they must also do it justly. However, expletive justice confers a right to punish with few *jus in bello* limits on its own. The resulting draconian punitive wars will still, to be sure, safeguard this basic standard of justice that separates the human from the animal. After all, the threat of punishment creates a disincentive for potential offenders where none previously existed. However, without an attributively prudent and theologically charitable moderation of these punishments – a moderation governed by a purposive and even redemptive vision and ordered toward the flourishing of victim and criminal alike – this human world will remain inhumane. A purely deontological standard shows little mercy to those who have offended. Indeed, the draconian chastisements of strict justice may only invite reprisals from the other side. The resulting condition will also be distinctively human rather than animal – not in its distinctive capacity for peace, but in its distinctive capacity for war without limit or end.[80]

Yet the challenge of appropriately carrying out punitive war is dwarfed by the challenge of undertaking it in the first place. In order for nations to legitimately protect their possessive claim-rights to territory or possessions, they must be willing to exercise their decidedly nonpossessive right to punish. The right to wage punitive war thus leads to the demanding responsibility to act on the right. Of course, this attributive responsibility to take up third-party punishment is never a perfect duty. It cannot be demanded in expletive justice. Hence, a nation commits no injustice by refusing to take it up. Yet if nobody takes it up, and carries it out well, international order will gradually succumb to a tragedy of the commons. If international outlaws remain unchecked, the protections of sovereign nationhood will come to mean little. In other words, the sovereign nationhood that exempts one from a perfect duty to punish international criminals may also undermine the very concept of sovereign diplomacy that promotes international order and guards against the descent into a war of all against all. The deontology of expletive justice provides a standard that different nations and civilizations should be able to agree on, but without attributive justice, this standard is unlikely to be realized.

This threat is substantial, no less in our own age than that of Grotius. As Grotius has pointed out, these higher virtues of attributive justice are unlikely to arise without the prospect of eternal reward and punishment. But this only seems to address the problem of punishment in the human realm by creating one in the divine realm – to kick the problem up one level. It is well and good to explore the importance of punitive war, but if divine punishment is the ultimate guarantor of a humane order, we must now turn our attention to that higher inquiry. And when we do, we will find the apex of Grotius' thought in his creative and enduring Atonement theology. Here he brings together his understanding of government and law, his distinction between liability and punishment, his concept of the higher (but individually distinct) virtues of prudence and charity, and – most of all – his outline of the limits of strict rights-based justice. After all, God holds the ultimate expletive right to eternally punish every sinful human being. But if this were the inevitable fate of every person, would anyone carry out – even partially – their expletive duty to honour God or obey his natural laws? The very possibility of virtue seems to require something that cannot be demanded as a matter of right: that God set aside his own rights.

Notes

1 Much the same question could have been asked of the Nuremberg trials, which punished the perpetrators of a Holocaust largely carried out within German territory.

2 For instance, see James Turner Johnson, *Sovereignty: Moral and Historical Perspectives* (Washington, DC: Georgetown University Press, 2014), 22–26, 84–85, 88–89, 105–06.

3 Yet it may be surprisingly timely, considering the increasing use of private military contractors.

4 Hugo Grotius, *The Rights of War and Peace*, ed. Richard Tuck, from the Edition by Jean Barbeyrac (hereafter *DJB*) (Indianapolis, IN: Liberty Fund, 2005), 1.3.2, 241–42; 1.3.4, 248–52; 2.20.1.2–3, 949–51; 2.20.3.1–2, 955–56; 2.20.7.2, 963–64; 2.20.8.5, 970–71. As Grotius states that these wars may be undertaken by "any magistrate whatsoever," it is not clear whether all individuals retain the right, or only those who occupy some form of political authority. However, it is clear that punitive war may justly be undertaken by nonsovereign individuals acting in their own name. Citations from *DJB* are occasionally taken from Hugo Grotius, *De Jure Belli ac Pacis (The Law of War and Peace)*, trans. Francis W. Kelsey, intro. James Brown Scott, Carnegie Classics of International Law, No. 3, Vol. 2 (New York: Bobbs-Merrill, 1925), or from this author's own translations of the Latin original.

5 Ibid., 1.3.4.1, 248–50.

6 Indeed, this is the theoretical approach of the English School of international relations, which accords Grotius pride of place as its intellectual progenitor.

7 David D. Corey and J. Daryl Charles, *The Just War Tradition: An Introduction* (Wilmington, DE: ISI Books, 2012), 21.

8 Ibid., 133.

9 James Turner Johnson, *Ideology, Reason, and the Limitation of War: Religious and Secular Concepts, 1200–1740* (Princeton, NJ: Princeton University Press, 1975), 170–71.

10 Grotius, *DJB* 2.1.2.1, 393.

11 Ibid., 2.1.5–11, 398–408.

12 Ibid., 2.1.4–9, 398–404. However, Grotius qualifies this by saying that the same reasoning does not apply to defence of property, because there is a great disparity between the value of the property and the value of life. Here the permissibility of taking life in order to defend property is valid only in regard to the morally guilty robber, which suggests a criminal law paradigm. Moreover, Christian charity invalidates this natural liberty even if life is at stake. In such a case, one is instead enjoined to give up their own innocent life rather than taking that of another. Even though this counsel restricts only Christians, one can already see the (attributive) mode of operation in which a higher virtue limits the exercise of the permissions afforded by natural law.

13 In regard to punitive war, there is no difference in the just titles to war; however, as we will see, Christian charity may motivate the sacrifices of war in a manner likely unavailable to natural reason.

14 James Turner Johnson, "Historical Roots and Sources of the Just War Tradition in Western Culture," in *Just War and Jihad: Historical and Theoretical Perspectives on War and Peace in Western and Islamic Traditions*, ed. John Kelsay and James Turner Johnson (New York: Greenwood Press, 1991), 9–10.

15 Johnson, *Sovereignty*, 162.

16 Augustine, *Questions on the Heptateuch*, 6.10, in John Eppstein, *The Catholic Tradition of the Law of Nations* (London: Burns Oates and Washbourne, 1935), 74.

17 *Augustine, Against Faustus the Manichean* 22.74, in Augustine, *Political Writings*, trans. Michael W. Tkacz and Douglas Kries, ed. Ernest L. Fortin and Douglas Kries (Indianapolis, IN: Hackett, 1994), 221; Augustine, *City of God* 1.1, in Augustine, *Political Writings*, trans. Michael W. Tkacz and Douglas Kries, ed. Ernest L. Fortin and Douglas Kries (Indianapolis, IN: Hackett, 1994), 3.

18 Aquinas, *Questions on Joshua*, Book VI, Question 16, in John Eppstein, *The Catholic Tradition of the Law of Nations* (London: Burns Oates and Washbourne, 1935).

19 Franciscus de Vitoria, *On the Indians*, trans. John Pawley Bate, in *De Indis et De Jure Belli Relectiones*, ed. Ernest Nys, *Carnegie Classics of International Law*, No. 7 (Washington: Carnegie Institute, 1917), 3.2, 3.5, 3.9, 151–56.

20 Franciscus de Vitoria, O*n Dietary Laws, or Self-Restraint*, in Pagden and Lawrence,

eds, *Francisco de Vitoria: Political Writings*, 1.5, 218–25; Franciscus de Vitoria, *On the Indians*, 2.16, in Nys, *De Indis et De Jure Belli Relectiones*, 147.

21 Vitoria, *On the Law of War*, 19, as cited in John Eppstein, *The Catholic Tradition of the Law of Nations* (London: Burns Oates and Washbourne Ltd., 1935), 102.

22 See Francisco Suarez, *On Charity*, Disputation 13: *On War*, Sections 2.1, 5.1–5.5, 8.2, in *Selections From Three Works of Francisco Suarez*, Gwladys L. Williams *et al.*, trans. (Oxford: Clarendon Press, 1944), 806–55.

23 Grotius, *DJB* 2.1.2.2, 395–96.

24 Ibid., 2.20.38, 1018.

25 Ibid., 2.20.39.1, 1018–19.

26 Michael Walzer, *Just and Unjust Wars*, 3rd ed. (New York: Basic Books, 1998), 58–63. The fifth plank of his paradigm is that "Nothing but aggression can justify war." Walzer does admit several important exceptions to his legalist paradigm, including that of humanitarian intervention (which he expands upon in the Preface to the third edition). Moreover, he views territorial aggression as a crime rather than a tort. However, it is noteworthy that his basic premise begins only with the crime of appropriation of the territory (property) of another state, rather than crimes against international society, humanity, or nature.

27 Some would argue that punitive damages already partakes of criminal punishment, not least in its very terminology, which is something of an oxymoron on its own terms – thus rendering the objection moot. Nonetheless, at the very least, punitive damages are assessed for property crimes in private law.

28 Grotius, *DJB* 2.20.40.3, 1022–24.

29 One might argue that Grotius' examples of punishment for dishonour *can* actually be framed along private law lines, by attempting to conceptualize honour as a possession that can be taken and subsequently restored (as in suits of defamation). However, this possessive framework becomes less credible considering that Grotius later includes the honour due to God. Indeed, this paradigm would be uniquely antithetical to Grotius, given that his understanding of the Atonement is less inclined to portray God's honour along possessive lines than any Christian thinker before him.

30 Hugo Grotius, *De Imperio Summarum Potestatum Circa Sacra (On the Power of Sovereigns Concerning Religious Affairs)*, critical edition with introduction, translation and commentary Harm-Jan Van Dam (Boston: Brill, 2001), 1.13, 174–79; 6.6, 298–99.

31 Grotius, *DJB*, 2.20.44, 1027–31; 2.20.51, 1051–52. In correlating religion and public morality, one might attempt to argue that Grotius is reducing religion to public morality. However, when he comments on the importance of religion, he cites figures such as Plato and Aristotle, not "two truths" thinkers like Averroes and Marsilius. Only once in his entire work does Grotius cite Marsilius, when he says that "things which are sacred are public" (Ibid., 3.5.2, 1305.) Even in this case, however, Grotius is making the point that sacred things can be governed by the ruler of a state because the ruler has care over things both sacred and secular, rather than because sacred things are simply instrumental to secular outcomes.

32 This is, of course, the Achilles heel of Hobbes' solution.

33 Grotius is also unmoved by counter-arguments that God should be able to punish crimes against himself; after all, God can also punish ordinary crimes against others, but this does not mean that human society should refrain from punishing them. (See Ibid., 2.20.44.2,1028.)

34 Ibid., 2.20.44.3–6, 1028–31; 2.20.46.4, 1037–38. Grotius' willingness to punish such grave impiety provides further context for his supposedly 'impious hypothesis.' If he is truly trying to subvert religious belief or render it irrelevant, it is strange that he should advocate punishing those who reject God's existence.

35 Ibid., 2.19.5.1–2, 943–45; 2.20.44.2, 1028. Grotius here raises the famous suicide of Cato the Younger. He argues that suicide is cowardly, as it exhibits an inability to live magnanimously under trials.

36 Richard Tuck, *The Rights of War and Peace: Political Thought and the International Order from Grotius to Kant* (New York: Oxford University Press, 1999), 102–03, 108. See also Michel Villey, *La Formation de la Pensée Juridique Moderne*, 4th ed. (Paris: Montchretien, 1975), 630–32.
37 Grotius, *DJB* 2.20.48–50, 1041–50.
38 Ibid., 2.20.46.1–4, 1035–38.
39 It is important to note that Grotius does not here indicate a moral relativism: this immunity would be valid only inasmuch as their religion is consistent with natural religion. To take one obvious example, Aboriginal religions living up to their own principles of human sacrifice (a live example in Grotius' day) would not be exempt from punitive war.
40 Grotius, *DJB* 2.20.51, 1051–52.
41 Ibid., 2.20.41–42, 1025–26.
42 Ibid., 2.22.12, 1106; 2.22.16, 1112–13.
43 Ibid., 2.20.43.1, 1026–27.
44 Ibid., 2.20.46.1, 1035.
45 Ibid., 2.20.44–47, 1027–41; 2.20.51, 1051–52.
46 Ibid., 2.20.38–39, 1018–21; 2.20.43.3, 1027.
47 Ibid., 2.20.9.1, 972; 2.20.23, 998–1000; 2.20.44.6, 1031.
48 Ibid., 2.20.23, 998–1000; 3.11.7.1, 1434–35.
49 Ibid., 2.24.1.1, 1133.
50 Interestingly, Grotius also asserts the inverse: one who performs a just action under the impression that it is unjust commits a wrong. See Ibid., 2.23.2.1, 1116.
51 Ibid., 2.20.43.2, 1027. One is reminded of the final element of Aquinas' definition of a law: promulgation.
52 Ibid., 2.23.13, 1130–32.
53 Johnson, *Sovereignty*, 22–26, 84–85, 88–89, 105–06. Here Johnson indicts the reticence of Vitoria and Grotius to punish Amerindians for violations of true religion as evidence that they espouse the Westphalian conception of sovereignty (which seems to lead to its attendant doctrine of nonintervention).
54 Johnson, *Ideology*, 18–21, 194. In this earlier work, Johnson is clear about Grotius' intent to make countries more scrupulous in *jus in bello*, rather than to become agnostic about *jus ad bellum*.
55 Grotius, *DJB* 2.21.17–19, 1092–94; 3.13.1–2, 1475–77.
56 This is also consistent with his argument that in order to protect one's own right to life while fleeing an assailant, one is justified in harming an innocent person who accidentally blocks one's escape.
57 Grotius, *DJB* 2.21.17–19, 1092–94; 3.13.1–2, 1475–77.
58 This tells against Villey's reading of Grotius as eliminating objective right. It also tells against the idea (of Wesley Hohfeld, among others) that all rights and duties are perfect (and thus reciprocal).
59 In *DJB* 2.25, Grotius again advocates actions that transcend strict duty in his discussion of wars on behalf of others, or humanitarian intervention. In such a case, a nation risks the lives of its own soldiers in the name of saving nationals of other countries. This further enjoins the common good of humanity over the rights of a country's own soldiers, who must potentially set aside their right to life.
60 Ibid., 2.20.15, 989.
61 Ibid., 2.20.5–9, 959–76.
62 Ibid., 2.20.8.4, 968–70; 2.20.40.1, 1021; 2.25.8, 1159–62. One might add the likelihood that all involved parties will have their hands dirty, thus failing to meet the moral condition of the right to punish.
63 Hugo Grotius, *De Satisfactione Christi (The Satisfaction of Christ)*, trans. Oliver O'Donovan and Joan Lockwood O'Donovan, in *From Irenaeus to Grotius: A Sourcebook in Christian Political Thought* (Grand Rapids, MI: Eerdmans, 1999), 2.6, 817.
64 Grotius, *DJB* 2.20.40.1–4, 1021–25.

65 One notably rare and worthy attempt to deal with Book III is Steven Forde, "Hugo Grotius on Ethics and War," *American Political Science Review*, Vol. 92, No. 3 (1998), 643–46.
66 Grotius, *DJB* 3.1.2–4, 1186–88.
67 Ibid., 3.4.9, 1283–84; 3.5.1–2, 1303–09.
68 Ibid., 3.10.1.1, 1411.
69 Ibid., 3.10.1.1–3, 1411–14.
70 Ibid., 3.8.1.1, 1374–76; 3.15.1–2, 1498–1500; 3.15.12.1–2, 1509–11.
71 To take one example among multitudes, see Ibid., 2.24.2.4, 1136–37.
72 Ibid., 3.15.1, 1498–99.
73 Ibid., 3.15.1–6, 1498–1503; 3.15.12, 1509–11.
74 Ibid., 3.4.2.1–3, 1271–74.
75 O'Donovan and O'Donovan, 791.
76 Rulers guilty of the same (or similar) offences would also be ineligible to punish him.
77 Of course, the wise (and thus legitimate) use of force can be subsequently limited by promises, wise or unwise.
78 In other words, international society should uphold a procedurally fair framework in which people can exercise their unique human freedom and international sociability. This means that self-interest is the guiding principle, but it is a self-interest that recognizes and respects the legitimate self-interest of others. International relations may be a self-interested competition to maximize one's rightful possessions, but it is one undertaken in the peaceful fashion uniquely available to human reason, rather than by the law of the jungle.
79 His much thicker list of crimes against humanity are punishable only inasmuch as they undermine the moral framework that supports the basic negative rights above.
80 See Oliver M. T. O'Donovan, "Law, Moderation and Forgiveness," in *Church as Politeia: The Political Self-Understanding of Christianity*, ed. Christoph Stumpf and Holger Zaborowski (New York: de Gruyter, 2004), 6.

8 Divine Government

Why You Can't Ever Really Pay for Your Crimes

Augustine inaugurated the just war tradition with the argument that war can be justified in the name of peace. Yet waging war for the goal of peace requires a challenging transition from the one to the other – especially after a civil war. This challenge has inspired a burgeoning recent literature around *jus post bellum*, or justice after war.[1] While the nascent field of "transitional justice" explores war crimes tribunals (such as the IMTFE), it also focuses on the alternative of reconciliation. The latter has only increased in prominence since South Africa's Truth and Reconciliation Commission (TRC). Yet the very substitution of truth commissions for criminal tribunals renders the term "transitional justice" something of a misnomer: truth commissions explicitly rule out the prison terms so often associated with the justice after war. One might instead describe these commissions as mediating between the mutually exclusive imperatives of strict justice and peaceful unity.

The South African TRC is often praised as a success because it relaxed strict justice in order to make peaceful unity possible. Nelson Mandela made the politically prudent and personally sacrificial decision not to punish the perpetrators of Apartheid. Yet if this mandate relaxed the punishments of strict justice, it was not a simple exoneration. It still decreed responsibilities for its participants. In order to avoid prosecution, perpetrators had to speak the truth about their crimes and personally apologize to the victims and their families. As TRC leader Archbishop Desmond Tutu stated, "It is not about ... turning a blind eye to the wrong. True reconciliation exposes the awfulness, the abuse, the hurt, the truth.... It is a risky undertaking."[2] Reconciliation required letting go of strict justice, but it still demanded some form of satisfaction for crime.

The same is true of the Christian theology whose inspiration permeated the TRC. Christianity allows for forgiveness of human sin against God, but that forgiveness is not cheap. Just as the state demands satisfaction for crime in expletive justice, God requires satisfaction for sin. According to orthodox Christianity, Christ's passion and death is not merely a manifestation of his perfect love, but also serves as the satisfaction for human sin. Without Christ's sacrificial atonement for human sin, humans could not escape their criminal status in God's moral government, no matter how well they followed Christ's moral example.

Nonetheless, it is not self-evident exactly how Christ's death atones for human sin. Nor is it a small matter. One's approach to the Atonement implies an associated doctrine of justification and sanctification: the respective doctrines of how a sinful person gains the status of entry to heaven and of how one's sinful character is purified. It was the conflict over these very doctrines that turned the Protestant Reformation from a protest over clerical corruption (of which there had been many over the centuries) into an irrevocable split of the Western church – one that indirectly led to the carnage of the Thirty Years' War and the fundamental refashioning of political order in the Treaty of Westphalia.

Hence, an understanding of the foundations of political reconciliation – and indirectly of the Westphalian order – suggests an examination of the Christian doctrine of the Atonement. Such a study often begins with two main theories: the satisfaction theory of Anselm (subsequently developed by Aquinas) and the penal substitution theory of Calvin. Yet theology textbooks identify at least three other options.[3] One of these was also developed during the age of the Reformation, and it belongs to none other than Grotius. Grotius' theological corpus is hefty; it includes an early work detailing the commonalities among the various branches of Christianity, an apologetic treatise that would be published over 100 times in twelve languages, and a massive four-volume Biblical commentary to which he devoted his final decade. However, his Atonement theory was his most substantive doctrinal contribution, and it retains wide currency today within Arminian Protestantism, particularly in the Methodist church. Nonetheless, there has been comparatively little study of this "governmental" theory, even though political theologian Oliver O'Donovan has suggested it as "one of his most valuable theoretical contributions."[4]

When scholars today do treat Grotius' theology, they often read him as a modern liberal. Some base this on Grotius' historical-critical methods of Biblical interpretation. Others point out Grotius' lack of identification with any specific Christian denomination, or read into his work a sympathy for Unitarianism. Such readings dovetail with the standard political narrative of Grotius as a modern rights-based political thinker who carves out significant swaths of politically (and morally) indifferent permissions. Yet a closer look at Grotius' Atonement writings reveals a theory less possessive, individualistic, and economic – and more classically communal and political – than any of the alternatives. Government is not simply a value-neutral referee of private property claims, but a public practice calling for classical and Christian virtues. Indeed, this theory shows a governing God who responsibly (and charitably) preserves the concept of politics by prudently not exercising his right to the full.

Grotius' governmental theory brings to a climax his political themes of rights, prudence, punishment, pardon, and sacrifice. By exploring divine punishment through the lens of expletive and attributive justice, he illustrates the stakes involved in conceptualizing political (and human) existence according to one or the other. This leads to his fullest treatment of the relationship between civil and criminal law. By conceiving of sin and atonement through the latter, he emphasizes the public realm of politics over the private realm of economics. He deepens this public emphasis in his corporate conception of human action. Humans are most free not when they passively avoid violations, but when they actively carry out positive virtues. Grotius also emphasizes law as the context-attentive guidance of an active ruler whose display of internal virtue cannot be reduced to unchanging and impersonal propositions. Likewise, he emphasizes the ruler's classical political virtue of prudence not simply as the highest natural virtue but even as a divine virtue. It mediates not only between extremes of vices but between extremes of metaethics and metaphysics, deepening its literal centrality to human existence. Grotius' commingling of government and divine virtue also illuminates the importance of trans-political virtue in human government, while reciprocally directing politics ahead to an orientation point that it can never claim to fully instantiate. These governmental virtues are grounded in the historical acts of God the Son, a vision that can inspire humanity more universally than any theory of pure reason.

In sum, Grotius' Atonement theology most fully expresses the limits of expletive justice and most richly outlines the virtues of attributive justice. Here he most compellingly demonstrates the imperative of exercising rights responsibly. Here he most clearly explores his interplay between nature and free will, his balance between intrinsic and extrinsic motives, his unity of naturalism and voluntarism, and his orientation of the right toward the good. Finally, in this theory he most deeply shows how strict justice undermines its own realization and points toward its own transcendence.

Satisfaction Theory of Anselm and Aquinas

The doctrine of the Atonement is central to Christian theology, while also containing an implicit philosophy of law, punishment, and justice. All orthodox Christians affirm that humans have violated God's first negative command: "of the tree of the knowledge of good and evil you shall not eat, for in the day that you eat of it you shall surely die."[5] The penalty for breaking the law is death, traditionally understood not simply as bodily death but as eternal damnation of the soul.[6] Every person stands guilty of original sin and unable to rectify the situation by human effort. Christ announces good news: the hope of felicitous eternal life. His passion, death, and resurrection make possible this hope of salvation from eternal punishment. But how? What is the nature of human sin, and how does Christ's death substitutionarily make possible a release from its just punishment? As with many Christian doctrines, the answer was not immediately clear to the early church. Christians immediately affirmed Christ's work as atoning for human sin and thus enabling salvation, but did not explore its operative nature until later.

In the eleventh century, Anselm of Canterbury proposed to explain the mechanism through his "satisfaction" theory. This theory is sometimes called the "commercial theory," because it employs the language of debt and repayment. It begins with the classical framework of justice, defined as rendering to those what they are due. God's eternal justice demands that each person pay him constant and perpetual honour to the fullest of their ability, which is due to him because of his nature as the all-holy, all-powerful creator. However, when humanity sins, each person fails to render this honour, and thus incurs an unjust debt of honour. What is more, these demerits can never be fully repaid. One might repent and then attempt to provide as much honour as possible to God at that time, but such an action would only meet the minimum current requirements of justice. One can never accumulate a surplus with which to pay off the prior debt. As a result, humans must suffer eternal punishment in the debtor's prison of the afterlife.

Christ the Son also owes God the Father such honour, which (unlike sinful humanity) he perpetually does offer. However, Christ also goes beyond what he owes the Father: he humbles himself to be made in human likeness, and offers his innocent life on the cross. As a result, he earns an infinite storehouse of merits – a massive surplus on the ledger, so to speak. Christ renounces his claim on these merits, and God then graciously promises to apply them to the debt of the whole church, allowing it to pay off its collective debt of honour. By joining the church, each member can satisfy his individual debt to God. In other words, God the Son's love in suffering an undeserved death makes it possible for humans to return to a condition of justice before God the Father.

Aquinas builds on Anselm's conception by introducing another element to sin. Sin does not simply fail to pay honour to God, but also gains for the sinner unjust temporal benefits or pleasures. While God's eternal justice still demands that sinners make a belated payment of honour to God, his temporal justice also demands restitution: sinners must take on temporal pains equal to the pleasures they gained from sin. These temporal pains – known as penance – are assigned by their confessor on behalf of God. They may include abstinence, prayer, fasting, or other sacrifices. Hence, justice requires a sinner both to satisfy the eternal debt of honour, which Christ does on his behalf, and to provide temporal restitution, which the sinner voluntarily undertakes himself.[7]

Once the sinner has both accepted Christ's substitutionary death (in the sacrament of baptism) and completed his penance (in the sacrament of reconciliation), he returns to a state of grace. After all, God has promised these merits to those who fulfil these two conditions, and is now obligated in justice to provide those merits.[8] This allows the sinner to receive the other sacraments of the church, such as the Eucharist, through which God infuses grace into his being. This enables a gradual and ongoing process (or "synergism") in which God both justifies and sanctifies the Christian. Justification changes his forensic status from "sinner" to "just," and sanctification changes his nature from sinful to virtuous.

One can be sure that one's baptism is valid, because the priest oversees and carries out the entire sacrament. However, one may be less sure that one's sacrament of reconciliation is valid, because one must carry out the assigned penance oneself without the active oversight of the confessor. Naturally, this invites one to cut corners. Hence, one may die under a valid baptism (having satisfied the debt of honour) but an invalid reconciliation (not having fully satisfied the debt of restitution). In such a case, one may still satisfy the requirements of the latter after death, as God will assign temporal pains in purgatory and fully oversee their completion. Both eternal and temporal justice must be satisfied; however, temporal justice may still be satisfied after death.

Although people cannot offer God more eternal honour than he is due (thus necessitating Christ's role), it is nonetheless possible for Christians – reflecting

Christ's sacrifice – to perform temporal service that goes beyond what God demands of them. Such acts of piety might include pilgrimages, chastity, voluntary poverty, and monastic obedience, and are called "supererogatory" acts. In response, God grants to those individuals temporal merits, just as he granted to Christ eternal merits for his supererogatory suffering and death. Individuals can then renounce their claim on these supererogatory temporal merits and add them to the divine treasury of merits, just as Christ renounced his claim on eternal merits. When individuals do so, the church (God's temporal agent) may apply these merits to offset the demerits of another individual in purgatory. This is known as an indulgence, and it may enable the release of that soul from purgatory.[9]

The designation of "satisfaction theory" or "commercial theory" is quite appropriate for this approach. God's moral economy demands satisfaction of the eternal debt of honour, as well as the temporal debt of restitution. The penalty for sin is grounded in the objective order of the universe. A particular sin implies an equal and opposite penalty. Once it is paid, the debt is satisfied. Having been fully repaid, it ceases to exist, as though the debt never existed in the first place. Furthermore, merits are transferable from one holder to another, and continue to hold the same currency in the eyes of God. The crux of the matter is the satisfactory value of the merit possessed by the person.

Penal Substitution Theory of Calvin

By the sixteenth century, the satisfaction theory was widely accepted in the Western church. However, the Protestant Reformation would introduce an alternative. The Reformation began when Martin Luther protested the sale of indulgences to fund the reconstruction of St Peter's Basilica in Rome. Yet Luther did not simply protest this abuse of indulgences; he opposed the very practice itself, denying the church's power to grant them. This led to an even deeper critique of the church's prevailing approach to justification and – by extension – its theology of penance. He argued that if people must voluntarily undertake temporal penance, then they can earn salvation on their own merit. Likewise, he believed that if God is then obliged in justice to grant salvation to the penitent, then salvation cannot be a truly free gift of God.[10]

John Calvin echoed Luther's criticism in his systematic (and widely adopted) Reformed theology. In it, he presented his "penal substitution" theory, which justified Christ's substitutionary atonement without requiring freely willed human action or subjecting God to the demands of justice. According to Calvin, justice demands that humanity follow God's original command. If humanity violates that command, justice demands that humanity be eternally punished, as stipulated in the command. In other words, justice demands meeting one of two conditions: following the law or being punished. Human sin creates an injustice because neither is met. The sinner might repent and never again sin, but he cannot meet justice until he suffers the eternal punishment for his past sin. This conception of sin and punishment – much like the commercial theory – is grounded in the 'objective' order of things: sin against God demands exact satisfaction. However, this theory sees satisfaction not as repaying God the honour due him, but assuaging God's righteous punitive anger at sin. Calvin thus clearly conceptualizes God's moral polity not according to civil law but to criminal law.

Hence, this penal substitution theory produces a subtly but critically different understanding of justice. Both theories agree that individuals who have not provided satisfaction to God must suffer eternal punishment. However, the commercial theory argues that eternal damnation does not fulfil justice; justice obtains only when God is repaid his honour. Thus, the damned are never in a relation of justice to God. By contrast, the penal substitution theory argues that justice obtains upon infliction of punishment equal to the crime. Thus, in damnation, there is a sort of justice that obtains in the order of the universe.[11] Hence, in the penal substitution theory, justice does not require that Christ suffer and die for humanity, because the punishment of universal damnation would in fact exactly fit the crime. God the Son need not lovingly suffer and renounce his merits in order to satisfy God the Father's justice.

However, there is an alternative that also satisfies God's justice while enabling a more felicitous outcome. In God's earlier covenant with the Hebrews, he had allowed the sacrifice of a spotless and innocent lamb to bear the punishment that sinful individuals deserved. However, these sacrifices were not effective forever or for all. Fortunately, God chooses to remedy the incompleteness of the Hebrew sacrificial system by offering a new and lasting covenant with the universal church. Here the innocent Christ lovingly condescends to earth in the Incarnation. In his passion and death, God lays on him the punishment for all the sins of those whom God predestined to salvation. Christ's punishment exactly fits the crime committed by the elect. This substitutionary assumption of human punishment satisfies justice without the need to universally damn humanity.

Because Christ's punishment fully fits the crime, no further act of human effort (such as the restitution of temporal merits in penance or purgatory) is needed to gain salvation. As a result, there is no need for indulgences. Nor could any such penitential acts oblige God in justice to grant salvation. Indeed, man's original sin results in the total depravity of his nature, which prevents his acts from earning any merit. Hence, there can be no supererogatory acts by which to enrich the treasury of merits. Nor can merits be imparted to the elect; sinful humanity merits only punishment. Rather, Christ's sacrifice gains merit *for Christ*. However, God then charitably determines the status of the elect by looking past their nonmeritorious nature to the meritorious Christ, who is their interceder and mediator. The merit of Christ is imputed on behalf of the elect, who are now seen by God as though their status were meritorious. Christ's death alone is both necessary and sufficient to justify the elect, enabling their eternal salvation.

When Christ bears the eternal punishment of the elect, he does so for sins past, present, and future, including those sins that the Christian has not yet committed. Thus, future penance for specific sins is unnecessary for justification.[12] Rather, the Christian's status changes instantaneously from "sinner" to "justified" at the death of Christ, and is made effective at the moment in which the Christian professes faith in Christ's substitutionary death. Justification is not a synergistic co-operative process, but a "monergistic" forensic status that changes at one point for all time.[13] For this reason, there is no need for further infusions of grace (such as regular Eucharistic communion) in order to justify the person.

Yet God (and the church) may continue to impose temporal punishments. God may give sanctifying grace through these punishments, as well as through other elements of Christian practice, thus changing the person's nature. The more the person's nature is changed, the more he will automatically carry out good works that are externally indistinguishable from the sacrifices of penance that are designed to secure an extrinsic heavenly reward. However, from an internal perspective, only now will these acts be truly virtuous, because they will be undertaken solely out of gratitude to God, independent of any resulting reward. As with any true gift, they are now offered purely for their own sake.

In sum, the penal substitution theory also demands a specific satisfaction grounded in the order of the universe; the sin of humanity implies a specific penalty. However, while the satisfaction theory focuses on the necessary substitutionary merits arising from Christ's loving willingness to die, the penal substitution theory focuses on Christ's necessary substitutionary role as a bearer of punishment. Thus, Calvin dissociates the idea of merit from any freely willed participation in the creation and employment of merits, whether by Christ or humans. Furthermore, he eliminates the need for God to contingently oblige himself, through his promises, to distribute merits to those individuals who have carried out good works. Satisfaction is not a matter of restoring merits, but of taking on the punishment merited by crime. Whereas humanity merited damnation, Christ's loving assumption of punishment merited salvation. Hence, a merit is not a unit of account, but an action.

Example Theory of Socinus

There are clear and important differences between the satisfaction and penal substitution theories. At the root of each, however, is an effort to understand the unique (and essential) role of Christ in enabling salvation. Late in the sixteenth century arose a theory that departed from this orthodox belief. Faustus Socinus was shaped by the scepticism of the Italian Renaissance and espoused an anti-Trinitarian belief that denied the divinity of Christ. In 1574, he wrote *de Jesu Christo Servatore*, which put forward a theory of the Atonement that (unsurprisingly) denies the essential role of Christ's death for human salvation.

Socinus' Atonement theory is comparatively simple. He begins by conceiving of sin through a civil law framework. Sin against God is a debt, one that injures God as metaphoric economic creditor. As Grotius has earlier established, a creditor in civil law holds a possessive claim-right to a particular sum under concessive natural Right. As creditor, God can exercise this concessive natural Right by demanding payment – or by not demanding payment. According to Socinus, God does the latter. As a benevolent and generous divinity, God exercises liberality (Grotius' third concept in *de Aequitate*), writing off the unpayable debt of humanity. God requires no additional satisfaction for sin, as his decision has no implications for public justice; he could even make it arbitrarily. Hence, God the Father does not need God the Son to suffer and die. Christ need not provide merits that can be applied against the human debt of honour, because God need not be repaid. And Christ certainly need not suffer as substitute punishment to merit salvation, because God as private plaintiff need not (and in fact cannot) punish. Hence, Christ is merely an example of a perfectly virtuous person who willingly gives up his life for his beliefs. He may serve as an example of virtue, but his death plays no more special role in human salvation than that of any other Christian martyr.[14] Unsurprisingly, both Roman Catholic and Protestant Christianity considered the Socinian theory heretical.

Governmental Theory of Grotius

Private Civil Law and Public Criminal Law

Grotius pens his 1617 Atonement theory in deliberate opposition to Socinus; indeed, the book title concludes "*adversus Faustus Socinus.*" His primary aim is to defend Christian orthodoxy. Nonetheless, he surely would have welcomed as a by-product a public recognition of his Christian fidelity. Many Calvinists had impugned his orthodoxy since the 1610 Articles of Arminian Remonstrance, and his citizenship in the international 'republic of letters' that included some Socinians only further inflamed Counter-Remonstrant suspicion.[15] Grotius' concern would be vindicated by events following the book's completion. The 1618 Synod of Dort (whose convocation Grotius had attempted to prevent in *de Imperio*) would end tolerance for Arminianism by mandating the Counter-Remonstrant 'five points of Calvinism.' It would conclude with trials and death sentences for Oldenbarnevelt and Grotius, the latter of which would be commuted to life imprisonment in the Loevestein castle. Two years later, Grotius would escape in a daring plan orchestrated by his wife, hidden from his captors' watch in a chest of books. He would be immediately welcomed at the royal courts of Paris, but from that time on would be *persona non grata* among the Calvinists now firmly in control of his home country.

If Grotius' primary intention had been to safeguard his reputation and protect his political interests, he surely could have composed a short apologetic speech-act reaffirming the penal substitution theory. Yet instead he constructed a long ten-chapter theological treatise defending the essential role of Christ's atonement. What is more, he advances a theory that is orthodox but non-Calvinist – an odd way to curry Calvinist favour. Indeed, the catholic purport in the work's extended title – *A Defence of the Catholic Church Concerning the Satisfaction of Christ (SC)* – would have surely further inflamed many Calvinists, who – having only recently secured independence from the hated Spanish – held little love for things Catholic. Yet nor would Grotius gain allies from the opposing Roman church, as his defence of Christ's necessary role also departs from the satisfaction theory. Nor would he allay Calvinist suspicion by using extensive

Biblical citation, even though he had a great familiarity with Scripture (which would later enable him to write a massive four-volume Biblical commentary). Rather, his theory would defend orthodoxy by reference to an overarching classical theological-jurisprudential-metaethical account that both illustrates his overall themes and illuminates his political thought. Grotius' supposed attempt to safeguard his reputation was ill-conceived and nearly dead on arrival, but his effort to give content to a central Christian doctrine endures to this day.[16]

Grotius begins his work by first establishing that Christ does not remove the sins of humanity; he bears them.[17] The penalty is not removed but carried out. As he has said in an earlier work, "a sin committed against God cannot be expiated by any penalty less than that of death."[18] As this work's title testifies, Christ fully bears the penalty and provides objective satisfaction, thus enabling forgiveness and redemption. Second, Grotius affirms that in the Atonement, God does not change or overturn the law itself. The law still condemns humans as guilty, and it still commands punishment. In other words, the equity Grotius outlines in *de Aequitate* does not call for God to judge humans as innocent. Humans cannot raise a point of constitutional law in their defence; they have broken not only a particular law of God but have offended against the essence of morality. Christ's death does not change the original guilty verdict.

With these basics in place, Grotius then firmly situates the Atonement within the realm of criminal rather than civil law. Following the penal substitution theory, the Atonement is not the mere remission of a debt to God; it is the deliverance from punishment proper.[19] God's action in the Atonement is not that of a private economic creditor concerned with attaining his strict expletive due; it is that of a public governor concerned with punishing in a contingent and imaginative fashion.[20] This unique emphasis has led subsequent readers to entitle Grotius' doctrine the "governmental theory" of the Atonement.

In Grotius' earlier treatment of civil and criminal law, he outlined several differences between the roles of economic creditor and governor. The seventh (and perhaps most important) distinction is that the expletive claim-right of a creditor to collect on a debt is an end in itself. It has no public effect, and it does not point beyond itself. Thus, an individual creditor has an absolute or radical liberty to release a debtor from his obligation if he wishes. In fact, if the creditor does not actively pursue legal action, such a release will be the de facto result. The creditor's private choice to collect or waive the debt has no wider bearing on anyone other than the debtor. By contrast, the expletive right to punish is not a claim-right but a duty that points beyond the immediate harms it inflicts. A governor thus has no right to arbitrarily release a criminal, as in the liberality Grotius enumerates third in *de Aequitate*. Rather, the governor has a wider responsibility to promote not only the future good of the criminal but of the entire polity that has suffered from the offence. To use theological terms, sin is an offence of treason against the entire moral universe of which God is creator and governor. As governor, God cannot allow such treason to stand.[21] God must testify to the goodness of his moral order as an objective, universal, and immutable truth. This is precisely what Socinus has denied.

Natural Law and Positive Will

Expletive justice thus demands satisfaction for sin, which in Grotius' criminal law conception means punishment. He describes it as "properly natural" that a sinner be punished, as it necessarily follows "from the relation of the sin and sinner to the superior." Indeed, the "merit of punishment" is one of the five fundamental elements of expletive justice.[22] This truth of expletive justice is universal and necessary in the "simple" sense; it is inherent in the structure of creation.[23] As an element of immutable preceptive natural Right, even God is bound by it.[24] Thus, expletive justice both grants to God the right to condemn sinners, and compels him to punish wrongdoing. Any punishment, no matter how severe, fulfils expletive justice.

Fortunately, some matters may be "less properly natural," which is to say that they are "convenient," or "fitting" (for example, that a son should succeed his father).[25] This corresponds to fitting natural Right, which is "becoming" or "appropriate," and has a "harmony with nature."[26] While the strict justice of preceptive natural Right immutably 'confers' on God the expletive duty to punish, and permits the ultimate sanction, it does not mandate any specific punishment, because it cannot determine what would conduce to the multiple purposes of punishment. If God's will were purely arbitrary, he could impose any punishment. However, God's will is not arbitrary, even if its dictates are sometimes inscrutable to humanity (as befits an infinite God). Hence, God always exercises his permissive natural Right according to attributive (or governmental) justice.[27] Hence, while deontology grants God the right to punish, teleology guides his exercise of punishment.

In God's original command, of course, he has mandated eternal death as the punishment for original sin. However, this command is not simply a reiteration of a "simple" or "universal" natural law of expletive justice.[28] Rather, this command and punishment is a divine positive law. God used it to teach obedience to law in a particular time and place. We know this because Grotius adverts to it in *Adamus Exul (The Exile of Adam)*, an early dramatic dialogue illustrating the Fall of man that some have described as a precursor to the *Paradise Lost* of Milton (an acquaintance of Grotius).[29] When the serpent initially asks Eve to elucidate the reason why God outlawed the forbidden fruit, Eve responds that it is enough to know that God forbids it.[30] Much like God issued the positive laws to the Hebrews regarding the indifferent things of the Levitical code in order to teach adherence to law, God gave to Adam and Eve a positive command regulating a naturally indifferent matter in order to test their fidelity to him. (If the Hebrews were in the infancy of religion, Adam and Eve were in the infancy of human existence.) This positive law carried with it an (eternal) death penalty.

However, as a positive law, one grounded not in the nature of things but in the will of God, it is flexible. All positive law emanates from the will of the governor, which means that the governor can will to change it at any time. One hopes, of course, that the governor will do so according to attributive natural Right, as time and place suggest – and one can be sure that the divine governor will do so. In regard to divine government, it is "sufficiently fitting to nature" (or counselled by attributive justice) that the punishment need not have an "inflexible rectitude." An alternative punishment might be "very fitting to the nature and order of things."[31] As ruler of the moral universe, God is required by nature to punish sin, but not to punish violations of his positive law with eternal death.

The right to punish follows from God's naturalistic modality as creator, but the exercise of punishment follows from his voluntaristic modality as governor. God's will continues to be active after creation, and he carries it out according to the teleological purposes of punishment. Because God as creator of expletive justice demands punishment in general but does not demand eternal damnation in particular, God the governor greets the humanity condemned to eternal punishment with indulgence (the second of Grotius' categories in *de Aequitate*). He does not act as judge exercising equity; if this were the case, God the judge would have to determine that God the legislator did not mean for humans to be punished so severely, or that God did not intend for the category of "sin" to include the types of actions that humans have actually committed.[32] Nor is God's action one of liberality, which by its private nature is irrelevant to punishment. Rather, relaxation of punishment is an act of indulgence or pardon.

Prudence and Extrinsic Motives

Because God acts not as generous creditor but pardoning governor, he cannot act arbitrarily. Generosity is a private act between the giver and the receiver, which means that one can act generously for any (or no) reason. However, pardon is a public act between the governor, the criminal, and the entire moral order, which means that the governor cannot pardon at random. Because God is responsible for the good of the entire moral universe, punishment cannot be relaxed for any "light cause"; it must conduce to this overarching common good.[33]

Fortunately, in the moral universe governed by God, there is such a weighty cause – one that perhaps illustrates most fully Grotius' fundamental Christian balance between intrinsic naturalism and extrinsic voluntarism. If the full punishment of rights-based justice were to prevail, all humanity would know that there was no release from eternal punishment. Such a harsh course of action would still be just in the strict sense, because God had the right to punish to the full.[34] However, much like in the Book of Job, there would be no relationship between one's future actions or character and one's future felicity or misery. Those who mend their evil ways would suffer the same punishment as those who do not. As a result, humanity could have no reasonable grounds for hope. With the prospect of inevitable eternal damnation to follow, there would be zero extrinsic motivation to worship God and practice religion. In a postlapsarian world, humans suffer intrinsic weakness of will, and need at least some external motives to act virtuously. Thus, the cultivation of Christian virtues of faith, hope, and charity would inevitably fade away. Such practices would remain intrinsically good, and could perhaps alleviate some suffering on earth, but all gains would be lost at death, when the torments of eternal damnation would presumably be unmitigated by these virtues. Hence, while this heavy punishment would be strictly just, it would ultimately cause an irreparable rupture in man's consciousness of the transcendent and his practice of virtue.[35]

On the contrary, if God were to simply waive the punishment of humanity (as Socinus conceives), all humanity would know that release from punishment was guaranteed. Much like the holder of the Ring of Gyges in Plato's *Republic*, one could kill the king, seduce the queen, and usurp the kingdom while remaining equally immune from punishment as the just person. An absolute remission of punishment would eliminate the credibility of God's threat to punish, creating no external incentive for people to reform their ways. The complete absence of extrinsic punishments for noncompliance would again tempt sinful humans beyond what they could bear. They would inevitably fail to fear God, ceasing to worship or to develop virtue.[36] Ironically, the extreme of complete mercy would produce the same result as the extreme of strict justice: the end of religion and virtue. A blunt deontological principle of mercy would be equally problematic as one of strictly just punishment.

Of course, either inflexible justice or absolute mercy would address the past sins of humanity, by justly punishing them or by mercifully removing them. However, either option would undermine the entire future toward which God's moral government must aim. Hence, in order to guard the future integrity of the moral universe, God must very carefully mediate between showing his displeasure with sin and showing mercy. Expletive justice does not permit a complete elimination of punishment, but it does permit a relaxation.[37] Thus, God must exercise prudence to determine the appropriate balance between the overly heavy – though naturally just – punishment permitted by the law, and the imprudently generous exercise of mercy.

One conceivable way to do this would be to simply damn some people and not others. However, such an option would do little to link sin and virtue to future punishment and reward. Moreover, while the punishment of some people for the sin of all would partially realize the purposes of punishment, it would leave something to be desired. For one thing, the punishment of only some would allow others (still guilty) to escape punishment. More substantially, the punishment of finite human beings with a dignity far inferior to God would only feebly demonstrate the infinite seriousness of sin against the superior dignity of God (and his moral government). This class of options would technically fulfil expletive justice, because God could say that sin has been punished. However, none of them would realize very effectively the purposes of punishment.

Hence, God prudently determined that the best way to demonstrate the seriousness of sin while widening the possibilities of salvation was through the substitutionary punishment of Christ. The suffering and death of the infinitely perfect second person of the Godhead qualitatively demonstrates the seriousness of sin in a better fashion than punishing any number of finite humans.[38] It also demonstrates the ultimate punishment which will befall unrepentant sinners: "Man sees the price that matches his sins."[39] This encourages man's moral reform and points him toward the salvation of his soul. However, it also releases God from the need to condemn any person who joins the church and accepts Christ's substitutionary atonement. Contrary to the penal substitution theory, the death and passion of Christ is not an exact punishment on behalf of the sins of humanity; in Grotius' view the exact punishment would be the damnation of all people. Rather, it is a prudent substitution of punishment that actually demonstrates the seriousness of sin in a *superior* fashion than would the exact punishment. Hence, God demonstrated his governmental wisdom by allowing an alternative punishment out of regard for the common good of the universe. In relaxing the punishment, but not eliminating it entirely, God achieves an ideal prudential balance between mercy and punishment. The result is not the deontologically 'right' punishment, because it is not the exact punishment or even the only possible punishment, but it is instead the punishment that best instantiates the teleological good.

Charity and Intrinsic Motives

While Grotius' Atonement theory particularly highlights God's role as prudent governor, this does not in any way derogate from God's charity. Just as God the Father demonstrates the fullest possible exercise of prudence, Christ the Son demonstrates the heights of charity. The perfect Christ, the only one who did not deserve punishment, suffers punishment not only on behalf of those who did deserve punishment, but in fact for those who sinned against him.[40] Although one might metaphorically say that God had a duty to act prudently as moral governor, one cannot say even metaphorically that Christ had a duty to act charitably as redeemer.

This additional element of charity adds to God's moral government and further helps to foster future virtue in his subjects. God's prudence promotes religion and virtue by maintaining the extrinsic balance between motives of reward and punishment, while Christ's charity inspires religion and virtue by arousing in humanity the intrinsic love of God. Because God's prudence already provides the best possible extrinsic motivations, this addition of intrinsic motives for worship and virtue is never strictly demanded in expletive justice. However, a good governor will go beyond the demands of strict justice and give his subjects intrinsic reasons to follow the law. Subjects who not only fear punishment but also admire the greatness and goodness of the state (and the governor who embodies it) will be further inspired to work toward the ends of its government. This is particularly true if the governor has shown not only intellectual wisdom but personal sacrifice.

In both *de Satisfactione* and his early *Meletius*, Grotius immediately illustrates this principle with the vivid example of the ancient Greek lawgiver Zaleucus. As governor, Zaleucus mandated a "wholesome and profitable" law that adultery be punished by the loss of both eyes. Some time after decreeing this law, his own son was caught in adultery, and brought to face his father as executor of the law. Zaleucus first removed one of his son's eyes, and then plucked out one of his own. This personal sacrifice maintained the dignity of the law while preserving his son's capacity for sight. As Grotius describes it, "So he rendered unto the law the due measure of punishment, through a wonderful and equitable moderation, having divided himself between a merciful father, and a just legislator."[41] Zaleucus did not demonstrate liberality, and he did not merely demonstrate prudent indulgence; he demonstrated sacrificial charity. In doing so, he inspired in his own people intrinsic reasons to follow the law.

While intrinsic motives are never strictly necessary in politics, a polity that relies solely on extrinsic motives faces several challenges. The first is practical. An exclusive reliance on extrinsic motives of fear might be theoretically sufficient to compel adherence to law. However, no government – at least no human government – can ever perfectly enforce the law. Hence, while extrinsic motives are theoretically sufficient, in the human world they are practically insufficient.[42] The second and greater problem is not practical but philosophical, and threatens not only human government but also divine. If virtue must be freely chosen, it cannot be compelled. Extrinsic motives of fear (or reward) always mandate some measure of compulsion, because one follows the law not for its own sake but to avoid negative consequences (or gain positive benefits). By contrast, when Zaleucus and Christ show charity, they demonstrate the exact virtues that they hope to foster. In the case of Christ, the charity is not merely human but actually divine, and thus creates the greatest possible intrinsic motives of gratitude. One is not simply grateful to truth for existing and being good; one is grateful to a person for his sacrifice. The consequent motives of gratitude and love never compel one to act from without; rather, these motives sweetly inspire one from within. Moreover, one needs no specialized theological knowledge to comprehend Christ's charity; one only needs to know the historical account of Christ's action. Unlike the depersonalized intrinsic motives of philosophy, Christ's personal inspiration is available to the wise and the simple alike (at least once it is promulgated). Likewise, a ruler might provide detailed intrinsic reasons to follow a particular law, but these will only motivate experts in jurisprudence. On the contrary, his personal sacrifices to uphold and promote the law can inspire the entire polity.

In God's balance between mercy and punishment, God prudently maintains a balance between two extrinsic factors. This shows an Aristotelian mean between negative extremes that would eliminate the future possibility of religion and virtue. By now showing a sacrificial charity, Grotius' God maintains a balance at a higher level: namely, a prudent balance between the extrinsic fear of God and the intrinsic love of God. Again, one sees an Aristotelian golden mean, but with two uniquely Christian re-conceptions. First, on this higher level, both ends of the spectrum – namely, the fear and love of God – are not vices but virtues. Second, if Christianity particularly emphasizes the infinite nature of virtue, neither of these virtues (the fear and love of God) are ever fully attainable. By maintaining a balance that reflects the impossibility of a finite human being attaining both ends, Grotius ensures that the quest for both remains alive. The incompleteness of the possible worldly instantiation of both sustains the longing for both. In doing so, it ensures that worldly existence never loses sight of the Sun that is ultimately beyond this world, and yet gives life to this world as the locus of the journey toward that infinite fulfilment.

Forgiveness as an Active Virtue

While Christ's charity adds intrinsic reasons for religion and virtue, it also demonstrates the actively virtuous character of God's action in the Atonement. This is especially visible when we contrast Grotius' God as governor with Socinus' God as economic creditor. The Socinian view requires of God only passivity, because God simply need not collect on his debt. This position is consistent with the pre-Christian understanding of forgiveness as an indifference to harm, one that falls under the virtue of temperance.[43] God might determine that, in his perfection, he does not need repayment, and that would be the end of the matter.

Grotius' theory indeed has echoes of the idea that God does not require restitution. God does not *need* anything from man. The honour that humanity fails to render to God does not detract from God's 'stock' of honour. God is omnipotent and never lacks in any way; he is not concerned to be "made whole," as in private law. Grotius does not appeal to the satisfaction theory because sin does not exactly incur a debt to God.[44] However, God does exercise a governing responsibility toward the good of his created subjects.[45] Although God is self-sufficient, he does not simply ignore humanity, as an extraordinarily rich creditor would ignore a debt of 100 dollars. Rather, he actively seeks out humanity, more like a law enforcement officer volunteering for a particularly dangerous job of protecting.

Indeed, this pursuit is particularly costly for God. The good of humanity is best served by Christ, his dear Son, actively suffering a punishment that God judges as fitting. This emphasizes Grotius' Christian (rather than pagan) understanding of forgiveness as an active virtue, rather than a passive one. God does not simply display liberality, giving to humanity from his own infinite 'stock.' Rather, he acts with indulgence toward humanity, which requires the costly act of suffering on behalf of humanity. This is especially appropriate for Grotius, who considers as virtuous only those actions that follow from an active intention.

Teleological Good over Deontological Right

Grotius' Atonement theory does not eliminate the idea of justice, but rather highlights the limits of justice. Like Aristotle and Aquinas, Grotius understands strict justice as giving people what they are due. All humans have offended against God's infinite dignity, which means that strict justice suggests eternal damnation. People might want to exercise caution before demanding justice; they do not deserve as much as they might imagine. Fortunately, while God may have an imperfect duty in justice to punish, he does not have a perfect duty in justice to punish to the full extent allowed by his right. Indeed, one might metaphorically say that he has an imperfect duty *not* to punish to the full extent.[46]

Hence, the Atonement demonstrates the limits of a rights-based approach to moral reality.[47] God gave up his "properly natural" right to punish to the full, in order to promote the higher theological goods of faith, hope, and charity: a course of action "sufficiently fitting to nature." However, this action promotes not only theological goods, but even the basic provisions of expletive justice. Without this prudent preservation of a connection between unjust acts and punishment (and between just acts and reward), nobody would carry out even the minimal level of basic justice. If God simply governed according to expletive justice, he would undermine the performance of even the basics of expletive justice in his subjects. (This echoes God's prudent leniency in permitting divorce and revenge to the Hebrews, rather than imposing on them a strict law.) The deontology of expletive justice undermines its own instantiation in the world; the teleology of attributive justice saves it.

Hence, while Grotius does have a deontological right-based component to his theory (namely, that sin must be punished), it is not constituted in the usual element employed by most deontological theories of punishment: retribution. Rather, the deontological component arises from the normative (indeed, teleological) purposes of government: the demand to care for the moral well-being of subjects. This means holding together the balance between extrinsic punishment and extrinsic mercy; God must be fearful without being too fearful. The governor has a deontological duty to uphold his government, which means refusing to act according to deontological principles of pure justice or pure mercy. Moreover, by adding intrinsic motives from charity, God cares for his subjects not only through an ideal balance of extrinsic motives, but by a balance of extrinsic and intrinsic motives.

Comparison to Dominant Theories

Public and Private

Grotius' theory is not radically new. Indeed, in many ways it follows one or both of the two dominant theories: the satisfaction theory and the penal substitution theory. A comparison with these two helps to draw out both the continuities and the changes in emphasis. The first element of comparison is the beneficiary of the Atonement. Here Grotius echoes the satisfaction theory. In the penal substitution theory, Christ dies for those individuals who have been chosen by God to receive his grace. Although one may collectively refer to these individuals as 'the elect,' such a term represents a simple aggregation of individuals, rather than a necessarily corporate body. The term arises only from the fact that more than one individual has been predestined by God to salvation, rather than from the social and political character of one's relation to (and with) God. In contrast, together with the satisfaction theory, Grotius sees God's grace as being given to the church. Only secondarily – by believing in Christ, repenting of sins, and being received into the church – do individuals then partake of that grace.[48] Thus, Grotius declines to side with the individualistic nature of the penal substitution theory.

In fact, Grotius emphasizes the corporate nature of salvation to a degree that even the satisfaction theory does not permit. While the satisfaction theory requires one to join the church in order to partake of salvation, such deliverance atones for a matter of denied honour that is between the individual and God.

Although the merits are given to the church, they are effective for the demerits of individuals. On the contrary, the governmental theory requires one to join the church because the matter at hand is the sin of all humanity. The entire moral universe (or at least the church) must be saved from every individual's sin. This builds on Grotius' conception of God as governor rather than judge, as sin is not simply committed against another individual, or against God, but against the entire moral order created and governed by God. (Of course, in sinning against God's order, one is also sinning against God; unlike the Sun King, the creator of the sun can well and truly say, "*l'etat, c'est moi.*")[49] The nature of God's moral government is not simply a one-dimensional relation between the governor and each individual person. Rather, it is a multi-dimensional relation between God and individuals as well as between individuals with each other.

Thus, while the satisfaction theory sees Christ's death as providing merits to the church, which subsequently provides them to its constituent members, Grotius' governmental theory sees Christ's salvation as directly effective for the church as a whole. One might even perhaps argue that this renders the effect of original sin more intelligible: just as the effects of Adam's original sin spreads to all of humanity, so do the effects of every subsequent individual sin.[50] Christ's death saves people not only from their own freely willed sin, but also from the effect that others' sin has on them, including the greater propensity it creates in them to sin. Like the broken window theory, Christ replaces the window not only on behalf of the sinner who is responsible (and inadequate) to restore it, but also on behalf of the community's weakened sense of order. Christ's death is necessary not only for the sin of the individual, but also to show others (who have not committed that sin) that the grace for their potential sins is not cheap.

Satisfaction as Subjective Action, Not Objective Merit(s)

Yet while Grotius' framework invites a public component that calls to mind the satisfaction theory, his emphasis on punishment instead of restoring a 'quanta' of honour now builds on the penal substitution theory. This does not mean that he entirely rejects all objective components of Atonement. After all, he opposes Socinus by insisting that expletive justice demands satisfaction for human sin. Indeed, the Latin term *explere* is often rendered as "satisfaction." Moreover, Grotius has identified satisfaction as one of three interrelated purposes of punishment.

Yet while Grotius' theory calls for objective satisfaction, it does not call for instantaneous satisfaction. In his treatise on punishment, he described satisfaction as necessary in order that the victim not remain disrespected and thus subject to further offences. In the sacred realm, the 'victim' to be vindicated is the dignity and integrity of God's moral government, something that carries forward indefinitely. Hence, satisfaction must have ongoing effects. For this reason, it cannot be retributive, because retribution looks backward to cancel out an original crime. Rather, satisfaction looks forward as God's instrument to cultivate virtue in (and thus to redeem and sanctify) the souls of his subjects. Its content cannot be deontologically set out by expletive justice; it is a matter for attributive justice. Thus, even the expletive necessity of satisfaction points beyond itself, because satisfaction is an action rather than a thing.[51]

Grotius' rejection of a quantitative conception of satisfaction also departs from the satisfaction and penal substitution theories. In both of these prior theories, the penalty or punishment must have a mathematically exact correspondence to the sin. There is a clear, objective, and logically straightforward relation between the depth of human sin and the height of Christ's substitutionary satisfaction, one that is grounded in the strict order of things. Consequently, in both of the prevailing theories, expletive justice can fully account for the Atonement. The penalty cannot be relaxed, because all particular sins must be punished. For this reason, both theories employ the language of merit(s). Both imply, in their individual ways, the idea of a credit of account that must reach a certain condition before a person can be justified in God's sight. Sin implies an objectively discernible remedy or punishment – one that, once completed, will return the sinner to a state of justification.

Grotius, too, argues that there is a need for punishment; contra Socinus, he understands expletive justice to demand satisfaction. However, his expletive justice does not demand specific punishment for *specific* sins; it requires punishment of sin *in general*.[52] Hence, the punishment undertaken by Christ does not have a value exactly equal to that deserved by humanity (or at least by the elect). After all, there is no such thing as an exact punishment in the realm of crime (or sin), as though the crime could be undone by an equal and opposite crime. The idea of 'an eye for an eye' has been tried and found wanting, just as providing a victim with immunity to burglarize the home of a convicted burglar would be absurd. Even when a criminal completes a prison sentence, the idea that "justice has been done" often rings hollow. (This is even more of an issue when one seeks punitive damages for intangible wrongs such as "pain and suffering"). In Grotius' theory, there is no reckoning of merits, because no sin or punishment can be assigned a specific merit-value. Punishment is always symbolic and requires prudence.

Grotius further underscores the inability of punishment to correspond exactly to crime in his corporate conception of action. Sinful actions (indeed, all actions) carry on into the world on an ongoing basis. Their consequences are unpredictable, potentially infinite, and undoable. They do not cease simply because the divine or human governor makes the forensic proclamation that justice has been served; the law cannot chase them down and find them. For this reason, one can never assign a finite negative value to any particular sin, a value to which a specific punishment could exactly correspond. Satisfaction seeks not to undo actions but to redeem them.[53]

This leads Grotius to reconceptualize the term "indulgence." For Aquinas, an indulgence is effectively a quantity of positive merits that the church can apply to an individual debt of the same size. Yet Grotius rejects the idea of merits as units of account that an authority can disburse at its discretion. Rather, indulgence is a relational act of mercy. It is not a noun, but a verb. God does not grant an indulgence; he acts indulgently. Indulgence deals not with objects and their transactions, but with personal subjects and their interrelationships.[54]

Status of Justification and Action of Sanctification

Grotius' conception of indulgence as an action rather than an object carries implications for his concepts of justification and sanctification. Here his concept of justification follows the penal satisfaction theory in its monergistic character. The status of humanity changes instantaneously at the moment in time when Christ suffers the punishment; salvation is now a possibility. This status is made effective for the Christian in the moment in which he apologizes to God, professes faith in Christ's Atonement, and joins the church in baptism.[55] Indeed, in keeping with perfect nature of expletive justice, an apology is described in the perfect tense, which connotes instantaneity: not "I am apologizing," but "I apologized." Justification requires no further temporal penance or purgatory. Once human sin is properly punished, humanity is justified.

Nonetheless, Grotius' concept of sanctification seems to be more akin to the satisfaction theory. While justification occurs at a moment in time, its effects carry on into the future. Christ instantaneously satisfies God's need to punish, but the purpose of this satisfaction is to uphold the ongoing dignity of God's moral government in order to promote future virtue and prevent future sin. Thus, as in the satisfaction theory, Grotius also believes that the Atonement is effective both for justification and sanctification. Indeed, because Grotius does not have an explicit conception of the sacraments of the church in infusing sanctifying virtue, he seems to envision the Atonement as playing a particularly robust role in inspiring sanctifying virtue. It is true that this divine co-operation, in the form of Christ's death, is monergistic, taking place at one time. However, its effect is synergistic, in that it contributes to the sanctification of the church in countless ongoing future instances.

When Grotius suggests that Christ's action inspires human virtue rather than immediately possessing a person's spirit and supplying the strength for virtue, he reaffirms the free nature of virtue. People do not have a (sinful) nature that is wholly determinative of their acts. Their apparently virtuous acts are not merely a manifestation of Calvinist operative grace that bypasses the person's naturally depraved will. Yet if Grotius' belief in free will opposes the penal substitution theory, it also goes beyond the measure of free will implied by the satisfaction theory, because it rejects the concept of penance. For Grotius, the Christian is motivated simply by gratitude for Christ's sacrificial charity, and will thus carry out virtuous acts of penitence even without any immediate extrinsic reward (such as the return to a state of grace). The absence of external inducements allows these acts to be entirely (rather than only partially) free. Indeed, no amount of penitential acts could ever make one fit for heaven; God's standard is not one of neutrality or even perfection, but one of infinity. Hence, Grotius emphasizes the relevance of sanctification and virtue in salvation, and yet paradoxically implies that no amount of virtue is ever enough to compel God to grant salvation.[56] In other words, he harmonizes the concern of Anselm and Aquinas for freely willed virtue with the concern of Luther and Calvin for the radical gift-nature of the Atonement.[57]

Forward to Glorification, not Backward to Innocence

Grotius' forward-looking concept of justification also contrasts with the satisfaction theory and especially the penal substitution theory. In the latter, the Atonement looks backward to original sin, seeking to cancel out the status of sin. The satisfaction theory also looks backward, seeking to cancel out the debt of honour owed to God (although such justification is ultimately connected to a forward-looking sanctification). Both seem to portray Christ's death as looking back to remove the negative status of "sinful" from the church or the elect. In Grotius' approach, such justification appears to align with strict justice, because it returns one to a condition of objective *jus:* "that which is not unjust." It is as if one is returned to the Edenic state of innocence, in the infancy of the human race.

However, such a state of innocence is not the same as the state of glorification. It seems that justification would return one to the innocent status of "law-abiding."[58] However, Grotius has repeatedly reminded us that mere avoidance of law-violation does not equate to positive virtue. Mere perfect Aristotelian continence may allow one to avoid eternal punishment but not to attain eternal felicity. What is more, the deeds of violation-avoidance are external, but do not automatically signify a virtuous doer. However, God is not ultimately concerned with external acts but internal actors. Indeed, it costs nothing to an omnipotent God to change external consequences, which is why Grotius sees as unintelligible the demand that humanity satisfy a debt to God. On the contrary, the one thing an omnipotent God cannot do is to forcibly change a person's will, because this would make the person good at the cost of his humanity. These distinct paths of return to innocence and ascent to virtue correspond to distinct Grotian doctrines: justification (which permits remission of guilt), and sanctification (which cultivates righteousness).[59] The governmental theory of the Atonement is not merely concerned with the justificatory expiation of divine justice, but also its sanctificatory manifestation; its interest is not primarily retrospective, but rather prospective.[60] Ultimately, the work of Christ does not point backward to the Edenic state of innocence, but forward to the Heavenly state of glorification.

Divine Government as Personal

Grotius' emphasis on the growth of one's being, rather than the change of one's status, is a further contrast with the penal substitution theory. In the penal substitution theory, salvation appears to be binary. It is an either/or condition: a status outside of time. All of the elect are in the same fundamental state of the soul; so are those unfortunate ones not predestined for glory. There is no middle ground. On the contrary, Grotius' emphasis on sanctification means that the status of justification is only the beginning. It enables the process of sanctification, in which a person is actually changed over time. Every individual may be in a different relationship to God and his perfection.

Indeed, the person is not in a relationship to a status but a divine Person.[61] Grotius' conception of God as not only naturalistic creator but voluntaristic governor emphasizes God's free will and personhood. If God were reducible to the natural laws of creation, then his will would merely be the mechanistic executive of his nature; he would be unable to act contingently and prudently.[62] However, while God's nature is unchanging, his will is rational and capable of deliberation, and he thus responds to particular situations – and particular persons – in particular ways. This shows that Grotius' God is not simply a deistic creator, but a governor capable of personal friendship with his subjects. Thus, glorification is not simply an intellectual condition of having knowledge about God, but of actually knowing God in an existential sense.[63] Because the Atonement is intersubjective, it is political, not economic.

The forward-looking nature of friendship with God also emphasizes the impossibility of reaching completion in this world. One can never say that one's relationship with another subject is ever fully complete. Rather, the best that one could say is that the relationship continues to grow. The idea of completeness implies a finality that requires one – at the very least – to transcend time. Indeed, when one says that his or her relationship with another person is "finished," it does not imply that the relationship has reached its ultimate goal. Rather, it indicates that the only way to reach finality with another person is in death, when the personal subject has been reduced to a bodily object.

Political Implications

What do these theological concepts of corporate salvation, active indulgence, forward-looking sanctification, and a personal God have to do with politics? In a rare article dealing with Grotius' theology, Knud Haakonssen seems to suggest an answer: very little. In his reading, Grotius' community with God is unlike community with people, because the former is the realm of the positive virtues following from the "special moral intervention of God." He continues, "God's authorship explains the fact but nothing about the form of human sociability ..." In contrast, if my reading is correct, Haakonssen's account is accurate only in regard to the expletive pre-conditions for society. One can indeed have a society ruled purely according to the natural law of expletive justice, one without any positive or uncoerced virtues. Such a society is a recognizably human society; it operates according to principles of justice rather than the law of the jungle in which parties contend by irrational force. Yet while the fact of society comes from the natural law authored by God as creator, the form of human sociability – and the virtues required for a truly humane politics – come from a wider natural Right anchored in the person of God as governor. Mere human society is at least theoretically possible in the absence of substantive virtue. However, a humane politics requires a shared notion of human flourishing that is grounded in an account of the person, one that – recognized or not – derives from the person of God. This vision is discerned in the virtuous examples of persons who instantiate this vision, reflecting (consciously or otherwise) the freely willed actions of God in history – most notably the Incarnation and Atonement of Christ. Hence, while Haakonssen asserts that "the whole form of Grotius's argument is thus in effect to narrow down the [fact of human sociability] to a question of faith and to expand the [form of human sociability] to a quest for explanatory knowledge,"[64] the opposite may actually be true. One can know the formal and depersonalized fact of human sociability through the natural law that Grotius (in)famously declares to be knowable "even if we should acknowledge … that God does not exist." Yet the substantive and teleological content of sociability requires a virtue that goes beyond nature: in Grotius' words, it is not enough simply to "live in accordance with nature."[65] One can carry out acts that avoid offending against "nature," but true community requires virtuous intentions and character. As Alexis de Tocqueville would later suggest, a rights-based politics requires a religious virtue that cannot be compelled by politics if a rights-based politics is to survive.

Yet if these virtues transcend nature, Grotius chooses surprising examples by which to illustrate them. His paradigmatic this-worldly example of prudent and charitable sacrifice is that of Zaleucus – a pagan pre-Christian.[66] For all of Grotius' Christian inspiration, he seems exquisitely conscious of the need to speak on nonparticularistic terms. His apparent pagan illustrations of theological virtue suggest that he understands his theology to be relevant not only for divine but human polity. This should not surprise us, as Grotius' uniquely political conception of God as both charitable and prudent has already shown that his politics is relevant to his theology.

This governmental concept of the Atonement thus suggests several important implications for politics. Grotius' rejection of the language of merits as a divine unit of account casts doubt on the thesis that he reduces politics to the protection of property. If Grotius were fundamentally concerned with restoring possessions, he could have espoused the Unitarian Atonement theology of Socinus, one that Locke would later implicitly embrace. Had he been concerned to dispel Calvinist perceptions of supposed heterodoxy, he could have instead taken the debt metaphor of the satisfaction theory to extremes, unambiguously framing the honour owed to God as a possession to be returned. Yet Grotius not only criticizes the Socinian theory on the very grounds of its overly debt-related framework, but he also rejects the dominant views by implying that their objective language of merits is uncomfortably close to that of Socinus. Instead, he sketches a different theory that reaffirms the essential role of Christ in salvation without recourse to possession of merits or even to a mathematical correspondence between Christ's death and human sin. In doing so, he argues for the very limits of an 'objective' approach, viewing the Atonement through attributive justice rather than simply through expletive justice. Government, whether human or divine, is ultimately concerned with the prudent interaction of persons rather than the mere protection of possessions.

Moreover, Grotius' belief that the Atonement takes place on behalf of the church rather than individuals further suggests that he does not see politics as an aggregation of individuals. To be sure, individuals must consent to create the state just as individuals must choose to join the church. However, their participation in the common life of their polity (whether state or church) is what brings them toward the fulfilment of their personhood. Grotius' forward-looking reconception of satisfaction further substantiates this corporate reading. Satisfaction is not a matter of returning a possession, but of repairing the integrity of the entire moral order. Even though the state cannot forbid all actions, all actions impact the integrity of the polity.

For this reason, the health of the political order may require that individuals decline to exercise the rights that the state (rightly) protects. Subjects should not simply act as they wish within their rights, trusting in political institutions to channel self-interest or check ambition. They should ask not what their country can do for them, but what they can do for their country. Likewise, governors should not simply provide (extrinsic) incentives, or merely "run the economy" (in the current parlance). They should treat their office as public service and set a moral example. A governor should ask not what his office can do for him, but what he can do for his office – and thus for the people he governs.

This positive account of politics as transcending the mere prohibition of offences coheres with Grotius' metaethics. Grotius is often portrayed as opposing Aristotle's belief that politics promotes a full human life, and substituting a proto-Hobbesian stance that sees politics as merely securing property and person. In other words, Grotius' politics is often depicted not as educative, but as reliant on force and fear. This conception would imply an all-powerful voluntaristic God rather than a good God who indicates truth to the world in nature. Yet Grotius' careful balance between naturalism and voluntarism suggests that the practice of government should not simply rely on extrinsic fear of coercion. At its best, it should also inspire intrinsic devotion to its ideals. However, it must always be guided by the virtue of prudence that determines the appropriate balance between extrinsic and intrinsic motives, depending on circumstances. Good government mediates between fear of coercion and love of country and ruler. Polities with a better internal constitution should be governed with more intrinsic reasons than extrinsic, and vice versa. In Aristotelian fashion, Grotius seems not to aim for an ideal state, but for a best practicable balance.

When Grotius does accentuate God's voluntaristic modality as governor over God's naturalistic modality as creator, he does so not to emphasize God's arbitrary power to re-create nature (as it were), but to emphasize God's prudence and equity in fitting his good will to particular persons and situations. By depicting strict law as subordinate to prudential government, Grotius orders the faculty of making (*techne* or *poiesis*) toward the higher reality of doing (*praxis*). In the human realm, the act of founding (which parallels God's creation) makes possible the practice of government (which parallels God's government). A state constitution may set out ideals (analogous to the order of nature in creation), but its static nature struggles to guide the growth of a less-than-perfect polity.

In other words, law-making and even constitution-making are only a prelude to doing politics. They are momentary reifications of their maker's dynamic will that is frozen in time in propositional form.[67] These laws may be temporally first, but they are not ontologically highest, because they cannot express the fullness of moral reality. God's government is primarily one of parliamentary (or rather, executive) supremacy, with only very limited judicial review. Law confers the right to punish lawbreakers, but even a judge who interprets the law with equity may be forced to give an inappropriate punishment. For this reason, good government calls for the prudent exercise of indulgence and mercy that does not impugn the equity of the judge but appeals instead to a higher standard. This allows for a teleological rule that fulfils a regime of rights rather than sweeping it away. Grotius sums it up well in one pithy statement, cited (appropriately enough) from the Ancients. Referring to the Atonement, he says that pardon is "not according to the law, yet not against it; but rather, above the law, and instead of it."[68]

Conclusion

South Africa's Truth and Reconciliation Commission (TRC) has been hailed as a model of success, inspiring many countries to copy it. Yet such efforts elsewhere have often been disappointing. Frequently, they are seen to offer undeserved pardon to unrepentant members of unlawful regimes. To draw the theological analogue, they are seen as a form of Socinian 'cheap grace' that simply washes away the debts of the offenders without changing their character. What allowed the South African TRC to avoid these pitfalls? A primary reason was Nelson Mandela's willingness to consider participation in the TRC as full satisfaction for the crimes of Apartheid. As a lifelong political prisoner, Mandela had suffered as much as anyone. If even he could forgive his Apartheid captors, how could ordinary South Africans insist on punishing them to the full? Just as the divine Christ's suffering uniquely enables God to pardon humanity, Mandela's suffering made him uniquely able to inspire forgiveness among his people.

Grotius himself was a political prisoner of a quasi-theocratic ultra-Calvinist-inspired regime. Yet he never used his many works – including those he wrote behind bars – to punish his Calvinist opponents.[69] In the same way, he suggests that governors – and perhaps subjects – should prudently relax their right to punish if they want to preserve their rights-based order. This does not mean that the governor demands no satisfaction; indeed, the integrity of the moral-political order demands it. However, the form of satisfaction may offer grace to criminals, whether enabled by the substitutionary punishment of Christ or the willingness to own up to one's crimes in the TRC. In doing so, satisfaction then fosters a flourishing moral-political order and enables the criminal's possibility of hope – one of the greatest of the Christian virtues.

Grotius' Atonement theory thus illustrates many of his political themes. He rejects the existing theories that implicitly view the Atonement through expletive justice. While Grotius' governmental theory may begin with expletive justice, it ends with attributive justice. He grounds this account on his distinction between private and public law, or between debt and punishment. Grotius' exclusive use of a criminal law framework, rather than the implicit private law framework of Socinus (and perhaps even Aquinas and Calvin), leads him to reject the category of merits. By avoiding a quantitative unit of economic account, he emphasizes (public) politics rather than (private) economics. He deepens this emphasis by highlighting the social and political nature of sin (and of action in general) as an act against the entire moral-political order. Fittingly, he sees the Atonement as effective for the church rather than simply for individuals. Together, these point not to a possessive individualist with a minimalistic and anti-Aristotelian rights-based approach, but a thinker concerned with the common good and the naturally political purposes of humanity.

Beyond these political implications, Grotius' Atonement theory brings together many of his wider philosophical themes. The first is the coexistence of deontology and teleology and the ordering of the former to the latter. This is intertwined with the second: the dual modalities of God as naturalistic creator and voluntaristic governor. As creator, God expresses his nature by authoring five strict natural laws, one of which deontologically demands that wrongdoing be punished. As constitution-maker for the moral universe, God then voluntaristically decrees a positive command in Genesis affirming this right without qualification, forbidding sin upon pain of death. This creates the strongest possible incentive for his subjects not to break the law and thus to remain in an ideal condition, attaining their *telos*. God the governor may carry out this ultimate sanction on those who break the law; such is his right in strict justice.

However, when one person breaks the law, he does not simply offend individually against God. Rather, he tears the fabric of the entire moral polity, undermines the dignity of God's law, provides incentives for others to offend, and instantiates a diabolical chain reaction in which others' social needs can now be fulfilled only by joining the ranks of the criminal.[70] God can justly condemn the original sinner and the inevitable multitudes who follow. However, such punishment does not allow criminal humanity any hope of re-entering the path toward their *telos*, because the severity of its permanent exile eliminates any incentive (and thus hope) of attaining future virtue. While universal damnation conforms to right, it is not the best punishment. Deontology thus undermines its own realization; violators of right, having lost their innocence, are now incapable of innocence, and will continue to violate right.

Yet nor can God simply pardon without any punishment: deontology demands punishment of some sort because its complete absence would absolutely disincentivize future virtue and thus guarantee future crime. Such everlasting punishment in the hereafter would be a uniquely human (rather than animal) punishment: its uniquely human duration (which transcends physical existence) would correspond to its uniquely human offence (which transcends physical damage). Indeed, this punishment would correspond to man's uniquely human capacity for deontological reason. However, it would not be a humane punishment, because it would not promote what is highest in humanity, nor correspond to man's teleological standard of action. For this reason, God the governor steps into this closed system of strict law and punishment. By exercising his personal free will, he pardons violators from exile and reopens the path to innocence. Deontology thus paradoxically seems to demand that one not punish according to the deontologically simple extremes of absolute punishment or absolute mercy; it points to its own transcendence.

The teleological call to relax the law of punishment illuminates a third theme: law points toward politics. Law is effective in setting an ideal and unchanging standard, but it can be truly effective only for agents lacking the free will to break it. In the non-ideal world of human existence, it is only a tool to advance a higher good, and ought to be altered when its ahistorical dictates fail to promote this good in a particular circumstance. However, only a personal governing ruler could alter it. This builds on the second theme that naturalism and voluntarism are ultimately unified in God. As governor, God issues positive commands whose binding force arises from his power to enforce them. However, the content of these commands is not morally arbitrary. Rather, they suit the purposes of government that inhere in God and that he makes as creator.

God's relaxation of punishment leads to the fourth wider theme: that prudence must be actualized in a person, because it cannot be defined but only illustrated. Grotius uniquely places prudence as coequal with charity at the centre of God's character, as God deliberates over a punishment that will best serve the common good of the entire moral universe. The result is a golden mean between the mathematically deontological extremes of universal condemnation and absolute mercy – one that demonstrates the seriousness of sin while maintaining a possible link between virtue and reward. God cannot deontologically mandate such a prudent relaxation of punishment as deistic creator; he must prudently determine it as Christian governor. Indeed, this prudence requires that God the Son enter into human history in human form to display the charity that is a requisite part of God's prudent plan.

The charitable action of God the Son also overcomes the limitations identified in the fifth wider theme: that deontology can protect only a minimum standard of violation avoidance in the realm of objects. Although the impersonal dictates of God as lawgiver of natural religion can outlaw wrongdoing, the moral-political life is more than the nonviolation of an impersonal legal code. Rather, it is the active instantiation of positive virtues. For this reason, the heights of God's charity are shown not in his legal prohibitions but in the personal actions of Jesus Christ in history. This points to a sixth theme: only God as personally charitable bearer of punishment can act in a mode of inspiration rather than compulsion. The extrinsically coercive mode of legal reward and punishment acts on people, treating them as objects. Yet the moral life is not simply adherence to a set of externally licit actions but the internal re-orienting of a soul to voluntarily choose the good. God's mode of inspiration preserves the free will of subjects while inspiring them to freely choose positive virtue. In theological terms, God's goal is not simply justification, which redresses damages and returns his subjects to a past innocence, but sanctification, which fosters (positive) participation in his divine reality. God's (natural) virtue of prudence makes possible the former, but God's (supernatural) virtue of charity makes possible the latter. Natural justice thus points toward the higher theological virtues of faith, hope, and charity. This develops Aristotle's teleology of prudence, by adding to it a charity that alone can truly inspire. Aristotle's *spoudaios* may set a high example to his countrymen, showing them a worthy path if they wish to attain to the same extrinsic honours. However, only Christ can set the fullest example, inspiring a higher path out of intrinsic gratitude for his example. Indeed, if perfection exists outside time, it can only be known to the human world if the perfect God enters into time from outside it – something that the *spoudaios* could not do if he wanted to (and would not do even if he could).

In conclusion, it is worth revisiting the observation that Grotius conceptualizes the Atonement through attributive justice in a way that the satisfaction or penal substitution theories do not, because it points to his understanding of nature and grace. What Grotius describes as "properly natural" or "necessary simply" is not the highest element of his thought. Nature itself, and the natural religion that is part of natural law, allows humanity to know the moral law. However, its punishments for breaking the law are unyielding in their strict justice, giving sinners their just desert but undermining any prospect of reward for future virtue. This points to Grotius' seventh and final wider implication: while natural religion and strict justice are theoretically coherent, they tend to undermine the likelihood of their own practical realization. Although Grotius holds both natural philosophy and pre-Christian religion in high regard, he argues that both call for a subsequent fulfilment that neither can itself bring forward on its own terms. For this reason, Grotius writes that "any religion has become obsolete which does not show the way to remission and reparation of sins."[71] This may explain why he words his impious hypothesis carefully: secular natural law would have only "a degree" of validity if one did not acknowledge God's existence. Grotius' natural law – known even to impious atheists – points to natural religion, and natural religion then points to the grace of God. In other words, nature points to a Creator-God, but a Creator-God is ultimately irrelevant to human action without a Redeemer-God who enters into nature to transform it. Nature points beyond nature.

In the same way, politics also requires something beyond politics. The analogy between theology and politics is admittedly imperfect, because politics has no comparable conception of original sin, and the political ruler lacks the perfect moral rectitude of the divine governor. Nonetheless, it is accurate enough, because crime against the political order – cosmic or temporal – produces the same result. Unlike debtors (or tortfeasors), expletive justice provides no way for sinners or criminals to undo their acts against the dignity and integrity of the political order. Once crime punctures the neat system, the impersonal law struggles to guide a diseased polity toward health. It works in (ideal) theory, but not in (non-ideal) practice. As long as crime remains a realistic possibility, the political order will struggle to sustain itself according to purely strict nature. Ultimately, justice is not enough.

Notes

1 See, for instance, Larry May, *After War Ends: A Philosophical Perspective* (Cambridge: Cambridge University Press, 2012); Colleen Murphy, *A Moral Theory of Political Reconciliation* (Cambridge: Cambridge University Press, 2012); Daniel Philpott, *Just and Unjust Peace* (Oxford: Oxford University Press, 2012).

2 Desmond Tutu, *No Future Without Forgiveness* (New York: Doubleday, 2012).

3 See, for instance, Millard J. Erickson, *Introducing Christian Theology*, ed. J. Arnold Hustad (Grand Rapids, MI: Baker Books, 1992), 243.

4 Oliver O'Donovan and Joan Lockwood O'Donovan, "Hugo Grotius," in *From Irenaeus to Grotius: A Sourcebook in Christian Political Thought* (Grand Rapids, MI: Eerdmans, 1999), 790.

5 Genesis 2:17, New King James Version.

6 Hugo Grotius, *Defensio fidei Catholicae de satisfactione Christi adversus Faustum Socinium* (hereafter *SC*), ed. Edwin Rabbie, trans. Hotze Mulder (Assen, NL: Van Gorcum, 1990) 1.35, 110–13. Quotations are customarily taken from Hugo Grotius, *Defensio fidei Catholicae de satisfactione Christi adversus Faustum Socinium (A Defence of the Catholick Faith Concerning the Satisfaction of Christ: Against Faustus Socinus)* (London: Printed for Thomas Parkhurst and Johnathan Robinson, 1692), and quotations from Chapter 2 are taken from Hugo Grotius, *Defensio fidei Catholicae de satisfactione Christi adversus Faustum Socinium*, trans. Oliver O'Donovan and Joan Lockwood O'Donovan, in *From Irenaeus to Grotius: A Sourcebook in Christian Political Thought* (Grand Rapids, MI: Eerdmans, 1999). Some translations may be the author's own from the Latin original.

7 Of course, he can only do so with the help of God's co-operative grace.

8 God is not naturally obligated through preceptive natural Right but positively (if unchangingly) obligated through his freely willed divine positive Right.

9 *Catechism of the Catholic Church*, Revised ed., trans. Geoffrey Chapman (London: Burns & Oates, 1999), Secs. 1471–79, 331–33.

10 An adherent of the satisfaction theory might respond that human free will is a necessary but insufficient condition for the works that lead to salvation. Thus, while works – on some level – lead to salvation, it is inaccurate to say that works done by human free will apart from grace lead to salvation.

11 To put this another way, the satisfaction theory argues that justice must be connected to a teleologically good outcome, while the penal substitution theory appears to argue that justice can be separated from goodness and virtue. (Of course, the latter sees God as choosing to act according to a goodness and virtue that transcends justice, rather than acting in a way that enables the realization of justice.)

12 Indeed, even to talk about specific sins is somewhat irrelevant from the Reformed understanding of justification. Because man's nature is corrupted by original sin and is totally depraved, all actions flowing from that nature are automatically sinful.

13 Of course, in order to participate in this justification, the individual must be baptized and believe. However, God foreknew who would do so, and provided justification on their behalf.

14 For a fuller description of Socinus' position, see Grotius, *SC*, ed. Parkhurst, 1, 44–49. Socinus sees the effect of Christ's death as displaying a supreme example of God's love for us. This position is similar to Peter Abelard's moral influence theory.

15 Henk J. M. Nellen, "In Strict Confidence: Grotius' Correspondence with his Socinian Friends," in *Self-Presentation and Social Identification: The Rhetoric and Pragmatics of Letter Writing in Early Modern Times*, ed. Toon Van Houdt (Leuven: Leuven University Press, 2002), 227–46.

16 In particular, the governmental theory has gained wide currency in the Methodist church.

17 Grotius, *SC* 1, 16–19.

18 Hugo Grotius, *Meletius*, ed. and trans. Guillaume H. M. Posthumus Meyjes (New York: Brill, 1988), 45, 117.

19 Grotius, *SC* 5, 134–42.

20 Ibid., 2.1–2, 815. This distinction also relates to the two different forms of *dominium*: sovereignty and ownership. Such might be the subject of an interesting study on Grotius, comparing him to other thinkers who emphasize ownership in politics.

21 Ibid., 2.3–5, 816–17; 2.13, 819; 5, 125.

22 Hugo Grotius, *The Rights of War and Peace*, ed. Richard Tuck, from the Edition by Jean Barbeyrac (hereafter *DJB*) (Indianapolis, IN: Liberty Fund, 2005), Prol.8, 85–86.

Citations from *DJB* are occasionally taken from Hugo Grotius, *De Jure Belli ac Pacis (The Law of War and Peace)*, trans. Francis W. Kelsey, intro. James Brown Scott, Carnegie Classics of International Law, No. 3, Vol. 2 (New York: Bobbs-Merrill, 1925), or from this author's own translations from the Latin.

23 Grotius, *SC*, 3, 85. In other words, there must be satisfaction for sin. Grotius also emphasizes this point in his *Adamus Exul*, or *Exile of Adam*. There the serpent tempts Eve by arguing that if she should feel regret after tasting the fruit, surely she could easily return to God's graces; after all, a good God should be an obliging God. By putting this implicitly Socinian argument for 'cheap grace' in the mouth of the serpent, he portrays it as diabolical. See Hugo Grotius, *Adamus Exul (The Exile of Adam)*, trans. Barham (London: Sherwood, 1839), 44.

24 Hugo Grotius, letter to Willem de Groot, 18 May 1615, in Herbert F. Wright, *Some Less Known Works of Hugo Grotius* (Leiden: Brill, 1928), 208–10.

25 Grotius, SC 3, 85.

26 Grotius, letter, 18 May 1615, in Wright, 208–10.

27 Grotius, *SC* 5, 122. Of course, there are a small number of principles – the fundamental principles of nature – that may be known as unchangeable laws.

28 Ibid., 3, 85.

29 See, for instance, Elizabeth Oldman, "Milton, Grotius, and the Law of War: A Reading of *Paradise Regained* and *Samson Agonistes*," *Studies in Philology*, Vol. 104, No. 3 (2007), 340–75.

30 Grotius, *Adamus Exul*, 29.

31 Grotius, *SC* 3, 87.

32 Ibid., 2.3, 816.

33 Ibid., 3, 87.

34 One might also suggest that there would be a mathematical balance between the sin committed and the punishment given, due to the infinite crime of original sin.

35 Ibid., 5, 116.

36 Ibid., 3, 81. Humans need not obey God solely out of fear; the further their sanctification, the more they will obey out of love. However, their continuing imperfect nature requires a healthy dialectic between obedience from love and obedience from fear, and the latter requires the credible threat of punishment.

37 Ibid., 6, 152.

38 Ibid., 5, 117, 121.

39 Grotius, *Meletius* 47, 117.

40 Grotius, *SC* 3, 88.

41 Grotius, *SC* 4, 108–09; Grotius, *Meletius* 48, 117–18.

42 This is an obvious challenge for Hobbes.

43 Montague Brown, "St. Thomas Aquinas on Human and Divine Forgiveness," *St. Anselm Journal*, Vol. 6, No. 2 (Spring 2009), 1–8.

44 In fairness to Anselm, the satisfaction theory conceptualizes the honour to God as an activity that humans render to God, not a possession on God's part.

45 See Grotius, *SC* 6, 134. Sam Storms thus argues that Grotius sees the final cause of the Atonement as ultimately external to God. Instead, the final cause consists in what the good of the moral universe (contingently) requires, rather than what the nature of God demands. As he says, "although God can remit the penalty of sin without satisfaction [to himself]," according to Grotius, "he cannot do so in view of the welfare of the created order." This is a perspicuous observation, but it seems to reject the possibility of an outward-looking concept of satisfaction based on the other-oriented character of Christian love. See Sam Storms, "Grotius and the Governmental Theory of the Atonement." www.enjoyinggodministries.com/article/24-grotius-and-the-governmental-theory-of-theatonement/, retrieved 20 July 2016.

46 Grotius, *SC* 3, 83–84.

47 This serves as a counter-point to Stephen Darwall's argument that moral rights are incompatible with eudaimonism, and that Grotius imports a rights-based paradigm not only into politics but into morality. See Stephen Darwall, "Grotius at the Creation of Modern Moral Philosophy," *Archiv für Geschichte der Philosophie*, Vol. 94 (2012), 296–325.

48 See Grotius, *Meletius* 50, 118.

49 Grotius thus has a rich conception of the idea of a sin against nature. This echoes Grotius' earlier justification of punitive war against countries that display impiety against natural religion.

50 In this sense, it would be compatible with the Eastern Orthodox doctrine of ancestral sin, which argues that humanity inherits from Adam and Eve not the guilt of sin but the infirmity that leads to death. Adam and Eve's descendants are not inherently responsible for bringing the plague (although they may through their own choices come to share this responsibility), but they nonetheless suffer its effects.

51 Even those who have given even cursory study to *de Satisfactione*, such as Christian Gellinek (in his *Hugo Grotius* (Boston: Twayne, 1983)), often read Grotius as denying the necessity of satisfaction. This is likely because of Grotius' complex conception: his book on the necessity of (objective) satisfaction actually vindicates (subjective) relaxation of punishment.

52 Indeed, according to Grotius, this is what enables the possibility of substitutionary punishment. See Grotius, *SC* 4, 101.

53 Hannah Arendt, *The Human Condition*, 2nd ed. (Chicago: University of Chicago Press, 1998), 231–33, 236–39.

54 Grotius' use of the term "merit" is closer to that of Calvin, who argued that humanity merited death, while Christ merited God's favour. However, Calvin appears to see an exact equivalence between the two; Grotius does not.

55 Grotius, *SC* 6.16, ed. Rabbie, 196–97.

56 This does, of course, raise the question of the 'standard' for admission to eternal paradise. Neither the justification of Christ's substitutionary punishment nor the sanctification of the freely willed virtue it inspires seem to be individually sufficient.

57 Grotius does the latter not by denying the co-operation of human will, but simply by arguing that because justice could have been served through universal damnation, justice did not compel Christ's action. Thus, it can be conceived as a pure gift of grace.

58 The penal substitution theory does assert that one is simultaneously made innocent and made fit for heaven, but Grotius would seem to argue that each requires a different mechanism.

59 Grotius, *SC* 1, ed. Parkhurst, 47–48.

60 Contra Sydney Cave, *The Doctrine of the Work of Christ* (London: Cokesbury Press, 1937), 177. Given that Grotius devotes a chapter in *de Satisfactione* to the subject of expiation, he would likely reject Cave's characterization.

61 Of course, this is an incomplete description, as seen in Grotius' emphasis on the corporate nature of the Atonement.

62 See W. G. T. Shedd, *Dogmatic Theology*, Vol. 2, 3rd ed. (New York: Charles Scribner's Sons, 1891), 355–58. In such a case, if God's nature includes both punishment and mercy, which one would apply?

63 Grotius might argue that this friendship with God is not dependent upon restitution of objects, as objective factors can never 'add up' to subjective growth; true friendship cannot be bought.

64 Knud Haakonssen, "Hugo Grotius and the History of Political Thought," *Political Theory*, Vol. 13, No. 2 (1985), 249–50.

65 Grotius, *Meletius* 86, 132.

66 Nelson Mandela is another example of statesmanlike forgiveness from someone who was not an identifiably orthodox Christian.

67 Grotius, *SC* 3, 83.
68 Ibid., 5, 121–22. See also Grotius, *Meletius* 50, 119.
69 Maria Rosa Antognazza, "Introduction," in Hugo Grotius, *The Truth of the Christian Religion*, ed. and intro. Maria Rosa Antognazza (Indianapolis, IN: Liberty Fund, 2012), xviii.
70 See Grotius' *Adamus Exul*, 39, in which the innocent Adam knows God's law but is undone by the ties of conjugal affection to postlapsarian Eve; his need to know human society – rather than to stand apart as its permanent judge – overwhelms his knowledge of the Good.
71 Grotius, *Meletius* 43–44, 116. He continues, "unless such a means [of forgiveness] is found there will be no religion at all."

9 Transcending Natural Rights, or Rethinking the Foundations of Modern Political Secularism

Grotius and the History of Political Thought

The roots of natural justice, as well as the value and limits of political institutions in realizing it, begins in the ancient world. Plato inaugurates this tradition by describing how political justice requires a particular formal ordering of society, with the philosopher-kings as rulers. Aristotle puts forward a more detailed study of political justice, which he divides into "arithmetic" and "geometric" justice. With arithmetic justice, he acknowledges the importance of restitution of goods. This form of justice is concerned with the procedures by which one acquires an object. Its relevant parties are private individuals, and its associated reason is quantifiable and calculative. Aquinas renames this category "commutative justice," but largely follows Aristotle in his understanding. It is the justice of objects; it is transactional, or procedural; and it is private rather than public. Aquinas is also enamoured of the idea of law, and of possibility that history may converge on universal truths. Thus, he endeavours to cast natural Right in terms of propositional laws wherever possible. While he does not deny the place of virtue, it is sometimes overshadowed by the Roman law conception of *jus* as corresponding to external states of being.

Many observers have argued, explicitly or implicitly, that this commutative justice, shorn of any reference to extra-political justice, comprises the whole of justice for Grotius. Indeed, Grotius' expletive (or "strict") justice emphasizes external goods and the procedural nature of their just resolution. He also emphasizes the potential universality of its associated laws, grounded as they are in pure reason, and draws out the possibility of perfection in their resolution. Indeed, in recasting this conception of justice as "expletive justice," Grotius actually develops the tradition. Expletive justice discerns the laws of nature inherent in God's creation, even if the reasoner does not acknowledge any divine origin. This corresponds to the first element of human nature that separates man from animal: the use of discursive reason to know and act according to general principles. Its static nature makes it amenable to systematization, with simple parameters that are clear to all, rather than complex subtleties properly interpreted only by the wise and prudent. The backward-focused nature of rectification also admits of perfect realization, fully undoing the injustice. Grotius also draws out the negative nature of its prescriptions, which aim at neutrality and demand only the absence of injustice. All are thus capable of meeting this mandate; none can claim that its dictates violate individual conscience. Indeed, because expletive rights are universal, they can be expected of (and thus coerced in) all people. They are suitable to a pluralistic world, bypassing the need for agreement on a teleological vision of human flourishing.

However, the classical tradition argues that there is more to justice than simply this. Plato's formal tripartite ordering of society mirrors the deeper reality of the soul. This political ordering requires rulers whose souls are able to participate in the substantive (and transcendent) justice of the Good. Because justice is located in the soul, this right by nature is fundamentally personal, and rational propositions of natural law are inadequate to its full truth. Likewise, the best kind of rule is not simply carried out according to legal formulations, but flows forth from the virtue of the ruler. Aristotle's concept of geometric justice lowers these lofty aims, but still emphasizes the fundamentally political character of human existence. Universal laws are inadequate to bring about justice, and a ruler must use equity to discern the good in particular situations. Likewise, governors require a knowledge of the internal character of the person(s) involved. This leads to a substantive outcome of rightness, not a simple ensuring of correct procedures of acquisition. Aquinas renames this category "distributive" justice. He acknowledges many of these Aristotelian themes, while developing the epistemological place of history in discerning them. He also recaptures Plato's concept of transcendent ideals in the supernatural Christian realm to which the natural realm of politics is ultimately ordered.

Few observers have seen in Grotius much (if any) room for this conception of justice. However, while Grotius' expletive justice may be the beginning, his attributive (or "wider") justice is the end. Like distributive justice, attributive justice is fundamentally concerned with the internal person rather than external objects. Its reasoning requires the practical virtue of prudence, as it considers particular situations and persons; universal propositions are inadequate. Indeed, it looks to the practice of politics rather than to the insensitive and impersonal dictates of law. Its emphasis on situational knowledge follows Grotius' empirical emphasis on history as a source of knowledge. Moreover, while Grotius does not align the public/private distinction with his categories of justice, he does re-emphasize the political nature of existence. What is more, Grotius' use of the Greek term *axian* to name attributive justice confirms its axiological character, which more generally points to Aristotle's final causality.

Beyond this, however, attributive justice also develops the tradition of distributive justice in a new and (appropriately) imaginative fashion. Grotius grounds his attributive justice in the historical element of his epistemology; it is not explained in treatises but manifested in the historical record of attributively just actions. This element of justice follows from the voluntaristic modality of a theistic God, who enters the otherwise immutable natural order to act in time – most obviously in the Incarnation. This grounds Grotius' other unique element of human nature: the imaginative ability to envision the contingent future and to judge better and worse outcomes. Grotius thus draws out Aristotle's emphasis on prudence by departing from Aristotle's overly mathematical terminology of "geometric" justice. He also particularly highlights the forward-looking nature of a political justice that seeks not simply to redress past injustices but to work toward developing future political virtue. Likewise, his emphasis on virtue over law points toward realizing positive goods rather than merely avoiding negative violations encapsulated in propositional formulations. Justice is not simply a status that one can possess; it resides in the character and subsequent actions of just souls. Grotius also emphasizes the necessarily imperfect character of attributive justice, as the indefinite virtues that it requires are never perfectly realizable. Most importantly, attributive justice is not merely a parallel category for Grotius; this "wider" justice is actually the higher of the two types of justice. While strict justice sets out the preconditions for procedurally just action, attributive justice governs the use of these expletive rights.

Perhaps because of Grotius' emphasis on the illustrative nature of history relative to systematic exposition, he does not always make his organizing structure of expletive and attributive justice especially clear. However, this distinction between expletive and attributive justice undergirds several important elements of his political thought. The first is his theory of state formation. Expletive justice grants to all people the modern-sounding right to choose whether or not to enter political society. However, where expletive justice is agnostic about exercising this liberty, attributive justice counsels the institution of government, because it conduces to the social and political ends of human life. Civil society then provides both coercive extrinsic reasons to follow natural Right, as well as adding intrinsic knowledge of natural Right. Moreover, as the locus of prudence, it allows for the discernment of fitting natural Right, which enables people to discover elements of natural Right unavailable to them outside political society. Hence, the right of consent (or refusal) points to the responsibility to use it – and to use it well.

Expletive and attributive justice then continue to shape the subsequent contours of governing authority. Expletive justice protects the possibility of positive law by virtually eliminating the right of rebellion. However, the expletive status of governing authority (or legal sovereignty) points toward the attributive practice of rule (or domestic sovereignty). However, Grotius' taxonomy of rule also shows that others may exercise rule inasmuch as they are more knowledgeable about natural Right than the governor. In fact, because the governor is largely concerned with peace and order rather than precepts and principles, Grotius expects that nongovernmental organizations such as the church will exercise significant indicative rule. If the governor fails to govern according to the higher standards of justice that his subjects counsel, those subjects will disobey the laws and render impotent his imperative domestic rule. The governor's failure to exercise his expletive right according to attributive justice does not affect the possession of his expletive right, but does undermine his ability to exercise it. The governor's status is nearly unimpeachable; his actions are under constant threat of civil disobedience.

The exercise of governing authority leads not only to law-making but to law enforcement. This may take the form of adjudicating disputes in civil law as well as punishing offences against criminal law. The former is strictly a matter of expletive justice. Here Grotius is able to protect rightful property without imposing criminal sentences for debts or torts. The fact that one unjustly holds an objective possession does not necessarily mean that one is subjectively guilty. In civil law, individuals are free to exercise their right to be made whole, or to generously choose not to pursue their claim-right. By contrast, criminal law demands only the proscription of acts that follow from a criminal intent against strict justice, thereby safeguarding private morality in liberal fashion. Indeed, when individuals offend against criminal law, expletive justice requires the virtue of equity to identify and avoid punishing apparently criminal acts that actually follow from innocent intentions. However, if guilt is found, the subsequent expletive 'right' of the punisher is not a claim-right but in fact a difficult duty. Moreover, while expletive justice demands this duty, it is mute about better and worse ways to carry it out. Even capital punishment is available to the punisher as a matter of strict justice, but the aims of deterrence, reformation, and even satisfaction instead call for the prudent and forward-looking punishments of attributive justice. These aims require a governor to consider respectively the sense of social trust, the character of the criminal, and the integrity of the moral-political order. In other words, the preservation of a liberal order depends on the prudent ability to discern and shape internal character; attributive justice safeguards expletive justice. This higher sense of justice may also call for an action beyond the strict dictates of the law, such as the prudent and charitable virtue of pardon that requires the governor to give up his right to punish offences against the moral order he represents.

Because individuals have conceded to the state the punishment of only domestic offences, the practice of punishment leads to the question of punitive war. Here Grotius outlines a just war understanding of punitive war that reveals a pre-Westphalian conception of sovereignty as responsibility to a higher standard. Just as attributive justice counsels the establishment of a state that will provide third-party judges, international relations allows third-party nations to punish offences against natural Right. However, the punishment of these offences is not a perfect right incumbent upon any particular nation. Thus, without the attributive (and charitably sacrificial) decision to undertake punitive war, international society is likely to be disorderly and anarchical. Nonetheless, because crime (unlike debt) involves active guilt, nations must punish only for offences that the offending nation could and should have known to be wrong. One cannot coerce virtue, as it must be inspired by the example of revelation known through a history unavailable to foreign civilizations; one can only enforce violations of expletive justice that are universally knowable through reason. However, even this secular expletive justice demands the belief in (and worship of) a righteous God, because the fulfilment of promises (especially those made outside the state) cannot be guaranteed without the extrinsic punishments and rewards of the afterlife. The secular natural law of expletive justice identifies the basic moral foundations for a society, but it struggles to be realized without motives inspired by something beyond secular nature.

The punishments of the afterlife raise the same conundrums as do punishments in domestic communities and international society. This leads Grotius to carefully and creatively address the doctrine of Christ's Atonement. In contrast to both dominant orthodox theories, Grotius primarily views the Atonement through the lens of attributive justice rather than expletive justice. His "governmental" theory portrays God not only as naturalistic creator of the cosmic moral-political order, but also as its ongoing voluntaristic governor. Expletive natural law demands that God punish human sin, but God's governorship allows him to prudently determine the content of the punishment. While his positive law penalty of eternal death serves as the strongest possible deterrent to sin, the inevitable eternal punishment of a humanity universally tainted by original sin would produce despair, and thus the end of religion and sanctification. On the contrary, arbitrary universal mercy would offend against the expletive demand for punishment, and its 'cheap grace' would also remove all incentives for worship and virtue. Thus, while God has every right to condemn humanity, he instead prudently relaxes the punishment, finding a golden mean that avoids the extrinsic extremes of pure judgment or pure mercy. This golden mean, of course, involves the substitutionary death of Christ. While this is not the *only* way to satisfy the demand that sin (in the collective sense) be punished, it is the *best* way both to demonstrate the seriousness of sin and to enable salvation for the church. Christ's charitable sacrifice also inspires intrinsic motives for virtue, thus creating a divinely prudent balance between two positive (though incompletely attainable) ends: the extrinsic fear and intrinsic love of God. Government is meant to provide wise extrinsic incentives, but also to cultivate education of intrinsic moral goodness and to inspire motives for acting on it. God's voluntaristic government is not a matter of arbitrarily re-creating nature like a capricious pagan divinity, but of prudently and charitably entering into time to redeem the infinitely dark consequences that humanity has visited upon a nature that is "no longer 'mother' but 'stepmother.'"[1]

Hence, the deontological demand for punishment is, on some level, a demand that the governor *not* act according to the deontologically simple principle of pure punishment or pure mercy, but rather according to a balance between these two mutually exclusive demands that best fosters sanctifying virtue. Pure expletive justice undermines its own realization. Because nature is fallen, it in fact points toward the need for a redemption that transcends nature without sweeping it away. While nature still forbids sin and demands punishment, the grace of God makes possible the adherence to the dictates of nature. This path is costly for the (divine) governor: it requires not the simple passive concession of a possessive right (or merit), but the active and sacrificial assumption of punishment. God does not grant an indulgence; he acts indulgently. This sacrificial act of punishment is effective on behalf of the entire ecclesial or national polity, which indicates that the sin or crime that necessitated it offends against the entire moral-political order. The matter is not an individual one between criminal and victim or even criminal and lawmaker, but a corporate one that emphasizes the inherently interpersonal character of action. Likewise, the effects of the sacrificial punishment (whether undertaken by Christ or a human Christ-figure) carry forward indefinitely. The Atonement does not aim to restore the victim to a condition of neutrality or innocence that cancels out the original crime; indeed, the crime can never be undone. Rather, it aims to redeem a relationship. This relationship points its parties toward the indefinite vision of human fulfilment from which politics takes its lead and yet which politics can never perfectly fulfil.

The shape of this multifaceted political argument about expletive rights and attributive responsibilities points to several supra-political implications that have in fact grounded this specific political thesis. The first theme is an implicit Grotian metaphysics that grounds rights in deontology and responsibilities in teleology. This distinction between deontology and teleology then maps onto the second theme, which is Grotius' dual metaethics of naturalism and voluntarism. These two seemingly incompatible elements are unified in a God who authors natural laws as creator but also commands positive laws as governor. Only the former are truly laws, because they are unchanging and universal; the latter are in fact acts of politics that respond to the particularities of time and place. Thus, positive statutes are not voluntaristic acts of pure will, but prudent instantiations of nature in particular circumstances. The sovereign does not create positive law *ex nihilo*; statutes depend on a pre-legal normative political vision. A related third theme is that law deals with unchanging objects while political action deals with subjects possessing free will. Hence, the former (Aristotle's *techne*) is amenable to epistemological systematization in a way that the latter (Aristotle's *phronesis*) is not. Nonetheless, the latter remains metaphysically superior. This leads to Grotius' fourth wider theme: because the teleological virtue of prudence cannot be systematically defined but only illustrated, it must be rooted in a historical person. Grotius' Christ supersedes Aristotle's *spoudaios* as its model.

Grotius' fifth wider theme is that the universality of deontological law renders certain acts inherently and universally coercible: those that protect basic natural rights. However, a politics that does not move beyond this to a teleological comprehensive doctrine can protect (and only protect) a minimum 'night watchman' standard of 'negative rights.' A related sixth theme is that Grotius carves out this basic realm of rights (or moral permissions) not in order to lower the moral standard, but to preserve the free will that is the precondition for genuine virtue. One can coerce others to avoid illicit acts, but one cannot coerce the intentions of positive virtue; one can only inspire them. A final theme is that while a deontological foundation benefits from its universal knowability, it suffers from a weakened hold on the souls of its adherents. Without reference to a teleology beyond it, it may undermine the practical possibility of adhering to even its minimal requirements. Only if liberty is understood as more than licence can it inspire the responsibilities needed to maintain a regime of rights.

Grotius as Classical

Natural Law and Classical Natural Right

The prevailing reading of Grotius identifies a modern thinker whose development of depersonalized natural rights eliminates the need for classical political virtue. His politics breaks with Aristotle by protecting only property and human life and excluding any account of the person. However, if the present reading of Grotius is correct, it suggests that Grotius is in fact deeply inspired by the classical idea of natural Right: the idea that propositions of law are inadequate to capture moral reality. This is a central element of attributive (or "wider") justice, which is not a formulation but a personal virtue. To be sure, expletive (or "strict") justice does include preceptive natural Right. This area outlines a few natural laws which compel or forbid, thereby enclosing off a small sphere of human action from the realm of free will. Expletive justice also includes concessive natural Right, the realm of individual natural rights. Finally, expletive justice also guarantees human positive Right, by mandating the fulfilment of promises. However, this large sphere of human freedom protected by expletive justice is not radically free. Much of it is governed by a higher conception of fitting natural Right, or attributive justice. One is never compelled to act according to this higher standard. All acts in this realm of freedom will be just in the strict sense of being valid. However, they will not be just in the wider sense – that is, they will not be virtuous – unless they are guided by the higher goods of attributive justice.

Thus, the attributive justice toward which expletive justice is ultimately directed is a practical virtue that builds on Aristotle's *phronesis*. Because there are few rules that are universally true in all situations, Aristotle's *spoudaios* must be able to discern the good in unique and particular historical contexts. For him, natural Right resides more in concrete decisions than in general propositions.[2] While Grotius' expletive justice provides the procedural conditions for the existence of politics, Grotius agrees with Aristotle that a *good* politics comes about only through such prudent political rule that cultivates virtue in the population.

Hence, Grotius reflects and even deepens Aristotle's emphasis on *praxis*. This explains why he rejects Aristotle's terms of "geometric" and "arithmetic" justice, because both are overly rationalist and insufficiently flexible. One must consider persons and not mathematical formulas. In other words, Grotius is led by Aristotle's practical account of virtue to criticize the overly mathematical connotations in Aristotle's very account of justice. Grotius demonstrates his own concept of equity by breaking with the letter of the *Nicomachean Ethics* in order to fulfil its spirit.[3] *Pace* Tuck, Grotius is not trying to show that a politics of natural rights must make a "final and public break" with Aristotle; on the contrary, he is trying to show that it is possible to conserve the spirit of Aristotle in a rapidly emerging modern world.[4]

For this reason, it may be even more accurate to look to Plato as a classical antecedent. Plato's conception of ethics as participation in the transcendent reality of the Good emphasizes that ethics is not simply a matter of theory, but a practical and even existential virtue. Socrates indicates the inadequacy of propositions to fully capture the essence of the moral world when he repeatedly hesitates to directly answer the questions of his interlocutors. Grotius reflects this attitude throughout his work, not least in his belief that Christianity is manifested in peace and harmony rather than in assent to detailed dogma. Likewise, Plato's *Republic* attempts to show how the good polis mirrors the well-ordered individual, in his argument that order in society can arise only through order in the soul of the philosopher-king. The wise ruler is a sort of 'living law,' because the law is contained within his soul. This explains why Grotius sees the law as residing in the will of the governor. While this emphasis on will may superficially resemble Hobbes' voluntarism, Grotius' teleology instead shows how it manifests a higher goodness that transcends definition.

In this way, Grotius' wider justice corresponds not to a state of satisfaction between two individuals, but to a state of rightness in the entire moral universe. Many observers (particularly Michel Villey) have argued that Grotius' initial definition of justice overturns objective right, focusing instead on the subjective right of expletive and attributive justice. On the contrary, Grotius' attributive justice actually points back toward an overarching ('objective') sense of Right – but it is one that (like criminal over civil law) emphasizes persons rather than objects, as befits a moral universe created and governed by a God who is personal. On the surface, Villey's concept of 'objective right' may appear to be a natural Right bulwark against relativism. However, Grotius shows that the fullest conception of Right must transcend objective formulas.[5]

Positive International Law and Classical Politics

This conception of a nonpropositional natural Right that transcends the concrete formulations of natural law points toward what appears, on the surface, to be the paradox of Grotius. Grotius the trained lawyer spends considerable energy gathering and codifying the propositions of Roman law. His *Jurisprudence of Holland* will serve as a central legal text for centuries to come, remaining in active use even until the twentieth century. His *de Jure Belli* is primarily a work of jurisprudence.

Indeed, Grotius' conception of God as indicative (naturalistic) provides an ontological grounding for natural law. There are a small number of propositions of natural law that bind all of existence. For example, humans are commanded to revere God, or to refrain from taking the lives of others. God then imperatively commands these natural laws, lending them even more weight. Grotius' first four purposes of government underscore the value of written constitutions, which further promulgate these natural laws and add physically compelling sanctions to protect and promote them.

Having provided a foundation for natural and human positive law, Grotius then goes on to outline the benefits of these propositional statutes. First, the role of expletive justice in guaranteeing human positive Right introduces a concretization of Right. The static nature of law allows for a systematic science, in the same fashion as a computer programming language allows for an algorithm. One knows exactly what duties are binding, and on whom they are binding. This supports Grotius' aim to methodologically separate law from politics.[6] Second, expletive justice guarantees the achievability of law. The very etymology of the term *explere* highlights the possibility of perfect fulfilment or satisfaction as a distinguishing feature of natural law. From this follows its emphasis on preventing negative actions rather than promoting positive ones. It requires subjects only to passively refrain from illegal acts. Indeed, the law does not judge as "virtuous," but only as "not guilty." Complete omission of negative (illegal) acts is theoretically possible, and thus legitimately demanded of all.

Yet, having finally established the desirable concretization and achievability of law, Grotius proceeds to present the inadequacy of both characteristics. He points to the limits of concretization in his discussion of equity – the penultimate concept with which Aristotle concludes his discussion of justice in the *Nicomachean Ethics*. Here Grotius shows that the law does not fully succeed even on its own terms. As a product that is made rather than an action that is carried out, it is static and outside of time. Because it is a second-order sign of the will that enacted it, interpretation is required even to discern its meaning. One can have a self-contained and systematic science of law without recognizing anything beyond it, just as an atheist can know some elements of natural law. However, one misses the broader context by ignoring the artificiality of the boundaries that one has placed on the indefinite horizon of true Right. Grotius may in fact narrow his expletive justice (as in the virtual absence of any *jus in bello* restraints) precisely in order to leave the reader wanting more – thus pointing the way toward attributive justice.

Grotius also gestures toward the limits of achievability in his recognition that the legal judgment of "not guilty" is incomplete. *Pace* Hobbes, moral existence is not simply about living the "not bad" life, but about living the good life; this accounts for the pejorative connotations of the term "legalism." A good political order does not simply require adherence to the laws, or *politeuma*, but the cultivation of a particular way of life, or *politeia*. However, the personal, virtue-based nature of positive goods also points to the difficulty of ascertaining positive standards of commission (as opposed to omission). At what point has someone carried out an act that is as beneficial as possible to the common good? After all, the spectrum of positive acts that build up the community is indefinite. Thus, government must transcend law. It must be personal, fostering political virtues by demonstrating them.

By identifying the limits of law, Grotius helps to vindicate the practice of politics itself. Surveys today show shockingly low popular approval ratings for legislatures. Many contemporary observers disparage politics as an odious contest of manufactured partisanship that serves as a mask for self-interest. Those who defend politics as a means for the common good generally evoke ironic smiles and elicit barely restrained guffaws. Yet the same jaded observers often see constitutional courts as beyond reproach, soaring above the messy fray of politics. They are guided only by well-defined charters of rights, purifying the individual justices from the taint of self-interest. However, Grotius shows the limitations of law, and the rights discourse implied therein. Indeed, his fifth purpose of government – 'prudentially producing' natural Right – highlights politics as the realm of practical judgment in which moral truth comes to be known. Practices may be a more accurate guide than purported beliefs, as historical circumstances reveal and clarify natural Right. Those inclined to a contextualist methodology might even note that Grotius' own temporal ascent from teenage lawyer to elder statesman prefigures his conceptual ascent from law to politics.

This apparent paradox of a Grotius who simultaneously defends law and limits it continues into his treatment of international relations. Grotius is so keen to carve out a space for positive law that he takes the bold and original step of suggesting that it is possible to institute positive law in relations between states. This obviously leads to his appellation as the "father of modern international law." Grotius endorses international law just as he endorses the institution of government, which allows for positive domestic law and formal mechanisms of third-party judgment and punishment. These institutions foster the social and rational ends of human existence, because they better facilitate the settlement of disputes through peaceful human reason rather than violent animalistic force. Yet the creation of a legal-judicial order, whether domestic or international, is never strictly necessary. Human sociability is already present in the 'state of nature,' whether that be the pre-civil condition, or the actual present condition of international relations. Shared and effective norms – and even the punitive enforcement of these norms – are possible outside a formal legal framework. Indeed, the very institution of government requires the prior existence of a "people," which suggests a common vision of political ends. Correspondingly, Grotius bases his international law on the existing pre-legal customs and practices of nations, rooted in the *jus gentium*. Much like domestic law, international law depends on a political consensus that pre-exists it. This opens up a space for genuine (rather than Morgenthauian) politics among nations, or what some English School theorists have termed "international human relations."[7] In doing so, Grotius offers a classical Aristotelian alternative to the so-called 'realist' position that sees no moral reality in international relations beyond formal peace. However, he also outlines a classical corrective to liberal internationalist positions that see no moral reality outside of law.

Indeed, many English School thinkers identify Grotius as the intellectual progenitor of their approach, referring to a "Grotian tradition" in International Relations.[8] However, a lack of attention to Grotius' actual works has created some ambiguity about the nature of this tradition. For instance, it has left the English School divided on one of the central questions of international society: the acceptability of humanitarian intervention. A closer look at Grotius' foundational understanding of justice helps to illuminate this debate between so-called pluralists (who reject intervention) and solidarists (who admit the possibility and perhaps even the imperative).[9] Grotius' placement of expletive justice within the overarching framework of attributive justice helps to solve this conundrum. While the procedural-legal status granted by expletive justice may confer a valid title to sovereignty, the subsequent exercise of governing authority is binding only when it follows the higher substantive-moral standard of attributive justice. As a result, while international society presupposes states with valid authority to pass international laws protecting their sovereignty, the violation of justice may remove the obligation of nonintervention by others. Nonetheless, sovereign heads of state must still employ prudence in determining whether to intervene, and in carrying out the consequent intervention. This reading of Grotius shows that the pluralist reading of Grotius is partially correct, but ultimately insufficient. It also helps to substantiate some elements of the solidarist reading, while yet guarding against 'League of Nations'-type ventures that would pursue universalist solutions that are deaf to political considerations.

Imperfect Rights and Classical Duties

Grotius' recognition of the limits of natural law also opens up the possibility of imperfect rights and duties. His conception of attributive justice shows that the realm of legal freedom is still governed by morality, even in the absence of a specific duty-bearer and right-holder. If virtue resides in the character of the person, it ought to flow forth regardless of whether any other person could claim its performance as a right. Indeed, how could someone claim the right to beneficent treatment? Even if one could identify a specific actor and recipient, it is unclear what degree of beneficence would satisfy the claim. For this reason, several commentators have identified Grotius as a key figure in the development of imperfect rights and duties.[10]

The need to include imperfect obligations in one's moral world – and the benefits of a theory that can do so – is evident in Grotius' conception of pre-civil society. Here there is an imperfect duty to punish, because expletive justice demands that criminals be punished. However, this duty does not rest on one single person or authority. Indeed, Grotius is clear that criminal law does not confer a punitive right on the victim, because the offence is ultimately directed against the entire community. Furthermore, justice is always better served when crimes are punished by someone other than the immediate victim. Punishment is, of course, a duty that calls for (and hence illustrates) the higher virtues of wider justice. A system without imperfect rights or duties would be unable to punish in pre-civil society – or in international relations.

Grotius' introduction of the concept of perfect and imperfect rights and duties may help to overcome existing difficulties in rights discourse. For instance, the claim of a starving orphan to food is sometimes seen as being less theoretically solid than the claim of a creditor to collect on a debt. This is because only the latter has what legal theorist Wesley Hohfeld describes as a perfect right: a definite claim on a particular individual that arises from an explicit consensual agreement. However, the notion of imperfect rights and duties shows that there may be a moral duty of care for others, even in the absence of voluntarily undertaken promises. This prevents rights discourse from being reduced to the individual accumulation of private possessions, and allows for a discussion of public and structural injustices. Recent studies by Martha Nussbaum and Charles Taylor have identified Grotius' development of the concept of international obligations.[11] However, an examination of Grotius' conception of imperfect rights and duties would help to provide philosophical grounds for this conception of an overarching good.

Grotius as Christian

Classical Nature and Christian Grace

If the conventional reading of Grotius sees him as modern, it also portrays him as a secularist who reclassifies Christianity as politically irrelevant (or worse). Only the justiciable dictates of secular expletive justice should guide politics.

However, while a closer study of Grotius' classical references underscores his appeals to the Ancient world of Greece and Rome, it also substantiates his Christian perspective. Grotius sees the classical world through the lens of Christian revelation. This is not a filter that writes off the pagan elements of the Ancient world as a sad chapter in the obsolete pre-history of humanity. Rather, Grotius takes seriously the role of the Ancients in discerning nature. Far from attacking Aristotle, he says that Aristotle "deservedly holds the foremost place" among philosophers.[12] However, he declares a stronger allegiance to the early Christians, who took from many philosophers but recognized the inability of any (or all) to be authoritative. Christianity need not be hostile to the pagan study of nature, but does recognize its limits: as Christ says, "I did not come to destroy [the Law or the Prophets] but to fulfil [them]."[13] Christianity takes the mode of attributive justice to another level: it does not sweep away nature, but adds a harmony with nature that brings another dimension to it. Just as natural expletive justice finds its fulfilment in natural attributive justice, the nature of the Ancients prepares the way for Christian grace.

If nature leads to grace, it is nonetheless conceptually separable from it. Throughout *DJB*, Grotius is very careful to distinguish between the progressively increasing moral loftiness of (natural) expletive justice, (natural) attributive justice, and (gracious) Christian charity. While he demands expletive justice of all, and enjoins attributive justice to all, he expects charity only from Christians. This is why he rejects punitive war against peoples who refuse Christianity, and endorses it only for offences against natural religion. The latter can be coerced because it is knowable to all in natural reason and because it is a precondition for the most purely procedural and nonteleological component of morality: the fulfilment of promises.

Indeed, Grotius exhibits remarkably high praise for natural religion. It identifies many true and salutary components of religion, such as belief in a righteous Creator-God who rewards virtue and punishes vice, and the worship and obedience of that God. However, it also points its discerning adherent toward the inherent limitations of natural religion: namely, the permanently "criminal" status it must impute to every person. This opens the door toward a Christianity whose divinely substitutionary punishment offers hope of escaping this status. But while Grotius will point the non-Christian beyond the limits of where natural justice will take him, he does not force the non-Christian to go beyond these limits.

Nonetheless, if Grotius does not require Christian virtue of all, he enjoins to all the attributive justice that prepares the way for Christian virtue. Although the attributive virtues are natural virtues, they cannot be coerced through the expletive means of extrinsic incentives. Their free exercise can only be inspired by intrinsic motives rooted in one's character. Classical knowledge of this higher attributive standard is insufficient to compel its application; as the Christians point out, one must still freely choose to follow it. This freely willed mode of attributive justice enables one to be most truly human, attaining their classical *telos*. Yet it further points the person (whether acknowledged or not) toward the divine archetype of freedom anchored in God's imperative omnipotence.

Classical Equity and Christian Forgiveness

Grotius's treatment of equity well illustrates the relationship and directionality between the natural classical virtues and supernatural Christian ones. Equity is a natural virtue that points beyond the law, as it judges an apparently illegal actor to be innocent of wrongdoing. This exonerates a person who broke the letter of the law but not its spirit. Because equity implies that a person deserves innocence as a matter of justice, many of the Protestant reformers rejected it under the belief that justice for sinful humanity means damnation. Despite his Protestant affiliation, Grotius seeks to conserve this classical natural virtue. One is entitled to equity as a matter of justice, and one's political order is strengthened when its executives seek the spirit of the law.

However, if spirit of the law is better than the letter, sometimes even the spirit of the law is harmful to the polity. Recognizing this fact, Christianity goes one step further. Its concept of pardon (or grace) shows how a governor may release from punishment even a criminal who wilfully broke the spirit of the law. In this way, it is not simply a deeper understanding of justice, but a transcending of justice. The enshrinement in statute law of strong legal punishments is salutary for its criminally deterrent effect, but even the equitable interpretations of these sanctions may be unduly harsh. (For instance, most observers envy Singapore's success in preventing drug use, but recoil at its automatic death penalty for drug traffickers.) Hence, Grotius counsels pardon even in some cases where equity does not exonerate the criminal.

Moreover, Grotius shows that while equity requires the classical intellectual virtue of prudence, pardon goes even further, calling for the Christian moral virtue of giving up one's honour. In the latter, the indulgent governor sacrifices the demand for full satisfaction of the offence against the state (and thus against himself). (Some satisfaction is always required in order to uphold the integrity of the state, but it is often less than the eye-for-an-eye satisfaction that would also satisfy the naturally vengeful desires of the governor.) While equity requires no sacrifice, pardon does. Indeed, by referencing the pagan lawgiver Zaleucus as his prime example of this-worldly pardon, Grotius further shows how natural attributive justice points to (and perhaps even participates in) Christ's higher form of sacrificial pardon.

Because the pardon offered by both Christ and Christ-figure Zaleucus transcends natural expletive justice, one wonders whether it is even appropriate to use the word "justice" in conjunction with attribution and its associated virtues. If it is not a strict duty of justice that can be coercively compelled, its performance would seem instead to be a (freely willed) gift. Perhaps the answer can be found in the practice of forgiveness, which is always a free gift, but whose character changes from the Ancient world of justice to the Christian world of charity. Aristotle places forgiveness under the virtue of magnanimity, or even temperance, because the forgiver does not hold tightly to what they are owed. In this way, it is a passive virtue, because it holds one back from demanding costly repayment from another person. One might conceptualize it as Grotius' category of liberality, in which one simply declines to press their right. It is also a self-oriented virtue, not an other-oriented one. This is because it allows the forgiver to move on from the other person and the wrong they committed, as though the offender were of no concern to (or even beneath) the wronged party. (Indeed, this stance follows from Aristotle's conception of God as that which thinks about only the greatest thing – namely, itself.)

The Christian conception of forgiveness shares this idea of holding loosely to things owed. However, the Christian understanding then adds a positive component that turns forgiveness from a passive virtue into an active one. Christian forgiveness is inherently outward-focused and actively engages the other in reconciliation. As a part of charity, its ultimate concern is not simply the external good, but the moral good of others – even one's enemies.[14] This explains why God's action in the Atonement is that of pardon, not liberality. Mere generosity costs nothing to God; as the all-powerful maker of all things, he can forgive debts at will without reducing his 'stock' of credit. If God were merely generous, and simply exhibited an Aristotelian indifference to the honour owed him, the Socinian theory would be sound. However, God's indulgence leads him to relax his right to punish a crime against the moral order he created, and hence a crime that has sullied his own dignity as its governor. God acts not according to what would most fully restore his own honour, but according to what would best promote the free exercise of virtue and religion among his subjects, and thus enable the possibility of their salvation. To use Plato's terms, God gives up not the possessions that are the focus of the producers (and which the soldiers willingly surrender in their quest for honour), but rather he concedes the honour of the soldiers (which the philosopher-kings must surrender in their quest for the wisdom of the sun). We will return to the full implications of this analogy momentarily. For now, we can see that God's eschewal of the ultimate restoration of his dignity is costly to God on its own terms. The fact that God does so through the voluntary interposition of the second person of the Godhead as bearer of punishment further reinforces both the cost to God and the humility of God.

This emphasis on forgiveness for the sake of a greater good rather than for one's own honour reinforces the fact that natural expletive justice points toward attributive justice. A realm cannot be governed exclusively by expletive natural law unless everybody is already law-abiding. The law can set out a standard, and can operate effectively as a closed system with full compliance. It need not account for the contingencies of human will entering this natural system from outside. However, if the monkey-wrench of crime ever jams up the mechanical engine of law, the machine is incapable of self-repair. Unlike a debt that can be repaid, human action cannot be undone. The law can only look backward in mechanistic fashion to determine conformity to or deviation from the law. Like a bug in a computer program, it can potentially identify its own problem, but it cannot fix it. Innocence is no longer possible; only redemption is. However, redemption requires a person outside the system.

Indeed, once an injustice has been committed, the strict punishments demanded in expletive justice may actually be an impediment to preventing future injustices. This is best illustrated in the practice of war. Any demand during hostilities that the other side be brought to full justice upon conclusion of the war may cause the other side to fight to the last man. Only an international political order that allows for the possibility of pardon can provide the grounds on which the losing party will be willing to accept a cessation of hostilities. Without forgiveness, there would be little hope of ending war.[15] Once one party acts unjustly, a strict adherence to expletive justice could very well result in a perpetual war of all against all. Thus, an order that demands strict justice is unlikely to produce peace or justice.

Grotius' idea of forgiveness as breaking the unending cycle of violence also prefigures Hannah Arendt's discussion of the political importance of forgiveness and of new beginnings. In *The Human Condition*, she suggests that the problem of action – that of unpredictability – can be overcome by forgiveness. Forgiveness is thus a precondition for promises – one of the central elements of political action, which (in Nietzsche's understanding) raises man from the level of beast. Indeed, Arendt even points out that the prerogative of modern heads of state to pardon criminals follows from Christ's proclamation of forgiveness. Thus, while Grotius uniquely emphasizes the importance of political action in understanding Christ's salvific role, Arendt reciprocally emphasizes the importance of Christ in understanding political action. Grotius' emphasis on forgiveness is not only prescient but relevant to a post-modern discourse of personal responsibility over law.[16]

Addressing the Objections

Grotius' Christianity helps to explain several elements of his thought that superficially appear as modern repudiations of classical politics. Indeed, a critic could raise several questions in response to the argument here for Grotius' substantial continuity with the classical tradition. The first is the following: if Grotius' attributive justice truly follows Aristotle and Aquinas' distributive justice, why does Grotius say nothing about the distribution of public honours – an essential element of Aristotle's geometric justice? The answer begins with a return to the earlier unfinished thought that when God relaxes the deserved punishment of humanity, he declines to pursue the honour that he is due. Christ's humiliation on the cross only deepens this willingness to give up honour. For this reason, the crucifixion is "foolishness to the Greeks"[17] such as Aristotle, for whom the surrender of possessions may be magnanimous, but the surrender of deserved honours is the vice of weakness of soul, an offence against justice, and a degradation of politics. Likewise, it is "a scandal to the Jews,"[18] as well as to other monotheistic religions that see such humility as incompatible with the great fearfulness of God's sovereignty. However, Grotius recasts satisfaction as the restoration of the honour of God's government only inasmuch as it serves the subjects of that government (much as Plato's philosopher-kings benefit the polis more truly than do his soldiers). Satisfaction is not a matter of restoring God's honour per se. Rather, the integrity of God's moral government is ultimately a matter of re-emphasizing in the hearts and minds of the people the importance of Right. While expletive justice demands some satisfaction for the government, a harsh mathematically exact restoration of honour may actually compromise the future goodness of subjects, most obviously in its demand of a life for a life. Correspondingly, the stature of God's government is not most fully expressed in God's self-contained 'stock' of honour, but in the way that he brings others into the divine life. *Pace* Machiavelli, true political glory rests not in the object of *lo stato*, but in the harmonious political life of the polity as a whole.[19] By declining to demand his full honours in justice, God the governor best promotes political virtue in his subjects. In this consists the true wisdom and goodness of the polity that in fact transcends the honour of the state, just as the wisdom of Plato's philosophers transcends the honour of his soldiers.

This is particularly appropriate in light of the Christian doctrine of the Trinity. God the Father is not self-contained; the Godhead is essentially relational. This helps to explain why creation should exist, as it allows God to further share his love with persons, and in turn calls for God's government as part of this relation between creator and created. God's involvement in his moral polity contrasts with Aristotle's man of pre-eminent virtue who must be made (as beast or god) to live outside the polis.[20] The better the *spoudaios* (or, for that matter, the Nietzschean *übermensch*), the greater his self-regard, and the less his interest in the others who constitute his political reality. Yet while the Christian God is wholly self-sufficient, and thus incurs no debts of justice to any others, he yet takes up moral governorship, exercising a virtue that transcends the natural duties of justice. (This also provides the unambiguous explanation that Plato lacked for why the philosopher should re-enter the cave.) Paradoxically, in so doing, it may even grant to politics a stature that Aristotle could not attain, because politics now includes a place for the greatest of all gods.[21]

Hence, just as God gives up his deserved honour and humbles himself for the good of others in the Incarnation, so individuals ought to regard public honours lightly. Grotius knows that this Christian teaching is a stumbling block for many: "It is a hard thing for them lightly to esteem of honours and other advantages; which they must do, if they would receive what is related concerning Christ . . ."[22] This is a clear contrast with Aristotle's geometric justice, which demands that the just man receive his honours, and grants him the 'right' (and perhaps even the duty) to pursue them. However, once the Aristotelian man actively begins to pursue the honours that match his virtue, the Christian can argue that he no longer acts on an intrinsic desire to contribute to the polis, but instead on an extrinsic desire to gain a reward. To Grotius, the pursuit of an honour that justly corresponds to one's virtue may actually demonstrate a lack of virtue, because one is no longer motivated by virtue for its own sake. Indeed, even if one does not actively pursue public honours, the mere existence of reward already creates an inducement to act, one that renders subsequent action less than fully free. It then becomes difficult to ascertain whether one is truly aiming for virtue as an end in itself, or only a means toward possessing honour.[23] Honours for virtue cannot be demanded in expletive justice; they are only truly honours when the governor freely bestows them as an unanticipated gift.[24]

This reading of Grotius as classical might arm the critic with a second question: if Grotius truly values the classical virtue of prudence, why does he explicitly take issue with Aristotle's conception of virtue as a mean? Already in the Prolegomena of *DJB*, Grotius argues that virtue cannot always consist in a mean. His rejoinder to Aristotle is consistent with his understanding of public honours: one can never be too contemptuous of pleasure or honour or, for that matter, of evil in general. Nor can one worship God or desire heaven too much. The same is true in the opposite sense. Aristotle would have said that one should not have too little of any of these positive goods. However, for Grotius it is unproblematic to accept less than one is owed, because justice (in the strict sense) is simply refraining from the goods of others.[25]

Many commentators have taken this as the modern rupture with Aristotle that it ostensibly appears to be. Yet for Grotius, it is problematic to imagine an Aristotelian spectrum of virtue as a mean between vices residing at the tangible, finite points at the end of the spectrum.[26] Aristotle would likely argue that his golden mean is not mathematically discernible and that it changes over time, as it is meant to require prudence rather than mathematical deduction of a finite end-point. Nonetheless, he would presumably have to acknowledge that this mean at least theoretically resides at a particular point on that spectrum. For Grotius, there can be no finite point. Rather, virtue is at the (metaphorical) end of a spectrum that has no fixed end-point, because it is grounded in a God whose holiness is infinite. Thus, by portraying virtue as infinite, Grotius expresses the ineffable, existential, and practical character of virtue even better than Aristotle does in characterizing it as a mean. Grotius breaks with the words of Aristotle in order to more fully develop the spirit of Aristotle.

Indeed, because virtue is unlimited, it can never be fully instantiated in politics. For this reason, Grotius cautions against looking for ultimate solutions. Perfect fulfilment can dwell only in the lower realm of expletive justice, which concerns negative freedom. In contrast, the positive fulfilment of the person must be an ongoing quest; no political program can ever truly satisfy it. Politics is not a problem to solve but a practice to live. Perfect justice for its human subjects could come only at the end of history. Grotius thus provides a critique of utopia and a warning against ideology. In matters of ultimate importance, politics can – at most – point the way.

The classical reading of Grotius faces a third question: if Grotius truly has an ancient conception of natural Right, why bother complicating the issue by adding the concept of subjective natural rights? In fact, don't individual rights allow one not to act according to the fullness of natural Right? Again, Grotius' likely response to these charges proceeds from his Christianity. Unlike the Greek world, Christianity more clearly introduces the idea of individual conscience and will. Where the ancients assumed that the problem was ignorance, Christianity highlights the problem of weakness of will: "for what I would, that do I not; but what I hate, that do I."[27] This leads to the aforementioned emphasis on the free and uncoerced character of virtue. For this reason, Christianity is less optimistic than the ancient pagan world about the possibility of politically incentivized virtue. Hence, individual rights guarantee a large realm of free choice, unconstrained by governmental interference (no matter how benign). Moreover, Christianity expands the frontiers of both good and evil to infinite lengths.

Government is not only morally but practically inadequate to demand the highest performance of goodness. Hence, political rights do not reduce morality to the mere negative duty of noninterference, but permit the subsequent exercise of a virtue that is beyond coercibility.

Likewise, by conferring individual rights on everyone, Grotius confers individual responsibility on everyone. Each must then decide how to exercise it. This may inspire bearers of rights to exercise them in a fashion worthy of their status. Indeed, Grotius might prefigure Alexis de Tocqueville's idea that the right of political participation is a way of ennobling individuals, who ultimately respond to their increased freedom with a concern for the common good. Rights need not shut down moral consideration; they may in fact call it forth.

Grotius' Christian emphasis on individual conscience and will further emphasizes that in the absence of consent, one can only have rights over things, not over people. Grotius' resultant limitation of substantive expletive rights to the protection of person and property should not lead us to believe that this is the entire subject-matter of politics. The fact that one has claim-rights to property means that property is not more important, but less. While a good polity should certainly ensure security of person and property, politics is not reducible to a flourishing economy. Just as Aristotle argued that household management was a precondition for political participation, Grotius argues that rights are only a precondition for virtue. The state protects possessions so that people can use them well. Rights are not an excuse to enlarge one's possessions to the greatest extent possible, while ignoring the rest of humanity under the guise that one is simply not violating anyone's rights. Indeed, Grotius warns against the "endlessly increasing avarice which destroys the heart and ruins tranquility."[28]

A final question for the classical Grotius is this: if Grotius is a conserver of natural Right, why does he talk about history as a source of knowledge? Some might suggest that an emphasis on history makes Grotius a proto-Hegelian enemy of natural Right: a historical relativist unwittingly contributing to the development of ideological and totalitarian regimes. Yet here again, Grotius' Christian development of the classical tradition sheds a more positive light on his use of history. Grotius' God is both a creator of nature and a person with free will. Hence, Grotius' understanding of *logos* is personal; the author of a massive four-volume Biblical commentary could hardly have missed the immense (indeed, history-altering) import of John 1:1.[29] Hence, God cannot be fully knowable through laws, as though he were part of nature. Rather, as the good governor of the moral universe, God is particularly known through his actions. Someone who takes the Old Testament as seriously as Grotius did – to the extent of consulting Jewish tradition on its interpretation – must surely be alert to the historical account of God's interaction with his people, such as the prudent positive laws God gives to them at particular times. Of course, the fullest source of *logos* is the Incarnation – an event in time whose historical veracity is not merely incidental for the Christian: "If Christ be not risen, then … your faith is vain."[30] Christ's action in history overcomes the strictness of law, revealing the spirit of the law, while also redeeming the fallenness of nature, enabling the virtue of hope. But even then, history continues after Christ; if it did not, Christianity would lack a coherent doctrine of the Trinity, of Christ as fully God and fully man, or even of original sin.

Indeed, one might see this Christian emphasis on history not as opposing Aristotle's political thought but as fulfilling it. If Aristotle's natural Right resides not in general propositions but concrete decisions, one presumably can know it only through a record of those decisions in time. If prudence cannot be defined but only illustrated, one needs the examples of virtuous people in history. If natural Right allows some free play for discovery in human action (rather than merely deduction), then one cannot rely simply on theory or metaphysics. In sum, if Aristotle is the father of the practical political virtue of prudence, he cannot but have an implicit epistemology of history. Grotius simply makes this explicit. If he did not, one might begin to question both his classical and Christian influences, and begin to wonder whether he is indeed a modern secular rationalist.

Rethinking the Foundations of Modern Political Secularism

If Francis Fukuyama may have overstated the case for liberal democracy as satisfying the political soul, he did not conjure up its popular appeal out of thin air. Populations from Bangkok to Harare to Tehran clamour for human rights and self-government. Indeed, the appeal to rights seems to be the primary language of justice around the globe today. Rights are perceived as both secular and impersonal, safeguarding their purity and ensuring their universal appeal. Few would ever want to give them up. Yet if a regime of rights protects against the worst abuses, it does not guarantee social and political harmony, or even good government. It is often said that countries with the right of democratic participation get the governments that they deserve – a truism invariably invoked as a wry commentary on the reduction of political discourse to the lowest common denominator. Rights can be used to absolutize claims and prevent compromise, to rationalize an individualism that neglects past and future, or to reframe political life as a free-for-all in which each party takes what they can legally get. As Rousseau lamented, "everyone knows his rights, but no one his duties."[31]

A Grotian conception of rights offers a way to ennoble rights discourse, because it sets out a concept of rights in full awareness of these potential pathologies. Grotius' notion of rights is inseparable from the responsibilities that flow from a wider standard of justice. While he does not coerce a particular exercise of rights, he is aware that the absence of such a guide will undermine the preservation of a regime of rights. Indeed, his liberal theory of rights refrains from coercing higher goods in order to preserve their truly virtuous character.

Grotius writes in an age of violent pluralism, fully aware that he can no longer take for granted a shared consensus on comprehensive doctrines. For this reason, he grounds the existence of rights on a pure reason that requires no assent to religion or even teleology, and is thus theoretically knowable to all. Yet this nonparticularistic defence of rights is ultimately grounded in his conception of God's indicative modality as creator of nature. This portrait of God also includes an imperative modality as governor that opens up the historical possibility of revelation, which is not only an alternative source of truth but in fact a higher one. It seems reasonable to surmise that Grotius writes of secular natural law not to enable Christians to ignore revelation, but to give non-Christians an entry point to truth that will eventually lead them to its source. Hence, Grotius does not aim to disenchant the world (in Charles Taylor's phrase); rather, he aims to speak to those who are already disenchanted in a fashion that preserves the possibility of re-enchantment.[32]

The first implication of this re-reading of Grotius is historical: a re-evaluation of the thesis that natural rights originated in a secular reaction against Christianity. Grotius' concept of natural rights is in fact part of a larger project to which Christianity is central. Indeed, to understand Grotius as a Renaissance man is to understand his metaethics, epistemology, and structures of justice, each of which is grounded in his aforementioned understanding of God. It is appropriate that Grotius' political themes reach their apex in his Atonement theology.

Grotius' epistemological separation between the spheres of reason and revelation that are yet both ontologically grounded in the same God leads to a second implication: the separability and yet potential coexistence of secular institutions and teleological content. Value-neutral institutions – such as a science of law protecting what Isaiah Berlin calls "negative rights" – are formally complete on their own. Human positive law is valid independent of its ontological goodness, and procedural political institutions provide an order that protects the conditions in which the heights of justice can emerge. Grotius may be a legal positivist (albeit not an exclusive one), and his conception of order as practical rather than theoretical in fact leads him to inveigh against the rule of metaphysician-kings. Yet formal government does not mean that the teleological perspectives should be silent. Although governors are secure in their position regardless of their 'teleological performance,' civil society (particularly the church) is called to exercise indicative rule over them. Indeed, only adherence to such rule can guarantee the governor's domestic sovereignty, which alone can give meaning to his legal sovereignty.

To put it another way, the epistemological quasi-independence of reason establishes a basis for human society in a world lacking a religious consensus. Religious difference need not mean radical disagreement that perpetually extends the warfare that formed the backdrop of Grotius' adult life, and whose conclusion after a 'mere' thirty years Grotius would not live to see. It is possible to achieve a nonsectarian consensus on procedures, one that allows fundamentally different visions of human flourishing to compete through the peaceful thrust and parry of word rather than sword. Nonetheless, while this most basic use of reason is a formally human practice that separates man from the animalistic law of the jungle, the use of reason as a safe outlet for *thymos* is not the substantive fullness of political existence. True political community not only protects human existence from violence but directs reason toward a truth and goodness that actually fosters human flourishing. A merely human society upholds basic expletive justice, but such justice would obtain if God condemned all sinners to hell, or if a governor sent all criminals to the gallows. A truly humane community calls for a higher standard.

Grotius' interplay between nature and supernature in establishing rights suggests a third implication: a re-evaluation of the contemporary pretence that religion is inimical to the human rights of a humane order. On the contrary, Christianity introduces a vision of the will whose dignity ought to be protected by right(s). This helps to situate a concept as apparently secular and nonteleological as simultaneous ostensible justice in war as a manifestation of a Christian focus on intent – one that counsels pardon for those whose consciences could not possibly have convicted them. Contra Skinner's protestations that Christianity is "dangerous," Grotius vindicates Taylor's identification of a humanism in Christianity.[33] Indeed, a post-Christian approach based on pure reason is more likely to counsel eye-for-an-eye retribution than a Christ-inspired one that envisions punishment as helpful to human flourishing. A purely rights-based approach to punishment allows for a ruler to exact the full measure of repayment for honour; on the contrary, Christianity allows for punishment to be redemptive. As the Atonement demonstrates, Christian charity allows for a prudent relaxation of the punishment permitted by secular expletive justice.

Finally, this reading suggests that the survival of a regime of rights may depend on sources beyond natural rights – that is, beyond nature. This may seem a particularly counter-intuitive proposition. For instance, Skinner argues that if Christianity reduces rights to negative rights, it then undermines even those rights. However, in Grotius' framework, the opposite is true: a Christian backdrop is in fact the best way to preserve rights. If Christianity takes away with one hand the republican concept of the *vivere libero* (one that may itself call for a heavy-handed government aiming for its own glory), it gives back with the other hand a vision of how to freely exercise the resulting negative liberty in a way that promotes a wider (indeed, higher) common good.[34] In fact, the likelihood of instantiating even a nonteleological regime of rights depends on exercising rights according to a substantive vision of human flourishing ultimately grounded in the Christian God. Natural rights can be known by (and demanded of) atheists – but so can the limits of natural rights, such as their inability to motivate the assumption of imperfect duties, their extremely limited *jus in bello*, and their licensing of harsh punishments. Indeed, a full prosecution of the natural right to punish untempered by the Christian virtue of forgiveness may result in an unending cycle of violent retribution.

For this reason, Grotius' solution to political disorder in an age of pluralism, war, and religious conflict – one surprisingly like our own – is not, *pace* Hobbes, the elimination of religion. Politics demands not an eclipse of man's ultimate end but in fact an ever-present consciousness of it. A renewed emphasis on the eternal rewards and punishments of religion may be the best guarantee of law and order in politics. No Leviathan, even a totalitarian one, can ever provide perfect extrinsic incentives for obedience. However, a God outside of time can threaten a punishment lengthy enough to dissuade vicious acts, and offer a reward excellent enough to induce virtuous acts. Moreover, only Christ enters history to demonstrate (in a manner comprehensible to all) the heights of other-oriented charity, which alone can truly arouse intrinsic motives of gratitude and thus inspire in return the gift of freely chosen virtue. Hence, the Christian mystery of a God both imperative and indicative holds together what Eric Voegelin calls the "divine-human tension": the mutual coexistence of the animal and the divine that constitutes human existence. If political man is neither fully beast nor fully god, the golden mean he must maintain between extrinsic and intrinsic motivations is most fully grounded in (and fostered by) a divine governor.

Transcending Natural Rights

Grotius' project as I have described it is the attempt to carve out a deontological sphere of pure reason enumerating a standard that can bind the conscience of a world lacking a shared conception of human flourishing, but to do so without eliminating the teleological sphere that recognizes human existence as purposive and sets out a substantive (if never perfectly definable) vision of a full human existence. He maintains a characteristically Protestant emphasis on the importance of individual conscience, but pairs it with a typically Catholic conviction that natural teleology is accessible to human reason. Furthermore, his project is the attempt to show that this deontological standard, while logically consistent, can only be sustained in the world of practice through the virtues that, on its own terms, it cannot demand. He attempts to maintain a balance between the needed yet mutually exclusive imperatives of nature and freedom in a way that ensures that the (always imperfect) quest for both remains alive. Hence, Grotius does not eliminate virtues in favour of formulations, but rather provides formulations as a way to speak to a pluralistic world lacking – perhaps unhappily – not so much a comprehensive doctrine as a comprehensive vision. Grotius' de-emphasis on the good in favour of the right is only meant to allow the later (and richer) re-emergence of the good. While the right may be temporally first, the good is ontologically highest.

Indeed, Grotius recognizes the need for Aristotelian prudence in discerning this teleological vision, but instead of pointing toward its fulfilment in the *spoudaios* who embodies a mean between vicious extremes, he points toward the person of an infinite God whose goodness dwells in a horizon unbounded by discernable end-points on any spectrum. Grotius' resultant Christian conception of person and individual conscience underscores not only the objective conformity of actions to this vision but also the subjective choice of will to follow it, which further accounts for his deontic conviction that one must have the right to choose or reject it. For this reason, the freedom that Grotius anchors in his realm of concessive natural Right is not licence for a radically unnormed human will, but an opening for the unique human capacity of free will to find its completion. This completion comes through participation in the divine life that originally made human free will possible, much like the human freedom to open one's eyes enables one to see (however briefly) the sun that – as Plato pointed out – makes possible the very faculty of sight.

In this way, Grotius might in some ways prefigure Kant's conception of imperfect duties as the duty to cultivate general maxims. Yet while such a duty is universally incumbent upon all, it is inadequate to identify the content that would constitute its own standard of success. Grotius seems to intuit what at least one recent observer has noted: that there exists no genuinely satisfying definition of imperfect duties.[35] That Grotius does this without a detailed metaphysics is perhaps all the more appropriate, because the very drive of metaphysics toward definitions is inadequate – and even potentially inimical – to the ever-continuing journey toward the indefinite end of human existence.[36] To return to Plato's brilliant metaphor, even the mind's eye can never fully see the sun; its journey never ends. Indeed, the journey is not a search that ends in the finality of answers, but an ever-richer participation in the transcendent source of *logos* that renders the concept of "answer" (and of "question") intelligible.

Notes

1 Hugo Grotius, *Meletius* 36, ed. and trans. Guillaume H. M. Posthumus Meyjes (New York: Brill, 1988), 114.
2 Leo Strauss, *Natural Right and History* (Chicago: University of Chicago Press, 1953), 159.
3 See, for instance, Hugo Grotius, *The Rights of War and Peace*, ed. Richard Tuck, from the Edition by Jean Barbeyrac (hereafter *DJB*) (Indianapolis, IN: Liberty Fund, 2005), 1.1.8.2, 146–47; 2.20.2.2, 951–52; 2.20.33, 1013; 2.23.1, 1115–16. Grotius has earlier stated that one must equitably interpret the scriptural commands of God according to God's perceived intentions, so his audacity in purporting to discern Aristotle's true intention is comparatively mild.
4 Richard Tuck, "Grotius and Selden," in *The Cambridge History of Political Thought 1450–1700*, ed. J. H. Burns (New York: Cambridge University Press, 1991), 506–07, 515–19.
5 Michel Villey, *La formation de la Pensée Juridique Moderne* (Paris: Motchretien, 1975), 619–20.
6 Grotius, *DJB* Prol.58, 131.
7 See Martin Wight, *Four Seminal Thinkers in International Theory* (New York: Oxford University Press, 2005) and Hedley Bull *et al.*, eds, *Hugo Grotius and International Relations* (New York: Oxford University Press, 1990).
8 Ibid.
9 Representative readings on the pluralist side include Hedley Bull, *The Anarchical Society*, 2nd ed. (New York: Columbia University Press, 1995) and Robert Jackson, *The Global Covenant: Human Conduct in a World of States* (New York: Oxford University Press, 2000); Bull's recent work incorporates some elements of solidarism. Older versions of solidarism include Cornelius Van Vollenhoven, *The Three Stages in the Evolution of the Law of Nations* (The Hague: Martinus Nijhoff, 1919), and Hersch Lauterpacht, "The Grotian Tradition in International Law," *British Yearbook of International Law*, 1946. A more recent (and nuanced) solidarist position is found in Nicholas Wheeler, *Saving Strangers: Humanitarian Intervention in International Society* (Oxford: Oxford University Press, 2000).
10 See Samuel Fleischacker, *A Short History of Distributive Justice* (Cambridge, MA: Harvard University Press, 2004), 17–25, and Jerome Schneewind, *The Invention of Autonomy: A History of Modern Moral Philosophy* (New York: Cambridge University Press, 1998), 77–80.
11 See Martha Nussbaum, *Frontiers of Justice: Disability, Nationality, Species Membership* (Cambridge, MA: Harvard University Press, 2006) and Charles Taylor, *A Secular Age* (Cambridge, MA: Harvard University Press, 2007).
12 Grotius shows a characteristically Renaissance attitude in his concluding remark: "Our purpose is to set always a high value upon Aristotle, but so as to reserve to ourselves the same liberty which he himself took with his masters, for the sake of finding truth." Grotius, *DJB* Prol.46, 123.

13 Matthew 5:17, New King James Version.
14 Montague Brown, "St. Thomas Aquinas on Human and Divine Forgiveness," *St. Anselm Journal*, Vol. 6, No. 2 (Spring 2009), 1–8.
15 Oliver M. T. O'Donovan, "Law, Moderation and Forgiveness," in Christoph Stumpf and Holger Zaborowski, eds, *Church as Politeia: The Political Self-Understanding of Christianity* (New York: de Gruyter, 2004), 6.
16 Hannah Arendt, *The Human Condition*, 2nd ed. (Chicago: University of Chicago Press, 1998), 236–40, 243–47. Some observers have argued that Grotius also puts forward a new theory of promise, which might offer further potential for dialogue.
17 I Corinthians 1:23, Common English Bible.
18 Ibid.
19 Or perhaps glory ultimately rests (paradoxically) in the person of the governor who is willing to compromise his stature for the good of his subjects.
20 Aristotle, *Nicomachean Ethics*, trans. C. D. C. Reeve (Indianapolis, IN: Hackett, 1998), 1.2 (1253a28–30), 5; 3.13 (1284a3–8), 89.
21 Aristotle does include a place for kingship, but it seems an uncomfortable fit for his conception of politics as "ruling and being ruled in turn."
22 Hugo Grotius, *The Truth of the Christian Religion*, ed. and intro. Maria Rosa Antognazza, trans. John Clarke (Indianapolis, IN: Liberty Fund, 2012), 2.19, 135–37.
23 One need only consider the resumés of contemporary college applicants, whose litanies of *pro forma* volunteer activities typically signify more opportunism than altruism.
24 This raises unanswered (and perhaps unanswerable) questions about Grotius' simultaneous emphases on the importance of virtue that has no inducements and on the need for extrinsic punishments and rewards in the afterlife. Grotius is never entirely clear about the requirements for entry into heaven, as he seems to portray justification and sanctification as each necessary but insufficient.
25 Grotius, *DJB* Prol.44–45, 114–21.
26 For a representative example, see Schneewind, *Invention of Autonomy*, 77–80.
27 Romans 7:15, King James Version.
28 Grotius, *Meletius* 78, 130.
29 "In the beginning was the Word [*logos*], and the Word [*logos*] was God, and the Word [*logos*] was with God."
30 I Corinthians 15:14, King James Version.
31 James Bernard Murphy, "Review: Rethinking Rights," *Perspectives on Politics*, Vol. 8, No. 4 (2010), 1191.
32 See Charles Taylor, *A Secular Age*, 115–27, 157–70.
33 Ibid.; Quentin Skinner, "Modernity and Disenchantment: Some Reflections," in *Philosophy in an Age of Pluralism*, ed. James Tully *et al.* (Cambridge: Cambridge University Press, 1995), 46–48.
34 Quentin Skinner, "Surveying the *Foundations:* A Retrospect and Reassessment," in *Rethinking the Foundations of Modern Political Thought*, ed. Annabel Brett *et al.* (Cambridge: Cambridge University Press, 2007), 256–60.
35 Andrew Schroeder, "Imperfect Duties, Group Obligations, and Beneficence," *Journal of Moral Philosophy*, Vol. 11, No. 5 (2014), 557–84.
36 The maxim of the contemporary Aristotelian Alasdair MacIntyre comes to mind:

> the good life for man is the life spent in seeking for the good life for man, and the virtues necessary for the seeking are those which will enable us to understand what more and what else the good life for man is.
>
> Alasdair MacIntyre, *After Virtue*, 2nd ed. (Notre Dame, IN: University of Notre Dame Press, 1984), 219

Bibliography

Primary Editions

Grotius, Hugo (1601). *Adamus Exul (The Exile of Adam)*. Translated by Barham. London: Sherwood, 1839.

Grotius, Hugo (1603). *De Jure Praedae (Commentary on the Law of Prize and Booty)*. Edited and Introduced by Martine Julia Van Ittersum. Translated by Gwladys L. Williams. Indianapolis, IN: Liberty Fund, 2006.

Grotius, Hugo (1611). *Meletius*. Critical edition with introduction, translation, and commentary by Guillaume H. M. Posthumus Meyjes. New York: Brill, 1988.

Grotius, Hugo (1613). Hugo Grotius, *Ordinum Hollandiae ac Westfrisiae pietas (The Piety of the States of Holland and Westfriesland)*. Critical edition with translation and commentary by Edwin Rabbie. New York: Brill, 1995.

Grotius, Hugo (1614). *De Imperio Summarum Potestatum Circa Sacra (On the Power of Sovereigns Concerning Religious Affairs)*. Critical edition with introduction, translation, and commentary by Harm-Jan Van Dam. Boston: Brill, 2001.

Grotius, Hugo (1617). *Defensio fidei Catholicae de satisfactione Christi adversus Faustum Socinium.* Critical edition edited by Edwin Rabbie. Translated by Hotze Mulder. Assen, NL: Van Gorcum, 1990.

Grotius, Hugo (1617). *Defensio fidei Catholicae de satisfactione Christi adversus Faustum Socinum (A Defence of the Catholick Faith Concerning the Satisfaction of Christ: Against Faustus Socinus)*. Translated by W. H. London: Printed for Thomas Parkhurst and Johnathan Robinson, 1692.

Grotius, Hugo (1617). *De Satisfactione Christi (The Satisfaction of Christ)*. Translated by Oliver O'Donovan and Joan Lockwood O'Donovan. In *From Irenaeus to Grotius: A Sourcebook in Christian Political Thought.* Edited by Oliver O'Donovan and Joan Lockwood O'Donovan. Grand Rapids, MI: Eerdmans, 1999.

Grotius, Hugo (1620). *Inleydinge tot de Hollantsche rechtsgeleertheit (The Jurisprudence of Holland)*. Translated by R. W. Lee. Oxford: Oxford University Press, 1926.

Grotius, Hugo (1625). *De Jure Belli ac Pacis (The Law of War and Peace)*. Introduced by James Brown Scott. Translated by Francis W. Kelsey. Carnegie Classics of International Law, No. 3, Vol. 2. New York: Bobbs-Merrill, 1925.

Grotius, Hugo (1625). *De Jure Belli ac Pacis (The Rights of War and Peace)*. Edited by Richard Tuck. From the Edition by Jean Barbeyrac. Indianapolis, IN: Liberty Fund, 2005.

Grotius, Hugo (1627). *The Truth of the Christian Religion.* Edited and Introduced by Maria Rosa Antognazza. Translated by John Clarke. Indianapolis, IN: Liberty Fund, 2012.

Grotius, Hugo (1635). *Sophompaneas, or Joseph. A Tragedy.* Translated by Goldsmith. London, Francis Goldsmith, 1652.

Grotius, Hugo (1645). *Annotationes* (Combined Editions). Translated by Lindsay. London: Penny, 1736.

Grotius, Hugo (1645). *Briefwisseling* (Correspondence, in English, French, Latin, Dutch). Edited by P. C. Molhuysen. Amsterdam: Martinus Nijhoff, 1928–2001. 17 vols.

Grotius, Hugo (1656). *De Aequitate, Indulgentia & Facilitate (Traité de l'equité, de l'indulgence, et de la facilité)*. In Hugo Grotius, *Le Droit de la Guerre et de La Paix*. Translated by Antoine de Courtin. The Hague: Adrian Moetjens, 1703.

Grotius, Hugo. *Some Less Known Works of Hugo Grotius.* Edited and Translated by Herbert F. Wright. Leiden: Brill, 1928.

Secondary Sources

Abegunrin, Olayiwola. "Review: Truth and Reconciliation," *African Studies Review*, Vol. 45, No. 3 (December, 2002).

Anselm of Canterbury. *The Major Works.* Oxford: Oxford University Press, 2008.

Aquinas, Thomas. *On Law, Morality, and Politics*, 2nd ed. Edited by William P. Baumgarth. Translated by Richard J. Regan. Indianapolis, IN: Hackett, 2002.

Aquinas, Thomas. *Summa Theologiae*. Translated by Fathers of the English Dominican Province. London: Burns Oates and Washbourne, 1920.

Arendt, Hannah. *Between Past and Future.* New York: Penguin, 1993.

Arendt, Hannah. *The Human Condition*, 2nd ed. Chicago: University of Chicago Press, 1998.

Aristotle. *Nicomachean Ethics.* Translated by Martin Ostwald. Upper Saddle River, NJ: Prentice-Hall, 1999.

Aristotle. *Politics*. Translated by Ernest Barker. New York: Oxford University Press, 1962.

Aristotle. *Rhetoric*. Translated by W. Rhys Roberts. In *The Complete Works of Aristotle*. Edited by Jonathan Barnes. Princeton, NJ: Princeton University Press, 1985.

Augustine. *Against Faustus the Manichean.* Translated by Michael W. Tkacz and Douglas Kries. In *Augustine: Political Writings*. Edited by Ernest L. Fortin and Douglas Kries. Indianapolis, IN: Hackett, 1994.

Augustine. *City of God.* Translated by Michael W. Tkacz and Douglas Kries. In *Augustine: Political Writings*. Edited by Ernest L. Fortin and Douglas Kries. Indianapolis, IN: Hackett, 1994.

Barbeyrac, Jean. *An Historical and Critical Account of the Science of Morality*, prefaced to his edition of Samuel von Pufendorf, *The Law of Nature and Nations.* London, 1749.

Baum, Bruce and Robert Nichols, eds. *Isaiah Berlin and the Politics of Freedom: 'Two Concepts of Liberty' 50 Years Later.* London: Routledge, 2015.

Benedict XVI. "Relationship between Magisterium and Exegetes." Address to the Pontifical Biblical Commission, in *L'Osservatore Romano*, Weekly Edition in English. 23 July 2003.

Bentham, Jeremy. *The Rationale of Reward.* London: R. Heward, 1830.

Berlin, Isaiah. "Two Concepts of Liberty." In *Four Essays on Liberty.* Oxford: Oxford University Press, 1969.

Besselink, Leonard. "The Impious Hypothesis Revisited." In *Grotius*, Vol. 2. Edited by John Dunn and Ian Harris. Lyme, NH: Edward Elgar Publishing, Inc., 1997.

Blom, Hans W., ed. *Property, Piracy and Punishment: Hugo Grotius on War and Booty in De iure pradae.* Leiden: Brill, 2009.

Blom, Hans W. and Laurens C. Winkel, eds. *Grotius and the Stoa.* Assen, NL: Royal Van Gorcum, 2004.

Bouldin, Wood. "Review: *Hugo Grotius as Apologist for the Christian Religion* and *Grotius and the Stoa.*" *Renaissance Quarterly*, Vol. 58, No. 2 (Summer 2005), 690–2.

Brett, Annabel. *Changes of State: Nature and the Limits of the City in Early Modern Natural Law.* Princeton, NJ: Princeton University Press, 2011.

Brett, Annabel. "Natural Right and Civil Community: The Civil Philosophy of Hugo Grotius," *The Historical Journal*, Vol. 45, No. 1 (March, 2002), 31–51.

Brown, Montague. "St. Thomas Aquinas on Human and Divine Forgiveness," *St. Anselm Journal*, Vol. 6, No. 2 (Spring 2009), 1–8.

Buckle, Stephen. *Natural Law and the Theory of Property: Grotius to Hume.* New York: Oxford University Press, 1993.

Bull, Hedley. *The Anarchical Society*, 2nd ed. New York: Columbia University Press, 1995.

Bull, Hedley. "The Grotian Conception of International Society." In *Diplomatic Investigations*. Edited by Martin Wight and Herbert Butterfield. London: George Allen & Unwin: 1966.

Bull, Hedley, Benedict Kingsbury, and Adam Roberts, eds. *Hugo Grotius and International Relations.* Oxford: Oxford University Press, 1990.

Calvin, John. *Institutes of the Christian Religion.* Translated by Henry Beveridge. Peabody, MA: Hendrickson, 2007.

Cave, Sydney. *The Doctrine of the Work of Christ.* London: Cokesbury Press, 1937.

Chapman, Geoffrey. *Catechism of the Catholic Church.* Translated by Geoffrey Chapman. London: Burns & Oates, 1999.

Chisholm, R. "Supererogation and Offence: A Conceptual Scheme for Ethics," *Ratio*, Vol. 5 (1963), 1–14.

Conley, Carey Herbert. *Milton's indebtedness to his contemporaries in 'Paradise Lost.'* Master's Thesis, University of Chicago, 1910.

Connolly, William. *Why I Am Not a Secularist.* Minneapolis: University of Minnesota Press, 1999.

Constant, Benjamin. "The Liberty of the Ancients Compared With That of the Moderns." In *Political Writings*. Translated by Biancamaria Fontana. Cambridge: Cambridge University Press, 1988.

Corey, David D. and J. Daryl Charles. *The Just War Tradition: An Introduction.* Wilmington, DC: ISI Books, 2012.

Cox, Richard. "Hugo Grotius." In *History of Political Philosophy.* Edited by Leo Strauss and Joseph Cropsey. Chicago: University of Chicago Press, 1963.

Darwall, Stephen. "Grotius at the Creation of Modern Moral Philosophy," *Archiv für Geschichte der Philosophie*, Vol. 94 (2012), 296–325.

De Vries, Tiemen. *Holland's Influence on English Language and Literature.* Chicago: W. B. Conkey, 1916.

Dumbauld, Edward. *The Life and Legal Writings of Hugo Grotius.* Norman, OK: University of Oklahoma Press, 1969.

Dunn, John. "What is Living and What is Dead in the Political Theory of John Locke." In *Interpreting Political Responsibility.* Cambridge: Cambridge University Press, 1990.

Edwards, Charles S. *Hugo Grotius: The Miracle of Holland.* Chicago: Nelson-Hall, 1981.

Edwards, Charles S. "The Law of Nature in the Thought of Hugo Grotius," *Journal of Politics*, Vol. 32, No. 4 (1970), 784–807.

Eppstein, John. *The Catholic Tradition of the Law of Nations.* London: Burns Oates and Washbourne, 1935.

Erickson, Millard J. *Introducing Christian Theology*. Edited by J. Arnold Hustad. Grand Rapids, MI: Baker Books, 1992.

Feenstra, Robert, ed. *The World of Hugo Grotius (1583–1645)*. Amsterdam: APA – Holland University Press, 1984.

Figgis, John Neville. *Political Thought from Gerson to Grotius, 1414–1625*. New York: Harper, 1960.

Finnis, John. *Natural Law and Natural Rights*. Oxford: Clarendon Press, 1980.

Fleischacker, Samuel. *A Short History of Distributive Justice*. Cambridge, MA: Harvard University Press, 2004.

Forde, Steven. "The Charitable John Locke," *The Review of Politics*, Vol. 71, No. 3 (July, 2009), 428–58.

Forde, Steven. "Hugo Grotius on Ethics and War," *The American Political Science Review*, Vol. 92, No. 3 (September, 1998), 639–48.

Frohnen, Bruce and Kenneth Grasso, eds. *Rethinking Rights: Historical, Political and Philosophical Perspectives*. Columbia, MO: University of Missouri Press, 2008.

Fukuyama, Francis. *The End of History and the Last Man*. London: Penguin, 1992.

Fukuyama, Francis. *Trust*. New York: Simon & Schuster, 1996.

Geddert, Jeremy Seth. "Beyond Strict Justice: Hugo Grotius on Punishment and Natural Right(s)," *Review of Politics*, Vol. 76, No. 4 (2014), 559–88.

Geddert, Jeremy Seth. "Hugo Grotius' Modern Translation of Aristotle." In *Concepts of Nature: Ancient and Modern*. Edited by Steven F. McGuire and R. J. Snell. Lanham, MD: Lexington, 2016.

Gellinek, Christian. *Hugo Grotius*. Boston: Twayne, 1983.

George, William P. "Grotius, Theology, and International Law: Overcoming Textbook Bias," *Journal of Law and Religion*, Vol. 14, No. 2 (1999–2000), 605–31.

Gillespie, Michael. *The Theological Origins of Modernity*. Chicago: University of Chicago Press, 2008.

Glendon, Mary Ann. *Rights Talk*. New York: Simon & Schuster, 1991.

Graybill, Lynn. "Review: Assessing South Africa's Truth and Reconciliation Commission," *Canadian Journal of African Studies*, Vol. 36, No. 2 (2002), 356–61.

Gready, Paul. "Review of Alex Boraine, *A Country Unmasked: Inside South Africa's Truth and Reconciliation Commission* and Dorothy Shea, *The South African Truth Commission: The Politics of Reconciliation*," *Bulletin of the School of Oriental and African Studies, University of London*, Vol. 64, No. 3 (2001), 447–49.

Guiloineau, Jean. *Nelson Mandela: The Early Life of Rohlilahla Mandela*. Berkeley, CA: North Atlantic Press, 2002.

Haakonssen, Knud, ed. *Grotius, Pufendorf and Modern Natural Law*. Aldershot: Dartmouth, 1998.

Haakonssen, Knud, ed. "Hugo Grotius and the History of Political Thought," *Political Theory*, Vol. 13, No. 2 (1985), 239–65.

Haakonssen, Knud, ed. *Natural Law and Moral Philosophy: From Grotius to the Scottish Enlightenment*. New York: Cambridge University Press, 1996.

Haakonssen, Knud, ed. "Review: The Rights of War and Peace," *Mind*, Vol. 111, No. 4 (April, 2002), 499–502.

Habermas, Jurgen. "A Conversation about God and the World." In *Time of Transitions*. Cambridge: Polity Press, 2006.

Haggenmacher, Peter. "Droits subjectifs et système juridique chez Grotius." In *Politique, Loi, et Théologie Chez Bodin, Grotius et Hobbes*. Edited by Luc Foisneau. Paris: Kimé, 1997.

Haggenmacher, Peter. *Grotius et la Doctrine de la Guerre Juste*. Paris: Presses Universitaires de France, 1983.

Hamilton, Alexander, James Madison, and John Jay. *The Federalist.* Edited by George W. Carey and James McClellan. Indianapolis, IN: Liberty Fund, 2001.

Hart, A. C. 't. "Hugo de Groot and Giambattista Vico." In *Grotius*, Vol. 2. Edited by John Dunn and Ian Harris. Lyme, NH: Edward Elgar Publishing, Inc., 1997.

Heering, J. P. *Hugo Grotius as Apologist for the Christian Religion: A Study of His Work De veritate religionis christianae (1640).* Translated by J. C. Grayson. Boston: Brill, 2004.

Heering, J. P. "Hugo Grotius' *De Veritate Religionis Christianae.*" In *Hugo Grotius: Theologian.* Edited by Henk J. M. Nellen and Edwin Rabbie. New York: Brill, 1993.

Hervada, Javier. "The Old and the New in the Hypothesis '*Etiamsi daremus*' of Grotius," *Grotiana*, Vol. 4, No. 1 (1983), 3–20.

Hobbes, Thomas. *Leviathan.* Edited by C. B. Macpherson. New York: Penguin, 1968.

Hunter, Ian. *Rival Enlightenments.* New York: Cambridge University Press, 2001.

Husak, Douglas. "Criminal Law Theory." In *The Blackwell Guide to the Philosophy of Law and Legal Theory*. Edited by Martin P. Golding and William A. Edmundson. Hoboken, NJ: Wiley-Blackwell, 2004.

Irwin, Terence. *The Development of Ethics: A Historical and Critical Study.* Oxford: Oxford University Press, 2007.

Jackson, Robert. *The Global Covenant: Human Conduct in a World of States.* New York: Oxford University Press, 2000.

Janis, Mark W. *America and the Law of Nations 1776–1939.* Oxford: Oxford University Press, 2010.

Jeffery, Renée. *Hugo Grotius in International Thought.* New York: Palgrave Macmillan, 2006.

Jenkins, Thomas E. *The Character of God: Recovering the Lost Literary Power of American Protestantism.* New York: Oxford University Press, 1997.

Johnson, James Turner. "Grotius' Use of History and Charity in the Modern Transformation of the Just War Idea." In *Grotius*, Vol. 2. Edited by John Dunn and Ian Harris. Lyme, NH: Edward Elgar Publishing, Inc., 1997.

Johnson, James Turner. "Historical Roots and Sources of the Just War Tradition in Western Culture." In *Just War and Jihad: Historical and Theoretical Perspectives on War and Peace in Western and Islamic Traditions.* Edited by John Kelsay and James Turner Johnson. New York: Greenwood Press, 1991.

Johnson, James Turner. *Ideology, Reason, and the Limitation of War: Religious and Secular Concepts, 1200–1740.* Princeton, NJ: Princeton University Press, 1975.

Johnson, James Turner. *Just War Tradition and the Restraint of War.* Princeton, NJ: Princeton University Press, 1981.

Johnson, James Turner. *Sovereignty: Moral and Historical Perspectives.* Washington, DC: Georgetown University Press, 2014.

Kant, Immanuel. *The Metaphysics of Morals.* Edited and Translated by Mary Gregor. Introduced by Roger J. Sullivan. Cambridge: Cambridge University Press, 1996.

Kant, Immanuel. *Toward Perpetual Peace.* Edited by Pauline Kleingeld. Translated by David L. Colclasure. New Haven, CT: Yale University Press, 2006.

Keene, Edward. *Beyond the Anarchical Society: Grotius, Colonialism and Order in World Politics.* New York: Cambridge University Press, 2002.

Kelly, J. M. *A Short History of Western Legal Theory.* Oxford: Clarendon Press, 1992.

Kelsay, John and James Turner Johnson, eds. *Just War and Jihad: Historical and Theoretical Perspectives on War and Peace in Western and Islamic Traditions.* New York: Greenwood Press, 1991.

Kelsen, Hans. *General Theory of Law and State*. Translated by A. Wedberg. New York: Russell and Russell, 1961.

Kelsen, Hans. *Pure Theory of Law*. Translated by M. Knight. Berkeley: University of California Press, 1967.

Koritansky, Peter Paul, ed. *The Philosophy of Punishment and the History of Political Thought*. Columbia, MO: University of Missouri Press, 2011.

Knight, W. S. M. *The Life and Works of Hugo Grotius*. London: Sweet and Maxwell, 1925.

Krasner, Stephen. *Sovereignty: Organized Hypocrisy*. Princeton, NJ: Princeton University Press, 1999.

Lagrée, Jacqueline. "Droit et théologie dans le *De Satisfactione Christi* de Hugo Grotius." In *Politique, Loi, et Théologie Chez Bodin, Grotius et Hobbes*. Edited by Luc Foisneau. Paris: Kimé, 1997.

Lauterpacht, Hersch. "The Grotian Tradition in International Law." In *British Yearbook of International Law*, 1946.

Lawler, Peter and Marc Guerra, eds. *The Science of Modern Virtue*. DeKalb, IL: Northern Illinois University Press, 2009.

Lee, R. W. *Hugo Grotius*. Oxford: Oxford University Press, 1930.

Locke, John. *Second Treatise of Government*. Edited by C. B. MacPherson. Indianapolis, IN: Hackett, 1980.

Maas, Willem. "Grotius on Citizenship and Political Community," *Grotiana*, Vol. 20–21, No. 1 (1999–2000), 163–78.

MacIntyre, Alasdair. *After Virtue*, 2nd ed. Notre Dame, IN: University of Notre Dame Press, 1984.

MacIntyre, Alasdair. *Whose Justice? Which Rationality?* Notre Dame, IN: University of Notre Dame Press, 1988.

May, Larry. *After War Ends: A Philosophical Perspective*. Cambridge: Cambridge University Press, 2012.

Médaille, John. *Toward a Truly Free Market*. Wilmington, DE: ISI Press, 2010.

Mitchell, Joshua. *Not By Reason Alone: Religion, History, and Identity in Early Modern Thought*. Chicago: University of Chicago Press, 1993.

Mitchell, Joshua. "Protestant Thought and Republican Spirit: How Luther Enchanted the World," *American Political Science Review*, Vol. 86, No. 3 (September, 1992), 688–95.

Murphy, Colleen. *A Moral Theory of Political Reconciliation*. Cambridge: Cambridge University Press, 2012.

Murphy, James Bernard. "Review: Rethinking Rights," *Perspectives on Politics*, Vol. 8, No. 4 (2010), 1191–92.

Nellen, Henk. *Hugo Grotius: A Lifelong Struggle for Peace in Church and State, 1583–1645*. Leiden: Brill, 2014.

Nellen, Henk. "In Strict Confidence: Grotius' Correspondence with his Socinian Friends." In *Self-Presentation and Social Identification: The Rhetoric and Pragmatics of Letter Writing in Early Modern Times*. Edited by Toon Van Houdt. Leuven: Leuven University Press, 2002.

Nellen, Henk J. M. and Edwin Rabbie, eds. *Hugo Grotius – Theologian*. Leiden: Brill, 1994.

Nussbaum, Martha. *Frontiers of Justice: Disability, Nationality, Species Membership*. Cambridge, MA: Harvard University Press, 2006.

O'Donovan, Oliver. "The Justice of Assignment and Subjective Rights in Grotius." In *Bonds of Imperfection: Christian Politics, Past and Present*. Edited by Oliver O'Donovan and Joan Lockwood O'Donovan. Grand Rapids, MI: Eerdmans, 2004.

O'Donovan, Oliver. "Law, Moderation, and Forgiveness." In *Church as Politeia: The Political Self-Understanding of Christianity.* Edited by Christoph Stumpf and Holger Zaborowski. New York: Walter de Gruyter, 2004.

O'Donovan, Oliver. "Review: *De Imperio Summarum Potestatum Circa Sacra*," *Theological Studies*, Vol. 64, No. 3 (September, 2003), 629–30.

O'Donovan, Oliver and Joan Lockwood O'Donovan. "Hugo Grotius (1583–1646)." In *From Irenaeus to Grotius: A Sourcebook in Christian Political Thought.* Edited by Oliver O'Donovan and Joan Lockwood O'Donovan. Grand Rapids, MI: Eerdmans, 1999.

O'Donovan, Oliver and Joan Lockwood O'Donovan. "Introduction." In *Bonds of Imperfection: Christian Politics, Past and Present.* Edited by Oliver O'Donovan and Joan Lockwood O'Donovan. Grand Rapids, MI: Eerdmans, 2004.

Oldman, Elizabeth. "Milton, Grotius, and the Law of War: A Reading of *Paradise Regained* and *Samson Agonistes*," *Studies in Philology*, Vol. 104, No. 3 (2007), 340–75.

Onuma, Yasuaki, ed. *A Normative Approach to War.* Oxford: Clarendon Press, 1993.

Pangle, Thomas L. and Peter J. Ahrensdorf. *Justice Among Nations: On the Moral Basis of Power and Peace.* Lawrence, KS: University Press of Kansas, 1999.

Philpott, Daniel. *Just and Unjust Peace.* Oxford: Oxford University Press, 2012.

Pocock, J. G. A. "Foundations and Moments." In *Rethinking the Foundations of Modern Political Thought.* Edited by Annabel Brett *et al.* Cambridge: Cambridge University Press, 2007.

Posner, Richard. "An Economic Theory of the Criminal Law," *Columbia Law Review*, Vol. 85, No. 6 (1985), 1193–1231.

Posner, Richard. "Optimal Sentences for White-Collar Criminals," *American Criminal Law Review*, Vol. 17, No. 4 (1980), 409–18.

Posthumus Meyjes, G. H. M. "Grotius as a Theologian." In *Hugo Grotius: A Great European, 1583–1645.* Edited by the National Committee for the Commemoration of Grotius' Birth. Translated by P. J. E. Hyams. Delft: Meinema, 1983.

Plato. *Republic.* Translated by G. M. A. Grube. Revised by C. D. C. Reeve. Indianapolis, IN: Hackett, 1993.

Plato. *Statesman.* Translated by J. B. Skemp. Revised by Martin Ostwald. Indianapolis, IN: Hackett, 1992.

Rapp, Hans. "Grotius and Hume on Natural Religion and Natural Law." *Grotius*, Vol. 2. Edited by John Dunn and Ian Harris. Lyme, NH: Edward Elgar Publishing, Inc., 1997.

Rathore, Aakash Singh and Alex Cistelecan, eds. *Wronging Rights? Philosophical Challenges for Human Rights.* London: Routledge, 2011.

Rawls, John. "The Idea of Public Reason Revisited," *The University of Chicago Law Review*, Vol. 64, 765–807.

Rawls, John. *Political Liberalism.* New York: Columbia University Press, 1996.

Regout, Robert Hubert Willem. *La Doctrine de la Guerre Juste.* Paris: A. Pedone, 1934.

Remec, Peter Pavel. *The Position of the Individual in International Law According to Grotius and Vattel.* The Hague: Martinus Nijhoff, 1960.

Rousseau, Jean-Jacques. *Political Writings*, Vol. II. Edited and Translated by C. E. Vaughan. Cambridge: Cambridge University Press, 1997.

Salter, John. "Sympathy With the Poor: Theories of Punishment in Hugo Grotius and Adam Smith," *History of Political Thought*, Vol. 20, No. 2 (1999), 205–24.

Schneewind, Jerome. *The Invention of Autonomy: A History of Modern Moral Philosophy.* New York: Cambridge University Press, 1998.

Schroeder, Andrew. "Imperfect Duties, Group Obligations, and Beneficence," *Journal of Moral Philosophy*, Vol. 11, No. 5 (2014), 557–84.

Shedd, W. G. T. *Dogmatic Theology*, Vol. 2, 3rd ed. New York: Charles Scribner's Sons, 1891.

Shuger, D. K. *The Renaissance Bible: Scholarship, Sacrifice, and Subjectivity*. Berkeley, CA: University of California Press, 1994.

Skinner, Quentin. *The Foundations of Modern Political Thought, Vol. 2: The Age of Reformation*. Cambridge: Cambridge University Press, 1978.

Skinner, Quentin. "Modernity and Disenchantment: Some Reflections." In *Philosophy in an Age of Pluralism*. Edited by James Tully *et al.* Cambridge: Cambridge University Press, 1995.

Skinner, Quentin. "Surveying the *Foundations:* A Retrospect and Reassessment." In *Rethinking the Foundations of Modern Political Thought*. Edited by Annabel Brett *et al.* Cambridge: Cambridge University Press, 2007.

Smith, Adam. *The Theory of Moral Sentiments*. Edited by Knud Haakonssen. Cambridge: Cambridge University Press, 2002.

Stanley, Elizabeth. "Evaluating the Truth and Reconciliation Commission," *Journal of Modern African Studies*, Vol. 39, No. 3 (September, 2001), 525–46.

Storms, Sam. "Grotius and the Governmental Theory of the Atonement." www.samstorms.com/all-articles/post/grotius-and-the-governmental-theory-of-the-atonement/. Posted 17 March 2009. Retrieved 20 July 2016.

Stout, Jeffrey. *Democracy and Tradition*. Princeton, NJ: Princeton University Press, 2004.

Straumann, Benjamin. "'Ancient Caesarian Lawyers' in a State of Nature: Roman Tradition and Natural Rights in Hugo Grotius' '*De iure praedae*,'" *Political Theory*, Vol. 34, No. 3 (June, 2006), 328–50.

Straumann, Benjamin. "Natural Rights and Roman Law in Hugo Grotius's *Theses LVI, De iure praedae* and *Defensio capitis quinti maris liberi*," *Grotiana*, Vol. 26–28, No. 1 (2005–2007), 341–65.

Straumann, Benjamin. "*Oikeiosis* and *appetitus societatis:* Hugo Grotius' Ciceronian Argument for Natural Law and Just War," *Grotiana*, Vol. 24–25, No. 1 (2003–2004), 41–66.

Straumann, Benjamin. *Roman Law in the State of Nature: The Classical Foundations of Hugo Grotius' Natural Law*. Cambridge: Cambridge University Press, 2015.

Strauss, Leo. *Natural Right and History*. Chicago: University of Chicago Press, 1953.

Stumpf, Christoph. *The Grotian Theology of International Law*. New York: Walter de Gruyter, 2006.

Suarez, Francisco. *On the Three Theological Virtues of Faith, Hope, and Charity*, Disputation 13: *On Charity*. Translated by Gwladys L. Williams *et al.* In *Selections from Three Works of Francisco Suarez*. Edited by James Brown Scott. Carnegie Classics of International Law, No. 20, Vol. 2. Oxford: Clarendon Press, 1944.

Syse, Henrik. *Natural Law, Religion and Rights*. South Bend, IN: St. Augustine's Press, 2007.

Taylor, Charles. *A Secular Age*. Cambridge, MA: Harvard University Press, 2007.

Ter Meulen, J. and P. J. J. Diermanse. *Bibliographie des écrits imprimes de H. Grotius*. The Hague, 1950.

Thomas, Jeremy. "The Intertwining of Law and Theology in the Writings of Grotius," *Journal of the History of International Law*, Vol. 1 (1999), 61–100.

Tierney, Brian. *The Idea of Natural Rights*. Grand Rapids, MI: Eerdmans, 2001.

Tierney, Brian. *Liberty and Law: The Idea of Permissive Natural Law, 1100–1800*. Washington, DC: The Catholic University of America Press, 2014.

Tierney, Brian. "Natural Law and Natural Rights: Old Problems and Recent Approaches," *Review of Politics*, Vol. 64, No. 3 (June, 2002), 389–406.

Tinder, Glenn. "The Almost-Chosen People: Abraham Lincoln's America," *Weekly Standard*, Vol. 6, No. 11 (2000).

Tooke, Joan D. *The Just War in Aquinas and Grotius*. London: S. P. C. K., 1965.

Trevor-Roper, Hugh. *From Counter-Reformation to Glorious Revolution*. Chicago: University of Chicago Press, 1992.

Tuck, Richard. "Grotius, Carneades, and Hobbes." In *Grotius*, Vol. 2. Edited by John Dunn and Ian Harris. Lyme, NH: Edward Elgar Publishing, Inc., 1997.

Tuck, Richard. "Grotius and Selden," in *The Cambridge History of Political Thought (1450–1700)*. Edited by J. H. Burns. New York: Cambridge University Press, 1991.

Tuck, Richard. "History." In *A Companion to Contemporary Political Philosophy*, 2nd ed. Edited by Robert E. Goodin *et al.* Chichester: Wiley-Blackwell, 2012.

Tuck, Richard. "History of Political Thought." In *New Perspectives on Historical Writing*, 2nd ed. Edited by Peter Burke. University Park, PA: Pennsylvania State University Press, 2001.

Tuck, Richard. *Natural Rights Theories: Their Origin and Development*. Cambridge: Cambridge University Press, 1979.

Tuck, Richard. *Philosophy and Government 1572–1651*. Cambridge: Cambridge University Press, 1993.

Tuck, Richard. *The Rights of War and Peace: Political Thought and the International Order from Grotius to Kant*. New York: Oxford University Press, 1999.

Tutu, Desmond. *No Future Without Forgiveness*. New York: Doubleday, 2012.

Urmson, J. O. "Saints and Heroes." In *Essays in Moral Philosophy*. Edited by A. Melden. Seattle, WA: University of Washington Press, 1958.

Van Dam, Harm-Jan. "*De Imperio Summarum Potestatum Circa Sacra*." In *Hugo Grotius: Theologian*. Edited by Henk J. M. Nellen and Edwin Rabbie. New York: Brill, 1993.

Van Dam, Harm-Jan. "Introduction." In Hugo Grotius, *De Imperio Summarum Potestatum Circa Sacra (On the Power of Sovereigns Concerning Religious Affairs)*. Critical edition with introduction, translation, and commentary by Harm-Jan Van Dam. Boston: Brill, 2001.

Van Gelderen, Martin. "The Challenge of Colonialism: Grotius and Vitoria on Natural Law and International Relations," *Grotiana*, Vol. 14, No. 1 (1993), 3–37.

Van Ittersum, Martine Julia. *Profit and Principle: Hugo Grotius, Natural Rights Theoriesand the Rise of Dutch Power in the East Indies (1595–1615)*. Boston: Brill, 2006.

Van Nifterik, Gustaaf. "Grotius and the Origin of the Ruler's Right to Punish." In *Property, Piracy and Punishment*. Edited by Hans Blom. Leiden: Brill, 2009.

Van Vollenhoven, Cornelius. *The Framework of Grotius' Book* de Iure Belli ac Pacis. Amsterdam: Uitgave van de N. V. Noord-Hollandsche Uitgeversmaatschappij, 1931.

Van Vollenhoven, Cornelius. "Grotius and the Study of Law," *American Journal of International Law*, Vol. 19, No. 1 (January, 1925), 1–11.

Van Vollenhoven, Cornelius. *The Three Stages in the Evolution of the Law of Nations*. The Hague: Martinus Nijhoff, 1919.

Vermeulen, B. P. and G. A. Van Der Wal. "Grotius, Aquinas and Hobbes: Grotian Natural Law Between *Lex Aeterna* and Natural Rights," *Grotiana*, Vol. 16, No. 1 (1995), 55–83.

Villey, Michel. *La Formation de la Pensée Juridique Moderne*. Paris: Montchrétien, 1975.

Vitoria, Franciscus de. *On Dietary Laws, or Self-Restraint*. Translated by Anthony Pagden and Jeremy Lawrence. In *Francisco de Vitoria: Political Writings*. Edited by

Anthony Pagden and Jeremy Lawrence. Cambridge: Cambridge University Press, 1991.

Vitoria, Franciscus de. *On the Indians*. Translated by John Pawley Bate. In *De Indis et De Jure Belli Relectiones*. Edited by Ernest Nys. Carnegie Classics of International Law, No. 7. Washington: Carnegie Institute, 1917.

Vitoria, Franciscus de. *On the Law of War and Peace*. Translated by John Pawley Bate. In *De Indis et De Jure Belli Relectiones*. Edited by Ernest Nys. Carnegie Classics of International Law, No. 7. Washington: Carnegie Institute, 1917.

Voegelin, Eric. *The Nature of the Law and Related Legal Writings, Collected Works* Vol. 27. Baton Rouge, LA: Louisiana State University Press, 1991.

Von Heyking, John and Thomas Heilke, eds. *The Primacy of Persons in Politics: Empiricism and Political Philosophy*. Washington, DC: The Catholic University of America Press, 2013.

Vreeland, Hamilton. *Hugo Grotius: The Father of the Modern Science of International Law*. New York: Oxford University Press, 1917.

Waldron, Jeremy. *Law and Disagreement*. Oxford: Oxford University Press, 2001.

Walsh, David. *After Ideology: Recovering the Spiritual Foundations of Freedom*. Washington, DC: The Catholic University of America Press, 1995.

Walsh, David. *The Growth of the Liberal Soul*. Columbia, MO: University of Missouri Press, 1997.

Walsh, David. *The Modern Philosophical Revolution: The Luminosity of Existence*. Cambridge: Cambridge University Press, 2008.

Walsh, David. *Politics of the Person as the Politics of Being*. South Bend, IN: University of Notre Dame Press, 2015.

Walzer, Michael. *Just and Unjust Wars*, 3rd ed. New York: Basic Books, 1998.

Ward, Lee. *John Locke and Modern Life*. Cambridge: Cambridge University Press, 2010.

Ward, Lee. "Locke on Punishment, Property and Moral Knowledge," *Journal of Moral Philosophy*, Vol. 6, No. 2 (2009), 227–28.

Ward, Lee. *The Politics of Liberty in England and Revolutionary America*. Cambridge: Cambridge University Press, 2004.

Webb, Adam K. *Deep Cosmopolis: Rethinking World Politics and Globalization*. London: Routledge, 2015.

Weed, Ronald and John Von Heyking, eds. *Civil Religion in Political Thought*. Washington, DC: The Catholic University of America Press, 2010.

Weiner, Greg. "Of Prudence and Principle: Reflections on Lincoln's Second Inaugural at 150," *Society*, Vol. 52, No. 5 (December, 2015).

Wheeler, Nicholas. *Saving Strangers: Humanitarian Intervention in International Society*. Oxford: Oxford University Press, 2000.

Wight, Martin. *Four Seminal Thinkers in International Theory*. New York: Oxford University Press, 2005.

Wight, Martin. *International Theory: The Three Traditions*. Edited by Gabriele Wight and Brian Porter. Introduced by Hedley Bull. New York: Holmes & Meier, 1992.

Wilson, Eric. *Savage Republic: De Indis of Hugo Grotius, Republicanism and Dutch Hegemony within the Early Modern World-System (*c.*1600–1619)*. Boston: Martinus Nijhoff, 2008.

Wilson, Richard A. *The Politics of Truth and Reconciliation in South Africa: Legitimizing the Post-Apartheid State*. Cambridge: Cambridge University Press, 2001.

Winkel, Laurens. "Problems of Legal Systematization from *De Iure Praedae* to *De Iure Belli ac Pacis*," *Grotiana*, Vol. 26–28, No. 1 (2005–2007), 61–78.

Wolf, Mark. "Quality of Mercy," *New York Times Review of Books*, 27 May 2001.

Woollacott, M. "Reconciliation, or Justice and Ashes?" *Guardian*, 17 February 1997.
Zagorin, Perez. "Hobbes Without Grotius," *History of Political Thought*, Vol. 21, No. 1 (2000), 16–40.
Zarka, Yves Charles. "The Mutation of the Right of Resistance in Grotius and Hobbes," *Grotiana*, Vol. 20–21, No. 1 (1999–2000), 35–48.

Index

Page numbers in **bold** denote figures.

For Product Safety Concerns and Information please contact our EU representative GPSR@taylorandfrancis.com
Taylor & Francis Verlag GmbH, Kaufingerstraße 24, 80331 München, Germany

www.ingramcontent.com/pod-product-compliance
Ingram Content Group UK Ltd.
Pitfield, Milton Keynes, MK11 3LW, UK
UKHW022117190926
475702UK00013B/1503
9781138368262